INTERNATIONAL ECONOMIC DISPUTE SETTLEMENT IN AFRICA

This book fills the urgent need for a comprehensive understanding of the law, institutions, and processes shaping international economic dispute settlement within and beyond Africa.

African economies are becoming increasingly central in global trade networks. Understanding the continent's dispute resolution mechanisms is more crucial now than ever. The book systematically analyses the existing sub-regional courts and arbitral tribunals, as well as their roles. It achieves this by focusing on the following five of Africa's leading socio-legal actors: African States, transnational corporations, African international law scholars, international organisations, and African emerging transnational actors in arbitration. These five pillars create an ecology of socio-legal actors, interacting and intersecting to generate a complex social, political, historical, and legal variation matrix for understanding African international economic dispute settlement.

The book covers the two main international economic dispute settlement divisions: international court litigation and international public and private arbitration. It also carefully analyses sub-regional international economic courts and international public and private arbitrations in Africa through a Third World Approaches to International Law (TWAIL) lens and socio-legal actors methodology.

International Economic Dispute Settlement in Africa provides invaluable insights for legal professionals, policymakers, researchers, and business leaders navigating the complexities of African dispute resolution.

Studies in International Trade and Investment Law: Volume 34

Studies in International Trade and Investment Law

Series Editors
Gabrielle Marceau
Krista Nadakavukaren Schefer
Federico Ortino
Gregory Shaffer

This series offers a forum for publication of original and scholarly analyses of emerging and significant issues in international trade and investment law - broadly understood to include the whole of the law of the WTO, the public international law of foreign investment, the law of the EU common commercial policy and other regional trade regimes, and any legal or regulatory topic that interacts with global trade and foreign investment. The aim of the series is to produce works which will be readily accessible to trade and investment law scholars and practitioners alike.

RECENT TITLES IN THIS SERIES:

The EU, World Trade Law and the Right to Food: Rethinking Free Trade Agreements with Developing Countries Giovanni Gruni

Patent Games in the Global South: Pharmaceutical Patent Law Making in Brazil, India and Nigeria Amaka Vanni

The Nationality of Corporate Investors under International Investment Law Anil Yilmaz Vastardis

The Regulation of Product Standards in World Trade Law Ming Du

Investors' International Law Edited by Jean Ho and Mavluda Sattorova

Rethinking, Repackaging, and Rescuing World Trade Law in the Post-Pandemic Era Edited by Amrita Bahri, Weihan Zhou and Daria Boklan

Flexible Regional Economic Integration in Africa: Lessons and Implications for the Multilateral Trading System Timothy Masiko

International Investment Law: An Analysis of the Major Decisions Edited by Hélène Ruiz Fabri and Edoardo Stoppioni

State Capitalism and International Investment Law Edited by Panagiotis Delimatsis, Georgios Dimitropoulos and Anastasios Gourgourinis

The European Union and International Investment Law: The Two Dimensions of an Uneasy Relationship Francesco Montanaro

Financial Market Infrastructure and Economic Integration: A WTO, FTAs, and Competition Law Analysis George A Papaconstantinou

International Trade Law and Global Data Governance: Aligning Perspectives and Practices Neha Mishra

Hong Kong as an Actor in International Economic Law: Multilateralism, Bilateralism and Unilateralism Julien Chaisse

Economic Cooperation in the Shadow of Contested Sovereignty Chien-Huei Wu, Ching-Fu Lin and Han-Wei Liu

International Economic Dispute Settlement in Africa: Courts and Arbitral Tribunals as Socio-Legal Actors Harrison Otieno Mbori

International Economic Dispute Settlement in Africa

Courts and Arbitral Tribunals as Socio-Legal Actors

Harrison Otieno Mbori

• HART •
OXFORD • LONDON • NEW YORK • NEW DELHI • SYDNEY

HART PUBLISHING
Bloomsbury Publishing Plc
Kemp House, Chawley Park, Cumnor Hill, Oxford, OX2 9PH, UK
1385 Broadway, New York, NY 10018, USA
Bloomsbury Publishing Ireland Limited, 29 Earlsfort Terrace, Dublin 2, D02 AY28, Ireland

HART PUBLISHING, the Hart/Stag logo, BLOOMSBURY and the Diana logo are trademarks of Bloomsbury Publishing Plc

First published in Great Britain 2026

1

A catalogue record for this book is available from the British Library.

Library of Congress Control Number: 2026936638

ISBN: HB: 978-1-50999-287-4
ePDF: 978-1-50999-289-8
ePub: 978-1-50999-288-1

Typeset by Amnet

For product safety related questions contact productsafety@bloomsbury.com

To find out more about our authors and books visit www.hartpublishing.co.uk. Here you will find extracts, author information, details of forthcoming events and the option to sign up for our newsletters.

To
Purity, Malloh, & Miich

Preface

THE ASSESSMENT OF MANY African international economic dispute settlement regimes portrays them as less authoritative versions of their European and international counterparts. This book argues that such evaluations are inaccurate and aim to further marginalize African institutions to the periphery of international economic dispute settlement. The study responds to such analyses using two critical, eclectic, and interdisciplinary theoretical and methodological approaches: The Third World Approaches to International Law (TWAIL) and the thick description approach. Consequently, using five socio-legal actors: African states, Transnational corporations (TNCs), African international law legal scholars and experts, International and Transnational Organizations (IOs), and African emerging transnational actors in arbitration, the study conducts a critical and in-depth assessment of sub-regional international courts and international public and private arbitration in resolving economic disputes in Africa. These actors are the five pillars (pentagon) that act as an ecology of socio-legal actors interacting and intersecting to generate a complex social, political, historical, and legal variation matrix for understanding African international economic dispute settlement. The study covers the two main divisions of international economic dispute settlement: international court litigation and international public and private arbitration. This study is the first attempt at carefully analyzing sub-regional international economic courts and international public and private arbitrations in Africa through a TWAIL lens and socio-legal actors methodology.

Acknowledgements

A BOOK, ESPECIALLY A book of this magnitude, is always a joint effort. This work began as part of my PhD at Loyola University in Chicago. First, I must thank the Almighty God for his grace, blessings, and favour over my life. Second, my late parents Evans Mbori and Jane Anyago for whom it would have been an immense pleasure to have witnessed this work and achievement but for the untimely cruelty of death. My adoptive parents, uncle Chillion Obuoro, aunt Lydia Kithinji, and my beloved paternal uncle, the late Maurice Owii Obuaya, have played an indispensable part in my life.

Third, my dear wife, Purity Maritim, whom I love immensely. I do not understand how I lived 30 years of my life without her. She is an incredible source of emotional, physical, psychological, spiritual, and ideational support and help. Fourth, my lead supervisor, mentor, friend, and co-TWAIL conspirator the indomitable Prof James T. Gathii. 'Prof' as I call him as a term of professionalism, respect, and fatherly endearment has been a reliable source of professional, intellectual, and personal support. It has been an immense pleasure to learn, debate, discuss, co-write, and disagree with one of the greatest jurists Africa has produced. Indeed Prof Gathii has been and continues to be a father-figure to me (and his wife Carol Mwangi a major source of motherly warmth and love).

Fourth, special thanks to my two supervision committee members: Prof Barry Sullivan and Prof Margaret Moses, I am more than grateful for their support and excellent supervision. Prof Sullivan especially has a special place in my heart for always being so gracious, kind, and caring, especially outside our professional engagements. I still fondly remember having weekly weekend online meetings with him over the COVID-19 pandemic lockdown period that literally kept me sane and mentally healthy.

Fifth, I would thank Prof Luis G. Franceschi and the entire Strathmore University community, including my former students and friends. Prof Franceschi's leadership, mentorship, and ability to make impossible things happen remains a vital part of my young career progression so far. Arnold Nciko deserves special mention for his research assistance with the Francophone aspects of Chapter 5 on OHADA.

Finally, I would like to thank Prof Hélène Ruiz Fabri and all my colleagues and friends at Max Planck Institute Luxembourg. I am grateful to Prof Ruiz Fabri for recruiting me into a vibrant, resourceful, and intellectually stimulating institute where many ideas in this book were conceived, written, debated, and presented. I especially thank my many colleagues at the institute: Dr. Ezéchiel

Cirimwami, Dr. Carlos Bichet, Dr. Tatiana Renno, Dr. Kritika Sharma, Dr. Bin Zhao, Dr. Olivier Baillet, Dr. Randi Ayman, Dr. Dominik Ornig, Dr. Somesh Dutta, Dr. Bianca Nalbandian, Arman Melikyan, Dr. Ezgi Özlü, Luis López Zamora, Arpita Sachdeva, Bruno Biazatti, Gustavo Becker, Dr. Habiba Abubaker, Allan Mulondo, Nathalie Perrin, Derek Stemple, and Sylvie Peyre.

Contents

List of Abbreviations

A

AAA	African Arbitration Academy
AfAA	African Arbitration Association
AALCO	Asian-African Legal Consultative Organization
AfCFTA	African Continental Free Trade Agreement
AB	Appellate Body
AFSA	Arbitration Foundation of Southern Africa
ABA	American Bar Association
AIIL	African Institute of International Law
ACJ	African Court of Justice
AIPO	African Intellectual Property Organisation
ACtHPR	African Court on Human and Peoples' Rights
AJS	Alternative Justice Systems
ACJHPR	African Court of Justice and Human and Peoples' Rights
AMU	African Maghreb Union
ACERWC	Africa Committee of Experts on the Rights and Welfare of the Child
ARIPO	African Regional Industrial Property Organization
ADR	Alternative Dispute Resolution
ASIL	America Society of International Law
AEC	African Economic Community
ATC	American Tobacco Company
AECCJ	African Economic Community Court of Justice
AU	African Union
AYA	Association of Young Arbitrators

B

BAT	British American Tobacco
BIAC	Beijing international Arbitration Centre
BEAC	*Banque des États de l'Afrique Centrale*
BITs	Bilateral Investment Treaties

C – D

CAJAC	Chinese-Africa Joint Arbitration Center
CIL	Customary International law
CAMC-O	Conciliation Center of Ouagadougou
CJEU	Court of Justice of the European Union

CCJ	COMESA Court of Justice
CLS	Critical Legal Studies
CCJA	Common Court of Justice and Arbitration
CNO	*Commission Nationales OHADA* - OHADA National Commissions
CEMAC	Central African Economic and Monetary Community
COMESA	Common Market for Eastern and Southern African States
CETA	Comprehensive Economic Trade Agreement
CREL	Centro de Resolução Extrajudicial de Litígios
CERDS	Charter on the Economic Rights and Duties of States
CRCICA	Cairo Regional Centre for International Commercial Arbitration
CFA	*Colonies Francaises d'Afrique*
CFP	*Colonies Francaises du Pacifique*
DSMs	Dispute Settlement Mechanisms

E

EABCo	East African Business Council
ECT	Energy Charter Treaty
EACA	East Africa Court of Appeal
ECOSOC	UN Economic and Social Council
EACJ	East Africa Court of Justice
ECOWAS	Economic Community of West African States
ECCAS	Economic Community of Central African States
EAIAC	East Africa International Arbitration Conference
ECJ	European Court of Justice
EECC	Eritrea Ethiopia Claims Commission
ECCJ	ECOWAS Community Court of Justice
EU	European Union

F – H

FCTC	Framework Convention on Tobacco Control
FOCAC	Forum of Chinese African Corporation
FDI	Foreign Direct Investment
GAC	Ghana Arbitration Center
FET	Fair and Equitable Treatment
GATT	General Agreement on Tariffs and Trade
FIP	Finance and Investment Protocol
HICs	High Income Countries
FTAs	Free Trade Agreements
HKIAC	Hong Kong International Arbitration Centre

I – J

IACs	International Arbitration Centers
IIL	International Investment Law

IACAs	International Commercial Arbitration Centres
IMAIL	Integrated Marxist Approaches to International Law
ICs	International Courts
IMF	International Monetary Fund
ICA	International Court of Arbitration
INCOTERMS	International Commercial Terms
ICC	International Chamber of Commerce
IOs	International Organizations
ICCPR	International Covenant on Civil and Political Rights
IP	Intellectual Property
ICDR	International Center of Dispute Resolution
IR/IL	International Relations/International Law
ICESCR	International Covenant on Economic, Social, and Cultural Rights
ISDS	Investor-State Dispute Settlement
ICJ	International Court of Justice
ITC	Imperial Tobacco Company
ICoA	International Co-operative Alliance
ITLOS	International Tribunal for the Law of the Sea
ICSID	International Centre for the Settlement of Investment Disputes
JCPC	Judicial Committee of the Privy Council

K – L

KIAC	Kigali International Arbitration Centre
LCIA	London Court of International Arbitration
LCA	Lagos Court of Arbitration
LMICs	Low and Middle Income Countries

M

MAIL	Mainstream Approaches to International Law
MFN	Most-Favored Nation
MAILS	Mainstream Approaches to International Law Scholarship
MIT	Multilateral Investment Treaty
MDGs	Millennium Development Goals
MSMEs	Micro, Small and Medium-Sized Enterprises

N – O

NAIL	New Approaches to International Law
NIEs	Newly Industrialized Economies
NAFTA	North-American Free Trade Agreement
NTBs	Non-Tariff Barriers to Trade
NCIA	Nairobi Centre for International Arbitration
OAU	Organization of African Unity
NGOs	Non-Governmental Organisations

OAMCC	Ouagadougou Arbitration and Mediation & Conciliation Centre
NIEO	New International Economic Order
OHADA	*Organisation pour l'Harmonisation en Afrique du Droit des Affaires*

P – R

PAIC	Pan-African Investment Code
PMC	Permanent Mandates Commission
PAIL	Positivist Approaches to International Law
PSNR	Permanent Sovereignty over Natural Resources
PCA	Permanent Court of Arbitration
PTAs	Preferential Trade Agreements
PFT	Plausible Folk Theory
RECs	Regional Economic Communities

S

SADC	Southern African Development Community
SCIA	Shenzhen International Court of Arbitration
SADCT	Southern African Development Community Tribunal
SIAC	Singapore International Arbitration Centre
SAN	Senior Advocate of Nigeria
SHIAC	Shanghai International Arbitration Centre
SCC	Stockholm Chamber of Commerce
SPSs	Sanitary and Phytosanitary Measures

T

TCC	Transnational Capitalist Class
TLO	Transnational Legal Order
TDR	Third-party dispute resolution
TNCs	Transnational Corporations
TFEU	Treaty on the Functioning of the European Union
TWAIL	Third World Approaches to International Law
TFTA	Tripartite Free Trade Area

U

UAs	Uniform Acts
UNGA	United Nations General Assembly
UAA	Uniform Act on Arbitration
UNCITRAL	United Nations Commission on International Trade Law
UN	United Nations
UNCTAD	United Nations Conference on Trade and Development
URA	Uganda Revenue Authority
UNCTC	United Nations Centre on Transnational Corporations

V – W

VAT	Value Added Tax
WHO	World Health Organization
VCLT	Vienna Convention on the Law of Treaties
WHA	World Health Assembly
WACA	West Africa Court of Appeal
WTO	World Trade Organization
WAEMU	West African Economic and Monetary Union
WWI	World War I
WG III	UNCITRAL Working Group III
WWII	World War II

List of Figures

List of Tables

Table of Cases

EACJ

ECCJ

OHADA CCJA

SADCT

Rwanda

Senegal

US

CJEU

WTO

Permanent Court of Arbitration

ICSID

ICJ

Other

Table of Statutory Instruments

SADC

OHADA

WTO

United Nations:

Arbitration Centres:

1

General Introduction

INTRODUCTION

THE PERVASIVE NARRATIVES ON international economic dispute resolution in Africa are gloomy. These narratives exist in the two main avenues of international economic dispute settlement: international court litigation and international arbitration. These narratives consciously and sometimes unconsciously ignore layers of pernicious colonial, post-colonial, and imperial continuities structured around the socio-legal actors involved in international economic dispute settlement in Africa. In Africa, states have mandated judiciaries at the sub-regional level, ie, within sub-regional economic communities, as custodians of community law and for the settlement of disputes. The narratives within the mainstream beltway of international law view Africa's sub-regional economic courts, developed under sub-regional economic communities (RECs), as less authoritative versions of their European and international counterparts. They mainly describe these courts as copy versions of the Court of Justice of the European Union (CJEU). The outcome is that when these courts falter, they are labelled imperfect copies, and when they thrive, they are praised as perfect copies of the CJEU.

These narratives are replicated in another format in public (Investor-State Dispute Settlement (ISDS)) and private (international commercial) arbitration in Africa. For ISDS, debates continue on how African states can become rule-makers instead of rule-takers in international investment dispute settlement.[1] Furthermore, mainstream approaches to international investment law continue to marginalise critical African scholarly voices and state practice within current debates for the reform of ISDS.[2] In international commercial arbitration, Africa remains the last frontier for the arbitration market, like in many other areas of economic or commercial endeavours.[3] Yet African arbitrators and arbitration

[1] Makane Moïse Mbengue and Stefanie Schacherer, 'Africa as an Investment Rule-Maker: Decrypting the Pan-African Investment Code' (2018) 23 *AfYIL* 81; Wolfgang Alschner and Dmitriy Skougarevskiy, 'Rule-Takers or Rule-makers? A New Look at African Bilateral Investment Treaty Practice' (2016) *Transanational Dispute Management* 1.

[2] See Wolfgang Alschner, Investment Arbitration and State-Driven Reform: New Treaties, Old Outcomes (Oxford University Press, 2022) 17–18.

[3] Kingsley Chiedu Moghalu, *Emerging Africa: How the Global Economy's 'Last Frontier' Can Prosper and Matter* (Penguin Books 2014).

centres remain marginalised. The Western metropoles of Washington DC, London, Geneva, and Paris still adjudicate the most consequential arbitrations involving African actors.

International Economic Dispute Settlement in Africa argues that these narratives are wrong and aim to further marginalise African institutions to the periphery of international economic dispute settlement. To unpack this argument, *International Economic Dispute Settlement in Africa* makes specific interventions and arguments at four primary levels: the doctrinal level, the epistemological level, the theoretical level, and the socio-cultural level. It centres on five socio-legal actors and their actions in shaping, justifying, and transforming the authority, functions, and outcomes of international economic dispute settlement in Africa. The five socio-legal actors are: African states, Transnational corporations (TNCs), African international law legal scholars and experts, International and Transnational Organisations (IOs), and African emerging transnational actors in arbitration. These socio-legal actors have variously impacted the role, authority, and legitimacy of African sub-regional economic courts and arbitral tribunals. These actors are the five pillars (or pentagon) that I refer to as the socio-legal pillars of understanding African international economic dispute settlement.

African states stand at the core of this ecology of actors.[4] They have structured the jurisdictional mandates of their sub-regional judiciaries in complex ways that militate against purely positivistic or doctrinal analyses. These purely doctrinal analyses have produced the mainstream narratives described and discredited above. This book responds to such analyses with two critical and interdisciplinary theoretical and methodological approaches: Third World Approaches to International Law (TWAIL) and the thick description approach. Such an analysis reveals a complex matrix of social, political, historical, and legal variations.[5]

As a central logic of analysis, *International Economic Dispute Settlement in Africa* argues that the processes of colonialism, neocolonialism, and neoliberalism have constituted and continue[6] to generate international economic law

[4] Susan Block-Lieb and Terence C Halliday, *Global Lawmakers: International Organizations in the Crafting of World Markets* (Cambridge University Press, 2017) 31–33 (offering a detailed theorisation of the sociological ecology theory).

[5] Obiora Chinedu Okafor, 'Critical Third World Approaches to International Law (TWAIL): Theory, Methodology, or Both' (2008) 10 *IntlCLR* 371, 375; James T Gathii, 'The Agenda of Third Word Approaches to International Law (TWAIL)' in Jeffrey Dunoff and Mark Pollack (eds), *International Legal Theory: Foundations and Frontiers* (Cambridge University Press, 2022) 158–167, (Arguing that TWAIL scholarship has three main themes: Tracing the roles of international law in constituting order and disorder, the centrality of history, and a commitment to reforming and remaking international law); James T Gathii, 'TWAIL: A Brief History of Its Origins, Its Decentralized Network, and a Tentative Bibliography' (2011) 3 Trade, Law and Development 26 (arguing that its decentralised nature means that it is not organised around vertical hierarchies of knowledge production).

[6] *See* Emma Hunter, 'The History of Political Thought in the African Political Present' in Annabel Brett, Megan Donaldson, and Martti Koskenneiemi (eds), *History, Politics, Law: Thinking Through the International* (Cambridge University Press, 2021) 208–228.

dispute settlement outcomes in Africa.[7] These ideas and phenomena continue to inform the current orientations of Africa's international courts and the TWAIL theoretical framework employed in this book. The mainstream narratives of international law ignore, under study and occlude the critical subjects of colonialism, neocolonialism, and neoliberalism.[8] The book engages with these three concepts through three TWAIL strands: TWAIL's socio-legal scholars from the TWAIL I and II movements;[9] the eclecticism of TWAIL;[10] and the Third World as a geographic, political, and epistemic location. TWAIL scholarship and praxis have continually challenged international law's institutionalised social, economic, political, and racial injustice.[11] TWAIL scholarship challenges the dominant Eurocentric historical and ontological orientation of international law. TWAIL theory directly challenges Mainstream Approaches to International Law (MAIL), Positivist Approaches to International Law (PAIL), and some critical approaches to international law.[12] MAIL and PAIL present international law as a set of principles, rules, obligations, practices, and understandings on the identification, interpretation, and enforcement of international law, devoid of their links to colonialism, neocolonialism, capitalism, imperialism, and patriarchy.[13]

One vital thread from the TWAILian approach, as presented in various chapters of this book, is the Marxist class-theoretical approach, embodied in the role of the transnational capitalist class (TCC).[14] The TCC is a group of individuals, corporate entities, and institutions that own and manage capital in leading means of production entities in more than one nation-state.[15] Transnational

[7] See Sara Dezalay, Lawyering Imperial Encounters: Negotiating Africa's Relationship with the World Economy (Cambridge University Press, 2024).

[8] Bhupinder S Chimni, *International Law and World Order: A Critique of Contemporary Approaches* (Cambridge University Press, 2017) 15.

[9] See Antony Anghie and Bhupinder S Chimni, 'Third World Approaches to International Law and Individual Repsonsibility in Internal Conflicts' (2003) 2 Chinese JIL 77.

[10] Antony Anghie and others, 'Introduction' in Antony Anghie and others (eds), *The Third World and International Order: Law, Politics and Globalization* (Martinus Nijhoff Publishers, 2003).

[11] Obiora C Okafor, 'Newness, Imperialism, and International Legal Reform in Our Time: A TWAIL Perspective' (2005) 43 *Osgoode Hall LJ* 171.

[12] Bhupinder S Chimni, *International Law and World Order: A Critique of Contemporary Approaches* (n 8) 10–14.

[13] Bhupinder S Chimni, 'The International Law of Jurisdiction: A TWAIL Perspective' (2022) 35 *LJIL* 29; *see also* Bhupinder S Chimni, 'An Outline of a Marxist course on Public International Law' in Susan Marks (ed), *International Law on the Left: Re-examining Marxist Legacies* (Cambridge University Press, 2008) 53–91.

[14] Akbar Rasulov, 'Nameless Rapture of the Struggle: Towards a Marxist Class-Theoretic Approach to International Law' (2008) 19 *FYBIL* 244, 268–273 (arguing that the global economic arena can be divided into three classes: the transnational capitalist class (TCC), the transnational working class (TWC), and the transnational middle class (TMC)).

[15] William I Robinson and Jerry Harris, 'Towards A Global Ruling Class? Globalization and the Transnational Capitalist Class' (2000) 64 *Science and Society* 11 (arguing that the TCC is composed of transnational corporations and financial institutions, the elites that manage the supranational economic planning agencies, major forces in the dominant political parties, media conglomerates, and technical elites and state managers).

corporations (TNCs) and private financial institutions embody the leading means of production entities at the core of the TCC.[16] The TCC is one of the primary beneficiaries and instigators of the unfair methods, practices, and understandings prevalent in mainstream international law. Importantly, fractions of the TCC as dominant elites are also ascendant in many parts of the global South. Yet this book does not merely present the Marxist class theory as its only logic of analysis. It is only one of the eclectic logics of analysis represented by TWAIL in this book. Indeed, a minority of the arguments presented in the book are doctrinal and representative of the mainstream approaches to international law (MAIL).

Additionally, *International Economic Dispute Settlement in Africa* borrows and applies two qualitative methods from anthropology and sociology: Clifford Geertz's thick description approach and Pierre Bourdieu's judicial fields approach.[17] The thick description aims to understand different phenomena in their context. Such context includes the political, social, economic, physical, historical, cultural, linguistic, moral, experiential, and affective.[18] This book thus expands the aperture of analysis for African sub-regional economic courts to cover political, social, economic, historical, and cultural issues. The thick description method employed in this book is thus not ethnographic in terms of data collection. I use it in the Geertzian sense to assess human action and account for their practices and aims. The book employs 'thick description' in the sense of interpreting context, capturing thoughts and emotions, assigning motivations and intentions, and providing a rich account of details that lend meaningfulness to the narrative. The book employs Pierre Bourdieu's reflexive sociology to translate the thick descriptions of the sub-regional economic courts in Africa.[19] Here, I focus on the international law elites as crucial agents of law and the conceptualisation of law as symbolic power. The focus on African international law scholars and experts, such as the renowned Senegalese international lawyer and scholar Kéba Mbaye, in the creation of the *Organisation pour l'Harmonisation en Afrique du Droit des Affaires* (OHADA) is an example of how the book employs these methods (chapter 4).

Consequently, *International economic dispute settlement in Africa* demonstrates that African sub-regional court jurisdictional structuring and public and private arbitration are complex and nuanced, even at their basic procedural and

[16] ibid: see also Bhupinder S Chimni, 'Capitalism, Imperialism, and International Law in the Twenty-First Century' (2012) 14 *Oregon RevIntlL* 17 (TCC consists of four fractions: Transnational Corporation (TNC) executives and their local affiliates (corporate fraction); globalising state and inter-state bureaucrats and politicians (state fraction); globalising professionals (technical fraction); and merchants and media (consumerist fraction).

[17] Joseph G Ponterotto, 'Brief note on the Origins, Evolution, and Meaning of the Qualitative Research Concept "Thick Description"' (2006) 11 The Qualitative Report 539; Clifford Geertz, *The Interpretation of Cultures* (Basic Books Incorporation Publishers, 1973); Pierre Bourdieu, 'The Force of Law: Toward a Sociology of the Juridical Field' (1987) 38 *Hastings LJ* 805.

[18] Gilbert Ryle, Collected Papers: Volume 2 1929–1986, xvii (2009).

[19] Pierre Bourdieu, 'The Force of Law: Toward a Sociology of the Juridical Field' (n 17).

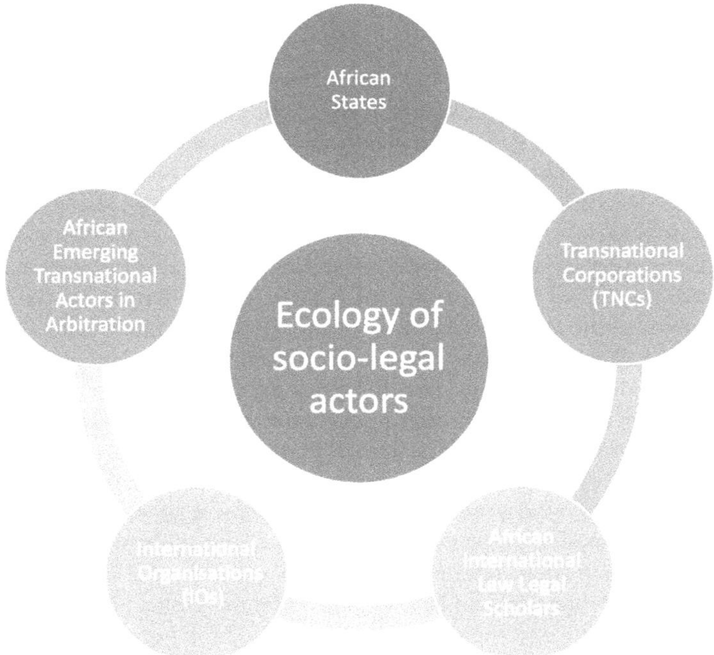

Figure 1 Ecology of socio-legal actors

doctrinal levels. This complexity produces three essential outcomes: the first is the outlook of courts that have mainly attracted human rights, governance, and domestic rule of law cases; the second is arbitration mandates that have not been fully exploited, and the third is a paltry docket of preliminary references or rulings. The broader outlook of these three outcomes is a general lack of economic disputes within these sub-regional judiciaries. Yet Africa remains home to the highest number of international courts of all the world regions. The sub-regional international economic courts analysed are established as an integral part of the African regional economic integration structure. They are designed in different ways and with different orientations. Some, like the East Africa Court of Justice (EACJ), the Economic Community of West African States (ECOWAS) Community Court of Justice (ECCJ), the Common Market for Eastern and Southern African States (COMESA) Court of Justice (CCJ), and the Southern African Development Community (SADC) Tribunal are community courts with jurisdiction to authoritatively interpret community treaties and laws. While another, the *Organisation pour l'Harmonisation en Afrique du Droit des Affaires* (OHADA) Common Court of Justice and Arbitration (OHADA CCJA), is a court of last resort on all OHADA harmonised commercial laws referred to as Uniform Acts (UAs).

I.I PILLAR ONE: AFRICAN STATES AS SOCIO-LEGAL ACTORS

African states act on international law in ways that display political, social, and legal outcomes. As social actors, states can only act through individuals (natural persons), since only individuals, from a sociological perspective, can possess intentions. The process of decolonisation, as a fundamental social occurrence, generated solidarity, which meant that states, especially those from the global South, would act together.[20] These state actions are manifested within the broader label of the Bandung spirit.[21] Colonialism, however, created a dual consciousness[22] in the psyches of African nation-states that has continued to influence the general trajectory of domestic and international African legal systems. The first manifestation of this duality in the law is the division between formally received law and informal legal systems. For international law, this duality is not pronounced in day-to-day application because the discipline, like most former colonial legal systems, is presented as a received system. Yet, it forms part of the general law applicable in African countries. The second duality is the paradox between rejectionism and reformism of international law among African scholars, especially those with a critical bent. Decolonisation introduced an ambivalent relationship towards international law from African states and critical international law scholars from the global South.

On the one hand, international law is criticised for perpetuating or acquiescing to existing systems of hegemony and subjugation, like slavery and imperialism and is thus in need of rejection. On the other hand, African states extol the emancipatory promise of international law for African communities, arguing that international law can be reformed for emancipatory purposes.[23] This is the duality and ambivalence that is also present in the TWAIL scholarship.[24] Yet, such duality and ambivalence do not render the pursuit of rejectionism and reformism of international law an objectionable endeavour. Indeed, as argued in Chapter 5 this book, the process of Africanisation of international law in Africa is constantly oscillating between these two poles. It is also a situation that all new nation-states that emerged in the twentieth and twenty-first centuries find themselves in. It is a dual move to reform and to affirm a system of law that is presented as universal, ie, as a law from nowhere and thus applicable everywhere, yet it is a law that is founded on European, imperial, and Christian values.[25]

[20] *See* Harrison Otieno Mbori, 'International Trade Solidarity Governance Split: Bretton Woods Solidarity vs Bandung Solidarity' in Cecial M Baillet(ed), *Research Handbook on International Solidarity and the Law* (Edward Elgar, 2024), 178–202.

[21] *See* Luis Eslava, Michael Fakhri, and Vasuki Nesiah, 'The Spirit of Bandung' in Luis Eslava, Michael Fakhri, and Vasuki Nesiah (eds), *Bandung, Global History, and International Law* (Cambridge University Press, 2017).

[22] *See* William Edward Burghardt Du Bois, *The Souls of Black Folk* (Oxford University Press, 2007 (1903)).

[23] See Sara Dezalay, Lawyering Imperial Encounters: Negotiating Africa's Relationship with the World Economy (n 7) 16 (describing the law's double bind, as both enabler and bulwark against domination).

[24] Mohsen al-Attar, 'Peculiar Double-Consciousness of TWAIL' (2022) 19 *Indonesian JIntlL* 239.

[25] Makau Mutua, 'What is TWAIL' (2000) 94 *AmSocIntlLProc* 31.

In chapter 3, I argue that the jurisdictional mandates of Africa's sub-regional economic courts and tribunals are complex, and commentators should avoid purely positivistic or doctrinal analyses of these courts. The chapter presents three specific examples of the current forms of Euro-American and Mainstream International Law Scholarship: Infantilisation, evaluative Western centrism, and systemic Western centrism. The chapter also demonstrates that a socio-historical appraisal of the jurisdictional posture of the African sub-regional economic courts and tribunals reveals a complex matrix of social, political, historical, and legal variation. Consequently, the chapter demonstrates how African states have established these courts, with distinct emerging characteristics. The following four characteristics are analysed: The multifunctionality of International courts in Africa, Courts specialising in human rights, Courts specialising in sub-regional economic law, and the phenomenon of non-judicialisation in North Africa. Finally, the chapter presents two factors that explain the low judicialisation of economic disputes within the sub-regional economic courts in Africa: the first is the presence, albeit limited use, and the contested nature of the arbitral function of these courts. The second is the low use of the domestic court references (Preliminary References/Rulings) to mandated African Sub-Regional Community Courts.

1.2 PILLAR TWO: TRANSNATIONAL COMPANIES (TNCS)

Transnational Companies (TNCs) are now integral as core actors in the global liberal market economy. Two diametric views have emerged regarding the impact of TNCs on the economic, social, political, legal, and environmental conditions of developing countries.[26] One view sees TNCs as agents of economic development, creating employment, transferring technological innovation and know-how, attracting further foreign direct investment (FDI), raising the standard of living, and fostering the rule of law and good governance. The shining example here from the global South is Costa Rica's attraction of Intel, making it a powerhouse in the microchip and semiconductor industry. The other view on TNCs argues that they have adverse effects on economic development, harm public and social interests, damage the environment, and weaken developing states' abilities to harness the potential benefits of economic globalisation.[27] An agnostic view suggests that both these views are extreme characterisations, each

[26] Bjørn Letnes, 'Transnational Corporations and Human Rights: Silencing the Ontological Controversy' (2004) 4 *Public Organization Review: A Global Journal* 259 (describing the view as the 'engines of development v. tools of exploitation debate).

[27] Ha-Joon Chang, 'Globalization, Transnational Corporations, and Economic Development: Can the Developing Countries pursue Strategic Industrial Policy in a Globalizing World Economy?' in Robert Pollin, Gerald Epstein and Dean Baker (eds), *Globalizing and Progressive Economic Policy* (1998) 97–113; Sara L Seck, 'Transnational Corporations and Extractive Industries' in Shawkat Alam and others (eds), *International Environmental Law and the Global South* (Cambridge University Press, 2015) 380–398.

assessing different aspects of the role of TNCS.[28] The first view applies statistical tools at the national level and finds that FDI generates positive economic and social rights outcomes.[29] The second view uses national and corporate case studies to illustrate numerous examples of human rights issues created by TNCs.[30]

International Economic Dispute Settlement in Africa leans more towards the second view than the first in demonstrating the specific role of TNCs within African sub-regional economic dispute settlement. Within the global supply chain, TNCs continue to drive globalised production in ways that promote and reproduce class, gender, and ethnic inequalities.[31] TNCs are one of the instruments that the Transnational Capitalist Class (TCC), comprising individual and corporate shareholders of TNCs, use to pursue their interests.[32] As sociological actors, the TNCs are one of the instruments the TCC uses to pursue globalist capital and accumulative interest. This book presents the TNCs as part of a socio-legal group of actors that carefully frame their actions to support crony capitalist interests. TNCs, thus, act at the margins of international law, carefully influencing the ensemble of methods, practices, and understandings of international law's identification, interpretation, and enforcement.[33]

TNCs are not new in the African legal, economic, cultural, and historical landscape. They were at the core of the legal formation of many African nation-states. The European colonial powers used the chartered companies as the desired instrument to herald empire in many parts of the global South.[34] Between the 16th and 19th centuries, the European version of the modern TNCs was the Royal Chartered company. They were the special-purpose vehicles that first came into contact with sub-Saharan Africa and heralded colonialism through armed intervention necessary to destroy African peoples' sovereignty and to lay the groundwork for colonial economies.[35] Before them, the European imperial powers, especially Britain and Portugal,[36] indicated that their interest in sub-Saharan Africa was philanthropic, namely, the suppression of the Arab slave trade.[37] The many expeditions that began in the late 19th century, led by

[28] Bjørn Letnes, 'Transnational Corporations and Human Rights: Silencing the Ontological Controversy' (n 26).

[29] ibid 259.

[30] ibid.

[31] David L Levy, 'Political Contestation in Global Production Networks' (2008) 4 Academy of Management Review 943.

[32] William I Robinson and Jerry Harris, 'Towards A Global Ruling Class? Globalization and the Transnational Capitalist Class' (n 15).

[33] Bhupinder S Chimni, 'Customary International Law: A Third World Perspective' (2018) 112 *AJIL* 1.

[34] Raj Kumar Trivedi, 'The Role of Imperial British East Africa Company in the Acquisition of East African Colony in the Second Half of the Nineteenth Century' (1971) 33 *Indian History Congress*.

[35] Walter Rodney, 'The Colonial Economy' in A Adu Boahen (ed), *General History of Africa: Africa under Colonial Domination 1880-1935* (1985) 337.

[36] Nazifa Rashid, 'British Colonialism in East-Africa during the Nineteenth Century' (2013) 1 *International Law Journal of Art and Art History* 22, 23.

[37] ibid.

Burton, Speke, Livingstone, Stanley, and Cameron, arguably started with a spirit of adventure and a quest for knowledge.[38] However, the motives of their financiers (the European imperial governments) were based on unabashed economic exploitation and the hope of eventual significant gains and profits.[39] The altruistic motives of ending slavery were a fig leaf for the British imperial government's plans to extend its political and economic influence to Africa.[40]

I have argued elsewhere,[41] using the *British American Tobacco v Attorney General of Uganda (EACJ), 2019* (BAT Case), that African sub-regional economic courts and tribunals would require two essential features to attract more international trade law disputes. The first is the product test. Here, the product at issue needs to be commercially, socially, politically, or culturally controversial. Tobacco is a good example, but many more products in the era of climate change and emerging global pandemics might also fulfil this characteristic. The second is the producer test. Here, TNCs easily qualify as the best examples of entities with the financial, legal, political, and even cultural power to drive international litigation, both directly and indirectly. The converse is thus correct in answering the vital question of why there has been low judicialisation of international trade law disputes within African sub-regional economic courts and tribunals. In many disputes, the product and producer tests articulated above are not present.

1.3 PILLAR THREE: AFRICAN INTERNATIONAL LAW LEGAL SCHOLARS AND EXPERTS

International law, as part of a cultural phenomenon, plays a vital role in the lives of international lawyers. African international law lawyers and scholars are integral norm entrepreneurs within African states, in TNCs, and in international organisations. These lawyers internalise thorough disciplinary training, the foundational concepts, and narratives of their discipline.[42] For African international lawyers, the effect of colonialism and its continuities has some indelible consequences. The colonial powers used the 'civilisation mission' as a veil for the actual and structural violence in the colonial process that forcefully and ideologically transplanted legal systems onto African soil. This process was achieved through Western social and cultural education,

[38] William Edward Burghardt Du Bois, *The World and Africa: Color and Democracy* (Oxford University Press, 1965) 71.

[39] ibid.

[40] *See* Rosa Luxemburg, *The Accumulation of Capital* (Routledge, 1913) (arguing that imperialism is a necessary outcome of capitalism and is linked to the very survival of capitalism).

[41] Harrison Otieno Mbori, 'Case Commentary on the British American Tobacco v. Attorney General of Uganda (EACJ) and GETMA International v. The Republic of Guinea (OHADA CCJA)' (2020)1 *AfJIEL* 344.

[42] Anne Orford, 'Embodying Internationalism: The Making of International Lawyers' (1998) 19 *Aust YBIL* 2–3.

or what the structural Marxist Louis Althusser called 'interpellation'.[43] Interpellation refers to the acquisition and internalisation of culture, in this case, legal culture. During colonisation and decolonisation, the educated and emerging African elite acquired and internalised two cultures: one from the Western colonial powers and the other from their traditional national cultures. Western thinkers had relegated these national cultures as backwards, primitive, uncivilised, and in many cases, repugnant to 'natural justice, equity, morality, humanity, and good conscience'.[44] The process of cultural relegation created a 'double consciousness'[45] inherent in the African political, social, cultural, and legal systems to date.

International Economic Dispute Settlement in Africa intervenes at this epistemological level to present the different African approaches to international law. The emergent international law scholars in Africa have inevitably faced the Du Boisian double consciousness described above. As an embodiment of the role of African international law scholarship, this book adopts, endorses, and applies James Gathii's categorisation of international law scholarship in Africa into two trends: Contributionist (weak) and Critical (strong) international law scholarship.[46] Proponents of the contributionist strand emphasise Africa's and Africans' contributions to international law. In other literature, contributionists are referred to as inter-civilisational approach scholars. Their main argument is that Africans and non-Europeans generally contributed to the identification, interpretation, and enforcement of international law.[47] Proponents of the critical strand examine Africa's subordination in international relations as a legacy directly traceable to international law.[48] They approach international law with this central question of how to defang international law of its imperialist and exploitative biases against the global South.[49] The dual categorisation of

[43] Louis Althusser, *On the Reproduction of Capitalism: Ideology and Ideological State Apparatuses* (Verso, 2014); *see also* Frantz Fanon, The Wretched of the Earth (Grove Press, 1963).

[44] Mohammad Shahabuddin, 'The Colonial 'Other' in the Nineteenth Century German Colonisation of Africa, and International Law' (2013) *AfYIL* 15; Antony C Diala, 'The Concept of Living Customary Law: A Critique' (2017) 49 *J Legal Plur Unofficial Law* 143; Godwin Eli Kwadzo Dzah, *Sustainable Development, International Law, and a Turn to African Legal Cosmologies* (Cambridge University Press, 2024), 207–212.

[45] William Edward Burghardt Du Bois, *The Souls of Black Folk* (n 22).

[46] James T Gathii, 'Africa and the History of International Law' in Bardo Fassbender and Anne Peters (eds), *The Oxford Handbook of the History of International Law* (Oxford University Press, 2012) 408–428; James T Gathii, 'Africa and the Radical Origins of the Right to Development' (2020) 1 *Twail Rev* 28.

[47] Tiyanjana Maluwa, 'Reassessing Aspects of the Contribution of African States to the Development of International Law through African Regional Multilateral Treaties' (2020) 41 *MichJIntlL* 327; Frans Viljoen, 'Africa's Contribution to the Development of International Human Rights and Humanitarian Law' (2001) 1 *AHRLJ* 18; *see also* Onuma Yasuaki, *International Law in A Transcivilizational World* (Cambridge University Press, 2017); Surya Prakash Sinha, *Legal Polycentricity and International Law* (Carolina Academic Press, 1996).

[48] James T Gathii, 'Africa and the History of International Law' (n 46).

[49] James Gathii, Obiora Okafor and Antony Anghie, 'Africa and TWAIL' 18(2010) *AfYIL* 9.

contributionist and critical, which I label as benign and radical, falls within the continuum of a critical tradition of international law scholarship.[50]

If the second strand sounds TWAILian in its content, it is because it is intended to be so. This book inevitably leans more towards the critical strand than the contributionist strand. Proponents of the critical strand are mainly early TWAIL scholars, such as the Algerian towering international law scholar and practitioner, Mohamed Bedjaoui, and Nigeria's leading scholar, Umozurike O. Umozurike. Many of the second-generation African TWAIL scholars, including Makau Mutua, Siba Grovogui, Issa Shivji, Sylvia Tamale, Joe Oloka-Onyango, Obiara Okafor, Joel Ngugi, Ibironke T. Odumosu, and Celestine Musembi, also fall squarely in this category. A new generation closely following the TWAIL II scholars is also emerging with some critical contributions to African international law in recent years. This group, which I cautiously label as TWAIL II plus,[51] includes scholars such as Mohsen al Attar, Olabisi Akingube, Achiume Tendayi, Babatunde Fagbayibo, and Christopher Gevers. Fagbayibo, for example, has argued for a third category or strand of 'intermediates' in addition to the two above.[52] Intermediates try to forge a path between the contributionist and critical approaches by emphasising the contextualisation and adaptability of Eurocentric conceptions of international law.[53] This approach does not dismiss ideas merely because of their Eurocentric origin but 'seeks to distil from them what can be used furthering cultural development and the strengthening of African human society'.[54]

Chapter 4 exemplifies the role of African international law scholars and experts as norm entrepreneurs (normpreneurs). The chapter examines the innovative structuring of the OHADA CCJA within the context of Françafrique's neo-colonial framework.[55] Françafrique refers to a system of continued dominance that contributes to the survival of France within the economic and military framework of its former colonies. This chapter centres the role of OHADA's main normpreneur: the towering Senegalese international law scholar, judge, arbitrator, and practitioner Kéba Mbaye.[56] The chapter supports the view of Kéba Mbaye as an intermediate within the three-part framework of African

[50] Harrison Otieno Mbori, 'Benign and Radical Africanization in International Investment Law and Investor-State Dispute Settlement in Africa' 24 (2023) *JWIT* 633.

[51] I remain conscious of the dangers and pitfalls of periodisation captured in TWAIL debates; *see* George Galindo, 'Splitting TWAIL?' (2016) 33 *Windsor YB Access to Justice*.

[52] Babtunde Fagbayibo, 'African Approaches to International Law' (Oxford Bibliographies, 2021).

[53] ibid.

[54] ibid.

[55] Boubacar Boris Diop, 'Françafrique: A Brief History of a Scandalous Word' *NewAfrican,* (3 March 2018) newafricanmagazine.com/opinions/francafrique-a-brief-history-of-a-scandalous-word/; see also Sara Dezalay, Lawyering Imperial Encounters: Negotiating Africa's Relationship with the World Economy (n 7) 38 ('the term "Françafrique" refers to France's sphere of influence (or "pré carré") over former French and Belgian colonies in sub-Saharan Africa').

[56] *See* Humphrey Sipalla, 'Not too many faces, one mask: A Kéba Mbaye Biographic' in Frans Viljoen, Humphrey Sipalla and Foluso Adegalu (eds), *Exploring African Approaches to International Law* (PULP, 2022).

international law scholarship discussed above. The chapter argues that despite OHADA's bleak neo-colonial outlook, the structure of the OHADA CCJA can allow for counteracting the internationalisation of investment contracts by making OHADA CCJA the 'domestic judicialised appellate court' on investment and other commercial disputes in Francophone Africa. Chapter 6 then proceeds to argue that the Africanisation narrative presented by another contemporary Senegalese international law scholar, arbitrator, and practitioner Makane Moïse Mbengue falls within the 'contributionist' (weak) category. The chapter additionally argues that Africanisation within the international investment law regime that leans towards the more 'critical or radical' (strong) category would result in more economic justice for the large sections of impoverished Africans. Finally, the chapter presents the following three attributes for such radical Africanisation: Focus on both inter and intra-African investment; engage substantive reforms; and finally, have an honest reckoning and engagement with the imperial history of international investment law generally and ISDS, specifically.

1.4 PILLAR FOUR: INTERNATIONAL AND TRANSNATIONAL ORGANISATIONS

International and Transnational organisations (IOs) are now easily considered indispensable to the current international law and governance architecture.[57] They cover all areas of important public policy questions today, from trade, health, and intellectual property to environmental governance. Increasingly, IOs act as administrative, regulatory organisations that formulate rules and monitor practices.[58] Two broad narratives tell the historical and contemporary role of IOs in international global governance. The first is the liberal and neoliberal account, which presents IOs as progressive, universalistic, and objective institutions for ordering specific and general transnational issues.[59] The second account is a critical account that engages with the IOs as a vast network of economic, social, and political instruments that First World states have carefully constituted and refashioned to actualise their interests and relegate those of the global South.[60] IOs seek to create, shape, join, understand, adapt, and resist transnational legal orders.[61] They form an integral part of the Transnational Legal Order (TLO). The TLO is a social order of individuals, national and international organisations, corporations, nation-states, and their networks

[57] Jan Klabbers, 'Introduction' in Jan Klabbers (ed), *The Cambridge Companion to International Organizations Law* (Cambridge University Press, 2022) 1–6.

[58] Susan Block-Lieb and Terence C Halliday (n 4).

[59] Bhupinder S Chimni, 'International Organizations, 1945-Present' in Jacob Katz, Ian Hurd and Ian Johnstone (eds), *The Oxford Handbook of International Organizations* (Oxford University Press, 2016) 113–130.

[60] Mohsen al Attar, 'Reframing the Universality of International Law in a Globalizing World' (2013) 59 *McGill LJ* 95.

[61] Susan Block-Lieb and Terence C Halliday (n 4).

that generate, apply, and enforce formalised legal norms that transcend more than one nation-state.[62]

This book focuses on economic regionalism as one of the critical trends in the trajectory of IOs. African regional economic communities (RECs) engage in a double-bind reaction to the liberal and neo-liberal model of international organisations. In the first sense, African states formulate these RECs as a counter-force to the World Trade Organization (WTO). They view the WTO as being a force that significantly limits their domestic economic sovereignty. African states, in this sense, want to be masters of their destinies. However, many different ideological forces and pressures have fractured the Pan-African spirit of solidarity that drives African unity. Secondly, the trifactor of colonialism, neocolonialism, and neoliberalism significantly limit the RECs' economic, social, and political sovereign autonomy. In this sense, African RECs are reactionary, rejectionist, and reformist. This is why this book engages with them on their own terms, without relying on the widespread scholarly comparative account that compares them to the European Union (EU). The African regional international organisations face many challenges that this book addresses on equal terms with their Western counterparts.

Additionally, the book focuses on the institutionalised Court of Arbitration of the International Chamber of Commerce (ICC) as a vital transnational non-governmental organisation involved in international commercial arbitration. The ICC indirectly orders private actors' commercial and trade relationships in less visible ways than other IOs, such as the United Nations Commission on International Trade Law (UNCITRAL). Chapter 6 of this book argues that most of the practices, rules, and structures of the emerging African International Arbitration centres (IACs) are modelled around the Paris-based International Court of Arbitration (ICA) of the International Chamber of Commerce (ICC). The ICC's nearly 100 years of commercial advocacy and policy lobbying with a neo-liberal political agenda tacitly influences its dispute settlement service. It is essential to distinguish the ICC as a chamber of commerce, as different from its dispute settlement service, the International Court of Arbitration (ICA), and its secretariat. The ICC carries out various functions, including advocacy and championing the free movement of goods, services, and capital across borders, which aligns with a neoliberal agenda. It also operates a dispute resolution service that encompasses mediation, arbitration, and expert proceedings. For arbitration, the ICC has an International Court of Arbitration (ICA), which is an institution that administers arbitration under defined rules. Chapter 6 thus argues that the politics of the ICC acting as a chamber of commerce, ie, as a group of business actors, tacitly and inadvertently affects and influences the role of its dispute settlement service, mainly encompassing legal actors. That influence is in the neo-liberal direction of the free movement of goods, services, and capital.

[62] *See* Terence C Halliday and Gregory Shaffer, 'Transnational Legal Orders' in Terence C Halliday and Gregory Shaffer (eds), *Transnational Legal Orders* (Cambridge University Press, 2015) 5–6.

1.5 PILLAR FIVE: AFRICAN EMERGING TRANSNATIONAL ACTORS IN ARBITRATION (LAWYERS, LAW FIRMS, AND LAW TRAINING INSTITUTIONS)

Lawyers, leading corporate law firms, and law training institutions in Africa are now intricately involved in brokerage and negotiation for the international arbitration market space and legitimacy.[63] *International Economic Dispute Settlement in Africa* argues that a small but increasing group of African lawyers can strategically position themselves through social, legal, political, and economic capital to create influential nodes of international arbitration governance. These lawyers can position themselves as either 'intermediary elites' or 'double agents;.[64] As 'double agents' in positions of power, they juggle neo-colonial corporate transnational influence and the promotion of the rule of law through arbitration. As 'intermediary elites', lawyers help structure, fix, and define private law doctrines and concepts that undergird arbitration.[65] In the highly judicialised format of arbitration described in chapter 7 of the book, lawyers negotiate the contracts that submit cases to arbitration, represent parties in arbitration proceedings, and are selected as arbitrators in arbitral proceedings. Lawyers are thus undeniably 'intermediaries' between the transnational elites, who are the primary builders of capital and capitalism, and the nation-state. They are also the primary source for international commercial arbitrators who play roles as 'judges', private service providers, legal officers, entrepreneurs, and academics.[66]

Law firms are the second level of emerging transnational actors in arbitration. African top-tier corporate law firms are increasingly making connections regionally and globally. Corporate law firms across many parts of the world are carefully expanding their domains of operation. Global capitalism requires a global vocabulary that is often wrapped up in the interest of exporting and importing the rule of law.[67] Law firms are the institutionalised vehicles that lawyers use to further their role as 'brokers' between social relations, actors, and the law.[68] Law firms serve as the institutional reputation capital drivers, enabling lawyers to accumulate social, legal, political, and economic capital. Law practice is a business in which financial profit is a strong incentive. The growth of transna-

[63] *See* Yves Dezalay and Bryant G Garth, 'Introduction' in Yves Dezalay and Bryant G Garth (eds), *Lawyers and the Rule of Law in an Era of Globalization* (Routledge, 2011) 1–16.

[64] *See* Sara Dezalay, 'Lawyers in Africa: Brokers of the State, Intermediaries of Globalization' (2018) *25 Indian Jof Global and LS* 639.

[65] *See* Ambreena Manji, *The Politics of Land Reform in Africa* (Zed Book Publishers, 2006), (presenting the role of lawyers in the global network of land reform); *see also* Ralf Michaels, 'Private Law Theory and the "Global Legal Community"' (2022) 23 *German LJ* 851 (arguing that non-European world private law theory remains unaddressed, marginalised, and ignored).

[66] Ralf Michaels, 'Roles and Role Perceptions of International Arbitrators' in Walter Mattli and Thomas Dietz (eds), *International Arbitration and Global Governance: Contending Theories and Evidence* (Oxford Academic, 2014) 48–73.

[67] Yves Dezalay & Bryant G Garth (n 63).

[68] ibid.

tional capital ventures in Africa means that leading African corporate law firms see arbitration as an essential avenue to amass economic and symbolic capital.

International Economic Dispute Settlement in Africa also demonstrates that the African arbitration scene is now growing, with emerging merchants of reputation.[69] These include individuals, institutions and associations that are invested in the arbitration rankings of arbitrators, lawyers, and law firms. The book shows the increasing number of African arbitration rankings and power lists. Based on Pierre Bourdieu's notion of symbolic capital, the desire for honour, prestige, and recognition generated by these arbitration rankings can be understood.[70] Bourdieu showed that the actors in any field, which he called 'habitus', are actively looking for symbolic capital, ie, in economic terms, money, and welfare, and in symbolic terms: honours, prestige, and recognition.[71] This is a truism in Africa as it is anywhere else in the world.

African regional international arbitration training institutions are the third and final arm of the emerging transnational actors in African international commercial arbitration. These are focused versions of training institutions designed to meet the demands of commercial arbitration practice.[72] The professionalisation of international arbitration has created a demand for such training institutions.[73] They aim to fill the gap created by the little attention given to international arbitration in African universities. These are not fully established institutions, such as universities or colleges. They are dedicated institutions with missions and visions focused on training qualified lawyers to acquire skills and gain accreditation in specific niche areas of international law, generally, and in arbitration specifically. In some parts of Africa, such as Kenya, branches of the Chartered Institute of Arbitrators in London serve as both a training institute and a leading international arbitration centre. Arbitration training institutions are set up for three primary purposes. The first is to supply a cadre of trained and thus well-prepared arbitrators and arbitral practice lawyers. The second is to professionalise the field, ie, the process of making a profession. The third and final role is to inculcate a distinct culture of international commercial arbitration.[74] The final section of Chapter 7 focuses on and analyses two African regional international arbitration training institutions: The African Arbitration Academy (AAA) and the African Institute of International Law (AIIL).

[69] Emmanuel Gaillard, 'Sociology of International Arbitration' 31 (2015) *Arbitration International* 10 (describing three arbitrations rituals: arbitral hearings, recognition tournaments, and periodic mass gatherings).

[70] See Pierre Bourdieu, Distinction-A Social Critique of the Judgment of Taste (Harvard University Press, 1984).

[71] Pierre Bourdieu, 'The Force of Law: Toward a Sociology of the Juridical Field' (1987) 38 *Hastings LJ* 805.

[72] Yves Dezalay and Bryant G Garth, *Law as Reproduction and Revolution: An Interconnected History* (California Press, 2021) 7.

[73] Mikaël Schinazi, The Three Ages of International Commercial Arbitration (Cambridge University Press, 2021) 195.

[74] Won Kidane, The Culture of International Arbitration (Oxford University Press, 2017).

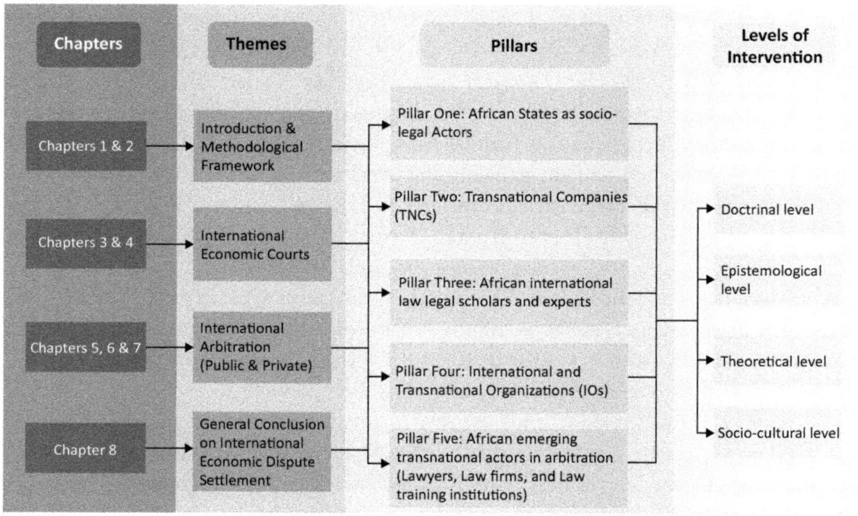

Figure 2 Summary of the book chapters, themes, and pillars of intervention

Increasingly, state-backed international arbitration centres like the Nairobi Centre for International Arbitration (NCIA) also offer training services.

1.6 HOW TO READ THIS BOOK AND CHAPTER OUTLINE

The chapters in this book are carefully arranged to provide the reader with a comprehensive view of the arguments presented in this general introduction. While the reader who wants the whole story is encouraged to read the book from beginning to end, I have also designed each chapter so that readers may profit by reading any of them on their own. This book has 8 chapters, including this general introduction. Overall, I have grouped the chapters into three broad themes as follows:

Theme 1 focuses on the Introduction and Theoretical and Methodological framework

Chapter 2: Assessing Sub-Regional International Economic Courts and Tribunals in Africa

This chapter offers two critical surveys of the different categories of international courts in Africa and the literature on these judiciaries. The chapter introduces Africa's international courts and tribunals. First, it showcases the categorical diversity of these courts and tribunals. There are four interrelated categories:

judicial, quasi-judicial, Free Trade agreements (FTAs) dispute settlement mechanisms (DSMs), and non-operational international courts. Second, the chapter offers the statement of the problem that underpins the analysis of the settlement of economic disputes in sub-regional Africa. Finally, the chapter critically reviews a select set of literature on Africa's sub-regional courts and tribunals.

Theme 2 focuses on Africa's sub-regional economic judiciaries

Chapter 3: The Complexities of Africa's Sub-Regional International Economic Courts and Tribunals

This chapter argues that African sub-regional economic courts and tribunals are complex in three different ways: analytically, in utility, and in functionality. The analytical complexity is demonstrated via the analysis of the present forms of Euro-American and Mainstream International Law Scholarship (MAILS) of African sub-regional International Economic Courts: Infantilisation, Systemic Western Centrism, and Evaluative Western Centrism. The utility complexity analyses the general multifunctional characteristics of African international courts and tribunals. This multifunctionality has produced three consequences: Courts specialising in international human rights; sub-regional courts that specialize in international economic law; and non-judicialisation in North Africa. Finally, the 'dormant' functional complexity aspect is analysed through two factors that explain the low judicialisation of economic disputes within the sub-regional economic courts in Africa. The first is the limited use and contested nature of the arbitral function of these courts. The second is the low use of domestic court References (Preliminary References/Rulings) to mandated African Sub-Regional Community Courts.

Chapter 4: The OHADA Court of Justice and Arbitration (OHADA CCJA): Innovation in the Shadow of Neo-Colonialism

This chapter argues that African states can and should innovate in designing sub-regional international economic courts and tribunals within the reality of neo-colonialism. Its focuses on OHADA and the OHADA CCJA as primary examples. The chapter first demonstrates the role that normpreneurs have played and continue to play in the development of international investment law. Within the OHADA CCJA, we see the role of Judge Kéba Mbaye as one of the leading normpreneurs within OHADA. The second part of the chapter presents OHADA as an institution woven within the 'Françafrique'[75] neo-colonial mould. The chapter demonstrates that the continued link of the CFA franc's currency with France means OHADA is firmly rooted in colonial foundations.

[75] Boubacar Boris Diop, 'Françafrique: A Brief History of a Scandalous Word' *NewAfrican* (n 55).

The chapter is, therefore, primarily structured around OHADA's Françafrique's origins and makes other institutional critiques of OHADA. Finally, the chapter argues that despite OHADA's bleak outlook, the structure of the OHADA CCJA can counteract the internationalisation of investment contracts. This structuring makes the OHADA CCJA a 'domestic judicialised appellate court'. The presence of uniformised laws allows investors to submit the OHADA CCJA itself to settle investment disputes and not ad hoc arbitral tribunals. This avenue is better structurally than ECOWAS' ECCJ because ECOWAS, unlike OHADA, does not have uniform law and is not as fully supranational as OHADA.

Theme 3 focuses on public and private (international commercial) arbitration

Chapter 5: Benign and Radical Africanization of International Investment Dispute Settlement in Africa

This chapter engages directly with the idea of Africanisation of ISDS. The chapter follows, adopts, and endorses the categorisation of international law scholarship in Africa developed by James Gathii into two trends: Contributionist and Critical International Law scholarship. The chapter argues that the trajectories of current reforms in African international investment law, now termed as Africanisation of international investment law, also fall into two categories: Benign Africanisation and Radical Africanisation, which respectively correspond with the contributionist and critical strands of international law scholarship proposed by Gathii. The chapter argues that to achieve international economic justice for the peoples of Africa, many of whom still face dire poverty, deprivation, and significant economic inequity and injustice, the radical form or approach of Africanisation must be deployed in reforming international investment law generally and ISDS specifically. As a central logic of analysis, the chapter argues that the process of colonialism and neocolonialism was and continues[76] to be a constitutive process of international investment law (IIL) dispute settlement in Africa and informs the current orientations and trajectories of reforms in international investment law in Africa. Colonialism was a process of wholesome cultural exportation and cultural dislocation at the domestic level. The colonial powers used the 'civilisation mission' as a veil for the real and structural violence in the colonial process that forcefully and ideologically transplanted legal systems into African soil.[77] The benign form

[76] *See* Emma Hunter, 'The History of Political Thought in the African Political Present' in Annabel Brett, Megan Donaldson & Martti Koskenneiemi, (eds), *History, Politics, Law: Thinking Through the International* (Cambridge University Press, 2021), 208–228.

[77] *See* Chen Lei, 'Contextualizing Legal Transplant: China and Hong', in Pier Giuseppe Monateri (ed.) *Methods of Comparative Law* (Edward Elgar Publishing, 2012) 192 (defining legal transplantation as the process by which law travels from one jurisdiction to another by way of transposition, imposition, reception or intended borrowing).

or approach of Africanisation will end up as window-dressing to the identified injustices of the current ISDS system without ever remedying the deeply seated colonial and neo-colonial continuities of unjust international investment law. in short, benign Africanisation will not reform IIL and ISDS sustainably to ensure economic, political, social, and environmental justice.

Chapter 6: International and African Regional Arbitration Centers as Competing Nodes of Governance for Economic Disputes with African Regional Courts and Tribunals.

This chapter examines the historical, substantive, institutional, and administrative frameworks of private and public arbitration. Most international arbitrations are now administered by national or International Arbitration Centres (IACs). The chapter argues that African regional IACs are emerging and are increasing the competition for arbitration disputes involving African parties with more established IACs, such as the International Chamber of Commerce (ICC). With its broad economic, political, and social tentacles, competing with the ICC is a challenge and will continue to remain so for the foreseeable future. However, the emergence and presence of these African regional IACs is a fact to be celebrated and encouraged. As long as they maintain a credible and high level of appeal for their services, in many cases supported by the state, the dominance of the more recognised IACs in the metropoles will not remain unchallenged.

Chapter 7: Three Emerging Transnational Actors within the African International Commercial Arbitration Scene

This chapter argues that the African marketplace of international professional dispute settlement analysis has thus far remained somewhat of a black box. This penultimate chapter of this book aims to fill a small section of this gap by focusing on the three emerging transnational actors within the African arbitration scene: international lawyers, law firms, and law training institutions. The chapter argues that three different but interconnected transnational socio-legal actors are emerging in the field of African international arbitration. These three are: First, well-established and emerging arbitrators; second, African top-tier corporate law firms connecting regionally and globally; and finally, African arbitration training institutions and professional centres.

Importantly, all three actors have African international lawyers at their core. The three actors are increasingly interconnected, navigating, and intermediating the African international arbitration scene. These actors are essential in shaping how arbitration practice is both globalised and localised for various interested parties.

2

Assessing Sub-Regional International Economic Courts and Tribunals in Africa

I. INTRODUCTION

AFRICA IS ARGUABLY THE best region to study as a laboratory of experiments in the judicialisation of international law. Examples of African international courts and tribunals are numerous in quantity and quality. With the proliferation of international courts and tribunals in the late twentieth and early twenty-first centuries, studying international courts and tribunals in Africa has become both compelling and urgent. States in Africa have established, are in the process of establishing, and have failed to establish regional and sub-regional international courts and tribunals. There are continuing successes and 'trials and errors' in Africa, making the continent an excellent laboratory for experiments in international adjudication. This book contends that assessing the legitimacy, role, or authority, of African international courts presents neither a case of complete gloom nor glory. This view differs from most mainstream accounts, which typically present these courts in a gloomy and pessimistic light.

Specifically, this book focuses on economic (including international investment) disputes in African sub-regional international judiciaries and tribunals. Sub-regional international courts in Africa are distinct from African regional international courts. The regional ones are established at the continental level, mainly by the African Union (AU). The sub-regional ones are nestled within sub-continental organisations such as the sub-regional Economic Communities (RECs). The subject matter covered in this book on international economic disputes is vast and encompasses a wide range of aspects of international economic law. In recent times, international investment law has received significant attention globally as a sub-branch of international economic law. This attention is focused primarily on the legitimacy of its chosen dispute settlement model, the Investor-State Dispute Settlement (ISDS).[1] However, little analytical

[1] Jürgen Kurtz, 'Building Legitimacy Through Interpretation in Investor-State Arbitration: On Consistency, Coherence, and the Identification of Applicable Law', in Zachary Douglas, Joost Pauwelyn, and Jorge E Viñuales (eds), *The Foundations of International Investment Law* (Oxford

and scholarly attention has been directed at the role of Africa's sub-regional judiciaries in addressing international economic law issues, including international investment, and how these courts can serve as avenues for the judicialisation of ISDS in Africa.

This chapter uses the term 'international courts and tribunals' to broadly cover methods and institutions offering third-party dispute settlement, authoritative – including binding – decisions and involving at least one recognised subject of international law.[2] This definition of international courts and tribunals or international adjudication is additionally based on the following five features: (1) deciding question(s) brought before them on the basis of international law; (2) following pre-determined rules of procedure; (3) issuing legally binding decisions or opinions; (4) being composed of independent members; and (5) requiring at least one party to a dispute to be a state or an international organisation. These criteria thus enables the expansion of the study in this area to include an analysis of the role of ISDS in Africa and the interlinkages between the African sub-regional judiciaries and ISDS as part of international adjudication, particularly in international economic law. Thus, although the area of ISDS encompasses arbitral tribunals, which are not permanent, ISDS can neatly fit into the criteria adopted above.

Before delving into the main arguments in the book, this chapter offers two critical surveys of the different categories of international courts in Africa and the literature on these judiciaries. The chapter aims to provide an introduction to Africa's international courts and tribunals. First, the chapter showcases the categorical diversity of these courts and tribunals. There are four interrelated categories: judicial, quasi-judicial, Free Trade agreements (FTAs) dispute settlement mechanisms (DSMs), and non-operational international courts. Second, the chapter offers the statement of the problem that underpins the analysis of the settlement of economic disputes in sub-regional Africa. Finally, the chapter critically reviews a select set of literature on Africa's sub-regional courts and tribunals.

Broadly, we can categorise African international courts based on their adjudicatory subject matters. On this count, many international courts and tribunals are increasingly specialised and accept disputes only in one or a limited number of categories of international law, such as human rights. Generalist international courts accept disputes in many or all areas of international law. The specialisation here means that the court or tribunal can only hear a case on a specific subject matter to which its constituent treaty is dedicated. Thus, at the international level, the International Tribunal for the Law of the Sea (ITLOS) hears only

Academic, 2014); Malcolm Langford and others, 'Special Issue: UNCITRAL and Investment Arbitration Reform: Matching Concerns and Solutions: An Introduction' (2020) 21 JWIT 167; Judith Knieper, 'UNCITRAL's Working Group III Discussion on Dispute Prevention' (2021) 17 *University of St. Thomas LJ* 455.

[2] Jorge E Viñuales, 'Experiments in International Adjudication: Past and Present' in Ignacio De La Rasilla and Jorge E Viñuales (eds), *Experiments in International Adjudication: Historical Accounts* (Cambridge University Press, 2019) 11.

disputes related to the law of the sea. In contrast, the World Trade Organization (WTO) dispute settlement system only accepts international trade-related issues. These typologies of specialisation and generalisation are also present in Africa.

2. A TYPOLOGY OF AFRICAN INTERNATIONAL COURTS

Africa's international courts and tribunals can be categorised into four main categories: judicial, quasi-judicial, FTAs, DSMs and non-operational international courts. In Africa, there is no court with general jurisdiction, except for the defunct African Court of Justice (ACJ) and the non-operationalised African Economic Community Court of Justice (AECJ). The AECJ was the only court designed to entertain cases on an unlimited number of subjects, from human rights to economic and trade issues. Still, both were only for states as disputing parties.

2.1 Operational/Active Judicial International Courts in Africa

Africa is home to at least eight active international courts or judiciaries[3] of regional and sub-regional character.[4] The following are the eight active international courts in Africa: (1) the African Court on Human and Peoples' Rights (ACtHPR) (established 1998); (2) the East Africa Court of Justice (EACJ) (established in 2001); (3) The Economic Community for West African States (ECOWAS) Court of Justice (ECCJ) (established in 2001); (4) The South African Development Community (SADC) Tribunal (established 2005); (5) the West African Economic and Monetary Union (WAEMU) Court of Justice (established in 1995); (6) The Organisation for the Harmonisation of Business Law In Africa Common Court of Justice and Arbitration (OHADA CCJA) (established in 1997); (7) the Common Market for Eastern and South Africa (COMESA) Court of Justice (established in 1998); and the (8) Court of Justice for the Central African Economic and Monetary Community (CEMAC) (established in 2000).

These eight international courts share three main vital features: they are operational with a varied degree of activeness, judicial, and international character. They are active not because of the number of cases in their dockets but merely because they are operational, with sitting judges (or have had sitting judges), and have heard some cases to conclusion.[5] They are judicial, not quasi-judicial,

[3] James T Gathii, 'African Regional Trade Agreements as Legal Regimes' (2011) 35 North *CarJ. IntlL* 564 (Referring to the courts established under Regional Trade Agreements as Judiciaries).

[4] James T Gathii and Harrison O Mbori, 'Reference Guide to Africa's International Courts: An Introduction' in James T Gathii (ed), *The Performance of Africa's International Courts: Using International Litigation for Political, Legal, and Social Change* (Oxford University Press, 2020).

[5] Cesare Romano, 'Trial and Error in international Judicialization' in Cesare Romano, Karen Alter and Yuval Shany (eds), *The Oxford Handbook of International Adjudication* (Oxford University Press, 2014) (describing some international courts that were unable to see the light of day and were thus nipped in the bud).

because they have the power to issue legally binding decisions between parties. They are international because they are established under international treaties and conventions as their constituent instruments. Quasi-judicial bodies review the compliance of state parties with treaty obligations but do not issue binding decisions. They only issue non-binding recommendations.[6]

Moreover, these eight courts above are permanent,[7] with standing judiciaries established by states under treaties to enforce the rights and obligations outlined in the various treaties. This permanency should be distinguished from international arbitral tribunals, which are established for the duration of a single dispute and are disbanded upon its conclusion. It is important to note that the traditional understanding was that the permanency of an international court distinguished it from a 'tribunal'.[8] Thus, non-permanent bodies, which in many cases are arbitral, are referred to as tribunals. Excellent examples include the Iran-US Claims Tribunal[9] and the Eritrea-Ethiopia Claims Tribunal.[10] This distinction has, in recent years, lost significance, as even permanent bodies are often referred to as tribunals, with a notable example being ITLOS.[11] These eight international African judiciaries also have broad subject matter jurisdiction over human rights, good governance, and economic and trade issues. The current active international courts in Africa are established as part of the African human rights systems under the auspices of the AU through the African Charter on Human and Peoples' Rights (Banjul Charter)[12] and the African regional and sub-regional economic integration systems.[13]

The number of international courts in Africa is the highest among other regions, including Europe and the Americas.[14] Like most international courts worldwide, the international courts in Africa have expanded significantly since

[6] ibid.

[7] Cesare P R Romano, 'A Taxonomy of International Rule of Law Institutions' (2011) 2 *JIDS* 241, 262. (arguing that permanence refers not to the court or tribunal itself as permanent rather that the group of judges who are sitting are not selected on an ad hoc basis by the parties to a given case).

[8] Chiara Giorgetti, *Introduction*, in Chiara Giorgetti (ed), *The Rules, Practice, and Jurisprudence of International Courts and Tribunals* (Martinus Nijhoff Publishers, 2012) 1.

[9] Christopher R Drahozal and Christopher S Gibson, *The Iran-U.S Claims Tribunal at 25: the Cases everyone needs to know for Investor-State & International Arbitration* (Oxford Law Pro, 2007); Rahmatullah Khan, *The Iran-United States Claims Tribunal: Controversies, Cases, and Contribution* (Martinus Nijhoff Publishers, 1990).

[10] Won Kidane, 'Civil Liability for Violations of International Humanitarian Law: The Jurisprudence of the Eritrea-Ethiopia Claims Commission in the Hague' (2009) 23 *Journal of Ethiopian Law* 36.

[11] Chiara Giorgetti, (n 8).

[12] Banjul Charter on Human and Peoples' Rights, 21 ILM 58 (1982).

[13] *See generally* James T Gathii, 'African Regional Trade Agreements As Legal Regimes' (n 3); *see also* Richard Frimpong Oppong, *Legal Aspects of Economic Integration in Africa* (Cambridge University Press, 2011).

[14] Karen Alter, *The New Terrain International Law: Courts, Politics, Rights* (Princeton University Press, 2014) 155–161 (8 courts in Africa out of 24 international courts overall globally).

the end of the Cold War.[15] This expansion is evidence of what scholars have referred to as the proliferation of international courts and tribunals.[16]

2.2 Quasi-Judicial International Courts in Africa

In addition to these active international courts, there are many active international quasi-judicial institutions in Africa. They include the African Commission on Human and Peoples' Rights (ACHPR);[17] the Africa Committee of Experts on the Rights and Welfare of the Child (ACERWC);[18] The High Commission of Appeal of the African Intellectual Property Organisation (AIPO/OAPI); and the Board of Appeal of the African Regional Industrial Property Organisation (ARIPO). Additionally, Africa has been and continues to be home to several critical hybrid[19] international courts and tribunals in the field of international criminal law. The examples are the defunct International Tribunal for Rwanda (ICTR)[20] and the Special Court for Sierra Leone (SCSL).[21]

2.3 Free Trade Agreement Dispute Settlement Mechanisms in Africa

In addition to the above judicial and quasi-judicial institutions, Africa also hosts the soon-to-be-activated/operationalised mechanisms for dispute resolution

[15] ibid 149.

[16] *See* Theresa Squatrito and others, 'A Framework for Evaluating the Performance of International Courts and Tribunals' in Theresa Squatrito and others (eds), *The Performance Of International Courts And Tribunals* 1 (Cambridge University Press, 2018) 1; Roger P Alford, 'The Proliferation of International Courts and Tribunals: International Adjudication in Ascendance'(2000) 94 *AmSocIntLProc* 160; Pemmaraju Sreenivasa Rao, 'Multiple International Judicial Forums: A Reflection of the Growing Strength of International Law or Its Fragmentation' (2004) 25 *MichJIntlL* 929; George Abi-Saab, 'Fragmentation Or Unification: Some Concluding Remarks' (1999) 31 *NYUJIntlL& Pol* 919; Lucy Reed, 'Great Expectations: Where Does the Proliferation of International Dispute Resolution Tribunals Leave International Law?' (2002) 96 *AmSocIntLProc* 219; Thomas Buergenthal, 'Proliferation of International Courts and Tribunals: Is it Good or is it Bad?' 14 (2001) *Leiden JIntlL* 267; Cesare P R Romano, 'The Proliferation of International Judicial Bodies: The Pieces of the Puzzle' 31(1999) *NYUJIntlL& Pol* 713.

[17] Rachel Murray, *The African Commission on Human and Peoples' Rights and International Law* (2000).

[18] ACERWC, reporting.acerwc.africa/committeeexperts.

[19] Kirsten Ainsley and Mark Kersten, 'Resilience and the Impacts of Hybrid Courts' (2020) 33 *Leiden JIntlL* (arguing that hybrid courts are different from tribunals in that they feature varying combinations of international and domestic staff, operative law, structure, financing, and rules of procedure and are usually established in partnership with a domestic government in the state where alleged crimes took place).

[20] Anne-Marie de Brouwer and Alette Smeulers (eds), *The Elgar Companion to the International Criminal Tribunal for Rwanda* (Edward Elgar Publishing, 2016).

[21] Tim Kelsall, *Culture under Cross-Examination: International Justice and the Special Court for Sierra Leone* (Cambridge University Press, 2009).

embedded in two emergent FTAs, commonly referred to as DSMs.[22] These are the Tripartite Free Trade Area (TFTA) that aims to consolidate the East Africa Community (EAC), the COMESA and the SADC into a single free trade area;[23] and the African Continental Free Trade Agreement (AfCFTA) that brings all 55 African states under one umbrella FTA.[24]

To understand these emergent FTAs, it is essential to note that before them, African states already had several different RECs. These older RECs are theoretically anchored in the yet-to-be-attained vision of an African Economic Community (AEC) as outlined in the Abuja Treaty of 1991.[25] Africa, unlike Europe, does not have a single REC but several different sub-regional economic communities. These RECs emerge out of Regional Trade Agreements (RTAs) (in this case, sub-regional trade agreements) in the form of treaties that are referred to as Preferential Trade Agreements (PTAs) in WTO parlance.[26] The term Regional Trade Agreement is used when states in the same geographic region sign agreements for more favourable trade terms among themselves.[27] Embedded within the TFTA and the AfCFTA are DSMs that are similar to the ad hoc panels and the standing Appellate Body, in the style of the WTO and its dispute settlement system.[28]

2.4 Non-Operationalised International Courts in Africa

There are also some non-operationalised international courts and tribunals in Africa. The most significant is the African Court of Justice and Human and Peoples' Rights (ACJHPR), which will replace the ACtHPR when it becomes operational.[29] Others include the Arab Maghreb Union Judicial Organ, the African Economic Community Court of Justice (AECCJ), the Arbitration Tribunal of the Economic Community of West African States, and the Court of Justice of the Economic Community of Central African States (ECCAS). Another significant non-operationalised court that will never see the light of day because subsequent developments have superseded it is the African Union Court of Justice (ACJ). At its inception in 2002, the AU had intended to establish

[22] *See* Robert Howse and others, 'Introduction' in Robert Howse and others, *The Legitimacy of International Trade Courts and Tribunals* (Cambridge University Press, 2018).

[23] East African Community, 'COMESA-EAC-SADC Tripartite' www.eac.int/tripartite.

[24] African Union, 'AfCFTA: African Continental Free Trade Area' au.int/en/ti/cfta/about (The AU decided to establish a single continental market for goods and services, with free movement of business persons and investments, thus pave the way for accelerating the establishment of the Customs Union).

[25] Treaty Establishing the African Economic Community, 30 ILM 1241 (3 June 1991) [AEC Treaty].

[26] General Agreement on Tariffs and Trade 1994, 15 April 1994, Marrakesh Agreement Establishing the World Trade Organization, Annex 1A, 1867 U.N.T.S. 187, 33 ILM 1153 (1994), art XXIV.

[27] Pravin Krishna, 'The Economics of PTAs' in Simon Lester and Bryan Mercurio(eds), *Bilateral and Regional Trade Agreements* (Cambridge University Press, 2009) 11.

[28] Olabisi Akinkugbe, 'Dispute Settlement Under the African Continental Free Trade Area Agreement: A Preliminary Assessment' (2019) papers.ssrn.com/sol3/papers.cfm?abstract_id=3403745&download=yes.

[29] *See* Charles Jalloh, Kamari Clarke and Vincent Nmehielle(eds), *The African Court of Justice and Human and Peoples' Rights in Context* (Cambridge University Press, 2019).

two separate courts, with the ACJ serving as the counterpart to the ACtHPR.[30] Article 18 of the AU Constitutive Act, adopted in 2001, established the African Court of Justice (ACJ). The Protocol for the establishment of the ACJ was adopted in 2003 and entered into force in 2009.

The ACJ remains non-operationalised to this day and will likely never be formed, at least not in the format initially envisaged. This outcome is possible because when the ACtHPR Protocol entered into force in 2004, the AU Assembly had already begun discussing a potential merger of the two courts (the AU ACJ and the ACtHPR).[31] These discussions have led to the formation of the ACJHPR discussed above, which is yet to be operationalised. Yet, the ACJHPR differs from the AECCJ, which was envisioned under the Abuja Treaty for the Establishment of the AEC in 1991 by the Organisation of African Unity (OAU).[32] Since the African Economic Community as an organisation has not yet been formed, this court also remains non-operational.

3. STATEMENT OF THE PROBLEM

This chapter addresses three specific problems that permeate the African international economic dispute settlement landscape. The first problem is that sub-regional judiciaries in Africa established under RECs have attracted few litigants and cases in the areas of international economic law, including trade, business, commerce, and investment. This situation exists despite high barriers to trade and commerce in intra- and extra-African trade. The most active of Africa's sub-regional International Courts: EACJ, the ECOWAS ECCJ, and, to some extent, the SADC Tribunal before its reorganisation in 2014, have dockets dominated by human rights, democracy, and rule of law cases. The exception is the OHADA CCJA), which adjudicates purely business, commercial, and investment disputes. Yet it is arguably the least studied and least visible African international court and tribunal in Anglophone academic literature compared to the other three.

Except for the OHADA CCJA, this characteristic of these courts repurposing their mandates is the first peculiarity of African sub-regional judiciaries. Despite being established under RECs, they have not attracted cases within international economic law areas. So far, the cases they have adjudicated are essential and relevant for African states' dispute settlement. The scarcity of disputes on trade, business, and investment in African sub-regional international economic courts and tribunals raises concerns about the roles, functions, performance, effectiveness, and legitimacy of these courts and tribunals.

[30] Max du Plessis and Lee Stone, 'A Court not Found?' (2007) *AHRLJ* 522, 538.

[31] Ademola Abass, 'The Proposed International Criminal Jurisdiction for the African Court: Some Problematical Aspects' (2013) *NILR* 31.

[32] Richard Frimpong Oppong, 'The African Union, the African Economic Community and Africa's Regional Economic Communities: Untangling a Complex Web' (2010) 18 *AfrJIntlCompL* 99.

The second problem is the path dependence produced by European regional economic integration experimental triumphalism. It is crucial to dissuade one dominant theme in scholarship that analyses these African international judiciaries analogously with their European counterparts. Proceeding from this line of scholarship, one leading international court scholar has concluded that the African courts are generally non-starters, foundering, languishing with paltry dockets, and too numerous for a region that is not economically and democratically developed enough (for the WAEMU Court of Justice and the ECOWAS Community Court of Justice).[33] Such views paint African international courts with broad strokes and in an out-of-context comparative manner with their Euro-American counterparts. This gloomy and pessimistic analysis is one of the most significant problems with the methodologies of legitimacy employed by many international court commentators about Africa. This kind of scholarship delegitimises and undermines the essential political, social, and economic roles these courts play while operating in a part of the world with many authoritarian and illiberal regimes. It is similar to the now well-discredited view that courts in authoritarian regimes serve as mere pawns of their rulers and thus lack independent political, social, and economic influence.[34]

Finally, the third problem is the legitimacy crisis that has currently plagued the settlement of disputes in international investment law. Africa is at the centre of this crisis, with many African states having been respondents in ISDS claims. In the African ISDS arena, three interrelated concerns emerge: first, the composition of African ISDS tribunals by non-African arbitrators, especially those from the global North. Second is the role of African arbitration centres in attracting arbitral disputes, and third is the Africanisation debates in international investment law currently raging among African states and leading African international lawyers and academics. Most African sub-regional international economic courts have jurisdiction to receive investment disputes; yet, foreign investors in Africa, understandably so, and intra-African investors still prefer institutional and *ad hoc* commercial arbitration and ISDS.

4. RESEARCH QUESTIONS

One of this book's central research questions is why sub-regional judiciaries in Africa established under Regional Economic Communities (RECs) have experienced under-judicialisation (ie fewer cases) in trade, business, commerce,

[33] Cesare P R Romano, 'Shadow Zones of International Judicialization & Trial and Error in International Judicialization' in Cesare PR Romano, Karen J Alter and Yuval Shany (eds), *The Oxford Handbook of International Adjudication* (Oxford Academic, 2014) 1.

[34] Mark Fathi Massoud, 'International Arbitration and Judicial Politics in Authoritarian States' 39 *Law and Social Inquiry* (2014).

and investment. Additionally, the book also answers the following research questions:

a) What are the roles and functions of international economic sub-regional courts and tribunals in Africa?
b) What explains the slow judicialisation of certain general substantive areas such as business, trade and investment disputes?
c) What roles have leading African international lawyers played in fashioning the sub-regional international economic judiciaries and ISDS?
d) What effects have the sub-regional international economic courts and tribunals in Africa had and can have on the general development of international economic law in Africa?
e) How far can Africa's international sub-regional courts and tribunals counteract the legitimacy crisis in ISDS for African states?

5. LITERATURE REVIEW

The literature on international courts globally and in Africa is now vast and differentiated. The approaches different scholars have taken are also varied, and there has been an infusion of an interdisciplinary approach in the literature. This section introduces a cross-section of the literature referenced throughout this book. The sub-section is not a comprehensive presentation of the literature covered in the book but rather focuses on the literature of African international courts, primarily written by African authors. The literature is connected to international law theorising as international courts have become one of the dominant features of the international legal order in the past three decades.[35]

Karen Alter's pioneering work asserts that a paradigm shift has occurred in the development of international courts.[36] She argues that the nature of international courts has changed since the end of the Cold War. The old-style international courts lacked compulsory jurisdiction and could only rely on defendant states' consent to adjudicate on cases.[37] New-style international courts, on the other hand, are overwhelmingly possessed of compulsory jurisdiction and allow non-state actors and private litigants to initiate litigation.[38] From a global vantage point, this might be empirically true, but the situation in Africa is slightly more complex.[39] Arguably, the most influential African regional court with a specific human rights mandate is the ACtHPR. This court would narrowly fall under

[35] Armin von Bogdandy and Ingo Venzke, 'Framing the Issue' in Armin von Bogdandy and Ingo Venzke (eds), *International Judicial Lawmaking* (Springer, 2012) 3.
[36] Karen J Alter, The New Terrain of International Law: Courts, Politics, Rights (Princeton University Press, 2014).
[37] ibid 5.
[38] ibid.
[39] See Luis G Franceschi, The African Human Rights Judicial System: Viewed from a Foreign Affairs Perspective (Cambridge Scholars Publishing, 2014).

Alter's new-style international court formulation, as it possesses compulsory jurisdiction only for AU contracting parties. For non-state actors and individual litigants, African states must enter an additional declaration allowing them standing. The African Court of Justice and Human Rights (ACJHR), which is yet to be operationalised, has a similar jurisdictional posture as the ACtHPR. Helfer and Alter also argue that the political salience of international court rulings has generated increased scrutiny of the legitimacy of international courts.[40]

Despite having the highest number of International Courts and tribunals, mainstream international law literature largely ignores African International Courts. For example, Yuval Shany gives the ACtHPR as an example of a court with limited jurisdiction compared with the International Court of Justice (ICJ). He focuses on the European courts as examples that best exemplify the new ethos of international norm advancement and the maintenance of international cooperative arrangements.[41] When African ICs are assessed, even by some leading African jurists, they are shrouded with a sense of pessimism.[42] As these courts have different backgrounds and set-ups and operate in varied contexts, this book demonstrates that using broad-stroke approaches to analyse their impact and performance is unfair. The analytical methods chosen for this book – TWAIL and thick description – eschew this Euro-American comparativist analysis.[43]

5.1 African Regional Economic Trade Judiciaries

Like other regional economic arrangements, African RTAs have specific judiciaries possessing jurisdiction to entertain disputes from a broad category of litigants.[44] James Gathii has written extensively on the international sub-regional courts and tribunals in Africa, with a particular focus on the EACJ[45] and the

[40] Laurence R Helfer and Karen J Alter, 'Legitimacy and Lawmaking: A Tale of Three International Courts' (2013) 14 *Theoretical Inquiries in Law* 479, 480.

[41] Yuval Shany, 'No Longer a Weak Department of Power? Reflections on the Emergence of a New International Judiciary' (2009) 20 EJIL 73.

[42] Makau Mutua, 'The African Human Rights Court: A Two-Legged Stool?' (1999) 21 *HumRtsQ* 342; Christof Heyns, 'The African Regional Human Rights System: In Need of Reform?' (2001) 2 *AfrHumRts* LJ 167 (arguing that the expanded jurisdiction of the African human rights courts could cause jurisprudential chaos) *cf* Adamantia Rachovitsa, 'On New 'Judicial Animals': The Curious Case of an African Court with Material Jurisdiction of a Global Scope' (2019) 19 *HumRtsLRev* 255.

[43] James T Gathii, 'Introduction: The Performance of Africa's International Courts' in James T Gathii (ed), *The performance of Africa's International Courts* (Oxford University Press, 2020).

[44] James T Gathii, *African Regional Trade Agreements as Legal Regimes* (Cambridge University Press, 2011) 265.

[45] James T Gathii, 'Mission Creep or a Search for Relevance: The East African Court of Justice's Human Rights Strategy' (2013) 24 *DJCIL* 249; James T Gathii, 'Variation in the Use of Subregional Integration Courts between Business and Human Rights Actors: The Case of the East African Court of Justice' (2016) 79 *Law and Contemporary Problems* 37; James T Gathii, 'Saving the Serengeti: Africa's New International Judicial Environmentalism' (2016) 16 CJIL 386; James T Gathii, 'The East African Court of Justice: Human Rights and Business Actors Compared' in Karen J Alter, Laurence R Helfer and Mikael Rask Madsen(eds), *International Court Authority* (Oxford University Press, 2018) 59.

COMESA Court of Justice.[46] His targeted scholarship in this area possibly began in earnest in 2013 with his seminal paper: *Mission Creep or a Search for Relevance: The East African Court of Justice's Human Rights Strategy*. He had decried the under-appreciation of the jurisprudence of Africa's regional trade Judiciaries earlier in 2010.[47] Gathii argued that it was already evident at this stage of the development of these international courts and tribunals that they do much less dispute settlement around trade issues than other issue areas. He also noted that there had been an exponential increase in the use of these judiciaries, without much acknowledgement in mainstream international law academic literature.[48]

It is possible that the latter observation motivated him to take on the challenge of ensuring increased visibility of these judiciaries in the academic literature of international courts. He made this evident in his 2020 American Society of International Law Grotius Lecture, aptly titled '*The Promise of International Law: A Third World View*'.[49] In it, he argued that the international field as we know it today is hindered by a limited geography of places and ideas that marginalises places such as Arusha, Tanzania, which until recently was host to three important international courts and tribunals in Africa.[50] This book engages directly with this challenge. It is part of a project aimed at increasing the visibility and showcasing the relevance of African international judiciaries in the existing academic literature. Until 2013, Gathii's scholarship had not yet zeroed explicitly in on sub-regional international courts in Africa. He had already established a credible reputation as one of the founders and leading scholars of the TWAIL II scholarship.[51] He had also written incisive and persuasive contributions on corruption,[52] the rule of law,[53] and economic governance.[54]

[46] James T Gathii, 'The COMESA Court of Justice' in Robert Howse and others(eds),*The Legitimacy of International Trade Courts and Tribunals* (Cambridge University Press, 2018) 314; James T Gathii, 'Sub-Regional Court or Employment Tribunal? The Legacy and Legitimacy of the COMESA Court of Justice' in Robert Howse and others(eds), *The Legitimacy of International Trade Courts and Tribunals* (Cambridge University Press, 2015).

[47] James T Gathii, 'The Under-Appreciated Jurisprudence of Africa's Regional Trade Judiciaries' 12(2010) *OrRevIntL* 245.

[48] ibid.

[49] James T Gathii, 'The Promise of International Law: A Third World View' (2021) 36 *AUILR* 377.

[50] ibid.

[51] *See* Mohsen al Attar, 'Subverting Racism in/through International Law Scholarship' https://opiniojuris.org/2021/03/03/subverting-racism-in-international-law-scholarship/ (describing Gathii as follows: 'Gathii is a jurist like no other. His ability to produce muscular scholarship on all matters international and legal is rivalled only by his commitment to confronting the inequities of the legal academy (his SSRN page is jaw-dropping in both respects)').

[52] James T Gathii, 'Defining the Relationship between Human Rights and Corruption' (2009) 31 *UPaJIntlL* 125.

[53] James T Gathii, 'Popular Authorship and Constitution Making: Comparing and Contrasting the DRC and Kenya' (2008) 49 *William and Mary L Rev* 1109; James T Gathii and Celestine Nyamu, 'Reflections on United States-Based Human Rights NGOS' Work on Africa' (1996) 9 *HarvHumRtsJ* 285; James T Gathii, 'The American Origins of Liberal and Illiberal Regimes of International Economic Governance in the Marshall Court' 54 (2006) *BuffLRev* 765; James Gathii, 'Human Rights, the World Bank and the Washington Consensus: 1949–1999' (2000) 94 *AmSocIntLProc* 144.

[54] James T Gathii, 'The Neoliberal Turn in Regional Trade Agreements' 86 (2001) *Wash L Rev* 421.

5.2 African Regional Trade Agreements as Flexible Regimes

Some scholars have suggested that regionalism in Africa, through RTAs and RECs, is the answer to the low level of intra-African trade.[55] The African integration model is far more flexible, unlike the European model, which is based on classic market-based customs union integration models (Vinerian Model).[56] Under the Euro-American model, economic integration begins with a free trade area, progresses to a customs union, then to a common market, and ultimately to a monetary union, with a political union as the final stage.[57] One of the African RECs' most emblematic flexibility features is the overlapping memberships. This feature may explain why regionalism in Africa has been unable to effectively address Non-Tariff Barriers to Trade (NTBs) generally and Sanitary and Phytosanitary Measures (SPSs) in particular.[58]

Overlapping memberships in several RECs and RTAs reflects Africa's many bilateral and multilateral RECs and RTAs. These multiple memberships are a perfect example of the phenomenon Jagdish Bhagwati referred to as the 'spaghetti bowl'.[59] Current African regional RECs are also amalgamating. The EAC, the COMESA and the SADC have set up the TFTA, bringing together the three already existing RECs without terminating them. One scholar sensationally and perhaps prematurely termed this amalgamation as 'possibly the most significant event in Africa since the formation of the OAU in 1963'.[60] This development is arguably not the most significant event since 1963 because it occurs in the context of African states having negotiated and completed the formation of the Africa Continental Free Trade Area (AfCFTA), which aims to create an Africa-wide free trade area.

Gathii's initial focus on international courts and tribunals in sub-regional Africa began in 2011, following the publication of one of the first books to specifically focus on international trade law in Africa, titled *African Regional Trade Agreements as Legal Regimes*.[61] Gathii's seminal book, published in 2011,

[55] John Kagochi and Nazif Durmaz, 'Assessing RTAs Inter-Regional Trade Enhancement in Sub-Saharan Africa' (2018) 6 *Cogent Economics and Finance*.

[56] James T Gathii, 'African Regional Trade Agreements as Flexible Legal Regimes' 35(2010) *North CarJIntl L& Comm* 571.

[57] Jacob Viner, *The Customs Union Issue* (Oxford University Press, 1950).

[58] *See* Harrison O Mbori, 'Combating Unjustified Sanitary and Phytosanitary Measures in the African Tripartite Free Trade Area (COMESA-SADC-EAC): SPS-Plus or SPS-Minus?' (2017) 58 *Hungarian JLStud* 409.

[59] *See* James T Gathii, 'African Regional Trade Agreements as Flexible Legal Regimes' (2010) 35 *North CarJIntl L& Comm* 571; *see also* Jagdish Bhagwati, 'U.S Trade Policy: The Infatuation with Free Trade Agreements' in Jagdish Bhagwati and Anne O Krueger(eds), *The Dangerous Drift To Preferential Trade Agreements* (AEI Press, 1995) (arguing that a 'spaghetti bowl' is a metaphor used to describe a system in which crisscrossing strands of bilateral trade agreements create a tangled mess of restrictions and regulations, ultimately disrupting rather than promoting trade).

[60] Calestous Juma and Francis Mageni, 'The Benefits of Africa's New Free Trade Area' www.belfercenter.org/publication/benefits-africas-new-free-trade-area-0.

[61] *See also* Richard Frimpong Oppong, *Legal Aspects of Economic Integration in Africa* (n 13) (written in the same year as Gathii's book but with a different theoretical and substantive bent).

followed and included ideas he had developed in his persuasive assessment of African RTAs as flexible regimes.[62] He argued in these works that it is crucial to understand African RTAs on their own terms because they have contextualising imperatives grounded in African history, politics, and realities that defy the straitjacket strapping of European or other non-African experiences.[63] This argument, as we shall see below, underpins Gathii's later work on international trade courts and tribunals in Africa, as well as his TWAIL writings to some extent. This book also adopts this argument, viewing it as an essential lens for assessing African international economic courts and tribunals.

The flexible regime theory refers to the following five defining features of African RTAs: (a) they establish flexible regimes of cooperation as opposed to containing rules requiring scrupulous and rigorous adherence; (b) they incorporate the principle of variable geometry (ie, adopting steps for meeting timetables and other commitments) as a central feature; (c) they demonstrate a particular preference for functionally specific objectives to undertake discrete projects and to serve as forums for the integrated development of common resources – such as river basins – that cut across national boundaries; (d) they demonstrate a remarkable commitment to the equitable distribution of gains from trade and corresponding weakness in the adoption of non-discrimination trade principles and the related objectives of trade liberalisation; and finally (e) they are characterised by multiple and overlapping memberships, exemplifying a classic case of the 'spaghetti bowl' this multiple membership illustrates the flexibility or open-door membership that African RTAs offer.[64]

Accordingly, this flexibility theory compels Gathii to avoid and discourage comparing African RTAs with their European counterparts.[65] He cautions against viewing this flexibility as a blank check for non-compliance with binding treaty obligations. Instead, he sees it as these states agreeing that they will not stringently enforce compliance because these commitments are balanced against a variety of safety valves, such as variable geometry and the equitable sharing of benefits of regionalisation.[66] Timothy Masiko's award-winning monograph has persuasively and successfully deployed the flexibility regime theory.[67]

Expectedly, even the most stringent advocate of flexibility would be interested to know why these courts have not attracted a critical mass of trade-related cases. This concern is especially nagging where tariff and non-tariff barriers significantly hinder intra-African trade. Gathii argues that business actors in the EAC, such as the East African Business Council (EABCo), have eschewed

[62] James T Gathii, 'African Regional Trade Agreements as Flexible Legal Regimes' (2010) 35 *North CarJIntl L& Comm* 571.

[63] James T Gathii, *African Regional Trade Agreements as Legal Regimes* (n 44) xvii.

[64] ibid, 2.

[65] ibid.

[66] ibid 5–6.

[67] Timothy Masiko, *Flexible Regional Economic Integration in Africa: Lessons and Implications for the Multilateral Trading System* (Hart Publishing, 2022).

litigation before the EACJ despite non-tariff barriers imposing high costs on trade in the EAC.[68] He understandably suspected that the first case brought by a business actor in the EACJ – *British American Tobacco* (BAT) *v Attorney General of Uganda,* EACJ Reference No. 7 of 2017[69] – would not have emboldened other business and trade actors to submit cases.[70] The win by BAT might have encouraged companies like Tanzania's Kioo Limited (a glass manufacturing company) to sue on a similar issue as in the BAT case (discrimination in internal taxation), but this time against the Republic of Kenya.[71] Two individuals, both erudite Kenyan lawyers, Christopher Ayiecko and Emily Osiemo (in the *Christopher Ayiecko* case), brought a claim against Kenya in connection with Kenya's negotiations with the United States regarding the signing of a FTA in 2020.[72] The *Christopher Ayiecko* case concluded with a setback for Kenya's negotiating position on third-party trade agreements that continues to date. The *Kioo* case was terminated due to changes in circumstances that rendered the case moot.

Gathii's flexibility theory also pays close attention to institutional and legal perspectives of states as unitary actors. The theory centres on social, historical, and economic factors that influence multiple actors, including regional trade officials and non-state actors such as business groups, institutions, and professionals.[73] This book cautiously sees some links between the flexibility approach and what Joost Pauwelyn, Ramses A. Wessel, and Jan Wouters have defined as informal international lawmaking. These are processes and policies set up through coordination between public and private actors, often across multiple levels of government and through informal networks.[74] Gathii argues that 'such informal decisions taken within the context of RTA commitments that are designed to take advantage of regional complementarities help in building and consolidating regional integration initiatives such as infrastructural projects'.[75]

[68] James T Gathii, *African Regional Trade Agreements as Legal Regimes xvii* (n 44) 5–6.

[69] *British American Tobacco (U) LTD v The Attorney General of Uganda*, Reference No. 7 of 2017, East African Court of Justice [EACJ] (26 March, 2019).

[70] James T Gathii, 'The East African Court of Justice: Human Rights and Business Actors Compared' in Karen J Alter, Laurence R Helfer, and Mikael Rask Madsen(eds), *International Court Authority* (Oxford University Press, 2018) 74.

[71] Luke Anami, 'Tanzanian Glass Company takes KRA to Court over a 25% Import Tax' *The East African* (7 June 2020) www.theeastafrican.co.ke/business/Tanzanian-glass-company-takes-KRA-to-court/2560-5572644-g0engkz/index.html; Harrison O Mbori, 'Case Commentary from The EACJ (BAT v Attorney General of Uganda) and OHADA CCJA (Getma International v Republic of Guinea)' (2020) *AfJIEL* 339.

[72] Luke Anami, 'Lawyers fight Kenya-US Trade Deal' *The East African* (21 March, 2020), www.theeastafrican.co.ke/business/Lawyers-fight-Kenya-US-trade-deal/2560-5499270-2iwjkyz/index.html.

[73] James T Gathii, *African Regional Trade Agreements as Legal Regimes* (n 44).

[74] Joost Pauwelyn, Ramses A Wessel, and Jan Wouters, 'Informal International Lawmaking: Framing the Concept and Research Questions' in Joost Pauwelyn, Ramses A Wessel, and Jan Wouters (eds), *Informal International Lawmaking* (Oxford University Press, 2012) 2.

[75] James T Gathii, *African Regional Trade Agreements as Legal Regimes* (n 44) 15.

Furthermore, Gathii argues that this flexibility theory foregrounds the enmeshment of African RTAs within diverse economies, political frameworks, and normative commitments of a particular regime.[76] The advantage here is that

> the parties to these formal and informal agreements are continuously reiterating their commitments and making new ones. This production loop contributes to gradually building the regime's norms and rules and the political will and economic investment necessary to give these norms and rules efficacy.[77]

Reading Gathii, it is difficult not to reflect further on the theory of informal international lawmaking. Jan Klabbers argues that informal international lawmaking is not a new phenomenon.[78] He argues that informal international law is a phenomenon of all times as it taps into the need for the effectiveness of political action.[79]

Gathii's flexibility theory also includes two other vital elements: the multiplicity of objectives and the African RTAs as bulwarks of self-reliance and economic independence. On the first element, Gathii argues that African RTAs are essential frameworks for developing a political consensus among members regarding regional challenges, including those involving development, politics, and security.[80] Thus, while developed under treaties, African RTAs serve as forums for addressing regional challenges and creating a political consensus on how to cooperate.[81] Secondly, on self-reliance and economic independence, Gathii first shows that African RTAs are motivated by eliminating economic dependence on former colonisers.[82] Consequently, he showcases how founding pan-Africanists, such as Kwame Nkrumah and Julius Nyerere, strongly argued for economic self-determination.[83] This debate led to the emergence of two camps on African integration. Libyan former president Muammar Gaddafi argued for the first formula, which insisted on a single African political system, the so-called United States of Africa. The former Nigerian president, Olusegun Obasanjo, argued for the second formula, referred to as the gradualist approach. This formula foregrounds a loose federation beginning with 'the regions of Africa which have already established affinity and moving gradually to wider continental unity'.[84] The gradualists now have the upper hand with their idea adopted

[76] ibid.

[77] ibid.

[78] Jan Klabbers, 'International Courts and Informal International Law' in Joost Pauwelyn, Ramses A Wessel, and Jan Wouters, *Informal International Lawmaking* (Oxford University Press, 2012) 222 (arguing that informal international law is possibly first theorised seriously in 1953 by James Fawcett in his classical contribution in the British Yearbook of International Law: *The Legal Character of International Agreements*).

[79] ibid.

[80] James T Gathii, *African Regional Trade Agreements as Legal Regimes* (n 44) 24.

[81] ibid.

[82] ibid 27.

[83] ibid.

[84] ibid 29.

under the Treaty for the Establishment of an African Economic Community and the African Continental Free Trade Area treaty. Gathii importantly mentions that 'both ideas for a political union and loose federation share a commitment to self-sufficiency as embodied in global South international economic solidarity initiatives such as the New International Economic Order (NIEO) of the 1970s'.[85]

5.3 African Sub-Regional Economic International Courts and Tribunals

Gathii follows through with his flexibility theory in his analysis of African international courts and tribunals. He showed how the EACJ exemplified a new trend in African regional human rights enforcement. Rather than serving as a tribunal to resolve trade disputes, as envisaged by its original designers, the court evolved into one that seeks to hold member governments accountable for human rights violations and to promote good governance and the rule of law.[86] He argued that the EACJ, like the ECOWAS ECCJ and the SADC Tribunal, had become human rights courts.[87] This repurposed mandate for the EACJ and the SADC Tribunal (before its restructuring in 2014) was remarkable, as their constitutive treaties do not include a specific grant of jurisdiction to entertain human rights cases. Thus, his use of mission creep is a vivid analogy.[88]

The EAC partner states, however, unsuccessfully resisted this strategy by the court to gain, promote, and protect their human rights institutional power as a subversion of their sovereignty.[89] Gathii argued that 'the remarkable rise of human rights case law in the EACJ represents a significant instance of building and forging judicial autonomy that derives from the entrepreneurship, resourcefulness, and creativity of the judges on the court and its long-standing registrar'.[90] He also shows how, except for its 2009 advisory opinion,[91] and despite the EAC becoming a customs union in 2005 and a Common Market in 2010, the EACJ had, up to that point, not received any economic integration cases.[92]

Finally, he has also carefully examined the inaugural human rights case in the EACJ in 2007: *James Katabazi v. The Secretary General of the East African*

[85] ibid 30; *see also* Antony Anghie, 'Legal Aspects of the New International Economic Order' (2015) 6 *Humanity* 144.

[86] James T Gathii, 'Mission Creep or a Search for Relevance: The East African Court of Justice's Human Rights Strategy' (n 45).

[87] ibid.

[88] ibid.

[89] ibid.

[90] ibid 252.

[91] re A Request by the Council of Ministers of the East African Community for an Advisory Opinion, Appl. No. 1 of 2008 (First Instance Division, 2009), www.eacj.org/wp-content/uploads/2019/03/Advisory-Opinion-No.-1-of-2008-The-Council-of-Ministers-of-the-East-African-Community.pdf.

[92] James T Gathii, 'Mission Creep or a Search for Relevance: The East African Court of Justice's Human Rights Strategy' (n 45).

Community[93] (Katabazi case) and the post-Katabazi cases: *Plaxeda Rugumba v Secretary General of the East African Community*,[94] *Independent Medical Legal Unit v Attorney General of Kenya*,[95] and *Sitenda Sebalu v Secretary General of the East African Community*.[96] Though not covered in Gathii's paper, after this, there have been other cases in which the EACJ has continued to assert its human rights jurisdiction: *Samuel Mukira Mohochi v the Attorney General of the Republic of Uganda*,[97] *Democratic Party v. Secretary General of the East African Community*,[98] *Mary Arivizah & Okotch Mondoh v Attorney General of the Republic of Kenya*,[99] and one delivered in 2019 in *Media Council of Tanzania v The Attorney General of the United Republic of Tanzania*.[100]

5.4 African Sub-Regional Economic International Courts as Human Rights Courts

One of the responses and disagreements towards James Gathii's scholarship and arguments on the EACJ has come from Ally Possi. Possi disagrees with Gathii's view first directly in his 2014 LLD (PhD) thesis, explicitly arguing that:

> According to Gathii, the EACJ exemplifies a new trend in African regional human rights enforcement. He is of the view that the EACJ was mainly established to deal with trade disputes, but it is able to find space for human rights, due to the nature of the EAC integration. It is the intention of this study to narrate how the EACJ has afforded to accommodate human rights-related disputes. Contrary to Gathii's argument, the EACJ is not adjudicating human rights disputes. The court's findings in

[93] *James Katabazi and 21 others v Secretary General of the East African Community and Attorney General of the Republic of Uganda* (Reference No 1 of 2007) www.eacj.org//wp-content/uploads/2012/11/NO._1_OF_2007.pdf.

[94] *Plaxeda Rugumba v The Secretary General of The East African Community* (Reference No 8 of 2010) First instance Division 1 December 2011 www.eacj.org//wp-content/uploads/2012/11/Plaxeda-Rugumba-2010-8-judgment-2011.pdf.

[95] *Independent Medical Legal Unit v Attorney General of Kenya* (Reference No 3 of 2010) First instance Division 29 June 2011 www.eacj.org//wp-content/uploads/2012/11/3-of-20101.pdf.

[96] *Hon. Sitenda Sebalu v The Secretary General of The East African Community* (Reference No 8 of 2012) First instance Division 30 June, 2011 www.eacj.org//wp-content/uploads/2013/09/Sitenda_Taxation_Ruling.pdf.

[97] *Samuel Mukira Mohochi v The Attorney General of the Republic of Uganda* (Reference No 5 of 2011) First instance Division 17 May, 2013 www.eacj.org//wp-content/uploads/2013/09/FI_Uganda_v_Muhochi.pdf.

[98] *Democratic Party v Secretary General of the East African Community* (Reference No 2 of 2012) First instance Division 29 November 2013 www.eacj.org//wp-content/uploads/2014/02/REFERENCE-NO-2-of-2012-Democratic-party-VS-SG-and-4-Others.pdf.

[99] *Mary Arivizah and Okotch Mondoh v Attorney General of the Republic of Kenya* (Reference No 7 of 2010 First instance Division 30 November, 2011 www.eacj.org//wp-content/uploads/2013/10/RULING-OF-1ST-DECEMBER-2010.pdf.

[100] *Media Council of Tanzania v The Attorney General of the United Republic of Tanzania* (Reference No 2 of 2017 First instance Division 29 March, 2019 www.eacj.org/wp-content/uploads/2019/03/Referene-No.2-of-2017.pdf.

cases that have human rights allegations are not even placing weight in human rights. The court is simply employing judicial activism, which indirectly protects human rights.[101]

Secondly, Possi specifically targets Gathii's categorisation of the EACJ as a human rights court, arguing that since the Protocol that ought to have granted the EACJ its human rights mandate has never been enacted, the EACJ is not a human rights court.[102]

Unlike Gathii, whose scholarship on African international courts is animated with a strong sense of cautious optimism and, in many instances, enthusiasm,[103] Possi's work, starting with his LLD thesis, falls squarely within the category of pessimistic scholarship on African international courts. He argues that while it is commendable that the EACJ, through 'judicial activism', has adjudicated over human rights cases, the fact that EAC partner states are also members of the ACtHPR might lead to conflicting jurisdiction. Such conflicts, according to Possi, may lead to forum shopping and jurisprudential concerns.[104] This view strongly echoes Christof Heyns' jurisprudential chaos argument concerning the ACtHPR.[105] Adamantia Rachovitsa has persuasively refuted these arguments, arguing that the risk of a jurisprudential chaos is highly overblown.[106]

Possi's first contention, which colours the contours of his LLD thesis on judicial activism/overreach, is challenging to accept, especially for a scholar from one of Africa's leading human rights institutions: the Centre for Human Rights at the University of Pretoria. Despite this book not focusing on human rights as a specific subject matter issue, I would be remiss if I did not address Possi's claims of judicial activism/overreach.

Possi would rather the court abdicate its mandate for protecting human rights to remain politically legitimate (what Samuel Moyn has referred to as judicial modesty).[107] Yet, denying this human rights mandate by the EAC partner states ensures the court remains obscure and irrelevant. Gathii responds to a similar view when he addresses Samuel Moyn's work on the counter-majoritarian difficulty

[101] Ally Possi, 'The East Africa Court of Justice: Towards Effective Protection of Human rights in the East African Community' (November, 2014) (unpublished PhD dissertation, University of Pretoria), 19, repository.up.ac.za/bitstream/handle/2263/46232/Possi_East_2015.pdf?sequence=1&isAllowed=y.

[102] Ally Possi, 'An Appraisal of the Functioning and Effectiveness of the East African Court of Justice' (2018) 21 PER/PELJ 24.

[103] This is easy to see even when he laments the legitimacy deficit of the COMESA Court of Justice, *see* James T Gathii, 'The COMESA Court of Justice' in Robert Howse and others, *The Legitimacy of International Trade Courts and Tribunals* (Cambridge University Press, 2018) 314.

[104] Ally Possi, (n 101).

[105] Christof Heyns, (n 47) (arguing that the expanded jurisdiction of the African human rights courts could cause jurisprudential chaos).

[106] Adamantia Rachovitsa, 'On New 'Judicial Animals': The Curious Case of an African Court with Material Jurisdiction of a Global Scope' (2019) 19 *HRLRev* 255.

[107] Samuel Moyn, 'On Human Rights and Majority Politics: Felix Frankfurter's Democratic Theory' (2019) 52 *Vanderbilt Journal of Transnational Law* 1135.

in global judicial review.[108] First, one of Gathii's main arguments is that African international courts are a new and increasingly important avenue for waging political, social, and legal struggles.[109] Expectedly, Gathii also draws a direct link between Moyn's judicial activism views and Possi's[110] and responds by making a direct reference to the *Katabazi* case.[111] He argues that considering the EACJ's assumption of jurisdiction as judicial activism misses the point embedded in the counter-majoritarian difficulty that would legitimise the authoritarian governance of regimes like the one in Uganda.[112] Additionally, the litigants in the human rights cases are using the courts as just one strategy together with a multitude of others, 'including street protests, working with allies in parliament, writing editorials in the media, and appealing to like-minded groups to advance their causes'.[113]

The second view by Possi on the EACJ not being a human rights court is also challenging to sustain, primarily because of the strict and pedantic reading of jurisdiction he suggests. Solomon T. Ebobrah, a leading African international court scholar, described a category of international human rights courts categorised as 'non-dedicated human rights courts'.[114] He curiously does not add the EACJ to the non-dedicated human rights courts category but specifically includes the ECCJ in this category.[115] He is perhaps following the cue from the restrictive and formalistic view arguably established at his alma mater. It is interesting to note that Ebobrah, in his 2009 LLD thesis focusing on the human rights mandate of the ECCJ, framed his thesis as follows: 'African RECs, in particular ECOWAS, can be effective vehicles for the realisation of human rights without compromising their original economic objectives, without upsetting their relations with their member states or the African Union and its institutions, and without jeopardising the work of continental institutions involved in the field of human rights'.[116]

[108] James T. Gathii, 'Beyond Samuel Moyn's Countermajoritatian Difficulty as a Model of Global Judicial Review (2019) 52 *Vanderbilt Journal of Transnational Law* 1237.

[109] James T Gathii, 'Introduction: The Performance of Africa's International Courts' in James T Gathii (ed), *The Performance of Africa's International Courts: Using International Litigation for Political, Legal, and Social Change* (Oxford University Press, 2020).

[110] James T Gathii, 'Beyond Samuel Moyn's Countermajoritatian Difficulty as a Model of Global Judicial Review' (n 108) citing Ally Possi, 'Striking a Balance Between Community Norms and Human Rights: The Continuing Struggle of the East African Court of Justice' (2015) 15 *AHRLJ* 192, 203 (arguing that 'despite the existing limitations to adjudicate human rights disputes, it is undeniable that the EACJ has adopted some kind of judicial activism when adjudicating cases with human rights allegations. In such circumstances, it is likely to provoke controversy among member states. It can also be propounded that the continuing politicization of the EACJ's human rights jurisdiction may have been caused by the Court's activism'.)

[111] ibid.

[112] ibid.

[113] ibid.

[114] Solomon T Ebobrah, 'International Human Rights Courts' in Cesare PR Romano, Karen J Alter and Yuval Shany (eds), *The Oxford Handbook of International Adjudication* (Oxford University Press, 2014) 227.

[115] ibid 228 (he does not even mention the EACJ once in this entire chapter).

[116] Solomon T Ebobrah, 'Legitimacy and Feasibility of Human rights Realisation through Regional Economic Communities in Africa: The Case of the Economic Community of West African States'

Ebobrah frames his thesis more in the mould of Gathii's flexibility theory described above. Curiously, when it comes to categorisation, Ebobrah is shy to categorise the EACJ as an international human rights court. This book, keenly following and applying Gathii's flexibility theory of Africa RTAs, views the EACJ as both an economic/trade international court and an international human rights court. For the same reason, the court can be an international arbitral institution (in fact, the EAC Treaty explicitly stipulates this). Based on the cases it has attracted, it can also serve as an employment tribunal, a tribunal for political and democratic disputes, and an international tribunal for environmental law. This flexibility is the essence and spirit of the flexibility theory, and the pigeon-holing argument by Possi seems to generate a lot of heat but little light.

It is worth noting that Richard Frimpong Oppong published a book on international trade law in Africa, focusing on economic integration, in 2011, the same year as Gathii. However, as I elaborate further below, his work, unlike Gathii's, employs relational and regime complexity theories to evaluate African RECs.[117] He develops what he refers to as a relational theory in the context of law and economic integration.[118] This theory is concerned explicitly with the following matters:

> relations between the laws of a community, its institutions and those of member states; a mechanism for normative exchange or communication between a community and its member states *inter se*; jurisdictional conflicts between a community and its member states; the allocation of competences between a community and its member states; individuals' access to community institutions; and the recognition of member state and community normative acts.[119]

Oppong seems to endorse or base his analysis on the linear approach (Vinerian model) to economic integration from FTAs, Customs Unions, Common Markets to total economic integration.[120] He explicitly refutes Gathii's flexibility theory, especially its emphasis on informal institutional structures, cooperation, voluntary compliance, and good faith in implementing objectives.[121] His theory foregrounds the law through legal and institutional structures, lawmaking processes, interactions between legal systems, and implementation and enforcement of laws.[122] He concedes that high levels of legalisation have only been witnessed thus far in Europe and that this took a long time to achieve.[123] Africa, he argues, should also patiently seek this high level of legalisation.[124] Here, one

(September 2009) (unpublished PhD dissertation, University of Pretoria), repository.up.ac.za/bitstream/handle/2263/27990/Complete.pdf?sequence=9&isAllowed=y.

[117] Richard Frimpong Oppong (n 13).

[118] ibid 8.

[119] ibid.

[120] ibid 6.

[121] ibid 9.

[122] ibid.

[123] ibid 10.

[124] ibid.

can easily see why his theory is at loggerheads with Gathii's. While Gathii abhors the focus on Europe as the telos of legal analysis (Eurocentricity), Oppong starts from this very basis of comparison with the European model as the poster child of economic integration. Gathii's view here again seems more persuasive as it is attuned to the context of African states being different economically, socially, and politically.

While Oppong insists on high legalisation for African RECs, he argues that this high level of legalisation is necessary but ineffective.[125] He subscribes to the theory of goal-based effectiveness, insisting that a REC is effective only to the extent that it can achieve the objectives outlined in its respective treaties.[126] This notion of effectiveness is similar to the one proposed by Yuval Shany to analyse the effectiveness of international courts.[127] From a legal perspective, Oppong argues that an effective REC should demonstrate the following:

> the free flow of goods, services, person, capital and property, including judgments within the community consistent with the stage of economic integration it has reached; the existence and development of a significant body of community laws including judicial decisions to regulate the integration process; integration of community law into the laws of member states; the existence of a carefully structured legal framework for addressing and managing the multiple relationships (for example, community–state, interstate, inter-community, inter-institutional) created by economic integration; the existence of institutions adequately designed, mandated and resourced to ensure the application of community law; the existence of well-outlined procedures for monitoring and addressing breaches of community law; adherence to community law in member states; and the existence and development of constituencies with interest in the community and their full integration into the activities and operations of the community at both national and community levels.[128]

He does not, however, insist on these criteria as an immediate requirement and states that their achievement is incremental and should be viewed as elements along a continuum.[129]

Oppong's scholarship, following the publication of his book, unfortunately, did not further explore the African sub-regional courts, unlike Gathii. Furthermore, Oppong does not seem irked by the underappreciation of these courts in mainstream literature. Gathii's background can at least explain this irritation with the under-appreciation of African institutions as a leading scholar in the TWAIL movement. Oppong, despite his later abandoning the African economic integration project for economic harmonisation scholarship,

[125] ibid.
[126] ibid.
[127] Yuval Shany, 'Assessing the Effectiveness of International Courts: A Goal-Based Approach' (2012) 106 *AJIL* 225.
[128] Richard Frimpong Oppong (n 13).
[129] ibid 11.

writes an entire chapter on Africa's community courts in his book, making some contributions to which this section now turns.

Oppong refers to these courts as community courts, with the mandate to legally safeguard the integration process, to enforce the benefits of integration, to act as agents who decide when breaches have occurred, to provide remedies for the breaches, and to serve as arbiters of the institutional tensions inherent in the RECs.[130] He adds that community courts are responsible for norm advancement, regime maintenance and exercise both judicial and 'political' functions.[131] Following through with his legalisation theory, he categorises the African community courts as supranational and legalistic.[132] He views the legalistic nature of these courts as remarkable because African states are 'traditionally perceived as having no litigation culture and with a fetishist attachment to state sovereignty'.[133] On the acquisition of human rights jurisdiction by sub-regional courts, like Possi, he exudes an essentially cautionary and implicitly negative tone:

> It is important that, until its (EACJ) jurisdiction is extended to include human rights claims, the court exercises caution in admitting, indirectly, human rights claims. Too many human rights claims are likely to burden the court and distract it from the economic integration agenda. It is also likely to breed tension between the court and already established forums for vindicating human rights, such as national courts, which should be allies of the court in promoting economic integration. Indeed, the 'transformation' of the community courts – either through legislation or judicial activism – into 'human rights courts' is an unnecessary move and should be avoided.[134]

This book will demonstrate that this cautionary and negative tale is arguably refutable, as courts like the EACJ have begun to receive economic integration disputes. Although it is too early to tell, there is an emerging possibility that these courts could become custodians of human rights protection and economic integration. Additionally, since Oppong does not cover the OHADA system, it is possible he would have viewed sub-regional courts more optimistically for economic disputes. Since OHADA primarily focuses on legal harmonisation, Oppong would have been more predictably comfortable, as his scholarship has centred more on regional economic harmonisation. To his credit, he takes the economic subject matter role of these African international courts much more seriously than Possi. However, it is also possible to distinguish the two by arguing that Possi is only concerned with the human rights mandate of these courts.

The other prominent scholar on African sub-regional judiciaries is Solomon T. Ebobrah, some of whose scholarship has already been introduced in the sections above. Unlike Possi, in his LLD thesis, he set out to argue against the

[130] ibid 117.
[131] ibid.
[132] ibid 119.
[133] ibid.
[134] ibid 126.

main challenges that sub-regional organisations face in their endeavour to add human rights realisation to their core functions.[135] It is worth noting that he was not dealing with any specific sub-regional court. As his topical area was on the ECOWAS Community, he arguably covered the ECOWAS ECCJ. He, like Gathii on the EACJ, displayed a general sense of cautious optimism regarding the human rights mandate of the ECCJ from an early stage in his scholarship.[136]

Ebobrah argued that although the ECCJ was initially established to exercise traditional competence as a dispute resolution mechanism for the community, as well as to oversee the conduct of states in the integration process, the ECCJ (following a 2005 amendment) was granted the authority to entertain human rights disputes involving non-state actors.[137] The court remained idle between 2001, when it was operationalised through the appointment of the first batch of judges, until 2004, when the first case, *Afolabi Olajide v the Federal Republic of Nigeria,* was instituted.[138] This case was a human rights case with the applicant requesting individual access to the court, alleging a violation of the right to free movement in Article 3(iii) of the revised ECOWAS Treaty.[139] Ebobrah argues that, interestingly, the ECCJ relied on the Nigerian domesticated statute of the African Charter.[140] He states that 'while the ECCJ declined jurisdiction, the fall-out of the case, linked with the new visibility of human rights in the Community agenda, prompted the amendment of the 1991 Protocol of the Community Court of Justice'.[141] This amendment explicitly granted the ECCJ jurisdiction over human rights.

Ebobrah further asserts that a liberal interpretation of the Revised Treaty would have allowed the court to assume jurisdiction over human rights.[142] He argues that the court shied away from such judicial activism and opted to leave room for legislative provision of judicial competence.[143] He thus states:

> the restraint by the ECCJ has resulted in a clear and unambiguous empowerment of the court by the lawmaking organ of the Community. Thus, the human rights mandate of the ECCJ is "a legislature-driven" mandate in the sense that the main decision-making organ of the Community expressly confers it.[144]

[135] Solomon T Ebobrah, 'Legitimacy and Feasibility of Human rights Realisation through Regional Economic Communities in Africa: The Case of the Economic Community of West African States' (n 116).

[136] Solomon T Ebobrah, 'A Rights-Protection Goldmine or a Waiting Volcanic Eruption: Competence of, and Access to, the Human Rights Jurisdiction of the ECOWAS Community Court of Justice' (2007) *AHRLJ* 307.

[137] ibid 177.

[138] *Afolabi Olajide v the Federal Republic of Nigeria* Unreported Suit no. 2004/ECW/CCJ/04.

[139] ibid.

[140] Solomon T Ebobrah, 'Legitimacy and Feasibility of Human rights Realisation through Regional Economic Communities in Africa: The Case of the Economic Community of West African States' (n 116).

[141] ibid 172.

[142] ibid.

[143] ibid.

[144] ibid.

This position might easily be Eborah's indictment of the EACJ's approach compared to the ECCJ. Expectedly, when writing in 2014, Ebobrah categorised the ECCJ as a non-dedicated human rights court, but did not categorise or mention the EACJ in the same manner.[145] In his thesis, he describes the ECCJ as a hybrid court with a partially specialised human rights competence (*sui generis* human rights court).[146] This categorisation represents a less restrictive view of the court as a human rights court than he offered in 2014, and a more optimistic view of the court's multiple roles. It is essential to note that Ebobrah has maintained a robust scholarly focus on African international courts in sub-regional Africa, including the SADC Tribunal,[147] and has indeed established himself as one of the leading scholars on matters related to the ECCJ. For five consecutive years, between 2008 and 2012, he wrote about human rights development in African sub-regional economic communities.[148]

Following closely after Ebobrah, in terms of time, on the ECCJ but with a different theoretical bent and approach, Karen J. Alter, Laurence Helfer, and Jaqueline R. McAllister in 2013 described the ECCJ as a 'new human rights court'.[149] They set out to explain how the ECCJ, initially established to help build a common market, was redeployed as a human rights court.[150] They note that little progress had been made in regional economic integration as trade flows among West African nations remained extremely low. Tariffs, customs regulations, and non-tariff barriers continue to significantly hinder cross-border economic transactions.[151] Despite this, in 2005, the ECCJ mandate changed, according to them, 'unexpectedly' with the expansion of the court's jurisdiction to include human rights complaints by private litigants.[152] They also note that

[145] Solomon T Ebobrah, 'International Human Rights Courts' in Cesare PR Romano, Karen J Alter and Yuval Shany (eds), *The Oxford Handbook of International Adjudication* (Oxford University Press, 2014) 227.

[146] Solomon T Ebobrah, 'Legitimacy and Feasibility of Human rights Realisation through Regional Economic Communities in Africa: The Case of the Economic Community of West African States' (n 116).

[147] Solomon T Ebobrah, 'Critical Issues in the Human Rights Mandate of the ECOWAS Court of Justice' (2014) 54 *JAfrL* (2010)1; Solomon T Ebobrah, 'Tackling Threats to the Existence of the SADC Tribunal: A Critique of Perilously Ambiguous Provisions in the SADC Treaty and the Protocol on the SADC Tribunal' (2010) 4 *Malawi LJ* 199.

[148] Solomon T Ebobrah, 'Human Rights Developments in Subregional Courts in Africa during 2008' (2009) 9 *AHRLJ* 312; Solomon T Ebobrah, 'Human Rights Developments in African Sub-Regional Economic Communities during 2009' (2010) 10 AHRLJ 233; Solomon T Ebobrah, 'Human Rights Developments in African Sub-Regional Economic Communities during 2010' (2011) 11 AHRLJ 216; Solomon T Ebobrah, Human Rights Developments in African Sub-Regional Economic Communities during 2011, (2012) 12 *AHRLJ* 223; Solomon T Ebobrah, 'Human Rights Developments in African Sub-Regional Economic Communities during 2012' (2013) 13 *AHRLJ* 178.

[149] Karen J Alter, Lawrence R Helfer and Jaqueline R McAllister, 'A New International Human Rights Court for West Africa: The Ecowas Community Court of Justice' (2013) 107 *AJIL* 737.

[150] ibid 738.

[151] ibid.

[152] ibid (this change was not unexpected as ECOWAS states were politically troubled with the outcome of the Afolabi case).

the court did not acquire its jurisdiction through judicial lawmaking but through the coordinated campaign of bar associations, Non-governmental organisations (NGOs), ECOWAS officials, and the ECCJ judges themselves.[153] This is an expanded narrative to the one set by Ebobrah, which is state-centric. They introduce a narrative that focuses on other players in the field to explain the evolution occurring in the ECCJ. This narrative ties well with the theory Alter later develops in her 2014 book, which she calls the theory of altered politics. This theory attempts to explain why states would delegate self-binding powers to international courts.[154]

Furthermore, her work with Laurence Helfer goes against rationalist theories of cooperation that explain how international courts are problem-solving devices to further states' functional goals.[155] They instead use the historical-institutionalist accounts, which expect institutions to evolve in response to political contestation and societal pressures.[156] This theorisation is part of Alter's contribution to the rigours of empirical research, which had not been applied vigorously to African international courts up to this point. She further extended this in 2016, when, together with Gathii and Helfer, she partnered to pen one of the most important works on African sub-regional courts, focusing on backlashes.[157]

Finally, Alter and Helfer brought immense comparative knowledge, especially from European courts to African international courts. They did this with a reduced sense of Eurocentric triumphalism. They especially argued that the judicially led repurposing of mandates by the EACJ and the SADC Tribunal was not unique to Africa, as the European Court of Justice had witnessed equivalent shifts in the 1970s.[158] Alter and Helfer were arguably late entrants in the ECCJ scholarship, despite having already written about the court as early as 2013.[159] Yet they provided these African sub-regional courts with visibility in the global international law circles, especially in Europe and the United States, that African scholars had not yet received. They also introduced a different theoretical framework that incorporated interdisciplinarity, providing rigorous theoretical and empirical explanations. This interdisciplinarity is arguably due

[153] ibid.

[154] Karen Alter, *The New Terrain International Law: Courts, Politics, Rights* (Princeton University Press, 2014) 155–161.

[155] ibid; Karen J Alter and Laurence R Helfer, 'Nature or Nurture? Judicial Law-Making in the European Court of Justice and the Andean Tribunal of justice' (2010) 64 *International Law Organisation* 563 (2010); Laurence R Helfer and Anne-Marie Slaughter, 'Toward a Theory of Effective Supranational Adjudication' (1997) 107 *Yale LJ* 273.

[156] Karen J Alter, Lawrence R Helfer and Jaqueline R McAllister, 'A New International Human Rights Court for West Africa: The Ecowas Community Court of Justice' (2013) 107 *AJIL* 739.

[157] Karen J Alter, James T Gathii and Laurence Helfer, 'Backlash against International Courts in West, East and Southern Africa: Causes and Consequences' (2016) 27 *EJIL* 293.

[158] Karen J Alter, Lawrence R Helfer and Jaqueline R McAllister (n 156).

[159] Laurence R Helfer and Karen J Alter, 'Legitimacy and Lawmaking: A Tale of Three International Courts' (2013) 14 *Theoretical Inquiries in Law* 479.

to Alter being a political scientist who has been able to strenuously carve out a niche in mainstream international law circles. By her own admission, this acceptance was not easy, even for a white woman with access to vital international law connections and resources. Unfortunately, she and Helfer have not escaped the path-dependent comparative analysis that compares African international courts to their European counterparts.[160] To their credit, however, their assessment of the human rights courts is marked by a cautious optimism. Notably, instead of labelling the judicially led repurposing of the EACJ and ECCJ as judicial activism, which is a term employed by Ebobrah and Possi, they use the more benign term 'judicial lawmaking'.[161]

6. CONCLUSION

This chapter has introduced Africa's international courts and tribunals. It has offered an introductory and critical survey of the different categories of African international courts and the literature on these judiciaries. It also highlighted the diverse range of Africa's international courts and tribunals. It discussed the following four types of these courts: judicial, quasi-judicial, FTAs and DSMs and non-operational international courts. Notably, the chapter also presented the three problems that pervade the analysis of Africa's international courts. The final section of the chapter critically reviewed a select set of literature on Africa's sub-regional courts and tribunals.

Unfortunately, this chapter cannot cover the entire breadth of scholarship in this area. There are other important works that this chapter has not mapped. The roles of African sub-regional judiciaries as centres for human rights, rule of law, and democracy issues have been vastly covered and theorised. The role of these judiciaries in resolving trade, business, and commercial issues has not been adequately covered and remains under-theorised. It is thus essential to explain and research the role of these courts in resolving economic disputes. This focus is not intended to overlook or downplay the role these courts have played and continue to play in human rights, democracy, and the rule of law. The more critical concern is not the labels of the courts but the role the courts play in ensuring economic, social, and political justice.

For this book, the flexibility theory of African RTAs may have had the unintended consequence of establishing the courts under these RTAs as 'non-economic' courts, or, even more pointedly, human rights or generalist courts. With the flexibility of RTAs in mind, referencing these sub-regional courts as 'economic' or 'trade' courts might be a misnomer. The chapter sets up an analysis in the other chapters of this book on why these courts have not attracted

[160] See also Karen J Alter and Laurence R Helfer, Transplanting International Courts: The Law and Politics of the Andean Tribunal of Justice (Oxford University Press, 2017).

[161] Laurence R Helfer and Karen J Alter (n 159).

disputes on trade liberalisation, business, or commercial issues. This situation exists despite being established with trade liberalisation as an essential objective. Indeed, one of the main features of the EACJ, ECCJ, and the SADC Tribunal (prior to its restructuring in 2014) is that these courts have been involved in non-economic disputes related to human rights, democracy, and the rule of law. This outcome should not be surprising if the argument on the flexibility of African RTAs is accurate.

3

The Complexities of Africa's Sub-Regional International Economic Courts and Tribunals

1. INTRODUCTION

THIS CHAPTER COVERS AN essential subset of a nation-state's adjudicative jurisdiction. From a socio-legal perspective, it observes how African states mandate, utilise, and respond to international court determinations and other actors as they activate the use of Africa's sub-regional international economic courts and tribunals. The states' jurisdiction to delegate their adjudicative powers to international courts and tribunals for dispute resolution is well-settled. States create and design international courts as the chief 'mandate providers'.[1] They have the jurisdiction in international law to delegate different mandates to international courts. This chapter explicitly covers the complexities of the mandate provision to African sub-regional international economic courts and tribunals. The chapter focuses on these courts' roles as economic arbiters (in commercial, trade, investment, and competition law). The aim is to trace the socio-legal and doctrinal complexity embedded within these courts.

Before delving into the argument above, it is essential to introduce the twin concepts of jurisdiction and sovereignty in international law. The definition of jurisdiction in international law might seem self-evident to many international lawyers. Yet, in the lingua franca of international law, the term jurisdiction is, in many cases, taken for granted. It is one of the most challenging words to delineate in the international law legal lexicon.[2] Bhupinder Chimni calls it the 'most undertheorised category of international law'.[3] Jurisdiction has many meanings and 'sits at the intersections of political and legal theory, technical

[1] Yuval Shany, *Questions Of Jurisdiction And Admissibility Before International Courts* (Cambridge University Press, 2015) 1.

[2] BJ George Jr, 'Extraterritorial Application of Penal Legislation' (1996) 64 *Mich L Rev* 6093; *United Phosphorus, Ltd v Angus Chemical Co*, 322 F 3d 942, 948 (7th Cir 2003) ('Jurisdiction is a word of many, too many, meanings').

[3] Bhupinder S Chimni, 'The International Law of Jurisdiction: A TWAIL Perspective' (2002) 35 *LJIL* 29.

doctrine, sovereignty studies, and critical social theory'.[4] In public international law, jurisdiction 'is an aspect of sovereignty and refers to judicial, legislative, and administrative competence' whose exercise is regulated by public international law.[5]

From the concept of the state's jurisdiction flows the state's entitlement to exercise its sovereignty by adopting laws and stating the law relating to persons, activities, or legal interests.[6] Jurisdiction is therefore the power of a sovereign to affect the rights of persons and any other subjects or objects in a state by legislation, executive decree, or court judgment.[7] These views encompass the typology of jurisdiction in international law, including prescriptive jurisdiction, enforcement jurisdiction, adjudicative jurisdiction, and universal jurisdiction. Prescriptive jurisdiction refers to the right of the state to make its laws applicable to the activities, relations, or status of persons, or the interests of persons in things through legislation, executive order, or administrative rule or regulation.[8] Enforcement jurisdiction refers to a state's authority to compel compliance or punish noncompliance with its laws or regulations, whether through the courts, executive or administrative action, law enforcement agencies, or other non-judicial means.[9] Adjudicative jurisdiction refers to the state's authority to subject persons or things to the process of its courts or administrative tribunals, whether civil or criminal in nature.[10] Notably, international law practice has developed additional heads of jurisdiction, including universal jurisdiction. Universal jurisdiction refers to a state's power to prosecute and punish foreigners who commit crimes outside the state's territory, regardless of whether the victim or perpetrator is a national of that state. This jurisdiction pertains to the exercise of such competence by national courts, not international courts, and is limited to crimes, not civil disputes.[11]

The concept of jurisdiction is thus directly related to that of sovereignty. Historically, 'the words sovereign and its abstract sovereignty are of feudal origin. The sovereign was a personal role applicable to a singular person. When one was a sovereign, all others were subjects; and their relations primarily pertained to land'.[12] The concept was therefore historically personal, and feudal

[4] Asha Kaushal, 'The Politics of Jurisdiction' (2015) 78 *Modern L Rev* 791.

[5] Lassa Oppenheim, *International Law* (Oxford University Press, 1992) 456; Ian Brownlie, *Principles of Public International Law* (Oxford University Press, 2008); Frederick A Mann, 'The Doctrine of International Jurisdiction Revisited after Twenty Years' (1984) 186 Recueil des cours (Collected Courses) of the Hague Academy of International Law 20.

[6] Cedric Ryngaert, *Jurisdiction In International Law* (Oxford Law Pro, 2015) 5.

[7] Joseph H Beale, 'The Jurisdiction of a Sovereign State' (1923) *HarvLRev* 241.

[8] Cedric Ryngaert (n 6).

[9] ibid 9.

[10] ibid.

[11] Lux Reydams, *Universal Jurisdiction: International and Municipal Legal Perspectives* (Oxford Academic, 2004).

[12] Philemon Bliss, *Of Sovereignty* (Little Brown, 1885) 4; *see also* Martin Loughlin, *The Idea of Public Law* (Oxford University Press, 2004) 72-98 (contesting the feudal origins of the concept of sovereignty).

communities explicitly tied it to monarchical kings or queens as heads of state and government.[13]

Republics and constitutional democracies have abandoned the monarchical historical connotation of sovereignty. In modern Republics, citizens directly endow themselves with the primordial sovereign power formerly held by the Crown. Sovereignty, therefore, originates from and is exercised by the citizens. Such an exercise of sovereignty is called popular sovereignty. Yet, in international law, the concept of sovereignty, like that of jurisdiction, is also challenging to define. Early twentieth-century international law analyst Lassa Oppenheim stated as follows on the concept:

> There exists perhaps no conception, the meaning of which is more controversial than that of sovereignty. It is an indisputable fact that this conception, from the moment when it was introduced into political science until the present day, has never had a meaning which was universally agreed upon.[14]

Despite this fluidity of the two concepts, international law analysts have attempted over the years to define and relate them.

The now well-contested concept of 'Westphalian sovereignty' covered a nation-state's right to monopolise the specific exercise of power concerning its territory and citizens.[15] It allowed a state to exercise the following functions: internal authority (supreme political authority and monopoly over the legitimate use of force), border control, policy autonomy, and freedom from external intervention.[16] Westphalian sovereignty is the international law doctrine that triumphantly declared that international law had overcome colonialism's aberration at the height of African states' decolonisation in the 1960s.[17] Antony Anghie demonstrated how early international law jurists, like Francesco de Vitoria, and nineteenth-century positivist scholars, like John Austin, formulated the doctrine to exclude non-Europeans from the realm of sovereignty.[18] Thus, sovereignty is not a fixed doctrine established by the Peace of Westphalia in 1648, but was progressively produced and reproduced as a juridical tool by European powers to expand imperialism.

Despite this credible and vital aberration, Westphalian sovereignty is still considered the essence of the modern nation-state. It still stands as the true north star upon which statehood focuses.[19] One scholar has defined the concept

[13] ibid.

[14] Lassa Oppenheim, *International Law* (Longmans, Green and Co, 1928) 66.

[15] John H Jackson, 'Sovereignty: Outdated Concept or New Approaches' in Wenhua Shan, Penelope Simons and Dalvinder Singh (eds), *Redefining Sovereignty in International Economic Law* (Hart Publishing, 2008) 4,8.

[16] ibid.

[17] Antony Anghie, 'The Evolution of International Law: Colonial and Postcolonial Realities' (2006) 27 *Third World Quarterly* 741.

[18] ibid.

[19] Gbenga Oduntan, *Sovereignty and Jurisdiction in the Airspace and Outer Space: Legal Criteria for Spatial Delimitation* (Routledge, 2012) 21.

of sovereignty in international law as 'the power states do have at any given moment of the development of the international legal system'.[20] As an international law concept, sovereignty plays the following vital roles: imbues states with a monopoly of power as stated above, anchors the idea of 'equality of nations' (which many commenters view as dysfunctional and unrealistic), defines the status and rights of nation-states and their officials, thus creating the idea of 'sovereign immunity', and implies a right from non-intervention by any foreign (or international) power.[21]

Following this introduction, the chapter is divided into three sections. Section 2, labelled Analytical Complexity, analyses the present forms of Euro-American and Mainstream International Law Scholarship (MAILS) analysis of African sub-regional International Economic Courts. These three are Infantilisation, Systemic Western Centrism, and Evaluative Western Centrism. Section 3, labelled 'Utility Complexity', analyses the general multifunctional characteristics of African international courts and tribunals. This multifunctionality has produced three consequences: Courts Specialising in International Human Rights; Sub-Regional Courts Specialising in International Economic Law; and Non-Judicialisation in North Africa. Section 4, labelled 'Dormant Functional Complexity', analyses two factors that explain the low judicialisation of economic disputes within the sub-regional economic courts in Africa. The first is the limited use and contested nature of the arbitral function of these courts; the second is the Low Use of Domestic Court References (Preliminary References/Rulings) to mandated African Sub-Regional Community Courts.

Finally, using the EACJ as an example, Section 4, under the sub-section on the low use of the preliminary reference procedure, offers three plausible explanations for the procedure's low use. The First is the limited judicialisation of economic/commercial disputes within the EACJ. Second, there is limited awareness of this jurisdiction among legal practitioners and domestic judges in the EAC Partner States 'courts. Third, there is limited and constrained collaboration between national courts and judges, as well as the EACJ, in terms of legal and political matters.

2. ANALYTICAL COMPLEXITY: FORMS OF EURO-AMERICAN AND MAINSTREAM INTERNATIONAL LAW SCHOLARSHIP TO JURISDICTIONAL ANALYSIS OF AFRICAN INTERNATIONAL ECONOMIC COURTS

The analysis of the jurisdictional setup of African international economic courts and tribunals is mainly Euro-American, mainstream, formalist, and positivistic in approach. Mainstream International Law Scholarship (MILS) is

[20] Antony J Colangelo, 'Spatial Legality' (2012) 107 *Nw UL Rev* 69.
[21] John H Jackson (n 15).

an 'ensemble of methods, practices, and understandings about the identification, interpretation, and enforcement of international law which, among other things, does not recognise their links with deep structures of capitalism, imperialism, [racism], and patriarchy [racism]'.[22] MILS thus articulates two notions that some TWAIL scholars have linked to international law: Western Centricism and Eurocentrism. I borrow the term Western Centrism from Salvatore Caserta, who argues that it expands Eurocentrism, as it encompasses the current status of global power and its narratives beyond geographical Europe.[23] According to Gathii, five themes represent an anti-Eurocentric analysis of international law: first is the revisionism of international law by decolonised countries to end colonialism and neo-colonialism; second is a critical analysis of the power and structural inequalities between developed and developing countries; third is Antony Anghie's cultural articulation of the encounter between the European and non-European in the construction of international law doctrines; fourth is the focus of international law in the cultural construction of minorities and subordinate groups; finally is the exploration of the first generation of Asian and African scholars of international law.[24]

This subsection challenges some Eurocentric analyses of Africa's international courts from a TWAIL perspective. The following three forms of analysis present the key features of Western centrism: Infantilisation, Evaluative Western centrism, and systemic Western centrism.

2.1 Infantilisation

Infantilisation is a form of analysis that consciously or unconsciously[25] refers to African international courts as young to denigrate their role, authority, and legitimacy.[26] The legacy of infantilisation is cultural and sociological. This analysis is a racist colonial heritage tied to always seeing Africans and their institutions as childlike.[27] It is a form of dominant colonial socialisation connected to Eurosupremacy that sees anything white/European as superior to anything non-white/non-European.[28] So African systems and institutions are easily prone

[22] Bhupinder S Chimni (n 3).

[23] Salvatore Caserta, 'Western centrism, contemporary International Law, and International Courts' (2021) 34 *LJIL* 321.

[24] James T Gathii, 'International Law and Eurocentricity' (1998) 9 *EJIL* 184.

[25] *See* Tom Gerald Daly and Micha Wiebusch, 'The African Court on Human and Peoples' Rights: Mapping Resistance against a young Court' (2018) 14 *Intl J L Context* 294; *see also* Daniel Abebe, 'Does International Human Rights Law in African Courts Make a Difference' (2016) 56 *Va J Intl L* 527.

[26] *See* Makau Mutua, 'The African Human Rights Court: A Two-Legged Stool' (1999) 21 *Human Rights Quarterly* 342 (a surprising and early criticism of the African Court of Human and Peoples' Rights from a very unlikely source).

[27] *See* David M Anderson, 'Punishment, Race and 'the raw native': Settler Society and Kenya's Flogging Scandals, 1895–1930' (2011) 37 J *Sthn Afr Stud* 479, 496.

[28] Natsu Taylor Saito, *Settler Colonialism, Race, and the Law: Why Structural Racism Persists* (NYU Press, 2020) 25.

to infantilised conscious and unconscious analysis. A Western-centric analysis emerges that critically suffers from what Mahmood Mamdani has referred to as a paralysis of perspective or analysis.[29] In the case of African systems, they work because they have copied their Western counterparts appropriately; in the case they don't work, they are merely bad imitators. In terms of age, the four main regional economic courts in Africa are relatively young, including the ECOWAS Community Court of Justice (ECCJ), the SADC Tribunal, the OHADA Common Court of Justice and Arbitration (OHADA CCJA), and the EACJ.[30] However, some of these courts have a long history that can be connected substantively and procedurally to former colonial courts within the British colonial empire.[31] The West Africa Court of Appeal (WACA) and the East African Court of Appeal (EACA) are excellent examples. The link the current African regional international courts have with their colonial counterparts makes some of these courts appear 'older' in terms of age than they would have been otherwise.

2.2 Systemic Western Centrism

African international courts, while established in a specific context, do not exist outside the contours of international law. One of these contours is the role of international law in constituting objects and subjects of the international order and governing the relationships between them.[32] Thus, international law can universalise provincial values and local claims.[33] The idea here is that international law has particularly intervened in non-Western societies to socially, politically, economically, and culturally transform them into a European image.[34] One dominant concept underlying this transformation is that of sovereignty. Viewed in this light, international courts can further produce and reproduce mainstream concepts in international law, such as sovereignty and its corollary concept of jurisdiction.[35] The procedural and substantive rules of African international courts, as well as the rationality of their decisions, are easily interspersed by this systemic nature of understanding and engaging

[29] Mahmood Mamdani, *Citizen and Subject: Contemporary Africa and the Legacy of Late Colonialism* (Princeton University Press, 1996) 3

[30] Jörg Kleis, *African Regional Community Courts and their Contribution to Continental Integration* (Nomos Verlagsgesellschaft mbH & Company KG, 2016) 33.

[31] *See* L L Kato, 'The Court of Appeal for East Africa: From a Colonial Court to an International Court' (1971) 7 *E Afr LJ* 1.

[32] James T Gathii, 'The Agenda of the Third World Approaches to International Law (TWAIL)' in Jeffrey Dunoff and Mark Pollack, *International Legal Theory: Foundations and Frontiers* (Cambridge *University Press,* 2019) 158–60.

[33] Dipesh Chakrabarty, *Provincializing Europe: Postcolonial Thought and Historical Difference (Princeton University Press, 2000); see also Walter D Mignolo and Catherine E Walsh, On Decoloniality: Concepts Analytics Praxis* (Duke University Press, 2018).

[34] Sundhya Pahuja, *Decolonising International Law: Development, Economic Growth, and the Politics of Universality* (Cambridge University Press, 2011) 3.

[35] Bhupinder S Chimni (n 3).

with international law. To further unpack the possible emanation of systemic Westerncentrism, we should also engage with the ideas of coloniality of power and knowledge that are embedded in African economic courts and tribunals.

Epistemological colonialism is another form of cultural colonialism. It occurs when the concepts and categories by which people understand themselves and their world are replaced or are adversely affected by the concepts and categories of their colonisers.[36] This form of colonialism creates what Boaventura de Sousa Santos referred to as cognitive injustice.[37] Territorial and political colonialism was closely linked to physical violence, stealing cultural artefacts, land grabs through the forcible occupation of lands, and the wanton extraction of natural resources and wealth. Maintaining the haemorrhage of natural wealth from the colonies to the metropolis formed part of the development of wealth enjoyed today in the developed world. To ensure this extractive system remained intact, the colonisers had to maintain political control of the colonies. The false belief in the cultural superiority of the colonisers sustained economic and political control.[38] The colonisers set out to conquer not only the land and goods of the colonised but also their culture, souls, and minds. The aim of cultural superiority formed the basis of the epistemic injustice that occurred during colonialism and continues today. Drawing on the post-colonial scholarship of Gayatri Spivak, Leela Gandhi describes this cultural appropriation and subordination as epistemic violence: the practice of 'othering and silencing' the subjects of any study to such an extent that what remains is the self-centred culture of the Western thinker.[39]

This section highlights this form of colonialism: epistemological colonisation of international law within African international economic courts and tribunals. Decolonisation epistemologies involve interrogating the coloniality and politics of knowledge and knowledge production centres.[40] This decolonisation involves posing epistemological and pedagogical questions about the politics of knowledge generation and dissemination, including the purposes and sources of knowledge.[41] The idea here is that knowledge is never neutral. The who, what, and where of knowledge production and dissemination colour the contours of the politics of knowledge.[42] This is because Western knowledge and modes of knowing were first placed outside the reach of the colonised, and they were then partially and selectively offered as a way of co-optation. Later, they were made seductive as a means of gaining access to power, so that the colonised would aspire to it for their 'development'.[43] The general progression of

[36] Rajeev Bhargava, 'Overcoming the Epistemic Injustice of Colonialism' (2013) 4 *Global Policy* 413.

[37] Boaventura de Sousa Santos, *The End of the Cognitive Empire* (Duke University Press, 2018).

[38] Rajeev Bhargava (n 36).

[39] Leela Gandhi, *Postcolonial Theory: A Critical Introduction* (Edinburgh University Press, 1998) 87.

[40] Aníbal Quijano, 'Colonilaity and Modernity/Rationality' (2007) 21 *Cultural Studies* 168.

[41] ibid.

[42] *See* Michael W Apple, 'The Politics of Official Knowledge: Does a National Curriculum Make Sense?' (1993) 14 *Discourse* 1.

[43] Aníbal Quijano, '*Colonilaity and Modernity/Rationality*' 21(2007) *Cultural Studies* 169.

legal education and the teaching and learning of international law in Africa follows this general pattern of denialism/repression, co-optation, and seduction. Epistemic decoloniality is thus based on liberating knowledge, institutional practices, and pedagogy from the shackles of coloniality.[44] For international law, this means paying close attention to how alternative and critical approaches and voices have been marginalised and 'de-marginalising' them. These critical, alternative and contemporary approaches to international law generate 'emergent ways of knowing, teaching, and learning international law'.[45]

2.3 Evaluative Western Centrism

Evaluative Westerncentrism refers to 'the narratives concerning international law and its institutions, and to the fact that Western institutions are often set as the standard against which their non-Western counterparts are scaled and ranked'.[46] Cesare Romano's view of African intra-regional integration as a 'general failure' is an excellent example of analysis based on evaluative Eurocentrism[47] or Westerncentrism.[48] Romano accurately points out that the prioritisation of national identities over regional ones, low intra-African trade, and the economic privileging of former colonial powers have contributed to what he characterises as 'general failure' of integration in Africa.[49] Such an outlook ignores the fact that the integration project in Africa follows a different model from that of Europe.[50] Romano's conclusion that African integration has failed leads him to conclude that African integration courts are imperfect copies of their European counterparts. Specifically, he states that these sub-regional courts have been 'nonstarters, have floundered after a few years, or are languishing with a paltry docket'.[51] It is thus no surprise that in his chapter on trial and error in international judicialisation, the only courts he categorises as experiencing 'growing pains' are in the global South: the Southern African Development Community Tribunal (SADC Tribunal), the Court of justice of the West African Economic and Monetary Union (WAEMU Court of Justice), the Court of Justice of the Common Market of Eastern and Southern Africa (COMESA Court of Justice),

[44] *See* Awino Okech, 'African Feminist Epistemic Communities and Decoloniality' (2020) 12 *Critical African Studies* 313, 314.

[45] ibid 315.

[46] Salvatore Caserta (n 23).

[47] James T Gathii, 'International Law and Eurocentricity' (1998) 9 *EJIL* 184.

[48] Cesare Romano, 'The Shadow Zones International Judcicialization' in Cesare Romano, Karen Alter and Yuval Shany(eds), *The Oxford Handbook of International Adjudication* (Oxford University Press, 2014) 99.

[49] ibid.

[50] James T Gathii, *African Regional Trade Agreements As Legal Regimes* (Cambridge University Press, 2011).

[51] Cesare Romano (n 48).

the Mercosur Permanent Review Tribunal, and Central American Courts.[52] He additionally ties the emergence of sub-regional courts in Africa to the search for development and the emergence of accountability democracy in Africa. Such sweeping claims would require careful analysis and investigation.

Jörg Kleis' monograph on African Regional Community Courts offers another excellent example of the comparison and benchmarking of African Regional Economic Courts with their European counterpart: the Court of Justice of the European Union (CJEU).[53] He argues that since African states are still in the early stages of their development, it would be of interest to focus on the early years of the European Court of Justice (ECJ) as a benchmark.[54] His argument is a path-dependent one that this book cautions against, as it seeks to understand the intricacies of regional courts in Africa, as well as regionalism and the law in Africa. Indeed, the economic, political, and cultural context of 1950s Europe militates against this direct comparativism. In any case, in many ways, African regional courts often emerge as imperfect copies of their European counterparts, based on the yardsticks employed in such studies.[55] Mikael Rask Madsen, Pola Cebaluk, and Micha Wiebusch, in a more nuanced analysis, have persuasively argued that the negative assessment by Romano above is, in a real sense, a critique of international courts and tribunals that can be applied to all international courts.[56]

3. UTILITY COMPLEXITY: THE GENERAL CHARACTERISTICS OF AFRICA'S INTERNATIONAL ECONOMIC COURTS AND TRIBUNALS

All the African sub-regional international economic courts share three distinctive features in common. First, except for the Arab Maghreb Union's (AMU) Judicial Organ and the AfCFTA dispute settlement mechanism, all of these mechanisms allow, or have allowed in the past, individuals and, in some cases, other non-state actors to file claims against states. Second, except for the African Court on Human and Peoples' Rights (ACtHPR) and the AMU's Judicial Organ, they have compulsory jurisdiction.[57] That they allow individuals and NGOs to

[52] Cesare Romano, 'Trial and Error in International Judicialization' in Cesare Romano, Karen Alter and Yuval Shany(eds), *The Oxford Handbook of International Adjudication* (Oxford University Press, 2014)111–134.

[53] Jörg Kleis (n 30).

[54] *ibid*.

[55] James T Gathii, 'The Promise of International Law: A Third World View' (2021) 36 *Am U Intl L Rev* 377–478.

[56] Mikael Rask Madsen, Pola Cebalak and Micha Wiebusch, '*Backlash against International Courts: Explaining the Forms and Patterns of Resistance to International Courts*' (2018) 14 *International Journal of Law in Context* 197.

[57] *See* Karen Alter, *The New Terrain International Law: Courts, Politics, Rights* (Princeton University Press, 2014)42–44.

file cases is a significant factor in why some have become active. Third, although all these courts, without exception, allow states to file cases against each other, except for a case between Ethiopia and Eritrea in the COMESA Court of Justice, there have been no cases between states filed in these courts. Fourth, except for the ACtHPR, the regional community courts are multifunctional. The following subsection will focus on this multifunctionality and its attendant consequences.

3.1 Multifunctionality of International Courts in Africa

International courts and tribunals in Africa, like most other international courts and tribunals, do not play the singular function of dispute settlement. They are multifunctional.[58] We should not, therefore, fixate on their roles as being one-dimensional in terms of functions, ie, dispute settlement or subject matter, eg, 'human rights courts' or 'guardians of regional integration courts'.[59] From this multifunctional perspective, we can understand international courts as policy instruments in the hands of two principal constituencies. First, their mandate providers, ie, the states and international organisations that establish international courts, fund, and support their operations.[60] Second, the parties to any specific dispute may choose to submit their disputes to adjudication before an international court.[61] Thus, international courts and tribunals, designed by these two constituencies above, play a legal, political, moral, and social function.[62] Leading scholars have also supported the view[63] that judicial function does not necessarily require the mandate providers to explicitly assign a function (in this case, jurisdiction) to a court.[64] Bogdandy and Venzke argue that a post-black-letter jurisprudence framework would militate against exclusive legal mandates. It does not limit itself to doctrinal constructions, but also seeks to grasp the law in its social and political contexts, going beyond its legally assigned functions.[65]

Sub-regional community courts in Africa play a vital role in dispute settlement, act as legal guardians of economic integration, enforce the benefits of

[58] Armin Von Borgdandy And Ingo Venzke, *In Whose Name? A Public Law Theory Of International Adjudication* (Oxford University Press, 2014) 5.

[59] *ibid* (arguing that any approach in which an institution or system always performs a single function is implausibly narrow).

[60] *See* Cesare Romano, 'The Price of International Justice' (2005) 4 *Law and Practice of International Courts and Tribunals* 281.

[61] Yuval Shany, *Questions Of Jurisdiction And Admissibility Before International Courts* (n 1)7-8

[62] Karen J Alter, *The European Court's Political Power: Selected Essays* (Oxford University Press, 2009); Karen J Alter, 'The European Court's Political Power' (2009) 19 West European Politics 458; Sally Engle Merry, *Colonizing Hawai'i: The Cultural Power of Law* (Princeton University Press, 2000) 17–18.

[63] James T Gathii, 'Mission Creep or a Search for Relevance: The East African Court of Justice's Human Rights Strategy' (2013) 24 *Duke J Comp & Intl L* 249, 253.

[64] Armin Von Borgdandy And Ingo Venzke (n 58).

[65] *ibid* citing Rudolf von Jhering, *Law as a Means to an End, vol 1 & 2* (Isaac Husik tr, The Boston Book Company, 1913).

regional economic integration, determine remedies for breaches of obligations, and arbitrate on institutional tensions.[66] African states have mandated international courts and tribunals for the traditional role of 'pacific settlement of disputes'.[67] One of the fundamental principles of the East African Community (EAC), Economic Community of West African States (ECOWAS), Southern African Development Community (SADC), Common Market for Eastern and Southern Africa (COMESA), and the African Continental Free Trade Area (AfCFTA) is the peaceful settlement of disputes.[68] For the OHADA, one of its primary objectives is to promote arbitration as a means of resolving contractual disputes.[69] Some of these courts, especially the three most active – The EACJ, the ECOWAS Tribunal, and the SADC Tribunal – have also re-purposed themselves and functioned as guardians of human rights, democracy, and the rule of law.[70]

Richard Oppong cautioned against the EACJ's acquisition of an indirect human rights mandate, stating:

> It is important that, until its jurisdiction is extended to include human rights claims, the court exercises caution in admitting, indirectly human rights claims, too many human rights claims are likely to burden the court and distract it from the economic integration agenda.[71]

He argued that re-purposing the court's mandates as human rights courts through legislation or judicial activism was unnecessary and should be avoided.[72] This view partly overlooks the multifunctionality of these courts and advocates for a unifunctional role for these courts that is not realistic. There is also no evidence that by not accepting human rights cases, these courts would attract economic disputes of the kind Oppong suggests. Multifunctionality is therefore a welcome development; these courts can adopt many different roles.

[66] Richard Frimpong Oppong, *Legal Aspects of Economic Integration in Africa* (Cambridge University Press, 2011) 117.

[67] U.N. Charter, ch VI.

[68] Treaty for the Establishment of the East African Community, art 6, 30 November 1999, 2144 UNTS 255 [hereinafter EAC Treaty]; Economic Community for West African States (ECOWAS) Revised Treaty, art 4, 24 July 1993, 2373 UNTS 233 [hereinafter ECOWAS Revised Treaty]; Treaty Establishing the Common Market for Eastern and Southern Africa, art 6, 5 November 1993, 33 ILM 1067 [hereinafter COMESA Treaty]; Consolidated Text of the Treaty of the Southern African Development Community, art 4, 17 August 1992 www.sadc.int/sites/default/files/2021-08/Consolidated_Text_of_the_SADC_Treaty_-_scanned_21_October_2015.pdf [hereinafter SADC Treaty]; Agreement Establishing the African Continental Free Trade Area, art. 4, 21 March 2018, 58 ILM 1028 [hereinafter AfCFTA].

[69] Traité relatif à l'harmonisation du Droit des Affaires En Afrique, preamble, 1 November 1997, 4 Journal Officiel [Jo] Ohada 1, jusmundi.com/en/document/pdf/treaty/en-treaty-on-the-harmonization-of-the-business-law-in-africa-ohada-treaty-sunday-17th-october-1993 [hereinafter Revised OHADA Treaty].

[70] James T Gathii, 'Mission Creep or a Search for Relevance: The East African Court of Justice's Human Rights Strategy' (n 63); Karen J Alter, James T Gathii and Laurence Helfer, 'Backlash against International Courts in West, East and Southern Africa: Causes and Consequences' (2016) 27 *EJIL* 293.

[71] Richard Frimpong Oppong (n 66).

[72] ibid.

3.1.1 Courts Specialising in International Human Rights[73]

One distinctive characteristic of Africa's sub-regional international courts is that although three are established as sub-regional economic/trade courts, they have primarily decided human rights cases. These are the EACJ, the SADC Tribunal and the ECOWAS ECCJ. Yet, only the ECCJ has an explicit jurisdictional mandate to decide human rights cases. By contrast, the EACJ and the SADC Tribunal, until the latter was suspended in 2010, have pursued a broad interpretive strategy to justify assuming jurisdiction over human rights. A significant feature of these courts is thus their re-purposing of their original mandate over trade disputes to become bold adjudicators of human rights cases and disputes of a political nature. The re-purposing of their mandates is evidence that these courts are enmeshed within regional movements aimed at advancing human rights at the national level, which are increasingly spreading to the regional and sub-regional levels.

Decision-making in human rights cases has been politically consequential, especially when these decisions align with the firmly held preferences of States found to be in violation. The SADC Member States formally removed the SADC Tribunal's jurisdiction to receive individual complaints in 2014. This removal was in reaction to the SADC tribunal deciding that the Zimbabwean government's land reform program constituted discrimination based on race and that Zimbabwe conducted it without due process. In East Africa, the EACJ Partner States revised the jurisdictional structure and rules of the EACJ following a politically sensitive case from Kenya. In West Africa, the Gambia unsuccessfully attempted to persuade ECOWAS states to review the jurisdiction of the ECCJ by denying it the right to receive individual petitions after the court ruled that it had violated the rights of journalists.[74]

In contrast to the broad interpretive strategy employed by East, West, and Southern African courts, the COMESA Court of Justice has adopted a more restrictive interpretive approach.[75] The COMESA Court of Justice has largely remained an industrial (employment) tribunal. Its case law has primarily arisen from employees of the regional integration organisation.[76] Unlike the other African sub-regional courts, this court has not decided on human rights cases. A significant part of the explanation for its unique trajectory in redeploying to become an industrial court, rather than a trade integration court, is the lack of

[73] James T Gathii and Harrison O Mbori, '*Reference Guide to Africa's International Courts: An Introduction*' in James T Gathii (ed), *The Performance of Africa's International Courts: Using International Litigation for Political, Legal, and Social Change* (Oxford University Press, 2020) 302–303.

[74] Karen J Alter, James T Gathii, and Laurence Helfer, 'Backlash against International Courts in West, East and Southern Africa: Causes and Consequences' (2016) 27 *EJIL* 293.

[75] James T Gathii, 'The COMESA Court of Justice' *in Robert Howse, Helene Ruiz Fabri and Geir Ulfstein(eds), The Legitimacy of International Trade Courts and Tribunals (Cambridge University Press, 2018) 314–348.*

[76] ibid.

civil society interlocutors to bring cases to the court, defend it, and lobby for court reform. Additionally, its location, first in Khartoum, Sudan and currently in Lusaka, Zambia, strongly suggests why the court has been unable to build a broader jurisdictional reach. In addition, although it shares similarities in its individual access and jurisdictional rules with other sub-regional courts, it is also limited by the exhaustion of domestic remedies rule, which, together with its restrictive interpretive strategy, has effectively rendered it an industrial tribunal.[77]

3.1.2 Sub-Regional Courts Specialising in International Economic Law[78]

Another set of Africa's international courts has focused on economic issues. They have begun to challenge and, in some respects, are breaking down the previously closed-off national legal regimes and their presumed hierarchical superiority over sub-regional, regional and international legal rules. The best examples come from the West African Economic and Monetary Union (WAEMU), where, since 2002, the Court of Justice has declared the supremacy of the WAEMU competition law over the national law of Member States.[79] This declaration has meant that Senegal, as a WAEMU Member State, has had to give up its ability to enforce competition law at the national level to the WAEMU Commission. The fact that Senegal unsuccessfully contested what it saw as a 'power-grab' by WAEMU, and eventually relented after losing the case in the WAEMU Court of Justice, demonstrates the efficacy of this court in addressing a supranational economic issue.[80]

Similarly, in the Central African Economic and Monetary Community (CEMAC), the Member States have surrendered to CEMAC sub-regional law and jurisdiction over banking regulation. A powerful sub-regional banking institution, *Banque des États de l'Afrique Centrale* (BEAC), has emerged. BEAC has asserted and successfully defended its competence to govern sub-regional banking law through the CEMAC Court of Justice. In addition, in what is perhaps the best example of supra-national economic regulation in Africa, the supra-national corporate, commercial, and business laws of the OHADA region. The OHADA Court of Justice is the highest judicial body charged with enforcing and monitoring compliance with OHADA law. The Member States of the OHADA region have accepted the authority of the OHADA Court of Justice.

Although business actors have not generally invited African sub-regional courts to decide more trade cases, the experience in the WAEMU, CEMAC, and OHADA sub-regional regimes demonstrates the emerging transnational

[77] ibid.

[78] James T Gathii and Harrison O Mbori (n 73) 304.

[79] Ouseni Illy, 'The WAEMU Court of Justice' *in Robert Howse, Helene Ruiz Fabri and Geir Ulfstein(eds), The Legitimacy of International Trade Courts and Tribunals* (Cambridge University Press, 2018) 349–364.

[80] James T Gathii and Harrison O Mbori (n 73).

regulation of economic activities. In addition, the EACJ and the COMESA Court of Justice have decided their first purely trade cases.[81] These cases may herald a new phase of litigation on trade issues, adding to the large number of human rights cases already before those courts.

3.1.3 Non-Judicialisation in North Africa[82]

The AMU Judicial Organ is the least active of Africa's international courts. Why has judicialisation been so difficult in North Africa? In previous co-authored work, four plausible explanations were offered.[83] First, North African countries in the immediate post-decolonisation period placed more emphasis on developing national cohesion than on establishing a pan-Arab sub-regional identity. Each of these countries faced irredentist movements within them, making the building of national cohesion an imperative. Second, the development of a sub-regional institutional framework within the Arab Maghreb Union was hindered by territorial conflicts among these states. Most significant is the dispute between Algeria and Morocco over Western Sahara. A war between 1975 and 1991 over this dispute culminated in the closure of the border between the two in 1994. That dispute spilt over into the International Court of Justice (ICJ) and the African Union (AU) and remains unresolved to date.

Additionally, disputes between Libya and Mauritania weakened the prospects for regional integration in the AMU.[84] Third, the Maghreb area countries have individually negotiated trade and other agreements with the European Union (EU), which remains their most important trading partner. So much so that Morocco attempted to join the EU in 1987 and had its bid rejected. In the words of William Zartman, 'Regional unity has made little headway in northern Africa. National rivalries and the Algerian war have kept pan-Maghrebism from solidifying; national consciousness and national ideologies have kept Nilotic unity, or even foreign policy cooperation with Egypt, from crystallising in north-east Africa'.[85]

Finally, some scholars have argued that judicialisation is not highly favoured as a dispute settlement mechanism among states with an Islamic background. According to Emilia Justyna Powell, countries to the north of Africa, which are predominantly Islamic, prefer mediation and negotiation over the kind of dispute settlement in international courts.[86] This view dovetails nicely with

[81] For the East African Court of Justice case, *see* James T Gathii, '*The East African Court of Justice: Human Rights and Business Actors Compared*' in Karen Alter, Laurence Helfer and Mikael Madsen (eds), International Court Authority (Oxford University Press, 2018) 59-81. For the COMESA case, see James T Gathii, 'The COMESA Court of Justice' (n 75).

[82] James T Gathii and Harrison O Mbori (n 73).

[83] *ibid.*

[84] Cesare Romano, '*Trial and Error in International Judicialization*' (n 52).

[85] William Zartman, *Government and Politics in Northern Africa* (Methuen & Co, 1964) 184.

[86] Emilia Justyna Powell, *Islamic Law and International Law: Peaceful Resolution of Disputes* (Oxford University Press, 2019).

Makane Mbengue's view that one of the axioms of inter-state dispute settlement in Africa is that many African states prefer solitary diplomacy to resolve, especially boundary disputes.[87] They thus eschew third-party adjudication. The combination of all these factors, compounded by the relatively weak to non-existent AMU as a sub-regional commitment, makes cooperation around any set of issues, including dispute settlement through an international court, next to impossible. However, in an evaluative Westerncentric tone, Romano has argued that the weakness in the rule of law in the Maghreb region, which is a precondition for international adjudication, partly explains why this court was 'nipped in the bud'.[88]

4. DORMANT FUNCTIONAL COMPLEXITY: THE TWO FACTORS EXPLAINING THE LOW JUDICIALISATION OF ECONOMIC DISPUTES IN AFRICAN SUB-REGIONAL JUDICIARIES

In addition to the multifunctionality of African international courts analysed above, two additional factors can explain the low judicialisation of economic disputes in African sub-regional courts. The first is the presence, the limited use, and the contested nature of the arbitral function of these courts. The second is the low utilisation of the preliminary reference/ruling procedure, which facilitates judicial dialogue and cooperation between community courts and national courts.

4.1 Low Use of the Arbitral Institutional Function: The Doorway to International Commercial Arbitration and Investor-State Dispute Settlement (ISDS)

When analysing African sub-regional economic courts and tribunals, few commentators have focused on them as International Commercial Arbitration Centres (ICACs).[89] Each of the African sub-regional economic courts and tribunals has treaty-conferred arbitration jurisdiction. The structure of this arbitral jurisdiction varies depending on whether the court itself, through its judges, hears the arbitration cases or maintains a list of arbitrators from which the parties can choose, thus granting the parties full autonomy. This subsection provides a brief analysis of the arbitral jurisdictional structures of the following

[87] Makane Mbengue, '*African Perspectives on Inter-State Litigation*' *in Natalie Klein(ed), International Law Disputes: Weighing the Options* (Cambridge University Press, 2014) 182.

[88] Cesare Romano, *Trial and Error in International Judicialization*' (n 52) 118.

[89] For an in-depth discussion on the role of Africa International Commercial Arbitration Centres, *see* Chapter 6 of this book.

African sub-regional economic courts and tribunals: the ECOWAS ECCJ, the SADC Tribunal, the EACJ, and the OHADA Common Court of Justice and Arbitration (OHADA CCJA).

4.1.1 ECOWAS Community Arbitration Tribunal

Article 16 of the ECOWAS Revised Treaty of 1991 establishes the ECOWAS Arbitration Tribunal. The provision states that the status, composition, powers, procedure, and other issues concerning the arbitration tribunal shall be as set out in a Protocol.[90] The ECOWAS Member States have not yet enacted such a protocol. The implication is that such a tribunal remains inoperative without the enactment of an instrument that sets out its exact jurisdictional and procedural contours. While the ECOWAS Community arbitration tribunal remains inactive, it is interesting to note that the ECOWAS ECCJ Supplementary Protocol, 2005, grants the court jurisdiction to act as an arbitration (arbitrator) tribunal.[91] Article 9(5) of the 2005 ECOWAS ECCJ Supplementary Protocol states that 'pending the establishment of the arbitration tribunal provided for under Article 16 of the Treaty, the Court shall have the power to act as arbitrator for the purpose of Article 16 of the Treaty'.[92] This provision truncates the envisioned Arbitration Protocol in Article 16 of the ECOWAS Revised Treaty, making the ECOWAS Court itself an arbitration tribunal. Article 9(6) of the Supplementary Protocol also states that 'the court shall have jurisdiction over any matter provided for in an agreement where the parties provide that the court shall settle disputes arising from the agreement'. Both provisions in Article 9(5) and 9(6) directly grant the court the power to hear cases as an arbitral tribunal, despite the Protocol envisaged in Article 16 of the ECOWAS Revised Treaty.

The move here by the ECOWAS Member States is commendable and exciting for two reasons. The first is the states' shortcut in making the ECOWAS Court an arbitration tribunal that could now act as an investment tribunal.[93] Such a shortcut would avoid the long process of adopting another protocol for arbitration and is thus a clever and innovative move. The second interesting point of note is that this move means that the ECOWAS Court, as an arbitral tribunal, can also receive international commercial arbitration cases in which the disputing parties select the court as their forum or arbitral institution.[94] In such cases, the ECOWAS Court acts simultaneously as an international arbitration

[90] ECOWAS Revised Treaty, art 16(2).

[91] Economic Community of West African States (ECOWAS) Supplementary Protocol, arts 9(5)–(8), 19 January 2005, A/SP.1/01/05 [hereinafter ECOWAS Community Treaty 2005 Supplementary Protocol].

[92] ibid art. 3.

[93] Mathew Happold, '*Investor-State Dispute Settlement using the ECOWAS Court of Justice: An Analysis and Some Proposals*' (2019) 34 ICSID *Rev* 496; Mathew Happold and Relja Radovic, '*The ECOWAS Court of Justice as an Investment Tribunal*' (2018) 19 JWIT 95.

[94] *See Petrostar (Nigeria) Ltd v Blackberry Nigeria Ltd*, ECW/CCJ/JUD/05/11 (18 March 2011).

institution/centre and an international court. It enters into the institutional world of arbitral institutions, thus competing with both global and regional arbitration centres, and simultaneously remains a regional international court. Chapter 6 of this study presents more analysis on the place of ICACs.

4.1.2 Southern Africa Development Community (SADC) Tribunal

SADC Member States adopted the now-repealed Protocol to establish the defunct Southern African Development Community (SADC) Tribunal on 7 August 2000 (Repealed SADC Protocol, 2000).[95] Article 9(1)(f) of the Declaration and Treaty Establishing the SADC, 1992, had envisaged the Protocol.[96] According to Article 16 of the Consolidated Text of the Treaty of the Southern African Development Community (SADC), the tribunal's role was to ensure adherence to the proper interpretation of the provisions of the Treaty Establishing SADC, 1992 and subsidiary instruments and to adjudicate upon such disputes as may be referred to it.[97] Unlike the other regional economic courts in Africa, the Repealed SADC Tribunal Protocol, 2000, and the SADC Protocol, 2014 do not mention arbitration nor grant the SADC Tribunal any arbitration powers.[98] This omission renders the SADC Tribunal an incomplete outlier within the arbitration jurisdictional framework of African sub-regional economic courts and tribunals.

Interestingly, the SADC Member States had adopted the Finance and Investment Protocol (FIP), 2006, which entered into force in 2010.[99] Article 16 of Annexe I to the Protocol concerns the settlement of investment disputes, allowing investors to initiate international arbitration. They may agree to refer the disputes to three separate avenues. The first of these avenues is, interestingly, the SADC Tribunal. The other two are ICSID and *ad hoc* arbitration. The famous *Campbell v Zimbabwe* case caused the SADC Tribunal's eventual demise and the extinguishing of the ISDS function.[100] This case would quintessentially be an ISDS arbitration case, but because of the Repealed SADC Protocol, 2000, it was interpreted to allow individual access for what was framed as a human rights case.[101]The Campbell decision saga also followed this provision in FIP, as the

[95] Protocol on the Tribunal in the Southern African Development Community, 7 August 2000 www.sadc.int/document/protocol-tribunal-and-rules-thereof-2000 [hereinafter 2000 SADC Tribunal Protocol].

[96] SADC Treaty, art 9(1)(f).

[97] ibid art 16.

[98] Protocol on the Tribunal in the Southern African Development Community 14 August 2014 ijrcenter.org/wp-content/uploads/2016/11/New-SADC-Tribunal-Protocol-Signed.pdf [hereinafter 2014 SADC Tribunal Protocol].

[99] SADC Protocol on Finance and Investment, 18 August 2006 investmentpolicy.unctad.org/international-investment-agreements/treaty-files/2730/download [hereinafter 2006 SADC FIP Protocol].

[100] *Mike Campbell (Pvt) Ltd and Others v Republic of Zimbabwe* (2/2007) [2008] SADCT 2 (28 November 2008).

[101] *See* Erika de Wet, '*The Rise and Fall of the Tribunal of the Southern African Development Community: Implications for Dispute Settlement in Southern Africa*' (2013) 28 *ICSID Rev* 45.

SADC Member States amended the FIP in 2016 by removing the ISDS jurisdiction.[102] The SADC Member States were directly reacting to the Permanent Court of Arbitration (PCA) decision instituted under Article 16 of Annexe I of FIP in *Swissbourgh Diamond Mines (Pty) Limited v Kingdom of Lesotho*.[103] Thus, the ISDS jurisdiction of the SADC Tribunal lasted only six years, from 2010 to 2016.

4.1.3 Common Market for Eastern and Southern Africa (COMESA) Court of Justice

The COMESA Court of Justice is established in Articles 7 and 19 of the treaty establishing COMESA as the Community's court, whose role is to ensure adherence to the law in the interpretation of the treaty.[104] Article 28 of the COMESA Treaty states that

> the court shall have jurisdiction to hear and determine any matter: (a) arising from an arbitration clause contained in a contract which confers such jurisdiction to which the Common Market or any of its institutions is party; (b) arising from a dispute between the Member States regarding the treaty if the dispute is submitted to it under a special agreement between the Member states concerned.[105]

The arbitration jurisdiction crafted in this clause is of a *sui generis* type. The second requirement is similar to the general jurisdiction of the International Court of Justice (ICJ) under its compromissory clause. It is essential to first note the obvious out of this structuring of the COMESA Court arbitration jurisdiction. The provision empowers the court itself to serve as the arbitrator of disputes. This setup is similar to the ECCJ, as seen above, where the court judges serve as arbitrators, rather than a separate roster of arbitrators.

Unlike the ECCJ, whose jurisdiction is wide open because of the provisions in Article 9(5)–(8) of the 2005 Supplementary Protocol that sets out the outer limits of its scope, Article 28(a) of the COMESA Treaty limits the arbitration jurisdiction of the CCJ to disputes where the Community or any of its institutions is a party. This limitation arguably closes private international commercial arbitration and investor-state dispute settlement to the COMESA Court's arbitration jurisdiction, making its scope so narrow as to be meaningless outside its institutional framework. In recent years, the court has sought to establish itself as an arbitral institution by training its judges in arbitration and revising its rules of procedure. These efforts appear futile, considering the court's arbitral

[102] *See* Henok Asmelash, '*The Legacy of the SADC Tribunal in International Investment Law*' in Helene Ruiz Fabri & Eduardo Stoppioni (eds), *International Investment Law: An Analysis of the Major Decisions* (Hart Publishing, 2020).

[103] *See Swissbough Diamond Mines (Pty) Limited, Josias Van Zyl, The Josias Van Zyl Family Trust and others v The Kingdom of Lesotho*, PCA Case No 2013–29.

[104] COMESA Treaty, arts 7 and 19.

[105] *ibid*.

setup.[106] The jurisdictional structuring limits the court to hearing employment claims; thus, even in its arbitration jurisdiction, the court will remain an employment or industrial tribunal.[107]

4.1.4 *East African Court of Justice (EACJ)*

Article 32 of the treaty for the establishment of the East African Community sets out the arbitration jurisdiction of the court as follows: The Court shall have jurisdiction to hear and determine any matter:

> (i) arising from an arbitration clause contained in a contract or agreement which confers such jurisdiction to which the Community or any of its institutions is a party; or
> (ii) arising from a dispute between the Partner States regarding this treaty if the dispute is submitted to it under a special agreement between the Partner States concerned; or
> (iii) arising from an arbitration clause contained in a commercial contract or agreement in which the parties have conferred jurisdiction on the court.[108]

The first two provisions above in (i) and (ii) are similar to those in the COMESA Treaty and have identical implications as analysed above.

The final provision in (iii) is an addition that does not exist in the COMESA Treaty. It makes the EACJ an international commercial arbitration centre and court, similar to the ECOWAS ECCJ, as described above. The roles of administration and dispute resolution by the court's judges, acting as an arbitral tribunal, are fused in this jurisdictional structuring. It effectively means that the EACJ, just like the ECOWAS ECCJ, enters into the world of arbitration centres. However, its roster of arbitrators is its judges, not independent arbitrators. It is possible in this case to add the EACJ as a potential avenue for international investment cases, ie an investment tribunal like the ECOWAS ECCJ.

While the fusion of structure here is commendable, the EACJ judges sitting as arbitrators have disadvantages that would make the court a less competitive avenue compared to international, regional, and even national arbitration centres (see Chapter 6). The first limitation is the restriction on party autonomy regarding the roster of arbitrators, which only includes judges, who may not be experts in international commercial or investment law. The second limitation is the perception among business actors that the judges are more comfortable with litigation and might not be well-versed in arbitral practice. Finally, with a limited budget provided by the Partner States, parties might not trust the court as an independent player in the arbitration process.

[106] Lombe Chibesakunda, 'COMESA: Dispute Settlement and Arbitration Developments' (2017) Paper presented during TRALAC Annual Conference, www.tralac.org/images/docs/11119/comesa-dispute-settlement-and-arbitration-developments-lady-justice-lombe-chibesakunda-tralac-annual-conference-april-2017.pdf.

[107] see James T Gathii, 'The COMESA Court of Justice' (n 75).

[108] *ibid*, EAC Treaty, art. 32.

4.1.5 OHADA Common Court of Justice and Arbitration (OHADA CCJA)

The OHADA CCJA, which will be a specific subject of another chapter in this book (Chapter 4), is the most peculiar of all the African international economic courts and tribunals in arbitration. The OHADA CCJA is an international economic court and a separately structured international arbitration centre and tribunal (IAC). This setup means that, unlike the ECCJ or EACJ discussed above, the OHADA CCJA has a separate roster of arbitrators that hear cases. The OHADA CCJA has supervisory jurisdiction over these arbitrations.[109] It is essential to note that this supervisory jurisdiction encompasses interstate arbitration and investor-state disputes.[110] The OHADA CCJA's arbitral jurisdiction can be invoked pursuant to an arbitration clause in a contract or by agreement.

Additionally, the court (through the appointment of arbitrators) can assume arbitral jurisdiction where any of the parties is domiciled or has its usual place of residence in the territory of a state party. The court also has jurisdiction where a contract is performed or will be performed wholly or partly in the territory of one or more state parties.[111] As noted above, it is not the OHADA CCJA judges that hear the arbitration cases. Instead, the court appoints or confirms arbitrators who keep the court informed of the proceedings' progress and submit the draft award to the court for approval, in conformity with Article 24 of the Treaty.[112] The court acts as an appointing authority when the parties fail to agree on a slate of arbitrators within thirty days or when the parties fail to agree on a sole arbitrator.[113] The treaty also empowers the court to approve the arbitrators that the parties choose.[114] The court selects arbitrators from an updated list of arbitrators, which is compiled annually, and ultimately decides any challenge to the appointment of an arbitrator made by a party to a dispute.[115] The treaty also empowers the court to verify the form of arbitral awards before they are issued as final awards by the arbitral panel.[116]

4.2 Low Use of the Domestic Court References (Preliminary References/ Rulings) to mandated African Sub-Regional Community Courts

One of the other features present among the African sub-regional economic courts and tribunals is the jurisdiction for preliminary references or preliminary rulings. The COMESA Court of Justice (CCJ), the ECOWAS ECCJ, the EACJ, and the SADC Tribunal, prior to the 2014 amendments, all had jurisdiction for

[109] OHADA Treaty, art 21.
[110] OHADA Uniform Act on Arbitration (2017), arts 2 & 3.
[111] OHADA Treaty, art. 21.
[112] ibid art 21.
[113] ibid art 22.
[114] ibid art 22.
[115] ibid art 22.
[116] ibid art 24.

preliminary references or preliminary rulings.[117] The preliminary ruling jurisdiction is absent in the 2014 SADC Tribunal protocol. It is safe to say that SADC Member States have eliminated this jurisdiction. The jurisdiction, however, remains present among the three other sub-regional courts. The usage of this jurisdiction remains considerably low among these courts. In many respects, the preliminary reference procedural requirements of the EACJ, ECCJ, and CCJ resemble those of the corresponding EU procedure.[118] Yet while the EU's preliminary procedure has been deployed effectively to fashion and enhance EU law, the corresponding African courts' procedure has had minimal use.

The preliminary ruling procedure is primarily a scheme of collaboration and cooperation between two different judicial systems.[119] For international courts and tribunals, this procedure enables national courts to collaborate, cooperate, and engage in dialogue with international courts in the interpretation of regional or community law. Mandate designers of international law institutions, especially those involved in the integration schemes of regional economic communities, can easily envision the procedure as a scheme of non-hierarchical and horizontal collaboration between national and international courts.[120] The procedure originates from the EU community law, specifically Article 267 of the Treaty on the Functioning of the European Union (TFEU). The rationale for the procedure is that most Community law is enforced and applied within the Member States.[121] This means that domestic courts, in many instances, are the first port of call for domestic litigants on matters that might involve community law. The Court of Justice of the EU (CJEU) and EU Member States national courts have deployed the preliminary ruling procedure so effectively that some commentators have described it as the 'jewel in the crown' of CJEU's jurisdiction.[122]

Taking the EACJ as the prime example in this section, despite the EACJ establishing sub-registries in the national courts of its Partner States, litigants have not yet widely utilised this procedure.[123] From its operationalisation in 2001 to the time of writing this book in 2025, over a 20-year period, the EACJ has

[117] COMESA Treaty, art 30; ECOWAS Community Treaty 2005 Supplementary Protocol, art 10 (f); EAC Treaty, art 34; and 2000 SADC Tribunal Protocol, art 16(2).

[118] *ibid*; *see* specially for the EACJ, John Eudes Ruhangisa, 'The East African Court of Justice: Ten years of Operation (Achievements and Challenges)' (paper presented at the Sensitisation Workshop on the Role of the EACJ in the EAC Integration, Imperial Royale Hotel, Kampala, Uganda, 1–2 November, 2011).

[119] Morten Broberg, 'Preliminary Ruling: European Court of Justice (ECJ)' in Helene Ruiz Fabri (ed), *The Max Planck Encylopedia of International Procedural Law* (Oxford University Press, 2018).

[120] Armin Cuyvers, *'Preliminary References under EU Law'* in Emmanuel Ugirashebuja and others (eds), *East African Community Law: Institutional, Substantive and Comparative EU Aspects* (Brill Nijhof, 2017) 117.

[121] *ibid*, 275.

[122] Paul Craig and Gráinne de Búrca, *EU Law. Text, Cases, and Materials* (Oxford University Press, 2008) 460; Paul Craig, '*The Jurisdiction of the Community Courts Reconsidered*' (2001) 36 *Texas Intl LJ* 555, 559.

[123] Caroline Nalule, 'Defining the Scope of Free Movement of Citizens in the East African Community: The East African Court of Justice and its Interpretive Approach' *(2018)* 62 *J Afr L* 1,6.

received only two preliminary reference requests. The High Court of the Republic of Kenya submitted the first in 2011 in *Saida Rosemary & Hassan Elijuma Agade v. The Commissioner of Police, The Commandant Anti-Terrorism Police Unit and the Attorney General of the Republic of Kenya ECJ Case 283/81*. The High Court of the Republic of Uganda submitted the second in *The Attorney General of the Republic of Uganda v Tom Kyahurwenda* on July 31, 2015. This second preliminary reference was heard and finally determined by the court. The EACJ stayed the first because the Kenyan high court judge who requested the preliminary ruling had been removed from office.[124] The Kenyan High Court has not given directions on the matter to date. The apathy displayed by the Kenyan High Court and the procedural technicality stance taken by the EACJ may be a possible manifestation of limited but increasing legal and political collaboration between Partner States' institutions and EAC institutions. Such apathy has resulted in the limited use of the preliminary reference procedure.

In the Kenyan High Court preliminary reference, it is unfortunate that the case was never heard and determined due to what seems like a procedural technicality. The matter is especially dire when the importance of the substantive facts is considered. The petitioners in the case were representatives of Hussein Hassan Agade, Idris Magondu, and Mohammed Adan Abdow, who were extradited from Kenya to Uganda as terror suspects for the July 2010 World Cup final bombings in Kampala, Uganda.[125] The petitioners made habeas corpus applications to the Kenyan high court for these individuals who had been arrested as terror suspects. As part of the defence of the Kenyan authorities was that the renditions were conducted pursuant to EAC law, the preliminary reference to the EACJ would have presented an excellent opportunity for the court to lay down the law on such renditions that did not follow the legal channels of criminal extradition under the Kenyan Extradition (Contiguous and Foreign Countries) Act, Cap 76 laws.

Despite the apparent failure in the Kenyan preliminary reference, the EACJ was able to render its first ruling on a preliminary reference in 2015 in *Attorney General of the Republic of Uganda v Tom Kyahurwenda*. The preliminary reference arose from a miscellaneous application before the High Court of Uganda arising from Civil Suit No. 298 of 2012 (*Attorney General of the Republic of Uganda v Tom Kyahurwenda* (*Kyahurwenda*)). In the proceedings at the Ugandan Court, the Plaintiff, Tom Kyahurwenda, lodged a civil appeal against the defendant, the Attorney General of Uganda, claiming that the defendant's actions had caused him pecuniary losses and had also breached Articles 6, 7, 8, and 123 of the EAC Treaty. The Plaintiff sought monetary compensation, which the

[124] Victor Lando, 'The Domestic Effect of the East African Community's Human Rights Practice' (September 2017) 59 (LLD Thesis, University of Pretoria Faculty of Laws), hdl.handle.net /2263/64619.

[125] Open Society Foundations, 'Counterterrorism and Human Rights Abuses in Kenya and Uganda: The World Cup Bombing and Beyond' (2013) www.justiceinitiative.org/uploads/1b4cef46-0f2f-498a -a16c-cfcefd9897ae/counterterrorism-human-rights-abuses-kenya-uganda-20130403.pdf.

defendant state challenged by questioning the court's jurisdiction to adjudicate cases relating to the interpretation of the EAC Treaty and award compensation, arguing that the issues were not justiciable before the Ugandan High Court.[126] The Ugandan High Court sought a Preliminary ruling from the EAC, posing two questions: a) whether Articles 6, 7, 8, and 123 read together with Articles 27 and 33 of the Treaty are justiciable in the National Courts of Partner States; and, b) whether Articles 6, 7, 8 and 123 read together with Articles 27 and 33 of the treaty are self-executing and confer sufficient legal authority on the national courts of the Partner States to entertain matters relating to Treaty violations and to award compensation and/or damages as against a Partner State.[127]

The EACJ Appellate Division first considered which courts could interpret the EAC Treaty and annul Community Acts, regulations, directives, and actions. It concluded that analysis is necessary to avoid a legion of interpretations of the EAC Treaty or inconsistent annulments, as this mandate exclusively rests with the EACJ.[128] Preliminary rulings therefore enable national courts to seek an interpretation of the treaty from the EACJ. They then can apply the interpretations in cases before them.[129] The only instance in which national courts have jurisdiction to interpret EAC law is when Partner States have chosen to contract outside this principle and grant concurrent jurisdiction to the EACJ and national courts and tribunals. If this happens, Article 33(2) of the EAC Treaty is invoked, with the interpretation of the EACJ taking precedence over that of the national court or tribunal.[130] As to the discretion of national courts in Article 34 regarding requesting preliminary rulings, the EACJ ruled that it was narrow and was only exempted in instances where the question is irrelevant or where the *acte éclairé* and *acte clair* doctrines apply.[131] Once this ruling is made, it is binding on the court or tribunal that sought it; it applies as an obligation *erga omnes*, ie on all national courts and tribunals in the EAC.[132]

Having dispensed with this, the court then addressed the first question raised by the Ugandan High Court regarding the justiciability of Articles 6, 7, 8, and 123, as read in conjunction with Articles 27 and 33 of the EAC Treaty. On Articles 6, 7, and 8, which lay out the principles and objectives of the Community, the court referred to its previous decisions, which had answered that question in the affirmative.[133] The treaty empowers the Summit to suspend any Partner State that fails to observe and fulfil the fundamental principles and objectives of the treaty and to expel any Partner State that grossly and persistently violates these

[126] *The Attorney General of the Republic of Uganda v Tom Kyahurwenda* CASE STATED NO. 1 of 2014, paras 2 & 3.
[127] *ibid*, para 5.
[128] *ibid*, paras 48–50 & 59.
[129] *ibid*, paras 51 &52.
[130] *ibid*, para 61.
[131] *ibid*, para 57.
[132] *ibid*, para 58.
[133] *ibid*, paras 62-69.

principles and objectives.[134] As for article 123, the court considered the fact that its sub-article 5 envisions that 'the Council shall determine when the provisions of paragraphs 2, 3 and 4 of this article shall become operative and shall prescribe in detail how the provisions of this article shall be implemented'. Since this had not occurred at the time of the case's determination, the court rendered those parts of Article 123 non-justiciable.

Regarding the second question posed by the Ugandan High Court, the EACJ reiterated that since Articles 6, 7, and 8 of the Treaty are justiciable before national courts, these provisions confer legal authority on the courts to entertain claims of their violations. However, since paragraphs 2, 3, and 4 of Article 123 were not yet in operation, the court answered that they were not yet justiciable.[135] In concluding the final matter, the EACJ found that national courts can award compensation and damages against a Partner State that has breached the Treaty provisions and occasioned damage to a plaintiff.[136]

4.2.1 *Some Preliminary Reasons for the Paucity of Preliminary Rulings in the EACJ*

One of the main features of the preliminary reference procedure in the EACJ has been its paucity of use. The feature cannot be easily gainsaid, seeing that only one preliminary reference case has been fully heard on its merits in the EACJ since its creation as an international court. While the case settled some fundamental substantive questions regarding EAC law, the possibility of the EACJ attracting more preliminary references would be highly welcome for the development of EAC law generally. We, therefore, must ask and answer the nagging question of why the EACJ has not attracted a larger number of preliminary references or, put another way, why have national courts and tribunals not submitted more preliminary references to the EACJ? I argue that three reasons can explain this scenario. The first is the limited judicialisation of economic/commercial disputes within the EACJ, which would form a basis for possible preliminary rulings. The second reason is the limited awareness of this jurisdiction among legal practitioners and domestic judges of the EAC Partner States' courts. The final reason is the limited and constrained legal and political collaboration between national courts, judges, and the EAC/EACJ.

The limited judicialisation of economic/commercial disputes within the EACJ

One enduring feature of the EACJ that it also shares with other sub-regional judiciaries in Africa is the limited judicialisation of economic/commercial

[134] *See* EAC Treaty, art 146(1) & 147(1); *Attorney General of the Republic of Uganda v Tom Kyahurwenda* Case Stated No 1 of 2014, para 66.

[135] *ibid*, paras 73–74.

[136] *ibid*, para 75.

disputes. The EACJ has attracted few litigants and cases in trade, business, commerce, and investment, though this is also slowly changing.[137] This situation is despite many tariff and non-tariff barriers to trade and commerce in intra- and extra-African trade. The EACJ, though established as a sub-regional economic/trade court, has primarily decided non-economic cases. Thus, an essential feature of the EACJ is its ability to re-purpose its original mandate over trade disputes to become a bold adjudicator of human rights cases. One of the immediate casualties of this desirable and laudable development has been the EAC economic law that aims to push the Community more substantively toward a common market. While the Partner States have enacted all the necessary legal instruments to create a common market within the EAC, the actual process of establishing a common market has been relatively slow. The judges in the national courts must see themselves as an essential constituency for submitting preliminary reference questions. This reason for the limited use of the procedure is similar to that offered by former judge and president of the EACJ, Emmanuel Ugirashebuja, who suggests that litigants in the EACJ have preferred the direct action avenue to institute cases, which is a possible explanation for the limited use of the preliminary reference procedure.[138]

The limited awareness of this jurisdiction among legal practitioners and domestic judges in the EAC Partner States courts.

Writing in 2017, Emmanuel Ugirashebuja identified the lack of awareness of the jurisdiction's existence as one of the reasons why the preliminary reference procedure has not been actively utilised in the EACJ.[139] John Eudes Ruhangisa, the former registrar of the EACJ, also pondered on the underutilisation of the preliminary ruling by national courts and tribunals. Writing in 2011, he argued that many national court judges, magistrates, and lawyers were unaware of this provision.[140] He also noted that by 2011, only the High Court of Kenya had referred one matter to the EACJ for a preliminary ruling (*Saida Rosemary and Hassan Elijuma Agade case*).

In recognition of this situation, the EACJ has sensitised the Partner States to make the preliminary rulings jurisdiction more known among judicial officers and practitioners. A case in point is in 2017 when the EACJ's president paid a courtesy call to the Chief Justice and the Minister of Industry, Trade, and EAC Affairs in Rwanda. They acknowledged that part of the visit was to establish collaboration between the Rwandan national courts and the EACJ through the preliminary rulings. During the visit, the EACJ's President informed Rwanda's

[137] See Chapter 4 of this study for more arguments on this issue.

[138] Emmanuel Ugirashebuja, '*Preliminary References under EAC Law*' in Emmanuel Ugirashebuja and others(eds), *East African Community Law: Institutional, Substantive and Comparative EU Aspects* (Brill Nijhof, 2017) 274.

[139] *ibid.*

[140] John Eudes Ruhangisa (n 118).

Chief Justice that this relationship needed to be strengthened by educating Rwanda's judicial officers on the workings of this jurisdiction so that they could use it when appropriate.[141]

The limited and constrained legal and political collaboration between national courts and judges and the EACJ.

One of the glaring challenges presented by the preliminary reference procedure is the requirement for coordination and cooperation between the national courts of the Partner States and the EACJ. This expectation presupposes an existing relationship of collaboration between national and Community institutions. The political rhetoric is robust that the EAC is an important supranational institution for cross-border economic, political, cultural, and social relations; yet, a deep-seated cultural suspicion and mistrust persist when it comes to applying community law. Gathii has documented the sentiments among Tanzanian lawyers who culturally mistrust Kenyan lawyers, viewing them as 'pushy'.[142] It is unlikely that, in the space of such mistrust from domestic judges to view the EACJ as a legitimate node of authority to build strong community norms and deeper integration. The EACJ itself has also not taken an active role in stamping its jurisdictional authority on preliminary references. The 2010/11 Kenyan reference was a lost opportunity, as the court would have issued its first preliminary reference. Ugirashebuja has also lamented the lack of robust judicial dialogue between the domestic courts and the EACJ as one of the reasons for the limited number of preliminary references to the court.[143]

CONCLUSION

This chapter has argued that African states have designed these courts with complex jurisdictional mandates that militate against purely positivistic, doctrinal, and formalistic analyses. The chapter focused on African states that delegated adjudicative jurisdiction to their sub-regional economic courts and tribunals. The first section analysed three examples of Westerncentricism in the scholarship of international courts in Africa. I borrowed the term Westerncentricism from the brilliant scholarship of Salvatore Caserta. The first, termed infantilisation, argues against analysing these courts as young courts to denigrate their role, authority, and legitimacy. Such denigration can be done either consciously or unconsciously. The second form of Westerncentricism is

[141] EAC, 'Court President pays courtesy to the Chief Justice & Minister of Industry, Trade and EAC Affairs in Rwanda' www.eac.int/press-releases/153-legal-judicial-affairs/795-court-president-pays-courtesy-to-the-chief-justice-minister-of-industry,-trade-and-eac-affairs-in-rwanda.

[142] James T Gathii, *African Regional Trade Agreements As Legal Regimes* (Cambridge University Press, 2011) 192.

[143] Emmanuel Ugirashebuja (n 138).

termed systemic Western Centricism. It focuses on how international law has particularly intervened in non-Western societies to socially, politically, economically, and culturally transform them into a European image. Finally, on evaluative Westerncentricism, Western institutions were shown to be typically set as the standard for non-Western institutions. This study has generally argued against the purely positivistic analysis that these three forms present.

The second section of the chapter was therefore framed in an anti-positivistic format to present the argument that the jurisdictional mandates of Africa's sub-regional economic courts and tribunals are complex. The first frame of such complexity was introduced in the context of the Multifunctionality of International Courts in Africa. This multifunctionality has produced three consequences: Courts Specialising in International Human Rights, Sub-Regional Courts Specialising in sub-regional Economic Law, and Non-Judicialisation in North Africa. Notably, the second frame of Africa's sub-regional economic courts' complexity was argued in the final section of the chapter. That section analysed two specific characteristics of the African sub-regional community courts that explain the low judicialisation of economic disputes. The first is the presence, limited use, and contested nature of the arbitral function of the African sub-regional courts. The chapter highlighted the OHADA CCJA as an outlier in this regard, as its arbitration function has been more active and differs from that of the other courts. This book dedicates Chapter 4 to a further nuanced analysis of the OHADA CCJA. The second factor contributing to the low judicialisation is the limited use of the preliminary reference jurisdiction by these courts. Using the EACJ as an example, the chapter argued that there are three plausible reasons for this limited use of the preliminary reference procedure. The first is the already notorious fact of the limited judicialisation of economic/commercial disputes among the African sub-regional economic courts and tribunals. Second is the little awareness of the procedure among legal practitioners and domestic judges within national jurisdiction. Finally, there is the limited and constrained legal and political collaboration between national courts and judges in the sub-regional courts.

ANNEXE I

Table 1 African States Membership to sub-regional courts

MM	State	ACtHPR	ACHRP	EACJ	ECCJ	SADC Tribunal	CCJ	OHADA CCJA	CEMAC CJ	AMU Judicial Authority
3	Algeria	✓	✓							✓
2	Angola		✓			✓				
4	Benin	✓✶×	✓		✓			✓		
2	Botswana		✓			✓				
4	Burkina Faso	✓✶	✓		✓			✓		
4	Burundi	✓	✓	✓			✓			
4	Cameroon	✓	✓					✓	✓	
2	Cape Verde		✓		✓					
3	Central African Republic		✓					✓	✓	
4	Chad	✓	✓					✓	✓	
5	Comoros	✓	✓			✓	✓	✓		
3	Côte d'Ivoire	✓✶×	✓					✓		
4	Democratic Republic of Congo (DRC)	✓	✓			✓	✓	✓		
2	Djibouti		✓				✓			

MM	State	ACtHPR	ACHRP	EACJ	ECCJ	SADC Tribunal	CCJ	OHADA CCJA	CEMAC CJ	AMU Judicial Authority
2	Egypt		✓				✓			
3	Equatorial Guinea		✓					✓	✓	
2	Eritrea		✓				✓			
2	Ethiopia		✓				✓			
4	Gabon	✓	✓					✓	✓	
3	Gambia	✓✶	✓		✓					
3	Ghana	✓✶	✓		✓					
3	Guinea		✓		✓			✓		
3	Guinea-Bissau	✓✶	✓		✓			✓		
4	Kenya	✓	✓	✓			✓			
3	Lesotho	✓	✓			✓				
2	Liberia		✓		✓					
4	Libya	✓	✓				✓			✓
3	Madagascar	✓	✓			✓	✓			
4	Malawi	✓✶	✓			✓	✓			
4	Mali	✓✶	✓		✓			✓		
3	Mauritania	✓	✓							✓

(*Continued*)

Table 1 (*Continued*)

MM	State	ACtHPR	ACHRP	EACJ	ECCJ	SADC Tribunal	CCJ	OHADA CCJA	CEMAC CJ	AMU Judicial Authority
4	Mauritius	✓	✓			✓	✓			
2	Morocco		✓							✓
3	Mozambique	✓	✓			✓				
2	Namibia		✓			✓				
4	Niger	✓✶	✓		✓			✓		
3	Nigeria	✓	✓		✓					
4	Republic of Congo	✓	✓					✓	✓	
4	Rwanda	✓✶×	✓	✓			✓			
2	Saharawi Arab Democratic Republic	✓	✓							
4	Senegal	✓	✓		✓			✓		
3	Seychelles		✓			✓	✓			
2	Sierra Leone		✓		✓					
2	Somalia		✓				✓			
2	South Africa	✓	✓			✓				
3	South Sudan		✓	✓			✓			
2	Sudan		✓				✓			

MM	State	ACtHPR	ACHRP	EACJ	ECCJ	SADC Tribunal	CCJ	OHADA CCJA	CEMAC CJ	AMU Judicial Authority
3	Eswatini		✓			✓	✓			
4	Tanzania	✓✶×	✓	✓		✓				
4	Togo	✓	✓		✓			✓		
4	Tunisia	✓✶	✓				✓			✓
4	Uganda	✓	✓	✓			✓			
3	Zambia		✓			✓	✓			
3	Zimbabwe		✓			✓	✓			
		33, ✶12 ×4	54	6	15	16	22	17	6	5

MM: Multiple Memberships in African International Courts

✶ Made Declaration under Article 34 (6) of the Protocol on the Establishment of the African Court on Human and Peoples' Rights, allowing court to receive cases from individuals and NGOs with observer status within the African Commission on Human and Peoples' Rights.

× Withdrawn the Article 34 (6) declaration above.

Adopted and Updated from Alter (2014)[144]

[144] Karen J Alter, *The New Terrain of International Law: Courts, Politics, Rights* (Princeton University Press, 2014).

4

The OHADA Common Court of Justice and Arbitration (OHADA CCJA): Innovation in the Shadow of Neo-Colonialism

I. INTRODUCTION

INTERNATIONAL TRADE IN AFRICA remains at low levels, and intra-African trade remains low.[1] Intra-African trade remains low, even though most informal cross-border trade among Africans remains uncounted.[2] Outside of trade, sovereign borrowing, and aid, many African countries viewed the quest to attract foreign direct investment (FDI) as a suitable spur to economic development. Despite this motivation to attract FDI, by the turn of the twenty-first century, the entire African continent (except South Africa) had received inflows worth an estimated US$ 8.2 billion.[3] This FDI flow, in comparison, equals the inward FDI flow attracted by Finland alone in the same year.[4] In 2020, with the COVID-19 pandemic ravaging the world, Sub-Saharan Africa's inward FDI flows decreased by 12 per cent to US$ 30 billion. In comparison, Singapore alone experienced a 20.7 per cent decrease in FDI inflows, bringing its total FDI inflows to US$ 90.6 billion.[5]

We continue to see ambivalence from African states in their attitudes toward international investment arbitration. On the one hand, under the principles of the New International Economic Order (NIEO), especially the critical UN

[1] UNCTAD, 'Economic Development in Africa Report 2019: Made in Africa, Rules of Origin for Enhanced Intra-African Trade' (2019) 19.

[2] Andrew Mold and Samiha Chowdhury, 'Why the Extent of Intra-African Trade is much Higher than Commonly believed-and what this means for the AfCFTA' www.brookings.edu/blog/africa-in-focus/2021/05/19/why-the-extent-of-intra-african-trade-is-much-higher-than-commonly-believed-and-what-this-means-for-the-afcfta/ (Brookings, 19 May 2021) accessed 22 November, 2022; Kimberle Williams Crenshaw, 'Race, Reform, and Retrenchment: Transformation and Legitimation in Antidiscrimination Law' (1988) 101 *Harv L Rev* 133.

[3] OECD, 'Foreign Direct Investment for Development: Maximizing Benefits, Minimizing Costs' (OECD Publishing, 2002).

[4] ibid.

[5] ibid 46.

Resolutions of the 1970s,[6] global South states rejected the view that international law would apply to concession and investment agreements. They also strongly advocated for the exhaustion of local remedies before protected investors invoked international arbitration. On the other hand, in the 1980s and early 1990s, these states signed Bilateral Investment Treaties (BITs) that elevated these contracts and many other types of investments to the level of international law. This elevation includes granting investors direct access to international commercial arbitration.

This chapter argues that African states can and should innovate in designing sub-regional international economic courts and tribunals within the reality of neo-colonialism. The *Organisation pour l'harmonisation en Afrique du droit des affaires* (OHADA) or, in English, the Organisation for the Harmonisation of Business Law harmonisation model and the OHADA Common Court of Justice and Arbitration (OHADA CCJA) are used as primary examples. The argument is developed in three core stages. The first is to demonstrate the role that norm entrepreneurs (normpreneurs) have played and continue to play in the development of international investment law. This argument addresses a vital aspect of socio-legal actors that influence the direction of African sub-regional international economic courts and tribunals. Within the OHADA CCJA, we see the role of Judge Kéba Mbaye as one of the leading normpreneurs.[7] One Francophone author has referred to him as *le grand architecte de l'intégration juridique africaine* (the great architect of African legal integration).[8]

The second part of the argument presents OHADA as an institution woven within the 'Françafrique'[9] neo-colonial mould. Here we see the role of OHADA's central normpreneur, Judge Kéba Mbaye, as he contests this labelling of OHADA as part of Françafrique. I argue that the continued link of the CFA franc's currency with France means OHADA is firmly rooted in colonial foundations. The aim here is to show that the interests of the transnational capitalist class (TCC) were heavily involved in OHADA's formation. This section is primarily structured around this discussion and makes other institutional critiques of OHADA. First, it provides a historical context to OHADA, which

[6] Extensively discussed in Chapter 6 of this book.

[7] Humphrey Sipalla, 'Not too Many Faces, one Mask: A Kéba Mbaye Biographic' in Frans Viljoen, Humphrey Sipalla and Foluso Adegalu(eds), *Exploring African Approaches to International Law* (PULP, 2022) 28 (arguing that Mbaye was a complex figure. On one hand Africanist in his role as an arbitrator in investment arbitration and human rights engagements but also willing to work with the French in his OHADA integration project); *see also* Claude E Welch, *Protecting Human Rights In Africa: Roles And Strategies Of Non-Governmental Organizations* (University of Pennsylvania Press, 1995) 164; Mahmoud Cherif Bassiouni, 'In memoriam Kéba Mbaye' (2008) 79 Revue internationale de droit pénal 299, 299–300; Makau Mutua, 'Typologies of Scholarship on Africa' (2014) 107 ASIL Proceedings 191; Emmanuel Roucounas, *A Landscape Of Contemporary Theories Of International Law* (Brill Nijhoff, 2019) 123.

[8] Alhousseini Mouloul, *Understanding The Organization For The Harmonization Of Business Laws In Africa* (Lambert Academic Publishing, 2009).

[9] Boubacar Boris Diop, 'Françafrique: A Brief History of a Scandalous Word' *NewAfrican* (London, 3 March 2018) newafricanmagazine.com/opinions/francafrique-a-brief-history-of-a-scandalous-word/.

exposes France's critical role in OHADA's origins and evaluates OHADA's place in the neo-colonialist 'Françafrique' model. Secondly, the section demonstrates that OHADA, in fulfilling its primary objective, has come closer to the 'uniformisation' of business laws rather than to their harmonisation. Thirdly, it will explore other critiques against OHADA's institutional framework, including its incompatibility with the common law legal system.

The third part of this chapter argues that despite OHADA's bleak outlook, the structure of the OHADA CCJA can counteract the internationalisation of investment contracts. This structuring makes the OHADA CCJA a 'domestic judicialised appellate court'. I argue that with uniformised laws, investors should not submit disputes to ad hoc or external arbitrators but to the OHADA CCJA itself to settle investment disputes. This avenue is better structurally than ECOWAS' ECCJ because ECOWAS, unlike OHADA, does not have uniform law and is not as fully supranational as OHADA.[10] This argument might realistically be challenging to sustain if the OHADA Uniform Acts (UAs) remain indirectly tethered to France's neo-colonialism. Suppose, however, OHADA's UAs are carefully borrowed from a mix of civil and common law heritages; this chapter's argument can then be sustained.

2. NORM ENTREPRENEURSHIP IN INTERNATIONAL INVESTMENT LAW

Herman Abs, the former international finance expert and director of the Deutsche Bank, and Hartley Shawcross, the former general counsel of the Royal Dutch Shell, formed the early inner cabal of investment and investor protection norm entrepreneurs' (normpreneurs).[11] Abs and Shawcross proposed the first prototype investment agreement that was highly pro-investor: the "Abs-Shawcross draft."[12] Herman Abs introduced his idea for a Magna Carta of investment protection in October 1957 at the International Industrial Development Conference in San Francisco.[13] His legal imagination appeared long before the radical principles of the New International Economic Order (NIEO) took place in the 1970s. The decolonisation movement in Africa was just beginning as this was the same year that Ghana, the second sub-Saharan country after Sudan, gained independence. The process of political decolonisation was thus taking place simultaneously while the reassertion of economic domination was occurring. In one of his

[10] See the discussion of ECOWAS Community Court of Justice (ECCJ) in Chapter 3 of this book.

[11] Nicolás M Perrone, *Investment Treaties and the Legal Imagination: How Foreign Investors Play by Their Own Rules* (Oxford University Press, 2021) 1–16.

[12] ibid.

[13] ibid.

seminal works, David Kennedy referred to this process as a simultaneous process of reform and retrenchment.[14]

Though intended for a multilateral draft that never succeeded, the proposals in the Abs-Shawcross draft now form part of the many pro-investor BITs.[15] These two normpreneurs and others supported by their own multinational companies and professional organisations such as the International Chamber of Commerce (ICC) and the Society to Advance the Protection of Foreign Investments, saw foreign investment as essential for securing Western liberal values.[16] The main idea of these normpreneurs was that 'foreign investors should have a direct right to sue states before international arbitral tribunals without having to exhaust local remedies'.[17] Simply, these normpreneurs intended to institutionalise Investor-State Dispute Settlement (ISDS) and to resist the channel of diplomatic protection in public international law that required the exhaustion of local remedies. Aron Broches, another leading normpreneur of the International Centre for the Settlement of Investment Disputes (ICSID) system and the World Bank's General Counsel from 1959 to 1979, was of the view that direct access to international arbitration by investors without exhaustion of domestic remedies would amount to extra-territorial status for all foreign investment.[18]

One way of bypassing domestic remedies and accessing international arbitration tribunals was to argue that investment contracts were international agreements that attracted the application of international law.[19] This was one of the contending points for Global South countries in the United Nations (UN) while arguing for the principle of Permanent Sovereignty Over Natural Resources (PSNR) and self-determination. In a system governed by the rule of law,[20] the first step towards investing (outside of portfolio investments) is to contract with the host state. Such a contract between a private entity and the host state is governed by domestic law.[21] Domestic law is the

[14] David Kennedy, 'When Renewal Repeats: Thinking against the Box' (2000) 32 *NYU J Intl L & Pol* 335; *see also* James T Gathii, 'Reform and Retrenchment in International Investment Law' (SSRN Paper No 3765169, 13 January 2021) dx.doi.org/10.2139/ssrn.3765169.

[15] Perrone (n 11).

[16] ibid 2.

[17] ibid 5.

[18] Aron Broches, 'The Present Need for a Permanent Arbitral Tribunal' (Address at the Institute on Permanent International Courts, Minnesota State Bar Association, 13 June 1962).

[19] Muthucumaraswamy Sornarajah, 'The Battle Continues: Rebuilding Empire through Internationalization of State Contracts' in Jochen von Bernstorff and Philipp Dann (eds), *The Battle for International Law: South-North Perspectives on the Decolonization Era* (Oxford University Press, 2019) 175–197.

[20] David Kennedy, 'The "Rule of Law," Political Choices, and Development Common Sense' in David M Trubek(ed), *The New Law and Economic Development: A Critical Appraisal* (Cambridge University Press, 2006) 95–173.

[21] Sornarajah, 'The Battle Continues: Rebuilding Empire through Internationalization of State Contracts' (n 20) 182.

law that has the closest link and the most dominant ties with the process of the contract. International investment contracts, especially concessions agreements, are volatile because of their long duration, the political and economic risk involved, the possibilities of changes in external circumstances, and the public interest tied to the contract.[22]

Decolonisation and the mass nationalisations that accompanied it forced the pro-investor normpreneurs to think of appropriate ways to protect their contractual benefits. Just as how overt racism in Jim Crow US was replaced by covert claims of colourblindness while the core of the economic benefits of racism continued,[23] these normpreneurs were determined to salvage the core of the economic benefits of empire. The first aim was to ensure that in any situation in which the contract was at risk, the investor would have access to remedies that would restore the investor to their position before the dispute.[24] The investor is afraid that such disputes cannot be resolved at the domestic courts as they would be biased (the home court advantage). Additionally, the investor also believed, especially in the years immediately after colonisation, that judicial review of government acts by the judiciary of constitutional legislation would be illusory.[25]

The common law system that former British colonies inherited exacerbated this illusion. The legislature was sovereign, and acts of parliament were presumed constitutional. The judiciaries did not have the power to strike down legislation for unconstitutionality. The plan was, therefore, to place investment contracts beyond the reach of the host state.[26] These contracts were to form part of public international law and not part of domestic law. The International Court of Justice (ICJ) thwarted this project in the Anglo-Iranian Oil Company case (United Kingdom v. Iran), by holding that an oil concession contract between Iran and the Anglo-Iranian Oil Company was not a treaty between Iran and the United Kingdom.[27] In this case, the positivist account of international law that strictly limited international law to states played in favour of developing host states, even though the same account had shielded Transnational corporations (TNCs) of the nineteenth and early twentieth centuries from responsibility for wars, slavery, and plunder.[28]

M. Sornarajah, however, argues that limiting international remedies to states and not extending the same right to TNCs was also beneficial to the TNCs and

[22] Muthucumaraswamy Sornarajah, *The International Law on Foreign Investment* (Cambridge University Press, 2017) 88–98.

[23] Richard Rothstein, *The Color of Law: A Forgotten History of How Our Governments Segregated America* (Liveright Publishing Corporation, 2017).

[24] Sornarajah, 'The Battle Continues: Rebuilding Empire through Internationalization of State Contracts' (n 19) 182.

[25] Federico Ortino, 'The Investment Treaty System as Judicial Review' (2013) 24 *Am Rev Intl Arb* 437.

[26] Sornarajah, 'The Battle Continues: Rebuilding Empire through Internationalization of State Contracts' (n 19) 182.

[27] Anglo-Iranian Oil Co., (*United Kingdom v Iran*), Judgment,) [1952] ICJ Rep 93.

[28] See Tirthankar Roy, *The East India Company: The World's Most Powerful Corporation* (Penguin Random House, 2012).

their home states.[29] Granting the TNCs direct international law protection would upset the existing theories of responsibility, as direct conferment of personality would also mean that TNCs became bearers of responsibilities.[30] The pro-investor norm entrepreneurs, their organisations, and their home states – which were by this point, developed countries – indirectly created another version of international law that would grant the investor the right to sue the home state but would avoid responsibility for any damage to the home-state interests.[31]

Additionally, the home state would be shielded from responsibility under the principles of the law of agency. Sornarajah argues that the claim for agency here was compelling as the TNC repatriated profits home, was taxed by the home state, and general benefits arose for the home state's responsibility.[32] To bypass domestic jurisdiction and apply the above aims for TNCs and host states, the investment contracts needed to be 'internationalised'. Internationalisation refers to identifying international law as the proper law of the investment concession contracts to elevate contractual obligations into international obligations.[33] Even though the declaration of investment contracts failed in the ICJ, the process succeeded through other means. Sornarajah traces the origins of internationalisation of investment contracts to the *Lena Goldfields Arbitration*.[34] In this case, Lena Goldfields sued Russia for nationalising mines after the Russian Revolution. As the contract had an arbitration clause, the investor sued Russia, and despite Russia not appearing in the hearing, the tribunal proceeded to issue an award against Russia.

Later arbitrations that developed the theme of internationalisation involved oil and gas in the Middle East. While the tribunals in these cases conceded that the applicable law to such cases was the host state's domestic law, they still went ahead to displace this law by arguing that the Middle Eastern states' law was not sophisticated enough to deal with such complex contracts. This view is yet another manifestation of Antony Anghie's dynamic of difference (ie, the endless process of creating a gap between two cultures, demarcating one as 'universal' and civilised and the other as 'particular' and uncivilised, and seeking to bridge the gap by developing techniques to normalise the aberrant society).[35] In this case, the laws of the 'uncivilised' are said to be inapplicable to complex commercial relations as a guise for the perpetuation of economic imperialism. To be sure, Yves Dezalay and Bryant G. Garth reach similar conclusions while

[29] Sornarajah, 'The Battle Continues: Rebuilding Empire through Internationalization of State Contracts' (n 19) 184.

[30] ibid

[31] ibid

[32] ibid

[33] Chin Leng Lim, Jean Ho and Martins Paparinskis, *International Investment Law and Arbitration: Commentary, Awards and other Materials* (Cambridge University Press, 2018) 37–50.

[34] *Lena Goldfields Limited v USSR* [1930].

[35] Antony Anghie, *Imperialism, Sovereignty, and the Making of International Law* (Cambridge University Press, 2005) 4.

describing how transnational private justice developed in the name of international commercial arbitration.[36]

3. OHADA AND FRANÇAFRIQUE: A NEO-COLONIAL COMMERCIAL LAW REGIME?

The *Organisation pour l'harmonisation en Afrique du droit des affaires* (OHADA) is a regional body that initially covered 14 CFA (originally 'franc des *Colonies Françaises d'Afrique*') countries. We must distinguish between the two different CFAs currently in sub-Saharan Francophone Africa: The West African CFA and the Central African CFA. The French, as colonial masters in the nineteenth century, created two federations: French West Africa (*Afrique occidentale françaises*, AOF) in 1895, and French Equatorial Africa (*Afrique équatorial françaises*, AEF) in 1910.[37] French West Africa consisted of Dahomey (present-day Benin), Côte d'Ivoire, Guinea, Upper Volta (present-day Burkina-Faso), Mauritania, Niger, Senegal, and Sudan (present-day Mali). French Equatorial Africa consisted of Congo, Gabon, Ubangi-Shari (present-day Central African Republic), and Chad. Together with Cameroon and Togo, these countries were the initial signatories to the OHADA Treaty in 1993.[38] The aim of harmonising business law among these CFA countries stemmed from the fact that, up to the 1980s, they each applied outdated laws inherited from the French colonialists.[39] Accordingly, the primary objective of OHADA became the 'implementation of a modern harmonised legal framework in the area of business laws in order to promote investment and develop economic growth'.[40]

Some of the outdated laws to be updated and harmonised included the French Commercial Code of 1807, and subsequent legislation made applicable to the colonies; namely, the French Civil Code of 1804 governed the general regime of companies; the French Law of July 24, 1867, governed Public Limited Companies and the French Law of March 7, 1925 governed the Limited Liability Companies. Before OHADA, there was some form of harmonisation of business law in these former French colonies.[41] This harmonisation faded away around the 1980s.[42] The

[36] Yvez Dezalay and Bryant G Garth, Dealing in Virtue: International Commercial Arbitration and the Construction of a Transnational Legal Order (University of Chicago Press, 1996).

[37] Fanny Pigead and Ndongo Samba Sylla, *Africa's Last Colonial Currency: The CFA Franc Story* (Pluto Press, 2020) 6.

[38] Mouloul (n 8) 7–10.

[39] Abdoullah Cisse, 'L'harmonisation du Droit en Afrique: L'experience OHADA a l'epreuve de sa Premiere Decenie' [2004] Revue Internationale de Droit Économique 197, 198 (assessment based on 10 years 1993–2003); *see also* Mouloul (n 8)

[40] Salvatore Mancuso, 'Trends on the Harmonization of Contract Law in Africa' (2007) 13 *Ann Surv Int'l & Comp L* 157.

[41] Mouloul (n 8) 9.

[42] ibid at 7.

Table 2 Comparison between membership of CFA v OHADA

	CFA 14 Members	**OHADA 17 Members**	
Members	*Date of Formation*	*Ratification/ Accession Date*	*Entry into Force*
Benin	December 26, 1945	March 8, 1995	September 18, 1995
Burkina Faso	December 26, 1945	March 6, 1995	September 18, 1995
Cameroon	December 26, 1945	October 20, 1995	December 3, 1996
Central African Republic	December 26, 1945	January 13, 1995	September 18, 1995
Chad	December 26, 1945	April 13, 1996	July 2, 1996
Comoros	**Not a Member**	February 20, 1995	September 18, 1995
Congo	December 26, 1945	May 28, 1997	July 17, 1999
Côte d'Ivoire	December 26, 1945	September 29, 1995	February 11, 1996
DRC	**Not a Member**	July 13, 2012	September 12, 2012
Gabon	December 26, 1945	February 2, 1998	April 5, 1998
Guinea	**Not a Member**	May 5, 2000	November 21, 2000
Guinea Bissau	1997	January 15, 1994	February 20, 1996
Equatorial Guinea	1985	April 16, 1999	August 13, 1999
Mali	December 26, 1945	February 7, 1995	September 18, 1995
Niger	December 26, 1945	June 5, 1995	September 18, 1995
Senegal	December 26, 1945	June 14, 1994	September 18, 1995
Togo	December 26, 1945	October 27, 1995	January 19, 1996

principle of 'legislative speciality' rendered the application of colonial law null and void unless there was a decree declaring it applicable as is or through alteration.[43] Based on this principle, each country started legislating in domains it found of priority.[44] However, this legislative exercise was many a time, following the legislative reforms that were taking place in France at the time,[45] effectively disregarding local socioeconomic realities.[46] For example, on August 10, 1990, Cameroon passed a law regulating commerce, and Mali and Niger adopted commercial codes in 1986 and 1992, respectively. Senegal adopted a code on commercial activities. Gabon adopted Law No. 7/86 of August 4, 1986, and the Central African Republic adopted the Ordinance Law No. 82 82-403 of September 6, 1982.[47]

[43] ibid at 9–10.
[44] ibid.
[45] ibid at 7.
[46] ibid at 9.
[47] Emmanuel Kagisye, 'Environnement Institutionnel des Affaires en Afrique: Contexte et Structure d'harmonisation du droit OHADA'(HAL, 2017) hal-auf.archives-ouvertes.fr/hal-01495556/document.

To some extent, it is against this backdrop that the establishment of OHADA was set in motion. Against these countries' repeated attempts to cohesively harmonise their laws, one may optimistically call OHADA's subsequent establishment a moderate success for these countries. On a broader level, its establishment may even be considered a success in Africa's long-standing attempts at integration. After all, OHADA bears the distinct characteristic of being the only legal framework that harmonises business laws in Africa – a feat that arguably distinguishes it from the various regional economic blocs in the continent.[48] While this optimism may paint a picture of OHADA as an innovative regime founded on these countries' common developmental priorities, a more critical and arguably accurate perspective paints a different picture of OHADA's origins. A critical appraisal of OHADA's history reveals that the organisation was not simply indigenously motivated but was a neo-colonial Françafrique construct couched in indigenous motivations.

3.1 The Birth of OHADA

In April 1991, Finance Ministers from the various CFA countries met in Ouagadougou, Burkina Faso, to seriously consider harmonising African laws.[49] This meeting was followed by another meeting in Paris in October of that same year. In this second meeting, France decided to fund a mission investigating the feasibility of harmonising business law in the CFA Franc Zone.[50] The mission was presided over by Senegalese jurist Judge Kéba Mbaye, a former judge of the ICJ and the lead African normpreneur of the OHADA system. It was composed of seven members, including lawyers and business specialists, working towards establishing OHADA.[51]

For 6 months, from March to September 1992, the mission collected information from highly ranked public officials, commercial actors, and local legislators in select countries in the CFA Franc Zone.[52] In a two-day seminar, from April 19 to 20, 1993, Kéba Mbaye presented the mission's findings. To sum them up:

> Indeed, everyone agrees that the law in force is no longer appropriate, that the rules vary from one country to another, that there is an undeniable uncertainty in the legal corpus of each state, that judicial insecurity, due to the inadequate specialised training of judges, lack of continued training system, and to the ethical issues, the paucity

[48] Charles Manga Fombad, 'Some Reflections on the Prospects for the Harmonisation of International Business'(2012) 59 *African Today* 51.

[49] Mouloul (n 9) 16.

[50] *See* Martin Kirsch, 'Historiquede l'Organisationpour l'Harmonisationdu Droit des Affaires en Afrique (OHADA)' (1998) *Revue Penant* 130.

[51] Mouloul (n 9) 16.

[52] ibid.

of legal information, the total lack of available resources to the judicial services and to many other causes.[53]

It is, therefore, not surprising that the institutions established under the OHADA Treaty are geared towards acting on the findings of Kéba Mbaye's mission in select CFA Franc countries. The OHADA Treaty has established 5 institutions: the Conference of Heads of State and Government, the Council of Ministers of Justice and Finance, Permanent Secretariat, The Common Court of Justice and Arbitration (CCJA), and the Regional Higher School of Magistracy (ERSUMA). The Common Court of Justice and Arbitration (CCJA) is the principal judicial organ based in Abidjan, Côte d'Ivoire. The Permanent Secretariat is based in Yaounde, Cameroon, and the Regional Training School of the Judiciary (ERSUMA), which is based in Porto Novo, Benin and is administratively attached to the Permanent Secretariat.[54]

France's role in funding this mission may at first appear to be that of a benevolent benefactor. However, its contributions to the reform process and its motives suggest otherwise. While other international actors also participated in the founding and funding of OHADA, France provided not only most of the funds but also the ideas.[55] Indeed, French experts prepared the early drafts of the OHADA treaty and UAs while the Africans, to whom the law was to apply, were only required to comment on these drafts.[56] It is, therefore, no exaggeration to describe the reform process as a top-down and French-led process.[57] Judge Kéba Mbaye praised what he saw as the fertile humus for OHADA: monetary union (CFA Franc), a common legal substratum inherited from French law, comparable savings, the same official language (French), and neighbouring political regimes.[58] He refuted the claim that the OHADA process was a French project intended to facilitate the installation of French companies in Africa as a rumour and the most tenacious slander.[59] He argued that while the OHADA harmonisation process favours the expansion of economic units, it did not make a difference regarding their nationality.[60]

Additionally, and most importantly, Kéba Mbaye argued that the idea of harmonising laws was very African.[61] He asserted that the idea was present

[53] ibid at 33.

[54] *Traité relatif à l'harmonisation du droit des affaires en Afrique*, Port-Louis, 17 octobre 1993, JO OHADA n° 4, 1 nov 1997, p 1, préambule et art 3 jusmundi.com/en/document/pdf/treaty/en-treaty-on-the-harmonization-of-the-business-law-in-africa-ohada-treaty-sunday-17th-october-1993 [hereinafter Revised OHADA Treaty].

[55] Fombad (n 48) 66.

[56] ibid at 67.

[57] Gustav Kalm, 'Building Legal Certainty Through International Law: OHADA Law in Cameroon' (Roberta Buffett Center for International and Comparative Studies Working Paper No 11-005, 2011) 11.

[58] *See generally* Kéba Mbaye, 'L'OHADA: Une Intégration Juridique en Afrique' in Emile Yakpo and Tahar Boumedra(eds), *Liber Amicorum Moahmmed Bedjaoui* (Kluwer Law International and Martinus Nijhoff Publishers, 1999) 585–594.

[59] ibid.

[60] ibid.

[61] ibid.

as early as May 1963 in a meeting of Ministers of justice of French-speaking countries led by Professor Rene David. Harmonisation as an idea at this point was in direct response to decolonisation. Small and economically weak African countries saw legal, political, and economic cohesion as a way toward economic development.[62] Kéba Mbaye's final reason for sanitising the role of France in OHADA was that the organisation was born to ensure legal and judicial certainty conducive to attracting investments. He surmises that the idea's origin mattered little if it promoted the development of the activities of companies, both foreign and national.[63] It is difficult not to sense some revisionism and non-critical engagement in Kéba Mbaye's explanation of the French connection in OHADA.

Considered one of the most erudite international law jurists from West Africa and a champion for the right of development,[64] his explanations for the French involvement in OHADA above are not as persuasive as expected. My conclusion on Kéba Mbaye's explanation is open to the charge of anachronism/presentism, ie that I am using current standards to judge a man operating in a different and distinct historical context.[65] But even under his constrained context, other pragmatic explanations would still be offered. I venture to think that either Judge Kéba Mbaye genuinely believed in the OHADA project[66] or that the failure of the NIEO in the 1980s and the triumph of neo-liberalism would account for Mbaye's defeatist and economic fatalistic explanation.

France's 'technical' and financial assistance was strongly tied to the Françafrique system and the CFA monetary zone.[67] Charles Fombad infers from Kéba Mbaye's writings that France's assistance with OHADA was given to progressively transform the CFA zone into an economic union with a singular

[62] ibid.

[63] ibid.

[64] *See generally*, Frans Viljoen, Humphrey Sipalla and Foluso Adegalu (eds), *Exploring African Approaches to International Law* (PULP, 2022) 28 (curiously lacking a chapter dedicated to Judge Kéba Mbaye's leading role in OHADA except for a few references); *see also* James T Gathii, 'Africa and the Radical Origins of the Right to Development' (2020) 1 *TWAILR* 28 (arguing that Judge Kéba Mbaye falls on the intermediate category between critical and contributionism in African international law scholarship and practice on the right to development); *see also* Humphrey Sipalla, 'Not too Many Faces, one Mask: A Kéba Mbaye Biographic' in Frans Viljoen, Humphrey Sipalla and Foluso Adegalu(eds), *Exploring African Approaches to International Law* (PULP, 2022) 30 (arguing that Issa-Sadegh who would later be a close collaborator of Kéba Mbaye in the construction of OHADA law asserted that as far back as 1971 Judge Mbaye had already conceptualized OHADA law, 'not necessarily the definite structures we know today, but through articulating a theory for the harmonization of law in Africa').

[65] *See* Lauren Benton, 'Beyond Anachronism: Histories of International Law and Global Legal Politics' (2019) 21 *J Hist Intl L* 7 (2019) (accusing TWAIL scholars and international lawyers of anachronism (partisan or instrumentalist misuses of history)); *contrast* Anne Orford, *International Law and the Politics of History* (Cambridge University Press, 2021) ch 3 (offering a concerted defence to international lawyers' historical methods); *see also* Samuel Moyn, 'International Law and the Politics of History' (2022) 116 *AJIL* 895 (making close to an ad hominem review of Anne Orford's book).

[66] Kalm, (n 57) 12–13 (arguing that Judge Kéba Mbaye was not a new convert to the idea of harmonisation as he had prior to that argued in favour of harmonisation).

[67] See Pigead and Sylla (n 17).

market.[68] As a result, Fombad concludes that OHADA's substantive aim to encourage foreign investment into the region 'may well be on terms dictated not by its members' interests, but by those who want to bring in the investment', ie, French TNCs.[69] Despite Kéba Mbaye's assertion that OHADA was an African idea, it is no surprise that OHADA's substantive laws were and, for the most part, continue to be ideationally French.[70] Indeed, in the organisation's early years, OHADA's laws were so similar to French business laws that they even contained the same grammatical errors.[71]

One still wonders why Judge Kéba Mbaye, who was sufficiently aware of the dangers posed by post-colonial relations of dominance between Europeans and Africans (particularly economic dominance),[72] would be at the head of a mission that had the potential of reproducing such ties. Mbaye recognised that colonial economic patterns were reproduced in the post-colonial era and that former colonial powers extended development assistance to facilitate product markets in their former colonies.[73] The danger of repeated economic patterns and the partiality of France's development assistance should have been reasonably evident. Reflecting on the issue of France's aid, Mbaye noted the following:

> One must distinguish two things. The idea is African... But you know our countries. Their means are limited. In order to improve the diagnosis and find a remedy, a long route demanding continuity, especially for the considerable financial effort, was necessary. Only France could help African countries in this matter. (...) If France had not provided material and financial means, we would have never achieved what we have today.[74]

We see the manifestation of how African elites fall within the Fanonian (Frantz Fanon) view that the psychology of the post-colonial African middle class was 'that of a businessman, not that of a captain of industry'.[75]

Not to border on speculation, but Kéba Mbaye's ideas on neo-colonialism were likely tempered in this case by his beliefs in a 'universal solidarity' and his notions of shared humanity.[76] Indeed, he pegged the international human right to development on this shared humanity.[77] Even more importantly, Mbaye's approach to international law in Africa did not inwardly look to 'African histories, epistemologies and experiences to define an African approach to international law.'[78] This outlook perhaps also explains why he did not find

[68] Fombad (n 48) 67.
[69] ibid.
[70] Kalm (n 57) 12–13.
[71] ibid.
[72] Gathii (n 64) 46–47.
[73] ibid.
[74] Kalm, (n 57) 10.
[75] Frantz Fanon, *The Wretched of the Earth* (Grove Press, 1963)119–120.
[76] Gathii (n 64) 47.
[77] ibid at 47–48.
[78] ibid at 48.

the uncritical duplication of French business laws particularly concerning. The dissonance between OHADA's substantive aim and France's motives produced two present-day implications. The first implication is that the OHADA legal framework is more attentive to TNCs and big businesses' needs than the smaller and informal businesses that predominate in Africa.[79] The second is that the OHADA regime does little to promote intra-African trade as a means to economic growth on the continent.[80]

3.1.1 Failure to Consider Local Investors

UAs inspired almost exclusively by norms and principles developed for international businesses might not fit the member countries' internal legal, judicial, and economic life.[81] Some UAs have cultural values that do not fit the member countries' context. This is the case with promoting large-scale commercial enterprises, namely the limited liability companies that draw publicly on the savings system. These must refer to the stock market, yet such a market's culture is almost non-existent in most OHADA countries – a large section of the economic structures in the OHADA space function in the informal sector.[82]

For the UA on contracts, the OHADA Council took a different approach. Following its meeting in Brazzaville in February 2002, the Council asked the Permanent Secretariat to contact the International Institute for the Unification of Private Law/*Institut International pour l'Unification du droit privè* (UNIDROIT).[83] UNIDROIT proposed that Marcel Fontaine, Emeritus Professor and Former Director of the *Center de Membre du Group d'Etudes d'UNIDROIT*, prepare the principles and develop the draft UA. Switzerland's *Direction du Development et de la Cooperation* agreed to fund this project where necessary. Marcel Fontaine knew that he had to consider African particularities with the UNIDROIT Principles as a model. So, he organised three trips to select OHADA Member States proposed by the Permanent Secretariat. These trips were in November 2003 (Senegal, Mali, and Burkina Faso), February 2004 (Gabon, Congo Brazzaville, and Cameroun), and April 2004 (Togo, Guinea-Bissau, and Guinea, Conakry). In each country, the Minister of Justice provided a facilitator to help organise focus groups between highly ranked public officials, judicial officers, lawyers, academics, and representatives of various economic sectors. In total, more than one hundred people

[79] Fombad (n 48) 67–68.

[80] ibid at 68.

[81] Bepyassi V Ouafo, 'Le droit issu de L'organisation pour L'harmonisation en Afrique du droit des Affaires et les Societes Africaines: Regard Critique sur une illustration du deni de l'essence Culturelle du droit'(2020) 61 *Les Cahiers de droit* 793.

[82] ibid.

[83] Marcel Fontaine, 'Note Explicative à l'avant-projet d'Acte Uniforme OHADA sur le droit des Contrats' (2008) 13 *Uniform L Rev* 561.

were interviewed to provide information that may help come up with a UA on contracts, as well as reactions and suggestions on the current state of contract law in different countries.[84]

The findings were that, generally, each country preserved the contract law inherited from colonial rule.[85] Further, Fontaine found that local jurisprudence on contracts was not well-known in most countries, and European legal reforms were not considered.[86] It was therefore hard to tell whether such a body as OHADA would qualify for African contract law, if it was based on autochthonous rules developed in African societies to regulate local contractual arrangements. He additionally found that such rules were not well known and that African customary law does not seem to have developed a general theory of contracts.[87] However, while conducting the interviews, some interviewees gave views on local usages that had existed in some form of contractual arrangements for millennia. But Fontaine still found that such local usages could only be fit for low-level economic activities, which could not be pertinent to capture in a UA on contracts.[88] His conclusion perfectly fits Anghie's concept of 'dynamic of difference,' ie, the continuous process of creating a gap between two cultures, demarcating one as 'universal' and civilised and the other as 'particular' and uncivilised, and seeking to bridge the gap by developing techniques to normalise the aberrant society.[89]

Two central problems, however, appeared to be essential to the mission of Marcelin Fontaine. One was rampant illiteracy in the countries studied, and the other was no legal certainty. When disputes occurred, the report found that very few could take recourse to the judicial system. Most people went for Alternative Justice Systems (AJS), or some would avoid any settlement. Fontaine simply sided with internationally accepted 'best practice rules' to develop the draft UA on contracts in OHADA, most of which the UNIDROIT principles had already provided. In his view, for a UA on contract law to attract investors, it had to be simple, easily understandable, and fit to integrate Member States into international trade and investment.[90]

3.2 OHADA, A Critical Historical Appraisal: Money as an Organising Logic of Neo-Colonialism

The influence of France in what is today known as the OHADA space can best be understood if one goes back in history. After the independence of

[84] ibid at 563.
[85] ibid.
[86] ibid.at 567.
[87] ibid.
[88] ibid.
[89] Anghie (n 35) 4.
[90] ibid at 568.

Francophone countries in Africa, France was able to and continues to 'circulate its currency, and nothing but its currency, in politically free countries'.[91] In 1931, the British pound officially began to float and was no longer convertible based on gold reserves. This change was the first fall of the gold-based monetary system or standard.[92] In 1933, the US also ended its gold standard.[93] Rampant bank runs caused the US Federal Reserve to declare the (first fall) of the gold standard.[94] This fall should be distinguished from the 1971 fall (second fall) of the gold standard, when the US officially stated that the US dollar would no longer be convertible to gold, effectively ending the Bretton Woods monetary system.[95] Between 1933 and 1971, the US effectively only maintained a quasi-gold standard.

In the aftermath of the first fall of the gold standard, France, between 1936 and 1939, followed Britain in creating its version of the 'sterling area' in the 'franc area.'[96] These areas were a core part of the 'colonial pact' logic.[97] This logic is centred on four fundamental rules: First, the colonial powers forbid their colonies from industrialising. The colonial governments deliberately discouraged entrepreneurship and skilled labour.[98] Second, the colonies were to supply raw materials to the metropole, which manufactured them into finished products and then resold them back to the colonies. Third, the metropole enjoyed a monopoly on colonial exports, imports, and the shipping of colonial products abroad. Finally, the metropole granted commercial preferences to the products from its colonies.[99] Both areas were common markets allowing trade within their borders and protectionism against the outside world. Additionally, the franc area allowed France to control the currency and coordinate foreign trade.[100] The colonial pact and cultural dislocation meant that no other continent suffered as much destruction of its social, economic, and political fabric through foreign imperial domination as Africa.[101]

France created the CFA franc in 1945 after World War II (WWII) to work as a monetary and trade defence system by bringing together territories under its

[91] Joseph Tchundjang Pouemi, Monnaie, Servitude et Liberté: La répression Monétaire de l'Afrique (Éditions Jeune Afrique 1980) 27; *see also* Fanny Pigead and Ndongo Samba Sylla, *Africa's Last Colonial Currency: The CFA Franc Story* (Thomas Fazi tr. Pluto Press, 2020) 5 (calling the CFA franc a 'colonial relic', a 'vestige of colonialism, or simply a 'neocolonial currency').

[92] John H Wood, 'The Demise of the Gold Standard' (1981) 5 *Economic Perspectives* 13.

[93] Craig K Elwell, 'Brief History of the Gold Standard in the United States' (Congressional Research Service, 23 June, 2011) 9–11 https://sgp.fas.org/crs/misc/R41887.pdf.

[94] ibid at 9.

[95] Jeffrey E Garten, *Three Days at Camp David: How a Secret Meeting in 1971 Transformed the Global Economy* (Harper, 2021) 15–16.

[96] Pigeaud and Sylla (n 91).

[97] ibid.

[98] Issa G Shivji, *Accumulation in An African Periphery: A Theoretical Framework* (Mkuki na Nyota Publishers, 2009) 3.

[99] Pigeaud and Sylla (n 92).

[100] ibid at 10.

[101] Shivji (n 98).

domination in Africa, Asia, the Pacific, and the Americas.[102] The government of the then president, General Charles de Gaulle, created two versions of the franc: the franc of the French colonies of the Pacific (*Colonies Francaises du Pacifique*, CFP) and the franc of the French colonies in Africa (*Colonies Francaises d'Afrique, CFA*).[103] Because of the reduction of trade during WWII in French colonies, France started relying on 'improvised' currencies that were pegged to other currencies, including the US dollar. Looking at the devaluation of its currency at home (the French franc) and cushioning the US from a substantial devaluation of the French franc, France ratified the Bretton Woods Agreements in 1945. It made its first declaration as a party to the International Monetary Fund (IMF).[104] This move came with the creation of the CFA to ease the exportation of resources from the colonies to France while reasserting France's authority over these territories.[105]

In 1958, the CFA Franc was declared the currency of the French Community in Africa. This declaration came after a referendum in which citizens of all French colonies, except Guinea, voted yes to joining the French Community in Africa.[106] This new French franc had a fixed parity – 1 French franc = 50 francs of the French Community of Africa (CFA) that lasted for 36 years.[107] Guinea, under the leadership of Sékou Touré, rejected the offer and left the Franc Zone in 1960 to set up its own currency.[108] In retaliation, French authorities, through their secret services, put many counterfeit notes in circulation in Guinea.[109] In 1962, Mali tried to leave, but came back five years later due to economic and monetary mismanagement and fierce political pressure from France and neighbouring countries.[110] Unsurprisingly to the critical eye, in 1963, the Togolese president was killed just before the launch of a new currency.[111] Further, as Ndongo Samba Sylla has observed, there were no well-trained African economists at the time in Francophone Africa.[112]

In 1994, instead of addressing the parity attached to the franc of the French Community of Africa, France, the IMF sided with a 50 per cent devaluation of this currency.[113] The rationale was that a uniform devaluation rate in the thirteen remaining CFA countries was advantageous for France in maintaining its monetary empire.[114] And these countries were left with the choice to either devalue

[102] Kai Koddernbrock and Ndongo Samba Sylla, 'Towards a Political Economy of Monetary Dependency: The Case of the CFA Franc in West Africa' (MaxPo Discussion Paper No 19/2, 2019) 33
[103] Pigeaud and Sylla (n 91).
[104] ibid at 12.
[105] ibid.
[106] ibid at 15.
[107] Koddernbrock and Sylla (n 102).
[108] ibid at 2–3.
[109] Ndongo Samba Sylla, 'Fighting Monetary Colonialism in Francophone Africa: Samir Amin's Contribution' (2021) 48 *Review of African Political Economy* 32, 33.
[110] ibid at 35.
[111] Koddernbrock and Sylla (n 102) 2–3.
[112] Sylla (n 109) 33.
[113] ibid at 35.
[114] ibid.

or to be cut from international aid.[115] Further, the 1999 substitution of the euro for the French franc could have been assumed to lead to the break between CFA African countries and France. This did not happen as France diplomatically convinced its European counterparts to peg the CFA francs to the euro.[116]

France's insistence on maintaining the CFA franc in the post-colonial era is strongly tied to its vision of the 'Françafrique', a 'system of dominance that contributes to the survival of the former metropole.'[117] This system has maintained France's neo-colonial role of extracting resources from the CFA zone and has ensured the consistent repatriation of profits to the former colonial power.[118] The French intended to extract resources from its colonies through the establishment of commercial regimes for the benefit of the metropole.[119] The French and the entire colonial economy were tailor-made for exploitation by colonial capital linked to metropolitan trade and capital circuits.[120] These colonial trade and commercial circuits persisted even after independence. The fact that OHADA was, at its founding, almost exclusively made up of CFA zone members is not a coincidence. In some ways, a history of OHADA's origins reveals that OHADA is a part of the neo-colonial Françafrique system.

3.3 Critiques against the OHADA Institutional Framework

The Council of Ministers is the legislative body of OHADA. It has the power to enact UAs. Article 10 of the OHADA Treaty states that UAs are directly and compulsorily applicable in Member States and take precedence over domestic legislation in case a conflict arises.[121] Article 10 has thus introduced the principle of supranationality and direct effect within the OHADA space.[122] The OHADA Common Court of Justice and Arbitration (OHADA CCJA) has taken the view that Article 10 applies to domains that are likely to be harmonised and that, at the community level, CCJA decisions have the force of enforcement like that of a decision of a national court.[123]

The supranational nature of the OHADA Treaty has raised constitutional law questions in Member States.[124] International relations are marked by the globalisation of trade, which assumes economic spaces in which geographical barriers

[115] ibid.
[116] ibid at 44–45.
[117] Pigeaud and Sylla (n 91) 86.
[118] ibid at 86–91.
[119] ibid at 6.
[120] Shivji (n 98) 3.
[121] OHADA Treaty, art. 10 (stating that Uniform Acts shall be directly applicable to and binding on the States Parties notwithstanding any previous or subsequent conflicting provisions of the national law).
[122] OHADA Treaty art 10.
[123] Cisse (n 38).
[124] *See* La Cour Consitutionelle Du Senegale arret no 3/C93 du Dec 16, 1996.

have no political significance.[125] These harmonised spaces aim to promote social and economic development and attract private investors by making markets attractive and national and community enterprises more competitive.[126] However, they do weaken the economic sovereignty that a country enjoys.[127] Article 54 of the OHADA Treaty provides that no reservation is allowed while ratifying the Treaty.[128] Articles 5 and 10 of the OHADA Treaty state that UAs come into force through a procedure that only indirectly involves Member States' legislative bodies.[129] The nature of the Member States' legislative powers therefore seems delegated by ratifying the OHADA Treaty.[130] This delegation is analogous to the supremacy of European Union (EU) law.[131] Additionally, a reading of Article 2 of the Treaty reveals that there is no predetermined area that UAs may not regulate, ie the provision does not have any carve-outs.[132]

Critiques against the OHADA CCJA and the Judiciary Regional Training School have focused on the issue of access to justice for a majority of the population. Indeed, in a zone of seventeen countries, a unique court with thirteen judges appears insufficient and might risk increasing a backlog of cases.[133] This risk would be accentuated if the focus were also on local investors and, if they had access, included information tailored to the needs of local economic actors.[134] But as we have seen above, this is not the case. The first sixteen OHADA members revised the OHADA Treaty in Quebec, Canada, on October 17, 2008. One of these amendments increased the official languages of OHADA from one, French, to four: French, English, Spanish, and Portuguese.[135] To serve a majority of the small and informal businesses, diversifying the working languages of OHADA could serve as a catalyst for more formal and informal economic growth.[136]

The founders of OHADA saw the need to give it institutional support to help develop OHADA law and promote legal certainty in business law.[137] They did this by creating the Regional Training School of the Judiciary, which has the

[125] Mouloul (n 8) 7.
[126] ibid.
[127] ibid at 5.
[128] OHADA Treaty, art 54.
[129] ibid arts 5 & 10.
[130] Akeret Muna, 'Is OHADA "Common Law Friendly"?' (2001) 3 *Intl L Forum du droit Intl* 176.
[131] Babatunde Fagbayibo, 'Towards the Harmonisation of Laws in Africa: Is OHADA the way to go?' (2009) 42 *Comp & Int'l LJ S Afr* 309; *see also* Thibaud Roujou de Boubée and Thomas Kendra, 'The Paris court upholds the supranational nature of OHADA in dismissing annulment application' (CA Paris 16/25484, December, 20, 2018), JDSUPRA, www.jdsupra.com/legalnews/the-paris-court-upholds-the-76318/.
[132] OHADA Treaty, art 2.
[133] Demba Mbow, 'L'attractivité juridique et économique de l'OHADA' Université de Franche-Comté,'(2020) 98
[134] Cisse (n 39) 217.
[135] OHADA Treaty, art 42.
[136] Fagbayibo (n 131).
[137] Anaclet Nzohabonayo, 'Préservation de la Sécurité Juridique et Judiciaire des Affaires à Travers les Formations: Cas de l'ERSUMA et des commissions nationales OHADA' (2018) 23 *Uniform L Rev* 131.

mandate to initiate, develop and promote research in African law and be the link between the OHADA CCJA and higher courts of Member States. The school must establish OHADA National Commissions (CNO) in each Member State. However, the CNOs have not been adequately developed due to many issues.[138] Sessions promoting the legal consultations on all matters OHADA could have been easily and regularly organised in all Member States under the auspices of the CNOs. The aim of the CNOs would target both formal and informal (specifically non-educated) economic agents.

3.4 Harmonisation vs. Uniformisation

One commentator noted that the OHADA legal framework goes closer to uniformising business laws rather than harmonising them.[139] The focus on attracting foreign investors by disregarding local realities seems to support this point. The question of attractiveness does not only concern OHADA law but also French law. There is such a close relationship between OHADA law and French law that some have questioned the legitimacy of OHADA laws in Africa.[140] Many of the legislative reforms brought about by OHADA are inspired by French law. This transplantation is supported by the fact that French or Belgian professors generally put together the UA drafts.[141] African professors and Member States typically intervene during the drafting of reports and annotations of the said UAs.[142]

One may then ask whether it is a coincidence that in Articles 81 and 82 of the OHADA Uniform Act on Commercial Companies and Economic Interest Groups, an accredited investor is a person or an entity with the necessary means and competencies to take into account the risk inherent in financial transactions.[143] This emphasis on an accredited investor is similar to the French law of July 2, 1998, on miscellaneous economic and financial provisions.[144]

We have seen that it is not fair to speak of innovation within the OHADA legal framework when it comes to commercial law, as it remains primarily inspired by French law. The proper term here is convergence with French law. This direct transplantation occurs because the OHADA legal framework has either developed French law or has maintained specific solutions that French law has abandoned. Also, this transplantation has not been significant enough to alter French commercial jurisprudence. An example is adopting a conformity

[138] ibid.

[139] Salvatore Mancuso, 'Trends on the Harmonization of Business Law in Africa' (2007) 13 *Annual Survey of International & Comparative Law* 157.

[140] Fombad (n 48) 67.

[141] Patrice S A Badji, 'Reflexions sur l'attractivité du droit OHADA' (2014) 2 *Bulletin de Droit Economique* 51.

[142] ibid at 52

[143] The Uniform Act on Commercial Companies and Economic Interest Groups (2014), arts. 81 and 82.

[144] Badji (n 141).

declaration (adoption de la declaration de conformité) in the OHADA Uniform Act on Commercial Companies and Economic Interest Groups. This declaration was instituted in the French law of July 24, 1966, and was deleted by a law of 1994. The aim to foster simplicity and the relevance of the 1966 law became obsolete. Under Article 6 of the 1966 law, the founders had to submit to the registry a declaration in which they had to explain which operations were conducted to constitute the company and whether such operations were done in line with relevant laws. Although these were deleted in 1994 when the powers of the registrar were expanded, they were still retained in the Uniform Act on Commercial Companies and Economic Interest Groups in Article 73.[145]

3.5 OHADA and Common Law countries

Anglophone Cameroonian lawyers successfully pushed for translating the OHADA Treaty and UAs in 2016 into English, but disparities in the texts remain.[146] The translation of UAs was initially done to permit the Cameroonian Anglophone jurisdiction to conform to OHADA. However, the translations are only literal/semantic and less than adequate on conceptual issues. They do not translate general principles, rules, and concepts of the common law system. They then allow most common law-trained judges and practitioners to apply the civil law-inspired new laws by sheer approximation. Where there is simply no equivalent of a legal concept, courts in the common law jurisdictions have continued to apply pre-OHADA law, which OHADA law had abolished by strict application.[147]

It is colonialism and imperialism that constructed this legal conundrum in Cameroon. We can trace the roots of the problem to the League of Nations mandate system. The mandate system divided the Anglophone and Francophone-speaking parts of the country. Cameroon was first a German colony, and after the Germans lost the First World War (WWI), the League of Nations offered it as a mandate of the French and the British.[148] The British took a small stretch of the Northwest and Southwest part of Cameroon bordering Nigeria.[149] In the twenty-first century, a secessionist armed conflict rooted in this colonial division has led to a claim for a new state in the Anglophone Cameroon region called Ambazonia.[150]

A report on OHADA UAs by the section of the International Law and Practice of the American Bar Association (ABA) and the International Judicial Relations

[145] Uniform Act on Commercial Companies and Economic Interest Groups, 2014, art 73; see also Part 2 Titre 2, 296–297.

[146] Ouafo (n 81).

[147] Muna (n 130) 175.

[148] Reginald Chikere Keke, 'Southern Cameroons/Ambazonia Conflict: A Political Economy' (2020) 23 *Theory & Event* 329.

[149] ibid.

[150] ibid.

Committee of the US Judicial Conference emphasised that the role of OHADA is to attract foreign investors. For this to happen, the reports argued, the legal concepts in the translated versions should match the accepted Anglo-American legal terminology and tradition.[151] However, with common law comes the introduction of foreign concepts such as know-how contracts, leasing, factoring, franchising, and trust. This language issue has raised questions about whether there is a need for a UA for special contracts that capture these particularities or whether OHADA Member States could integrate them into the UA on general commercial law. The concept of leasing, for example, is not yet integrated into OHADA law.[152]

Furthermore, although today-working languages of OHADA have expanded beyond just French to capture English, Spanish and Portuguese, the French language takes precedence in case conflict arises in interpretation.[153] As a conduit of culture, this arrangement declares the French culture superior to Spanish, Portuguese, and English cultures.[154] And even more importantly, French, Spanish, Portuguese, and English supremacy further marginalise African culture. After all, English, French, Spanish, and Portuguese are all foreign languages and cultures in Africa that were introduced and imposed by the violence of colonialism. Ngugi wa Thiong'o, the famous Kenyan novelist, playwright, literary scholar and critic, argues that imperialism is the source of this language's Eurocentricity and hegemony.[155] He argues that Africans have accepted the fatalistic logic of the unassailable position of English [and other European languages] in their literature [and other disciplines] mainly through colonial imposition.[156]

4. OHADA CCJA AND INTERNATIONALISATION OF INVESTOR-STATE DISPUTE SETTLEMENT (ISDS)

Chinua Achebe, the famous Nigerian novelist, literary scholar, and critic, tells a fascinating story in one of his non-fictional works: *The Education of A British Protected Child*.[157] He narrates how in 1976, Henry Kissinger, the then US Secretary of state, decided to meet the then Nigerian Foreign Minister Joseph Garba at the United Nations headquarters in New York. At this point, the foreign relations between the US and Nigeria were at an all-time low because of how the US had handled the Angolan-Cuban-South African crisis. In what Achebe describes as a gambit of condescending pleasantness, Kissinger asked Garba

[151] Muna (n 130) 175.
[152] Badji (n 141) 52.
[153] OHADA Treaty, art 42(2).
[154] Ouafo (n 81) 777.
[155] Ngugi wa Thiong'o, Decolonising the Mind: The Politics of Language in African Literature (East African Educational Publishers, 1981) 9.
[156] ibid.
[157] Chinua Achebe, The Education of a British-Protected Child: Essays (Knopf, 2009) 24.

what he thought America was doing wrong in Africa. Garba replied plainly: 'Everything!' Kissinger then answered: 'Statistically, that is impossible. Even if it is unintentional, we must be doing something right'. Achebe regrettably admits that Kissinger's answer was true and that this exchange would easily be accurate about colonialism.[158] In this sub-section, I argue that this exchange would easily be accurate about OHADA CCJA's structure and functioning to deal with or possibly address the issue of internationalisation of ISDS in the OHADA region.

The issue over internationalisation of ISDS, as illustrated in the first sub-section of this chapter, was two-fold. First, the investment contract was elevated from a domestic contract to an international agreement, in some cases, a 'quasi-treaty'. This elevation is disadvantageous to the host state as its domestic law is no longer applicable. This possibility explains why the NIEO Resolutions advocated for the exhaustion of local remedies, the use of diplomatic protection, and the removal of foreign investment from the discipline of international law and relocating it to domestic law.[159] Second, international law or transnational law (in many cases, the law of European states) is applied to resolve the conflict. Secondly, in many cases, the investor has a direct recourse to international arbitration in cases where the contract has an arbitration clause.

M. Sornarajah described the famous ISDS case of *Asian Agricultural Products Ltd (AAPL) v Sri Lanka*[160] as the original sin in international investment adjudication.[161] The case was decided in 1991 and opened treaty-based investment arbitration.[162] In *AAPL v Sri Lanka*, the arbitral tribunal (with a strong dissenting opinion from Samuel K.B Asante)[163] held that a dispute settlement provision in a treaty decoupled from the contract between the investor and the state could create compulsory jurisdiction in the nominated tribunal.[164] The case thus embodies what Jan Paulsson, another important pro-investor normpreneur,[165] a few years later, after AAPL in 1995, called and is now famous as a fad in explaining ISDS: 'arbitration without privity.'[166] The unilateral avenue for the complete bypassing of domestic courts, one of the main aims of the 1960s normpreneurs, had been opened. An adjudication system that prevents the internationalisation of investment contracts by ensuring that disputes do

[158] ibid

[159] See Chapter 6 of this book for detailed analysis of the NIEO.

[160] *Asian Agricultural Products Ltd (AAPL) v Republic of Sri Lanka* ICSID Case No. ARB/87/3.

[161] Muthucumaraswamy Sornarajah, Resistance and Change in the International Law on Foreign Investment (Cambridge University Press, 2015) 139.

[162] *See generally* Evelyne Lagrange, 'SPP v Egyp, AAPL v Sri Lanka: Some Revolutionary Steps?' in Hélène Ruiz Fabri & Edoardo Stoppioni(eds), *International Investment Law: An Analysis of the Major Decisions* (Hart Publishing, 2022) 79–98.

[163] See generally Richard Frimpong Oppong and Kissi Agyebeng (eds), *A Commitment to Law, Development, and Public Policy: A Festschrift in Honour of Nana Dr. SKB Asante* (Wildy, Simmonds and Hill Publishing, 2016).

[164] *Asian Agricultural Products Ltd v Republic of Sri Lanka* ICSID Case No. ARB/87/3.

[165] Yvez Dezalay and Bryant G Garth, Dealing in Virtue: International Commercial Arbitration and the Construction of a Transnational Legal Order (University of Chicago Press, 1996).

[166] Jan Paulsson, 'Arbitration without Privity' (1995) 10 *ICSID Review* 232.

not go directly to an ISDS tribunal counteracts the idea of internationalisation. The OHADA CCJA system partially counteracts this pro-investor move toward complete delocalisation and, thus, complete internationalisation.

Article 21 of the OHADA Treaty provides that pursuant to an arbitration clause or submission agreement, any party to a contract may submit a contractual dispute to arbitration as provided for in Part 4 of the Treaty, where one of the parties is domiciled or has his usual place of residence in the territory of a State Party, or where the contract is performed or will be performed wholly or partly in the territory of one or more State Parties. The import of this provision up to this point is that the OHADA CCJA has jurisdiction to hear two types of arbitrations, international commercial arbitrations and investor-state arbitrations, where prior contracts or submission agreements state so, and one of the parties is domiciled or has their usual place of residence in an OHADA state party, or the contract is performed wholly or partly in the territory of one or more State Parties. The legal test for an OHADA CCJA tribunal to have jurisdiction is therefore prior consent for the arbitration and domicile/residence or contract performance in a state party.

For ISDS cases, where consent to arbitration is presented in a concession contract or investment contract (broader forms of investments like portfolio investment would present a challenge here), the OHADA CCJA would have jurisdiction and not the domestic courts of the State Party. From the perspective of bypassing domestic jurisdiction and thus 'depoliticising' and 'delocalising' the dispute, the foreign investor would be happy with such an arrangement. However, as the OHADA CCJA is a supranational institution headquartered in one of the state parties and applying uniform law, the host state is also happy (from an NIEO perspective). In such a case, the dispute is not entirely delocalised procedurally and is only partially delocalised substantively in treaty-based claims. Additionally, unlike in treaty-based arbitration, the host state can initiate a dispute in the arbitral tribunal, and thus the arrangement offers the possibility for investor accountability.

However, the second paragraph of Article 21 of the OHADA treaty makes a further provision that might easily jeopardise the advantage of the host state to avoid complete internationalisation. It states that the OHADA CCJA 'shall not itself settle such a dispute. It shall appoint or confirm arbitrators who shall keep the Court informed of the progress of the proceedings and submit the draft award to the Court for its approval in conformity with article 24'. Article 24 then provides that 'before signing a partial or final arbitral award, the arbitrator shall submit the draft to the CCJA. The Court may only propose amendments to the form of the award'. This setup means that it is not the OHADA CCJA as a court that hears OHADA CCJA arbitrations, but *ad hoc* arbitrators on a pre-defined list. The OHADA CCJA, however, maintains tight control of the arbitration. This control has caused controversy in the GETMA case.[167] This

[167] *GETMA International v Republic of Guinea (I)* CCJA Case NO.001/2011/ARB.

controversy was between the OHADA CCJA secretariat and arbitrators over remunerations.[168]

In March 2016, OHADA appointed a group of consultants from Jones Day in Paris to undertake legislative reform of OHADA's arbitration and mediation laws.[169] The Jones Day team was led by Michael Bühler, a partner at its Paris office.[170] From appointing Judge Mbaye in 1993 as the lead drafter of the OHADA laws to appointing a German and US-trained lawyer based in Paris, the trajectory of OHADA laws sociologically still pointed to the metropole in 2018. One of the consultant's radical recommendations was that OHADA abandon its current structure and instead create a regional independent mediation and arbitration centre.[171] This recommendation would not be so radical as the OHADA was already effectively operating as an arbitration centre. Article 3 The Uniform Act on Arbitration (UAA) provides that arbitration can be based on an arbitration agreement or 'an instrument regarding investment, in particular an investment code or bilateral or multilateral investment treaty.'

The OHADA CCJA thus emerged more like a permanent arbitration centre.[172] It has three competencies as an ad hoc commercial arbitration tribunal, as an ISDS (contract and treaty-based tribunal), and as a permanent arbitration tribunal/centre similar to the Permanent Court of Arbitration (PCA).[173] So, while the OHADA CCJA attempts to limit the judicialisation of ISDS, it does not do so completely. This limitation is because it allows external arbitrators who, in many cases, are still drawn from the global North to preside over cases. But what are the advantages of complete judicialisation of ISDS for OHADA? We can draw some lessons from the European Union (EU) on this question from the Court of Justice of the European Union's (CJEU's) Achmea case saga.

As we have seen before, ISDS has been the subject of various criticisms in the recent past.[174] These criticisms have led to the proposal of various solutions to tackle the challenges that the regime currently faces. Among the solutions proposed is the formation of an appellate mechanism, which some have opined

[168] Kwadwo Sarkodie and Joseph Otoo, 'GETMA v Republic of Guinea – implications for African arbitration' (2017) 33 *Arbitration International* 167, 168; Harrison O Mbori, 'Case Commentary on the British American Tobacco v Attorney General of Uganda (EACJ) and GETMA International v The Republic of Guinea (OHADA CCJA)' (2020) 1 *AfJIEL* 341.

[169] Michael Bühler, 'Out of Africa: The 2018 OHADA Arbitration and Mediation Law Reform' (2018) *J Intl Arb* 517.

[170] ibid at 519 (stating that Jones Day was among the few pre-qualified firms that had been invited to bid. Led by the author of this article, Jones Day won the bid, and became, as of Mar 2016, OHADA's Consultant for the Reform); *see also* Chapter 9 of this book on the role of law firms in African international arbitration.

[171] ibid at 519.

[172] See comparison of this structure to other international sub-regional economic tribunals in Africa in Chapter 3 of this book.

[173] *See* Nisuke Ando, 'Permanent Court of Arbitration' in Rüdiger Wolfrum(ed). *The Max Planck Encyclopedia of Public International Law* (Oxford University Press, 2006).

[174] Pia Eberhardt and Cecilia Olivet, 'Profiting from Injustice. How Law Firms, Arbitrators and Financiers Are Fuelling an Investment Arbitration Boom (Corporate Europe Observatory (CEO) and the Transnational Institute (TNI)' (2012); Sornarajah (n 163).

should be modelled on the WTO Appellate Body. The UNCITRAL Working Group III has been considering whether an appeals mechanism should form part of the reforms of ISDS.[175] OHADA CCJA's structure is not that of an appellate standing body but more of an arbitration centre with supervisory and administrative mandates over arbitrations.

One key reason for introducing an appellate judicialised mechanism is that it will arguably lead to more security and predictability within ISDS jurisprudence.[176] This introduction will be through adopting a form of *de facto* precedence in ISDS by requiring subsequent arbitral panels to consider and adopt the 'Appellate Body's' reasoning, absent cogent/compelling reasons not to.[177] As noted above, the OHADA CCJA cannot achieve this as it is not the Court determining the cases. The differences in the application of the CJEU decision in *Slovak Republic v Achmea BV (Achmea decision)* by subsequent arbitral tribunals indicate the need for judicialisation and precedent within ISDS.[178]

In the Achmea decision, the CJEU ruled that the arbitration clause contained in Article 8 of the Netherlands-Slovakia BIT had an adverse effect on the autonomy of EU law, thus was incompatible with EU law.[179] This incompatibility meant ISDS in intra-EU-BITs had to be cancelled in favour of the jurisdiction of the CJEU. This was therefore a claim for complete judicialisation within the EU of investment disputes. Subsequent arbitral tribunals interpreted the Achmea decision differently, particularly on the applicability of the decision to multilateral agreements such as the Energy Charter Treaty (ECT). *Masdar Solar v Spain* considered that the Achmea decision did not apply to multilateral agreements like the ECT, and *Vattenfall v Germany* ruled that EU law should not override multilateral agreements like the ECT.[180] However, the EU Commission argued that the Achmea decision should be extended to multilateral agreements like the ECT.[181] The varied and contradictory application of the Achmea decision by tribunals does little to ensure predictability in ISDS. Instead, they leave the

[175] Marike Paulsson, 'UNCITRAL Working Group III: Reforms in the Realm of Investor-State Disputes – UNCITRAL's Proposals for an Appellate Mechanism and its Impact on Duration and Cost' (Kluwer Arbitration Blog 26 March 2020) http://arbitrationblog.kluwerarbitration.com/2020/03/26/uncitral-working-group-iii-reforms-in-the-realm-of-investor-state-disputes-uncitrals-proposals-for-an-appellate-mechanism-and-its-impact-on-duration-and-cost/?print=print.

[176] Ian Laird and Rebecca Askew, 'Finality Versus Consistency: Does Investor-State Arbitration Need an Appellate System?' (2005) 7 *The Journal of Appellate Practice and Process* 294.

[177] United States – Final Anti-dumping Measures on Stainless Steel from Mexico (US – Stainless Steel (Mexico)) WT/DS344/AB/R (2008) para 160; *see also Saipem SpA v The People's Republic of Bangaladesh*, ICSID Case No ARB/05/7, Award (30 June 2009), para 90.

[178] *Slovak Republic v Achmea B.V* (Case C-284/16).

[179] Clement Fouchard and Marc Krestin, 'The Judgment of the CJEU in Slovak Republic v Achmea – A Loud Clap of Thunder on the Intra-EU BIT Sky!' (Kluwer Arbitration Blog 7 March 2018) legalblogs.wolterskluwer.com/arbitration-blog/the-judgment-of-the-cjeu-in-slovak-republic-v-achmea-a-loud-clap-of-thunder-on-the-intra-eu-bit-sky/.

[180] Deyan Draguiev, '2018 in Review: The Achmea Decision and Its Reverberations in the World of Arbitration' (Kluwer Arbitration Blog, 16 January 2019) arbitrationblog.kluwerarbitration.com/2019/01/16/2018-in-review-the-achmea-decision-and-its-reverberations-in-the-world-of-arbitration.

[181] ibid.

decision's application in a state of flux. OHADA CCJA would easily consider going in the CJEU direction, but this move could only be limited to intra-African BITs. Such BITs have, unfortunately, not been the focus of many African ISDS cases. But this move would be bold and positive.

Moreover, given that, since 2017, OHADA CCJA has dealt with both contract-based and treaty-based disputes, the issue of treaty-based disputes might arise in the future. Creating an appellate mechanism would arguably be suitable for the OHADA CCJA as it would ensure security and predictability in applying certain substantive norms in BITs that are not within the OHADA CCJA's jurisdiction. This view is in direct contradiction to Michael Bühler's radical proposal to make the OHADA an independent mediation and arbitration centre. My position is that OHADA CCJA is already an independent mediation and arbitration centre and needs to include a judicialised mechanism within the Court as an appellate mechanism. Alternatively, African states could even establish such an appellate mechanism under the current African Continental Free Trade Agreement (AfCFTA). The AfCFTA's investment appellate mechanism could be linked to all the other sub-regional economic courts and tribunals to create a singular ecosystem. Such a move would be a better case of critical and innovative Africanisation.[182]

4.1 An African Appellate Investment Permanent Court?

An African appellate mechanism would also remedy the chaos of parallel proceedings and inconsistency witnessed in *CME v Czech Republic* and *Lauder v Czech Republic*.[183] The factual circumstances of the two disputes were similar. One was filed by CME and the other by Mr. Lauder. The two proceedings resulted in conflicting awards.[184] A similar attempt at parallel proceedings was made in *Orascom TMT v Algeria* and *Orascom Telecom v Algeria*. The tribunal in *Orascom TNT v Algeria* dismissed the claim as inadmissible.[185] Related entities instituted multiple proceedings in different fora in these cases on the same basic facts. An African appellate judicialised mechanism in ISDS would arguably ensure consistency, predictability, and coherence in ISDS by ensuring that disputes arising from the same or related facts are coordinated and adjudicated similarly. The GETMA case from OHADA, though, limits such an expectation, as the case was further litigated in the US Federal District Court of the District

[182] *See* Harrison Otieno Mbori, 'Benign and Radical Africanization in International Investment Law and Investor-State Dispute Settlement in Africa' (2023) 24 *JWIT* 633.

[183] Lise Johnson, '*CME v Czech Republic, Lauder v Czech Republic,* Investment Treaty News: International Institute for Sustainable Development' (18 October 2018) www.iisd.org/itn/en/2018/10/18/cme-v-czech-republic-lauder-v-czech-republic/.

[184] Hans Bagner, 'How to Avoid Conflicting Awards: The Lauder and CME Cases' (2004) 5 *JWIT* 32.

[185] Zongnan Wu, '*Orascom TMT Investments v Algeria*: A New Trend on the Doctrine of Abuse of Rights in the Context of Parallel Proceedings?' (2019) 34 *ICSID Review* 197.

of Columbia (DC), US.[186] Additionally, the claimants instituted a parallel treaty-based claim and successfully litigated it at ICSID.[187] The claimants were awarded €449,000 (plus interest) for actions of public authorities that were not necessary for the termination of the concession agreement.[188]

ISDS has also been criticised for the lack of independence and impartiality of party-appointed arbitrators.[189] In the case of OHADA CCJA arbitrations, this is a glaring concern. Introducing an African appellate judicialised mechanism with appellate body members selected by all contracting parties, similar to the defunct WTO Appellate Body, would create a sense of objectivity in the system. Closely related to independence and impartiality is the practice of 'double-hatting', in which arbitrators act as counsel of experts in other ISDS cases where issues might be the same as those which they were presented with as arbitrators.[190] An African ISDS appellate mechanism should prohibit this practice by barring arbitrators in the appellate body from acting as counsel or experts during the tenure of their appointment.

Some analysts have objected to introducing an appellate judicialised mechanism because adding another 'step' to the arbitral processes will be much longer, more costly, and increase the risk of an adverse decision to the claimant.[191] This process increased duration and cost might benefit the well-resourced parties, which has been a critique of ISDS. However, designing the mechanism to act as a 'one-stop-appellate-shop' in which appellate body members can adjudicate on matters covered in different investment treaties can remedy the issue of costs. This innovation is suitable for a multilateral appellate judicialised mechanism but not a regional one. That is why I have suggested it within the AfCFTA. This structure would require the development of prerequisite qualifications for persons appointed to the appellate body. This idea of a 'one-stop-appellate-shop' has already been introduced in emerging trade agreements such as the EU-Vietnam Free Trade Agreement and the Comprehensive Economic Trade Agreement (CETA).[192] Moreover, a centralised system would shift the panel's cost from being covered by the parties to an institutional format in which permanent members cover costs. This structure would create a reprieve for parties, which are primarily developing states, from the excessive arbitrator's fees requested by the arbitrators, as in *GETMA International v Guinea*.[193]

The fragmented nature of ISDS currently allows an investor to file parallel proceedings before different arbitral bodies, in which case arbitral bodies risk

[186] Mbori (n 168).
[187] ibid at 400.
[188] ibid at 394–400.
[189] Elsa Sardinha, 'The New EU-Led Approach to Investor-State Arbitration: The Investment Tribunal System in the Comprehensive Economic Trade Agreement (CETA) and the EU-Vietnam Free Trade Agreement' (2017) 32 *ICSID Review* 628.
[190] ibid at 648.
[191] Laird and Askew (n 176) 298.
[192] Sardinha (n 189) 625.
[193] Mbori (n 168) 391–393.

rendering different awards on the same case. The centrality of an appellate judicialised mechanism would avert this risk by requiring an investor to withdraw or discontinue any proceedings before beginning another dispute settlement mechanism on the same measures. It would also bar an investor from initiating another proceeding once the matter is at the appellate level, which would act as the final arbiter in the case. Finally, an appellate judicialised mechanism process modelled on the WTO creates transparency within ISDS. This would require certain documents to be made public, such as a consultation requests. While arbitration may be preferred for its confidential nature, transparency is necessary to ensure harmonisation of procedural aspects and substantive norms and claims in ISDS. Such changes not only reinforce the system's security and predictability but also provide vital critiques of ISDS, presenting an opportunity for reform.

Using the WTO Appellate Body as the systemic (hierarchical) reform basis to address the coherence and legal error problems in investment law is further supported by its arguably efficient structure.[194] The Appellate Body has only three standing (division) members, compared with the ICJ's fifteen, who sit on a single case.[195] Coupled with the strict timelines under the WTO Dispute Settlement Understanding, the WTO's Appellate Body's structure can enhance efficiency and coherence in ISDS. Additionally, there is a high level of trust in the WTO system, based on its widespread use.[196] The culmination in 2019 of the non-appointment of Appelate Body members spearheaded by Trump's US government has dealt a massive blow to this assumption of trust. Despite these advantages, the WTO system is a closed system that applies only WTO law, and states have consistently resisted the inclusion of investment law as part of its subject matter. Thus, making investment law part of the WTO system would require treaty amendments that are currently not practically possible in the WTO.

OHADA CCJA's partial judicialisation of ISDS offers a possible experiment in counteracting the internationalisation of investment claims and ensuring investor accountability. Happold and Relja have also argued that the ECOWAS Community Court of Justice (ECCJ) can also serve as an investment tribunal.[197] Happold and Relja base their argument on Article 9(6) of the 2005 ECOWAS Supplementary Protocol.[198] Article 9(6) provides that the Court shall have jurisdiction over any matter provided for in an agreement where the parties provide that the Court shall settle disputes arising from the agreement. It is upon this

[194] Jürgen Kurtz, *The WTO and International Investment Law: Converging Systems* (Cambridge University Press, 2016) 259.

[195] ibid.

[196] ibid.

[197] Happold Mathew and Radovic Relja, 'The ECOWAS Court of Justice as an Investment Tribunal' (2018) 19 *JWIT* 95.

[198] The Supplementary Protocol A/SP.1/01/05 Amending the Preamble and arts 1, 2, 9 and 30 of Protocol A/P.l/7/91 relating to the Community Court of Justice and Article 4 Paragraph 1 of the English Version of the Said Protocol (signed 19 January 2005, entered into force provisionally 19 January 2005)

provision that Happold and Relja argue that the ECCJ can act as an investment tribunal. Indeed, these provisions mean that the ECCJ, unlike the OHADA CCJA, is fully judicialised. This is accurate because, in the OHADA CCJA, the parties must appoint *ad hoc* arbitrators, while in the ECCJ, the Court itself sits to hear the dispute.

The ECCJ thus has all the advantages of a judicialised dispute settlement mechanism described above. However, suppose the parties in ECCJ select international law as their choice of law, reference is then made to a BIT as the applicable law; the ECCJ would apply international law and immediately lose this advantage. Unfortunately, the ECCJ has affirmed that, as an international court, it applies international law and would likely apply it to such disputes.[199] While the ECCJ does have substantive investment provisions in the form of the ECOWAS Supplementary Act on Investments, ECOWAS Community law is unlike OHADA UAs, which are entirely binding over domestic law and form part of domestic law. While ECOWAS seems a better procedural forum, if the OHADA UAs were to serve the interests of OHADA states (which, as we saw above, they do not), the OHADA system might be the preferable structure. But as it stands currently, both courts in OHADA and ECOWAS have their merits and demerits.

CONCLUSION

The overarching argument of this chapter was that African states can and should innovate in designing sub-regional international economic courts and tribunals, considering the reality of neo-colonialism. The undeniable fact that OHADA is a regional economic integration system that displays French neo-colonial ambitions in the Françafrique mould is used as a core part of this chapter's argument. The argument is nuanced, and I developed it in three separate and specific stages. The first objective was to highlight the role of norm entrepreneurs in the field of international investment law. This argument served as a precursor to the role of African international law scholars as socio-legal actors. The example used in this chapter is that of the indomitable and towering Senegalese jurist, scholar, and Judge Kéba Mbaye.

The second sub-section set the stage to introduce OHADA and its historical background. This second part of the chapter argued that OHADA is an institution woven within the Françafrique neo-colonial mould. This section showed that Judge Kéba Mbaye, the leading African OHADA normpreneur, downplayed this argument as neither well-supported nor persuasive. With the CFA franc's currency continued link to France, it is hard to reach any other conclusion. The final argument to support the chapter's overarching claim was

[199] Mathew and Relja (n 197).

that, despite OHADA's neo-colonial Françafrique origins, the structure of the OHADA CCJA's arbitrations could be capable of clawing back the internationalisation of investment contracts. The OHADA CCJA challenges the almost total acceptance, in the twenty-first century, that internationalised investment agreements are now part and parcel of an internationalised dispute settlement system.

5

Benign and Radical Africanisation of International Investment Dispute Settlement in Africa

I. INTRODUCTION

AFRICANISATION IS AN IDEA in international discourse and process that emerged strongly with the formation of the idea of Africa as a continent and increasingly with mass decolonisation in the 1960s. Social and political theorists and philosophers have persuasively shown that Eurocentric systems of knowledge generation invented Africa as a geographic location and idea.[1] The process of African and Africa invention also constituted and contrasted Africa, especially sub-Saharan Africa, to Europe as the teleos of civilisation.[2] Africa was backward, its peoples were savages and unevangelised, its history and cultures were static and thus generally uncivilised. As it is better known as the civilisation mission, the process of civilisation started in the centuries of slavery and culminated in the twentieth century. Its intention was to 'civilise' the savage, primitive, and backward peoples of Africa, and in the process, Africans lost their sense of cultural identity. Compared to the condition of the African-Americans in the US, Africans also developed a double cultural consciousness.[3] On one side of the consciousness, the African could not easily let go of his indigenous scripts of social and cultural identity, and on the other, the educated African, that emerged in a critical mass in the twentieth century, endeavoured to become more like their European colonial master.

Africanisation emerges as a reactionary idea that responds to the invention, constitution, and the marginalisation of Africa, Africans, and Africaness. It is therefore an all-encompassing idea and process that covers many facets of life: social, economic, cultural, legal and political. The idea also forms a core part

[1] V.Y. Mudimbe, *The Invention of Africa: Gnosis, Philosophy, and the Order of Knowledge* (James Currey, 1988); Ali A Mazrui, *The Africans: A Triple Heritage* (Little, Brown, and Company, 1986); Lewis R Gordon, *An Introduction to Africana Philosophy* (Cambridge University Press, 2008); Achille Mbembe, *Out of the Dark Night: Essays on Decolonization* (Oxford University Press).

[2] *See* Frantz Fanon, *The Wretched of the Earth* (Penguin Books 1967).

[3] William Edward Burghardt Du Bois, *The Souls of Black Folk* (Oxford World's Classics, 2007 (1903)).

of Africa's historiography. According to historians and African studies scholars, Africanisation is defined as 'the process by which knowledge about Africa is rendered "more African"'.[4] This definition is of epistemology and not necessarily of other social phenomena like law or politics. But since knowledge forms the foundation of any social system, speaking of Africanisation from an epistemological perspective would apply to the epistemology of politics, the law, and any other social phenomenon. In this sense, Africanisation can be both a deeply theoretical and a practical idea.

For municipal and international law, Africanisation counter mingles with the idea of decolonisation. In the early years of mass decolonisation, at the political level, the idea simply involved replacing the white colonial masters with Africans in all the positions of power they occupied. The idea of Africanisation also stands within a similar frame of the African nationalism that emerged with mass decolonisation. African nation-states demanded nationalisation of political, social, and in some cases economic functions. Different African nation-states thus came up with '..nisation' policies. These would be referred directly with the states' name; for example, the Kenyanisation and Nigerianisation policies, or it would form part of a reform package presented by early national leaders such as Tanzania's Mwalimu Julius Nyerere's 'Ujamaa' policy.[5] As imperialism and colonialism denigrated the existing legal systems of African nationalities, Africanisation should not have meant only staffing the colonially created legal systems with African personnel but should have also meant a deeper change of legal systems in ways that were culturally, socially, and politically African.

The Africanisation that took place at the African domestic level with municipal law was only benign and not radical Africanisation in the sense that this study defines these terms. This is because the changes occurred in the Fanonian[6] sense of replacing the white colonial master with a black 'interpelleted' African elite. Interpellation refers to the acquisition and internalisation of a culture, in this case, legal culture.[7] The educated and emergent African elite during the process of colonisation, acquired and internalised two cultures, one from the Western colonial powers and the other from their customary national cultures that Western thinkers had relegated as backward, primitive, uncivilised, and in many cases as repugnant to 'natural justice, equity, morality, humanity, and good

[4] Esperanza Brizuela-Gracia, 'The History of Africanization and the Africanization of History' (2006) 33 History in Africa, 85–100; *see also* Toyin Falola & Christian Jennings, 'Introduction' in Toyin Falola & Christian Jennings (eds), *Africanizing Knowledge: African Studies Across the Disciplines* (Transaction Publishers, 2002), 1.

[5] *See* Issa G. Shivji, *Development as Rebellion: A Bibliography of Julius Nyerere* (Mkuki Na Nyota, 2020) 162-230.

[6] *See* Fanon (n 2).

[7] *See* Louis Althusser, *On the Reproduction of Capitalism: Ideology and Ideological State Apparatuses* (Verso, 2014); *see also* Fanon (n 2).

conscience'.[8] The process of cultural 'othering' created a 'double consciousness'[9] that is inherent in the African political, social, cultural, and legal systems to date.

A proper background for understanding and engaging with the idea of Africanisation should be premised on the dismantling of the falsification and fixation of African history as static, mundane, and undocumented.[10] Most of the African peoples, communities, and nations present in present-day Africa had organised their customs, politics, ideals, and economic transactions in significant autonomy for millennia before the advent of European evangelisation and conquest. Before the advent of the Westphalian (modern) State formation patterns, communities in present-day Africa were already exercising the breadth of practices that would cumulatively constitute their cultural and socio-political identity. Realistically, in the century before the start of European conquest in Africa, the 'Precolonial Century', Africa had already witnessed great paradigms shifts in its socio-economic and political structures.[11]

The two main proselytising religions, Islam and Christianity, had already taken a strong foothold in most of Africa, playing important roles in shaping socio-economic and political structures. Africa in the pre-colonial century (before the European scramble, partition, and the establishment of colonial rule) therefore had its main linguistic and cultural populations established.[12] The idea that Africa did not have a history is itself a falsification of history. This idea dehumanises the African as illiterate, apolitical, and ahistorical. This falsification of history therefore meant that any previous systems of knowledge, governance or social order were relegated to subordinate levels and thrown out of the confines of civilisation. Africanisation as an idea responds to and seeks to revise this contested history.

Additionally, the history of pre-colonial Africa before the nineteenth century is unique, lively, and adequately documented. One easily identifiable and unique phenomenon of this period was rapid population mobility.[13] African subsistence and economic activities were practised in extensive areas, moving from one

[8] *See* Mohammad Shahabuddin, *The Colonial 'Other' in the Nineteenth Century German Colonisation of Africa, and International Law*, in African Yearbook of International Law 15–39 (2013); Antony C Diala, 'The Concept of Living Customary Law: A Critique' (2017) 49(2) The Journal of Legal Pluralism and Unofficial Law, 143–165; Olaf Zenker & Markus Virgil Hoehne, 'When the State has to deal with Customary Law' in Olaf Zenker & Markus Virgil Hoehne, (eds), *The State and the Paradox of Customary Law in Africa* (Routledge, 2018) 1–40.

[9] Du Bois (n 2).

[10] B Jewsiewicki and VY Mudimbe 'Africans' Memories and Contemporary History of Africa' (1992) 31 *History and Theory* 1–11.

[11] *See* P Curtin, S Feierman, L Thompson and J Vansina, *Africa History* (Longman, 1978).

[12] Jacob Festus Adeniyi Ajayi, 'Africa at the Beginning of the Nineteenth Century: Issues and Prospects' in Jacob Festus Adeniyi Ajayi (ed), *General History of Africa VI: Africa in the Nineteenth Century until the 1880s* (Heinemann & UNESCO, 1989), 30.

[13] Jan Vansina, 'Population Movements and Emergence of New Socio-Political Forms in Africa' in Bethwel A Ogot (ed), *General History of Africa V: Africa from the Sixteenth to the Eighteenth Century* (Heinemann & UNESCO, 1992) 73.

field of land to another each year. Historians have shown that between 1500 and 1800 no African community remained in the same place.[14] Population mobility informed the socio-cultural practices of the communities of the whole continent.

These constant movements caused the Portuguese to describe the migrants as 'the antithesis of a settled, well-regulated people: they were barbarians as opposed to civilised people'.[15] During the period between 1500 and 1800, the African social, economic, and political structures were continuously transformed.[16] By 1800, African communities were already capable of claiming (legal) rights over their own portions of land.[17] 'By as late as 1880, about as much as 80 per cent of the continent of Africa was being ruled by its own kings, queens, clan and lineage heads; in empires, kingdoms, communities, and polities of various sizes and shapes'.[18] The most fundamental and dramatic, though tragic, of changes in Africa occurred within the short period between 1890 and 1910. That period saw the conquest and occupation of virtually the whole continent by imperial powers and the establishment of the colonial system. One of the main aims of the colonial authority was the destruction of communal autonomy.

This chapter engages directly with the idea of Africanisation of Investor State Dispute Settlement (ISDS). The chapter follows, adopts, and endorses the categorisation of international law scholarship in Africa developed by James Gathii into two trends: Contributionist and Critical International Law scholarship. The chapter argues that the trajectories of current reforms in African international investment law (IIL), now termed as Africanisation of IIL, also fall into two categories: Benign Africanisation that corresponds with the contributionist strand of international law scholarship proposed by Gathii, and Radical Africanisation that corresponds with the critical strand of international law scholarship by Gathii. The chapter argues that to achieve international economic justice for the peoples of Africa – many of whom still face dire poverty, deprivation, and significant economic inequity and injustice – the radical form or approach of Africanisation must be deployed in reforming IIL generally and ISDS specifically.

As a central logic of analysis, this chapter argues that the process of colonialism and neocolonialism was and continues[19] to be a constitutive process of IIL dispute settlement in Africa and informs the current orientations and trajectories of reforms in IIL in Africa. At the domestic level, colonialism was a

[14] ibid.

[15] Ibid.

[16] P Diagne, 'African Political, Economic and Social structures during this period' in Bethwel A Ogot (ed), *General History of Africa V: Africa from the Sixteenth to the Eighteenth Century* (Heine mann & UNESCO, 1992), 24–30.

[17] Jacob FA Ajayi, *Africa at the Beginning of the Nineteenth Century: Issues and Prospects* in General History of Africa VI: Africa in the Nineteenth Century until the 1880s 30 (Jacob FA Ajayi ed., 1989), 30.

[18] A Adu Boahen, 'Africa and the Colonial Challenge' in A Adu Boahen (ed), *General History of Africa VII: Africa under Colonial Domination 1880–1935* (Heinemann & UNESCO, 1989) 2.

[19] *See* Emma Hunter, 'The History of Political Thought in the African Political Present' in Annabel Brett, Megan Donaldson, & Martti Koskenneiemi, (eds), *History, Politics, Law: Thinking Through the International* (Cambridge University Press, 2021) 208–228.

process of wholesome cultural exportation and cultural dislocation. The colonial powers used the 'civilisation mission' as a veil for the real and structural violence in the colonial process that forcefully and ideologically transplanted legal systems into African soil.[20] The benign form or approach of Africanisation will end up window dressing the identified injustices of the current ISDS system without ever remedying the deeply seated colonial and neo-colonial continuities of unjust IIL. Benign Africanisation will not reform IIL and ISDS sustainably to ensure economic, political, social, and environmental justice.

The chapter proceeds as follows, and the first section begins by distinguishing between benign Africanisation and radical Africanisation. This distinction is adapted from the pioneering work of James Gathii on African scholarship engagement with international law, in which he categorises African international law scholarship into contributionist/weak and critical/strong approaches. This study adopts such categorisations, labelling the contributionist strand benign Africanisation and the critical strand radical Africanisation for purposes of IIL in Africa. The next section shows the three manifestations of benign Africanisation: Exclusive Focus on Intra-African Investment; Ambivalence towards ISDS Reforms; and Soft Engagement with the Imperial history and origins of IIL. The third section analyses the three possible manifestations of radical Africanisation: Focus on both Inter and Intra-African Investment; Engaging Deep-seated (substantive) reforms of ISDS; and a Real acknowledgment and engagement with the imperial history of IIL. The chapter also briefly analyses a possible intermediate form of Africanisation labelled Agnostic Africanisation. The chapter concludes that if the three manifestations of radical Africanisation are implemented in the reform of African international law, there is a possibility for the achievement of demonstrable economic justice for the peoples and communities of Africa.

2. BENIGN (CONTRIBUTIONIST) AND RADICAL (CRITICAL) AFRICANISATION IN INTERNATIONAL LAW

James Gathii in his seminal work on international law in Africa has argued that the scholarship of international law in Africa can be divided into two distinct trends from a historical perspective.[21] He labels the first trend 'contributionist' since its proponents emphasise Africa's contributions to international law. He labels the second 'critical' since its proponents examine Africa's subordination in

[20] *See* Chen Lei, 'Contextualizing Legal Transplant: China and Hong' in Pier Giuseppe Monateri (ed) *Methods of Comparative Law* (Edward Elgar Publishing, 2012) 192 (defining legal transplantation as the process by which law travels from one jurisdiction to another by way of transposition, imposition, reception or intended borrowing).

[21] James T Gathii, 'Africa and the History of International Law' in Bardo Fassbender & Anne Peters (eds), *The Oxford Handbook of the History of International Law* (Oxford University Press, 2012) 408–428.

international relations as a legacy traceable to international law.[22] Contributionism is framed on the idea that Africa and Africans contributed and continue to contribute to international law.[23] Gathii argues that Nigerian legal titan, the one-time Judge of the International Court of Justice, Taslim Olawale Elias is an example of an African contributionist scholar. Contributionist scholars – also referred to as inter-civilisational approach scholars – insist that Africa and indeed other non-European peoples have acted as 'innovators and generators' of international law.[24] This chapter refers to this trend as benign Africanisation for purposes of IIL. It is benign because it does seek to 'Africanise', ie emphasise, the contribution Africa and Africans have made in international law. Still, it does not seek to radically transform the root causes of the injustices perpetuated by IIL. The second trend, according to Gathii is represented by African scholars such as Mohamed Bedjaoui, Umozurike O. Umozurike, Makau Wa Mutua, Siba Grovogui, Kamari Clark, Ibironke Odumosu, and Obiara Okafor. They form both parts of the second and first generation of Third World Approaches to International Law (TWAIL) scholars. TWAIL is a critical theory of international law that aims to provide the intellectual instruments to 'unmask the institutionalised, harmful lies that sustain and legitimate social injustice and the political impulse to struggle against them'.[25]

TWAIL scholars, therefore 'problematise and contest dominant historically Eurocentric accounts of the origin of international law and its claims of universality, justice, and equality'.[26] The second trend on African international scholarship is therefore TWALian and represents an engagement with 'the manner in which modern international law continues the legacy of colonial disempowerment, while providing spaces for resistance and reform'.[27] However, the Critical approach presented by Gathii presents a paradox between rejectionism and reformism of international law among these TWAIL African scholars. On the one hand, international law is criticised for perpetuating or acquiescing to existing systems of hegemony and subjugation such as slavery and imperialism and is thus in need of rejection as a purveyor of social injustices. On the other hand, these states and scholars extol the emancipatory promise of international law for the communities of Africa, arguing that international law can be reformed and renovated for emancipatory purposes. This is the duality and ambivalence that is also present in the TWAIL scholarship. Yet such duality and ambivalence do not render the pursuit of both rejectionism and reformism an objectionable endeavour. Indeed, the process of Africanisation of international law in Africa constantly oscillates between these two poles. It is also

[22] ibid.

[23] ibid.

[24] See Onuma Yasuaki, *International Law in A Transcivilizational World* (Cambridge University Press, 2017).

[25] See also Boaventura De Sousa Santos, *Epistemologies of the South: Justice Against Epestimicide* (Routledge, 2016) viii.

[26] Karin Mickelson, Ibironke Odumosu & Pooja Parmar, 'Situating Third World Approaches to International Law (TWAIL): Inspirations, Challenges and Possibilities', (2008) 10 *International Community Law Review* 351.

[27] Gathii (n 21), 409.

a situation in which all new states that emerged in the twentieth and twenty-first centuries find themselves. It is a dual move to reform and affirm a system of law that is presented as universal ie as a law from nowhere and thus applicable everywhere, yet it is a law founded on European, imperial, and Christian values.[28]

At African state practice level, the paradox of acceptionism and rejectionism/reformism has also persisted in the engagement with international law. For rejectionism, African states have been a critical part of the rejectionist/reformist movement described in the previous years such as the New International Economic Order (NIEO). On the acceptionism side, many African states involuntarily found and still find themselves bound by rules, principles, and doctrines of international law formulated when their sovereignty was denied or forcefully exercised on their behalf.[29] These rules are referenced as customary international law and therefore binding on all states despite their formulation in Euro-American praxis.[30] This is in addition to the strong critique that most customary international law norms lack legitimacy and authority since they are not customary in the sense of widespread, consistent, and legal binding force.[31] This critique is premised on the view that while customary international law is intended to be inductive, inferred from the repeated acts of states believed to be in adherence to the law, 'these norms have become a device for judges, advocates, and self-interested states (mainly from the global North) to deduce or create new norms without regard to the beliefs or participation of the vast majority of states and their peoples'.[32]

This does not mean that the deductive version of customary international law produced by dedicated norm entrepreneurs and ISDS arbitral tribunals have not affected the trajectory of current customary international law for African states.[33] The current clamour for reform in IIL is historically linked to the norms of reform generated by Third World states and form part of the NIEO.[34] Additionally, recent reform claims are anchored on the expansive interpretations of international investment standards such as fair and equitable treatment and most-favored nation standards by ISDS tribunals that have continued the involuntary deductive production of customary international law for African states.[35] Despite the involuntarily

[28] *See* Annelise Riles, 'Aspiration and Control: International Legal Rhetoric and the Essentialization of Culture', (1993) 106 *Harvard Law Review* 723; Babatunde Fagbayibo, 'Some Thoughts on Centering Pan-African Epistemic in the Teaching of Public International Law in African Universities' (2019) 21 *International Community Law Review* 170–89.

[29] Bhupinder S Chimni, 'Customary International Law: A Third World Perspective' (2018) 112 *American Journal of International Law* 1–46

[30] ibid.

[31] Patrick J Kelly, 'The Twilight of Customary International Law' (2000) 40(2) *Virginia Journal of International Law* 449–543.

[32] ibid.

[33] Bernard Kishoiyian, 'The Utility of Bilateral Investment Treaties in the Formulation of Customary International Law' (1993) 14(2) *Northwestern Journal of International Law & Business*, 327–375.

[34] Mohammed Bedjaoui, *Towards a New International Economic Order* (UNESCO 1979); Jagdish Bhagwati, (ed), *The New International Economic Order: The North South Dialogue* (MIT Press, 1977).

[35] John Linarelli, Margot E Salomon and Muthucumaraswamy Sornarajah, *The Misery of International Law: Confrontations with Injustice in the Global Economy* (Cambridge University Press 2018) ch 3.

acceptionism of international law discussed above, African states have also voluntarily accepted and voraciously defended doctrines of international law that have proved disadvantageous to them. A good example of this is the doctrine of *uti possidentis juris* that the now-defunct Organization of African Unity (OAU) Member States unreservedly accepted in the 1960s and which cast in stone the European set colonial boundaries with complete abandon to the communities present in these spaces.[36] Here, the critique to earlier[37] and more recent[38] scholarship is that African states positive contribution to international law has been downplayed and only aspects of negative or what Olabisi Akingube in an agnostic review of African states to the International Centre for the Settlement of Investment Disputes (ICSID) regime has called 'reverse' contributionism[39] are salient in mainstream international law.

The African contribution to international law is a complex narrative that can be divided into many different streams. This study engages with the scholarship of Senegalese scholar and international practitioner Makane Moïse Mbengue that African contribution to IIL should be acknowledged and celebrated, while arguing that Makane Moïse Mbengue's scholarship falls into the milder version of benign contributionism to international investment law in Africa.[40] However, it would be better if African states both within the internal creation of regional community laws and general international law focused on wider international economic justice engendered in the radical Africanisation approach. This study argues in favour of the second stream of critical and impactful engagement with IIL or radical Africanisation as a more desirable move by African states.

2.1 Benign (Contributionist) Africanisation in International Investment Law

An increased number of scholarship in international investment dubbed 'Africanisation' has emerged in the years after 2010.[41] Makane Moïse Mbengue

[36] Makau Mutua, 'Why Redraw the Map of Africa: A Moral and Legal Inquiry' (1995) 16(4) *Michigan Journal of International Law* 1113–1175.

[37] Chuks F Okoye, *International Law and The New African States* (Sweet & Maxwell, 1972); Taslim O Elias, 'Africa and the Development of International Law' (Richard Akinjide ed, 2d ed 1988); and Josephmarie Bipoum-Woum, *Le Droit International Africain: Problèmes Généraux, Règlement Des Conflits* (1970).

[38] Jeremy Levitt, 'Introduction—Africa: A Maker of International Law,' in Jeremy Levitt (ed.) *Africa: Mapping New Boundaries In International Law*, (Hart Publishing, 2008) vii; Tiyanjana Maluwa, 'Reassessing Aspects of the Contribution of African States to the Development of International Law Through African Regional Multilateral Treaties,' (2020) 41 *Michigan Journal of International Law* 327–415.

[39] Olabisi D Akinkugbe, 'Reverse Contributors? African State Parties, ICSID and the Development of International Investment Law' (2019) 34 *ICSID Review - Foreign Investment Law Journal* 434–454.

[40] Carl Landauer, 'Things Fall Together: The Past and Future Africas of T.O. Elias's Africa and the Development of International Law' (2008) 21 *Leiden Journal of International Law* 351–375.

[41] Olabisi D Akinkugbe, 'Africanization and the Reform of International Investment Law' (2021) 53 *Case Western Reserve Journal of International Law* 7–32. Rose Rameau, 'The African Perspective: The Development of Investment Laws, the Pan-African Investment Code (PAIC), and the African

argues that Africa has contributed substantively in the development of the investment regime and in the creation and active utilisation of the ICSID.[42] He is responding directly to the claim in mainstream international law that African states have been 'investment rule takers' and not 'investment rule makers.'[43] Mbengue argues that over the over sixty years that IIL grew steadily from the mid-twentieth century, African countries were perceived to be at the margins of the field.[44] He does not specifically mention who had this perception but it is safe to assume that the assumption is from global North countries and mainstream international law scholars. Mbengue notes that despite African countries clamouring for reform in the NIEO, they signed pre-drafted Bilateral Investment Treaties (BITs) that did not anticipate any obligations for foreign investors nor integrated any human rights dimensions.[45] These were the early iteration of BITs that fully meant to protect the interest of investors. He notes that these early BITs were not intended to serve the development needs of African states but were merely conduits for the increase of Foreign Direct Investment (FDI).[46] Despite this gloomy outlook, he celebrates the African states involvement in the negotiation, drafting, and entry into force of the ICSID Convention, which he describes as innovative.[47] He interestingly also endorses Aron Broche's view that the formation of ICSID was instigated by African countries' request to the World Bank to help resolve investment disputes.[48]

Additionally, Mbengue argues that the first of the four consultative meetings convened to discuss the Preliminary ICSID Draft Convention was held in Addis Ababa, Ethiopia with 52 African delegates present on 7 January, 1964.[49] He notably mentions that Taslim Olawale Elias' who was then participating as Nigeria's Attorney General commended the Preliminary ICSID Draft Convention as 'an attempt not only to restore the confidence of the investor but also to codify certain principles of customary law and to engage the progressive development of international law'.[50] It is not surprising that Mbengue finds and endorses

---

Continental Free Trade Area in the "New Economic World Order"' (2020) 114 *American Society of International Law, Proceedings of the Annual Meeting* 62–67; Makane Moïse Mbengue & Stefanie Schacherer, 'The 'Africanization' of International Investment Law: The Pan-African Investment Code and the Reform of the International Investment Regime' (2017) 18 *The Journal of World Investment and Trade*, 414–448; Oladapo Fabusuyi, 'Africanisation of International Investment Law: Prospects and Challenges' *Afronomics Law*, 18 October 2019, www.afronomicslaw.org/2019/10/18/africanisation-of-international-investment-law-prospects-and-challenges; Emmanuel T Laryea & Oladapo O Fabusuyi, 'Africanisation of International Investment Law for Sustainable Development: Challenges' (2021) 20(1) *Journal of International Trade Law and Policy* 42–64; Anna Hankings-Evans, 'The Africanization of International Investment Disputes-from Past to Present' *Verfassungsblog*, 23 July 2020, verfassungsblog.de/the-africanization-of-international-investment-disputes-from-past-to-present/.

[42] Makane Moïse Mbengue, 'Africa's Voice in the Formation, Shaping and Redesign of International Investment Law' (2019) 34 *ICSID Review - Foreign Investment Law Journal* 455–481.

[43] ibid.

[44] ibid.

[45] ibid, 458.

[46] ibid.

[47] ibid.

[48] ibid.

[49] ibid.

[50] ibid.

Elias' view on the Preliminary Draft of the convention since both scholars can here be categorised as endorsing a contributionist or benign approach to the engagement with IIL, which in this case, took the form of the procedural aspect of creating an international arbitration house for ISDS under the auspices of the World Bank. To both, it would be enough that African states and stakeholders significantly participated without a deeper introspection on the effect of the resultant institutions on Africans, especially the most deprived. Such a move does not seek to critically question the inadequacies and deficiencies of the ICSID system that embedded an asymmetrical dispute settlement system in which only investors (who many would be from the global North) could institute claims. This support could be and should be contrasted to the NIEO claim on the exhaustion of domestic remedies under the Calvo Clause.

Mbengue continues to show that out of the twenty required ratifications for entry into force, 15 came from African states.[51] Tunisia was the first state on 5 May 1965 to sign the Convention, and Nigeria was the first state to ratify the convention on 23 August 1965. He points out the important role played by two Africans, both Egyptians, Ahmed El Kosheri and Ibrahim Shihata both of whom served in senior positions in ICSID in its early history.[52] It is interesting to note the role that Ahmed El Kosheri played in the case *AAPL v Sri Lanka*.[53] M. Sornarajah describes the case as the original sin in IIL as it created and endorsed compulsory consent to investment treaty arbitration under BITs that was never intended or accepted by state parties to the BITs.[54] Ahmed El Kosheri, the African figure Mbengue arguably extols as making a great contribution to the creation of ICSID, would easily be judged as being the architect of this origin sin. He sat as the presiding arbitrator in this ovarian case that was decided in favour of the investor; according to Gus Van Harten, the case sparked a transformation of international law in favour of the wealthy and to the detriment of sovereignty.[55]

We see the limits of contributionistic scholarship here as a deeper engagement with the role of El Kosheri would be similar to that played by other pro-investor protection arbitrators that form the core figures that have promoted ISDS in its current form. This form of contributionism represented by El Kosheri is a manifestation of the idea of African interpellation for the purposes of protecting investors. His involvement should be contrasted with that of Samuel Kwadwo Boaten Asante, the Ghanian legal titan who also sat in the same *AAPL v Sri Lanka* tribunal and delivered a dissenting opinion.[56]

[51] ibid.

[52] ibid.

[53] *AAPL v Sri Lanka* (1990) 4 *ICSID Rpts* 245.

[54] Muthucumaraswamy Sornarajah, *The International Law on Foreign Investment* (3rd edn, Cambridge University Press 2010) 139.

[55] Gus Van Harten, *The Trouble with Foreign Investor Protection* (Oxford University Press 2020) 39.

[56] *See* Richard Frimpong Oppong & Kissi Agyebeng (eds), *A Commitment to Law, Development and Public Policy: A Festschrift in Honour of Nana Dr. SKB Asante* (Wildy Simmonds & Hill Publishing, 2016).

In another benign contributionist formulation, Mbengue also argues that as African states have had many cases at ICSID, this should be noted as a contribution in ICSID's jurisprudence. Such a view is a strange twist of the logic of jurisprudential contribution as in ISDS cases, states participate only as respondents and non-disputing third-parties. Having many African states at ICSID, rather than being a cause célèbre for jurisprudential contribution, is actually a cautionary tale indicating that ICSID is serving the needs of powerful multinationals with the financial muscle to sustain expensive international litigation against African states. Here we witness yet another disadvantage of contributionism or benign Africanisation that masks injustices beneath the surface in a phenomenon that would seem beneficial without digging any further. The Africanisation here is only tokenist or, as Joe Oloka-Onyango and Sylvia Tamale have described it, in relation to mainstreaming third-world discourse: the 'add and stir' approach.[57]

The Africanisation involved in benign Africanisation is not African in its essential and critical elements. It is foreign essentially, and the additions of 'black' faces in case states are intended as a token or as an addition to the mainstream agenda to add flavour for the benefit of a select group of individuals or states. The same concern can be raised with gender diversity reforms. For example, while a code of conduct is helpful if all or most arbitrators are appointed from the Global North, only two women receive the bulk of female appointments (Gabrielle Kaufmann-Kohler and Brigitte Stern); the perceptions of bias against ISDS will therefore continue.[58] Gabrielle Kaufmman-Kohler has, in fact, herself stated that 'we cannot claim arbitration is the global dispute resolution method unless actors from all regions can participate'.[59]

On addressing the idea of Africanisation, the recurrent theme in Makane's scholarship is the notion of sustainable development, balancing obligations between investors and states, and the addition of the right to regulate.[60] The classic examples here are the Nigeria and Morocco BIT and the Pan-African Investment Code (PAIC), both of which are yet to enter into force at the time of writing. This chapter now identifies and analyses three elements that emerge in the process and engagement of benign Africanisation: the first is its exclusive focus on intra-African investment, the second its ambivalence towards ISDS, and the final one is its soft engagement with the imperial history of IIL.

[57] Joe Oloka-Onyango & Sylvia Tamale, '"The Personal is Political," or Why Women's Rights are Indeed Human Rights: An African Perspective on International Feminism' (1995) 17 *Human Rights Quarterly* 704.

[58] Andrea K Bjoklund, Daniel Behn, Susan D Franck, Chiara Giorgetti, Won Kidane, Arnaud de Nanteuil, and Emilia Onyema, 'The Diversity Deficit in International Investment Arbitration' (2020) 21 *The Journal of World Investment & Trade* 410–440.

[59] Gabrielle Kaufmann-Kohler, 'The Arbitrator and the Law: Does He/She Know it? Apply it? How? And a Few More Questions? (2005) 21 (4) *Arbitration International* 631–638.

[60] Mbengue (n 42); Makane Moïse Mbengue and Stefanie Schacherer, 'The "Africanization" of International Investment Law: The Pan-African Investment Code and the Reform of the International Investment Regime' (2017) 18 *Journal of World Investment & Trade* 414.

2.1.1 *Exclusive focus on intra-African investment*

One of the significant makers of benign Africanisation of IIL is the exclusive focus of the regional instruments on investment on the regulation of intra-African investment. FDI inflows into Africa have remained low compared with other regions in the years of the twenty-first century.[61] Intra-African FDI grew from 9 per cent in 2002 to 13 per cent in 2017 but was significantly affected in 2020 by the COVID-19 pandemic. The COVID-19 pandemic slashed FDI in Africa by about 16% to US$ 40 billion from US$ 47 billion in 2019.[62] Traditionally, African countries have relied on Europe and the US as the main sources of FDI, but in recent years China, which now accounts for almost half of Asian FDI, is making a strong presence in Africa.[63] In a 2015 speech at the China-WTO Roundtable, the WTO deputy director-general Anabel Gonzalez said that: 'Africa has integrated with the rest of the world faster than with itself'.[64]

The Pan-African Investment and the now enacted negotiations on a Protocol on Investment under Africa Inter-Continental Free Trade Agreement (AfCFTA) are part of the legal processes underway to deal with this low intra-African trade. There exist investment focused rules within the patchwork of African regional economic communities (RECs). The Common Market for Eastern and Southern African States (COMESA) has the COMESA Common Investment Area Agreement (CCIA), 2017.[65] The Economic Community of Western African States (ECOWAS) has the ECOWAS Common Investment Code (ECOWIC), 2018.[66] The Southern African Development Community (SADC) has the Protocol on Finance and Investment, 2006.[67] The SADC FIP Annex 1 was substantially reformed in 2016 and its approach is now much more 'rejectionist' than the one of PAIC.[68] And the East Africa Community (EAC) has the EAC Model Investment Code, 2002.[69]

[61] ECMR, 'Intra-African Foreign Direct Investment (FDI) and Employment: A Case Study' (2020) Working Paper Series N° 335, African Development Bank, Abidjan, Côte d'Ivoire.

[62] UNCTAD, 'COVID-19 slashes Foreign Direct Investment in Africa by 16%' 21 June 2021, unctad.org/news/covid-19-slashes-foreign-direct-investment-africa-16.

[63] ChristineZhenweiQiang,PeterKusek,*etal*,'TheRoadtoRecoveryinSub-SaharanAfrica:Capitalizingon TranformativeOpportunitiesfromshiftingFDIPatterns'WorldBanksBlogs,27May2021,blogs.worldbank .org/africacan/road-recovery-sub-saharan-africa-capitalizing-transformative-opportunities-shifting-fdi.

[64] Anabel Gonzalez, Senior Director, World Bank Group, Statement by Anabel Gonzalez at the Fourth China-WTO Accessions Roundtable: International Economic Cooperation and African Perspectives on the Future of the Multilateral Trading System, Nairobi, Kenya (Dec. 14, 2015), www.worldbank.org/en/news/speech/2015/12/14/deepening-african-integration-intra-africa-trade -for-development-and-poverty-reduction.

[65] COMESA, Investment Agreement for the COMESA Common Investment Area, 2017, https:// investmentpolicy.unctad.org/international-investment-agreements/treaty-files/3092/download (accessed on 17 December 2021).

[66] ECOWAS, ECOWAS Common Investment Code (ECOWIC), 2018, https://investmentpolicy .unctad.org/international-investment-agreements/treaty-files/6441/download.

[67] SADC, Protocol on Finance and Investment, 2006 www.sadc.int/files/4213/5332/6872/Protocol _on_Finance__Investment2006.pdf.

[68] Tomasz Milej, 'Reclaiming African Agency: The Right to Regulate, the Investor-State Dispute Settlement and 'Africanisation' of International Investment Law' in Rainer Hofmann, Julian Scheu, Stephan Schill, Christian Tams (eds), *Investment Protection, Human Rights, and International Arbitration in Extraordinary Times* (Nomos, 2021).

[69] EAC, 'Investment Framework: Key Features' www.eac.int/investment/investment-framework.

The flagship legal instrument regulating FDI in the continent is the non-binding PAIC, 2017, developed under the auspices of the African Union (AU). Ndanga Kamau describes the PAIC as 'the first pan-African expression of investment policy'.[70] Makane who was the led expert and negotiator for the African Union in the period between 2014 and 2016 when the PAIC was drafted, described it as the shining example of Africa's participation in IIL rulemaking as opposed to rule-taking.[71] He argues that the PAIC reflects the continent's own context, priorities, and realties.[72] This view again encapsulates the benign Africanisation idea as, in a globalised world where in reality intra-African investment FDI remains law, African states legislating on their own conception would have little impact on enhancing radical economic, social, and environmental justice for the majority of the African poor. This view does not take away and should not be read to take away from African countries' needed and valuable input on standards and rules that can be replicated in other parts of the world.[73]

Kamau criticises the PAIC for 'creating a two-track investor protection system that disadvantages African investors'.[74] Kamau's critique here is within a mainstream approach to international understanding since she presupposes the utility and usefulness of broad investor protection provisions in other investment agreements. As this study has already argued that these traditional investor protection rights are framed in a manner that disfavours the state's right to regulate for public benefit, indigenous communities, the environment, and socioeconomic rights of economically marginalised Africans, it does not make logical sense to argue that African investors should also enjoy them and PAIC denies them these rights. Thus Kamau's framework and understanding of the economic and social injustices perpetrated by IIL are not in line with this study and would be worse in outcome (for purposes of economic justice) than the outcome of benign Africanisation. This is because the logical consequence of her view is that African states should protect their investors just like global North countries have done. Such a view would only benefit the few elite Africans who Bhupinder Chimni would well describe as the Trans-National Capitalist Class (TCC).[75]

Kamau also cites Won Kidane as another protagonist against PAIC. Kidane has argued that the PAIC as drafted is not an 'African solution to an African problem'.[76] Yet Won Kidane's argument can be slightly contrasted to Kamau's. Kidane argues that PAIC's:

[70] Ndanga Kamau, 'Investment Law and Treaty Reform in Africa: Fragments and Fragmentation' (2020) 1(1) *African Journal of International Economic Law* 216.

[71] Mbengue (n 42) 471.

[72] ibid.

[73] Mbengue & Schacherer (n 60).

[74] Kamau (n 70) 216.

[75] William I Robinson, *Global Capitalism and the Crisis of Humanity* (Cambridge University Press 2014) ch 2.

[76] Won Kidane, 'Contemporary International Investment Law Trends and Africa's Dilemmas in the Draft Pan-African Investment Code' (2018) 50 *George Washington International Law Review* 572.

> restriction of investor rights and its broadening of the host state's regulatory space would have been desirable solution to the perceived one-sidedness of the investment protection regime vis-à-vis investors from the North because of the advantaged position that they have occupied. But as long as the objective of the Code is to encourage intra-Africa investment, denying itself of the kind of courtesy that Africa historically accorded to its Northern investors might be punishing oneself for the perceived wrongs of another.[77]

Kidane focuses on the imperial and Euro-American origins of investor rights and sees a real solution for Africa as tackling such legacy directly instead of creating a different and more favourable regime for African investors. It is this focus on African investors and not on extra-African investors that makes the Africanisation approach in the eyes of this study benign and not radical. Makane's response to Kidane's criticism is unfortunately not as persuasive.[78] He responds by merely repeating the innovative aspects of the PAIC, which Kidane already accepted but criticised for being deployed against the wrong target.

2.1.2 Ambivalence towards ISDS reforms

The benign Africanisation approach is ambivalent towards the reforms on ISDS. On the one hand, this approach insists that the ISDS regime requires deep reforms that are not only surface reforms ie, procedural reforms. On the other, the approach begins by accepting the inevitability of ISDS. The starting point of the use of ISDS in Africa is itself a colonised view that African judiciaries are not competent enough to resolve ISDS disputes and thus they should be 'delocalised'. This position is formulated in the civilisational trajectory of imperial thinking. It is a view that is presented within Antony Anghie's dynamic of difference: 'jurists using the conceptual tools of positivism postulated a gap, understood principally in terms of cultural differences, between the civilised European and uncivilized non-European world; having established this gap they then proceeded to devise a series of techniques for bridging this gap, of civilising the uncivilised'.[79]

PAIC further embodies benign Africanisation in its state-state dispute resolution provision in Article 41 (1) by stating that: where Member States agree to arbitration, the arbitration shall be conducted at any established African public or African alternative dispute resolution center. Again, here there is a favourable insistence on using African Alternative Dispute Resolution centres without deep introspection on these institutions. The claim that African judiciaries are not competent enough to resolve ISDS disputes has been sustained by normpreneurs who have systematically used ISDS to protect investors and the TCC.[80]

[77] Kidane (n 34) 572.
[78] Mbengue (n 42) 471–472.
[79] Antony Anghie, *Imperialism, Sovereignty and the Making of International Law* (Cambridge University Press 2005) 37.
[80] Bhupinder S Chimni, 'International Institutions Today: An Imperial Global State in the Making' (2004) 15 *EJIL* 1.

Importantly, national and regional arbitration centres, such as the national branches of the Chartered Institute of Arbitrators in London, also attract ISDS disputes. While there is no sovereign legislator within these networks of International Arbitration Centres (IACs), the older global IACs have the greater transnational reach than African IACs, and the elites who govern them are tightly networked in a stable, competitive, and market-based field.[81] In this atmosphere of IACs market-based competition for a limited market, the African arbitration centres cannot compete favourably or even equally against these global IACs without some form of binding obligations. Most African IACs are modelled around the Paris-based International Chamber of Commerce (ICC's) near hundred years of settling disputes and driving a neo-liberal agenda of dispute settlement.

PAIC's provision on ISDS has some interesting features that should be highlighted as part of a benign contributionist Afiricanisation. The first is Article 42's continuation of ISDS as means of dispute settlement. The provision, however, introduces the use of language that is intended to promote state regulatory space like: 'in line with their domestic policies' and 'subject to the applicable laws of the host state/or the mutual agreement of disputing parties'. The language here is meant to grant more autonomy to the states and the disputing parties. In the era of 'arbitration without privity'[82] as an anchoring logic of ISDS consent, the singular initial consent by the state in the BIT or multilateral investment treaty is controlling of consent to arbitration and states' autonomy is highly limited.

PAIC to its credit reintroduces the requirement of exhaustion of local remedies before ISDS is invoked and thus forms an important reaffirmation of the Calvo doctrine. Since the invocation of the Calvo doctrine is an emanation of a principle in the NIEO, we see here how the PAIC is ambivalent towards ISDS by accepting yet at the same time limiting party autonomy a fundamental principle in arbitration to exhaustion of domestic remedies. The same provision in PAIC also refers to the resolution of such disputes in African public or African private alternative dispute resolution centers and using the United Nations Commission on International Trade Law (UNCITRAL) rules. As argued above the provision on the use of African arbitration centers squarely falls within the four corners of benign Africanisation.

2.1.3 Soft engagement with the imperial history and origins of IIL

Any scholarship of legal instruments that does not engage meaningfully with the imperial and colonial heritage of ISDS yet seeks to reform it falls within benign Africanisation. Such scholarship and legal instruments are in many cases part of mainstream and positivism-based international law approaches. Some of these international law praxes do in many cases accept or acknowledge

[81] Yves Dezalay & Bryant G Garth, *Dealing in Virtue: International Commercial Arbitration and the Construction of a Transnational Legal Order* (The University of Chicago Press, 1996).
[82] Jan Paulsson, 'Arbitration Without Privity' (1995) 10(2) *ICSID Review* 332–257.

this history but in some cases, it is minimised or tokenised without serious engagement with the impact of imperialism, colonialism, and its continuities.

An example of such scholarship is Ndanga Kamau's article on investment treaty reform in Africa.[83] In her article, Kamau does engage with the inconsistencies of practice among African states in relation to investment treaty reform in Africa and argues that there are many disunities and single-country approaches. She, however, does not engage or mention the imperial and colonial histories of IIL and how this might inform or informs her arguments. Another example is Kariuki Muigua's paper on Africa's role in the reform of IIL and ISDS.[84] Muigua does mention colonialism and does not engage with the history of ISDS critically to inform African states current practices. Both authors mentioned above are active arbitrators. And one could easily surmise that their taking a soft-ball approach could have been informed by their status as active arbitrators possibly involved in ongoing disputes or seeking future appointments.[85]

Kamau's, Muiga's and arguably Mbengue's scholarship above can be contrasted with Ibironke Odumuso-Ayanu's, Olabisi Akinkugbe's, and James Gathii's scholarship on ISDS reform in Africa. Odumuso-Ayanu has, for example, explored the relationship between transnational capital, South-South investment treaties and African peoples' socio-economic well-being.[86] James Gathii in a 2021 keynote address, faulted the ISDS-centric focus of the UNCITRAL Working Group III and ICSID Rule processes as inadequate to addressing the most fundamental challenge in IIL.[87] Olabisi's Akinkugbe's has also categorised the Africanisation of IIL into two streams: one moderate and the other radical.[88] He argues that the current reform efforts or Africanisation efforts are moderate because they do not address the systematic inequalities in the IIL regime.[89] His categorisation of moderate Africanisation fits well within the categorisation in this study of benign Africanisation. Indeed moderate Africanisation, like benign Africanisation, will not transform the systemic inequalities within the ISDS regime and IIL as the reforms remain nestled within the neoliberal paradigm.[90] Akinkgube, unlike Kamau, Muiga, and even

[83] Kamau (n 70) 216.

[84] Kariuki Muigua, *Africa's Role in the Reform of International Investment Law and the Investor State Dispute Settlement (ISDS) System* (2020), http://kmco.co.ke/wp-content/uploads/2020/08/Africas-Role-in-the-Reform-of-International-Investment-law-and-the-Investor-State-Dispute-Settlement-ISDS-System-Kariuki-Muigua-August-2020.pdf.

[85] Bryant G Garth, 'One Window into the State of Insiders' Arbitration Scholarship' (2018) 19 *JWIT* 155.

[86] Ibironke T Odumosu-Ayanu, 'South-South Investment Treaties, Transnational Capital and African Peoples' (2013) 21 *African Journal of International & Comparative Law* 172–201.

[87] James Thuo Gathii, 'Reform and Retrenchment in International Investment Law' Keynote Remarks prepared for the Santander Roundtable Discussions on International Economic Law, co-hosted by Kenyatta University School of Law, (Nairobi); Riara Law School, (Nairobi); and the International Investment Law Center, at University of Cologne, January 13, 2021.

[88] Akinkugbe (n 41) 7–32.

[89] ibid.

[90] ibid.

Mbengue above, begins with and engages with empire as a practice and structure of unequal international integration that reveals the enduring continuities between the global North and global South.[91]

2.2 Radical (Critical) Africanisation in International Investment Law

Radical Africanisation unlike benign Africanisation, goes beyond asking the involvement of African states in IIL and attempts to excavate and deal with its unfair, asymmetric dispute settlement, unequal and unjust rules. For this approach to be manifested in Africa, this study proposes three lines of action: first African states in their reforms must focus on both inter and intra-African investment; second, the reforms must engage deeply (seated) substantive reforms in addition to the procedural reforms currently being debated at the UNCITRAL Working Group III; and finally African states must have a real reckoning and engagement with the imperial history of IIL generally and ISDS specifically.

2.2.1 *Focus on both extra and intra-African investment*

We have seen above that one of the identified weaknesses of the PAIC has been its sole focus on intra African investment and investors. This focus on intra African investors balances rights and obligations between African investors and African states but leaves the relationship of African states with non-African investors intact in its hegemonic framing. For the innovative features of the PAIC to have a strong impact on IIL in Africa and embody radical Africanisation, its application would have to be extended to non-African investors. African states like many other states in the Global South should not approach ISDS reforms from a neutral and benign viewpoint. They should instead offer proposals that will radically transform the system.

John Nyanje in his 2020 Afronomics blog post argued that African states should search for a 'working formula' to reform ISDS.[92] This study has argued that it is difficult to fathom a working formula in a system founded on a history of subjugation, imposition, and colonial continuities. How African States can remain neutral and in search for a working formula in such a system is difficult to imagine.[93] It is difficult to deny that ISDS is facing a serious legitimacy crisis

[91] ibid, citing Adom Getachew, *Worldmaking after Empire: The Rise and Fall of Self-Determination* (Princeton University Press 2019) 31-32.

[92] John Nyanje, 'Hegemony in Investor State Dispute Settlement: How African States Need to Approach Reforms' 7 September 2020, *Afronomics Law*, www.afronomicslaw.org/2020/09/07/hegemony-in-investor-state-dispute-settlement-how-african-states-need-to-approach-reforms.

[93] Harrison Mbori, 'Exit is the Only Way Out: A Polemic Response to John Nyanje's "Hegemony in Investor State Dispute Settlement: How African states need to Approach Reforms' 10 September 2020, *Afronomics Law*, www.afronomicslaw.org/2020/09/10/exit-is-the-only-way-out-a-polemic-response-to-john-nyanjes-hegemony-in-investor-state-dispute-settlement-how-african-states-need-to-approach-reforms.

from many quarters. Yet African and other states from the Global South have been reluctant about this system since its inception and it is only now that is has also proven burdensome for the Global North that serious efforts at reforms are on the table.[94] The explanation for this 'lateness of reaction from developed States lies in the fact they are now becoming targets of mechanisms that were devised against developing states in a past era of foreign investment relations'.

The era for NIEO targeted this hegemony that has been present from the beginnings of imperialism and has mutated over centuries to continue serving the interests of transnational and mobile capital. If the system is not reformed from its roots, the new reforms that emerge will be another transition towards retrenchment. This is the reason why African States cannot and should not face ISDS reform from a neutral perspective. Part of this radical Africanisation proposal is that it forms part of the erasure of history and epistemicide that African countries have faced for the past.[95] Like many other areas of international law, IIL promotes neo-colonialism and neo-liberalism. I therefore completely agree with Mathias Kumm that 'The idea of investment arbitration as a field with its own separate dispute resolution infrastructure should be seen as an inherently dubious transitional phenomenon – perhaps comparable to the League of Nations Mandate System or the UN Trusteeship System – that deserves to wither away over time, rather than being reformed'. This idea is well traced and supported by Antony Anghie in his seminal book on Imperialism, Sovereignty, and the Making of International Law.

2.2.2 *Engage Deep-seated (substantive) reforms of ISDS*

John Nyanje argued that African states are only against ISDS as a perception informed by Terence Halliday's Folk Theory at the heart of his argument. It is difficult to understand how the egregious sins of colonialism and its continuities – if we agree that this is a strong origin of ISDS – are mere perceptions. TWAIL-oriented scholars, from earlier ones like Judge Mohammed Bedjaoui[96] and M. Sornarajah[97] to more recent ones like Amr A. Shalakany[98] and, Antony Anghie, have already demonstrated how the ISDS system is founded on weak foundations and original sins. African states are therefore not using unverified assertions as a basis for the rejection of ISDS.

[94] Muthucumaraswamy Sornarajah, 'The New International Economic Order, Investment Treaties and Foreign Investment Laws in ASEAN' (1985) 27(2) *Malaya Law Review* 440–458.

[95] Santos (n 25).

[96] Bedjaoui (n 34).

[97] Muthucumaraswamy Sornarajah, *Resistance and Change in International Law on Foreign Investment* (Cambridge University Press 2015).

[98] Amr A Shalakany, 'Arbitration and the Third World: A Plea for Reassessing Bias under the Specter of Neoliberalism' (2000) 41 *Harvard International Law Journal* 419–468.

Specifically, on the perception claim, Chile, during the UNCITRAL Working Group III negotiations, pointed out in response to Mauritius and South Africa on the importance of facts and not perception. We should, however, not reject any perception claims as having nothing to do with the failed ISDS system. Perceptions are part of the sociological claims of the illegitimacy of ISDS. To require only facts devoid of perception is not possible. This does not mean that perceptions are non-factual only that they are subjective. Perception is indeed a subjective sociological phenomenon that cannot be easily measured empirically. Yet perceptions remain important in the research on ISDS. In fact, a recent study by Andrea K. Bjoklund, Daniel Behn, Susan D. Franck, Chiara Giorgetti, Won Kidane, Arnaud de Nanteuil, and Emilia Onyema uses the criteria developed by Nienke Grossman on sociological (perceived) legitimacy of international tribunals.[99] Grossman points out that to judge the sociological legitimacy of international tribunals one should use the following criteria: (1) there must be a perception that a tribunal is fair and unbiased; (2) there must be an identifiable commitment to the underlying normative regime, which will be affected by the quality of the decisions made about norms in addition to the norms themselves, (3) there must be some commitment to transparency and other democratic institutional norms.[100]

Thus, the Mauritius and South African ISDS rejection claims are 'perceived folk' theories that are not only supported by historical and factual evidence but by sociological theory too. In that sense, they are not merely folkloric. The seven scholars in the study above, out of whom as I know, only two are Africans, have verified and used a sociological perceptions-based study to anchor their research. Additionally, M. Sornarajah has spent a large chunk of his illustrious career making similar claims to those of South Africa and Brazil that have culminated in his support of the South African position.[101] Additionally, the normative framework of investment arbitration itself – the protection of investors – is founded on an imperial bedrock. Won Kidane has also persuasively shown how the cultural deficit of appointing mainly 'white, old, men' from the Global North further exacerbates this problem.[102]

2.2.3 *Real acknowledgement and engagement with imperial history of IIL*

The mainstream position has been that FDI is a union of convenience and that it offers benefits on both sides. The evidence of this in Africa is lopsided with mixed and contradictory evidence on the increase of FDI as a result of

[99] Bjoklund, Behn, Franck, Giorgetti, Kidane, Nanteuil & Onyema (n 289).

[100] Nienke Grossman, 'Legitimacy and International Adjudicative Bodies' (2010) 41 *George Washington International Law Review*, 107–161.

[101] Muthucumaraswamy Sornarajah, 'The Unworkability of "Balanced Treaties" and the Importance of Diversity of Approach among the BRICS' (2018) 112 *American Journal of International Law Unbound* 223–227.

[102] Won Kidane, *The Culture of International Arbitration* (Oxford University Press, 2017).

investment treaties.[103] Some studies have found little evidence that the signing of BITs stimulates additional investment.[104] The FDI referred to here was first protected by colonialism and is now protected by neo-liberal imposition, for which ISDS is a prime example.[105] The truth that African countries are capital importers is also tied to the history of extractive colonialism and continuities of colonialism through neo-liberal imposition.[106] Global North countries and institutions of the neoliberal era have forced the African States into a cul-de-sac. History, especially imperialism, has conspired to make African States economic dependents of the Global North for FDI. It is not these African States desire to 'view' themselves as capital importers. The truth is that through imperialism and neo-liberal imposition, transnational mobile capital is generated, disseminated, and regulated in the Global North. The external force of powerful institutions like the Bretton Woods Institutions (World Bank and IMF) have made African States perpetual capital importers.

2.3 Agnostic Africanisation: The Curious Case of Olabisi Akingube's Reverse Contributionism

Despite the involuntarily acceptionism of international law discussed above, African states have also voluntarily accepted and voraciously defended doctrines of international law that have proved disadvantageous to them. A good example of this is the doctrine of *uti possidentis juris* that the OAU Member States unreservedly accepted in the 1960s and which cast in stone the European set colonial boundaries with complete abandon to the communities present in these spaces.[107] Here, the critique to earlier[108] and more recent[109] scholarship is that African states' positive contribution to international has been downplayed and only aspects of negative or what Olabisi Akingube in an agnostic review of African states to the ICSID regime has called 'reverse' contributionism[110] are salient in mainstream international law. As we have seen above, the African contribution to international law is a complex narrative that can be divided into many different streams. This study is not against contributionism of benign Africanisation

[103] Jonathan Bonnicha, 'Assessing the Impacts of Investment Treaties: Overview of the Evidence' (2017) International Institute for Sustainable Development, www.iisd.org/system/files/publications/assessing-impacts-investment-treaties.pdf.

[104] Mary Hallward-Driemeier, 'Do Bilateral Investment Treaties Attract FDI? Only a bit…and they could bite' (2003) Policy Research Working Paper: No. 3121. World Bank, Washington, DC.

[105] Muthucumaraswamy Sornarajah, 'The Return of the NIEO and the Retreat of Neo-Liberal International Law' in Sharif Bhuiyan, Nico Schrijver & Phillipe Sands, (eds), *International Law and Developing Countries: Essays in Honour of Kamal Hossain* (The University Press Limited, 2017), 32–59.

[106] *See* Anghie (n 32).

[107] Mutua (n 269).

[108] Okoye (n 270); Elias (n 270); Bipoum-Woum (n 270).

[109] Levitt (n 271) vii; Maluwa (n 271).

[110] Akinkugbe (n 16) 434–454.

as framed. The study agrees with the scholarship of celebrated Nigerian scholar and international practitioner Taslim Olawale Elias that African contributions to international law should be acknowledged and celebrated, while also acknowledging the credible and well established narrative that Taslim Olwale Elias' scholarship falls into the milder version of weak contributionism to international law in Africa.[111] This is the same position the study has taken with the scholarship of Makane Moïse Mbengue and his brainchild the PAIC.

However, it would be better if African states both within the internal creation of regional community laws and general international law focused on broader international justice. This study has argued in favour of this second stream of critical and impactful contributionism by African states and offered elements of applying this radical form of Africanisation and what it would look like if such an attempt was made to reform IIL in Africa.

3. CONCLUSION AND OUTLOOK: PROPOSALS FOR REFORMS: TREATING DEEP ROOTED PROBLEMS, NOT SYMPTOMS

In this study's view, after presenting the root causes of the ISDS problem, the study suggestions for reform reject the many proposals in vogue at the UNCITRAL and ICSID reform processes as merely palliative (symptoms oriented) and not curative (root cause/problem-oriented). After presenting a correct diagnosis, it is possible, even desirable, to prescribe effective remedies. Unfortunately, the benign Africanisation approach remedies remain at the shallow end of the pool of problems. Proposals, such as a code of conduct for arbitrators (ICSID reform), early dismissal procedure, and opt-in multilateral treaty (UNCITRAL'S Mauritius Convention) have only attracted five state parties since it entered into force on 18 October 2017. None deal with deep-rooted historical, sociological, and normative causes of the rot in ISDS. The radical reforms proposals suggested above can deal with the deep-rooted historical, sociological, and normative causes of the rot in ISDS for African states. Importantly, substantive concerns, such as the asymmetrical nature of the regime, arbitrators pro-investors treaty interpretation, and broadly worded treaty standards need to be urgently addressed. And while a multilateral investment court might deal effectively with most procedural challenges, what about the normative challenges that current reform processes have mainly ignored? It is thus easy to see why South Africa and Tanzania have arguably both rejected the benign Africanisation approach/view on systemic incremental changes from a multitude of fora.

On the outlook for African states in the future, one question might linger: What is an appropriate alternative if the current international investment regime were to be rejected? A robust domestic rule of law standard anchored in strong

[111] Landauer (n 273) 351–375.

substantive and procedural administrative justice is a good starting point. Such an administrative law justice system would broadly address other non-economic concerns such as human rights and the protection of indigenous community rights that form part of the corpus of many constitutional bills of rights. While an increasing number of African countries have relatively strong administrative justice standards, as we have witnessed global North countries with equally strong administrative law justice standards facing ISDS claims, such an alternative will not completely remedy the malaise. It has the potential of rhetorically rebuffing the view that IIL is intended to ensure the rule of law in countries with weak rule of law systems. Such an outlook also would reintroduce the exhaustion of local remedies more robustly and justifiably as the SADC FIP, 2016 has done. The exhaustion of local remedies rule will grant all countries, not just African countries, an opportunity to engage with unfairly treated foreign investors domestically before being dragged to an international tribunal. This will not signal a complete death knell for IIL, as some have suspected, but a redirection or reversal of international law trajectory. Such redirection or reversal would significantly reduce the direct role of private actors such as transnational corporations in international dispute settlement. In a real sense, the SADC FIP, 2016 amendment that goes back to diplomatic protection to settle investment disputes is a welcome future outlook for African states.

6

International and African Regional Arbitration Centres as Competing Nodes of Governance for Economic Disputes with African Sub-Regional Economic Courts and Tribunals

INTRODUCTION

Arbitration as a form of dispute settlement presupposes consent between the disputing parties to have their dispute heard and bindingly settled by a third-party neutral or decision-maker called an arbitrator; the consent-based nature of arbitration grounds the consensual theory of international (commercial) arbitration.[1] The consensual grounding of arbitration makes the 'delocalisation' and 'denationalisation' of international arbitration possible.[2] The delocalisation here refers to the separation or detachment of international arbitration from connected national law.[3] Delocalisation does not occur fully in international arbitration, as the parties require domestic law to recognise and enforce arbitral awards. Delocalisation allows the parties to mutually agree not to have the dispute settled within either the territory from which the dispute arose from or apply the law of that territory.

The 'jurisdiction theory' in arbitration opposes the consensual theory in arbitration articulated above. It was classically formulated by Francis Mann in 1967, who emphasised that arbitration must occur somewhere. Only the law of the 'locality' in which arbitration is held conclusively permits it to exist.[4] Whichever side of the theoretical divide we fall on, we cannot entirely deny the legal, sociological, political, and economic legitimacy and reality of domestic

[1] *See* Andrea Marco Steingruber, *Consent in International Arbitration* (Oxford University Press, 2012).

[2] Joshua D H Karton, *The Culture of International Arbitration and The Evolution of Contract Law* (Oxford University Press, 2013) 42.

[3] Nigel Blackaby and others, *Redfern and Hunter on International Arbitration* (Oxford University Press, 2015).

[4] *See* Francis A Mann, 'Lex Facit Arbitrum' in Pieter Sanders (ed), *International Arbitration: Liber Amicorum for Martin Domke* (Martinus Nijhoff, 1967) 241.

and international arbitration in the twenty-first century. We therefore witness international private commercial arbitration when disputing parties domiciled in different nation-states engage in private transnational commercial transactions. Since Phillip Jessup's definition of transnational law as 'all law which regulates actions or events that transcend national frontiers',[5] drawing neat lines between what demarcates international arbitration from transnational arbitration can be difficult. The preferred formulation among international lawyers is international arbitration.

International arbitration can therefore generally cover public arbitration involving two disputing nation-states or a nation-state on the one hand and a private entity, such as in investor-state dispute settlement (ISDS), on the other.[6] Additionally, private international arbitration, commonly referred to as international commercial arbitration, covers disputes between private disputants. This chapter examines the historical, substantive, institutional, and administrative frameworks of private and public arbitration. Most international arbitrations are now administered by national or International Arbitration Centres (IACs). I argue that African regional IACs are emerging and increasing the competition for arbitration disputes involving African parties with more established IACs, such as the International Chamber of Commerce (ICC). With its broad economic, political, and social tentacles, competing with the ICC is challenging and will continue to remain so in the foreseeable future. However, the emergence and presence of these African regional IACs is a fact to be celebrated and encouraged. As long as a credible and increasingly high appeal for their services – in many cases supported by the state – is maintained, the dominance of the more recognised IACs in the metropoles will not remain unchallenged.

The chapter is divided into four broad sections and proceeds as follows. The first section introduces the nature of transnational law and governance, as well as the position of African sub-regional international courts and tribunals within this framework. This section argues that alternative dispute settlement, as currently practised in Africa, is an invented tradition practised with its Euro-American legal and socio-cultural attributes. Alternative Dispute Resolution (ADR), as is presently practised in Africa, is a panoply of legal techniques invented as appropriate modes of dispute settlement in Africa. One of the additional avenues for shifting international economic law-based disputes in Africa is international arbitration administered by an increasing number of global, regional, and national arbitration centres. The second section examines the origins of arbitration in medieval Europe, showing that the less judicialised version of arbitration emerged alongside the strengthening of nation-states' powers. This part illustrates how a system with minimal state regulation gradually developed a governance system that has become highly judicialised in the twenty-first century.

[5] Philip C Jessup, *Transnational Law* (Yale University Press, 1956).

[6] Margaret Moses, *Principles and Practice of International Commercial Arbitration* (Cambridge University Press, 2017) 15.

The third section follows the continued judicialisation of international arbitration through the leading international arbitration centre, the International Chamber of Commerce (ICC). It presents the historical origins of the ICC and how it represents the gold standard in terms of activities and rules of IACs. A recent survey found that the five most preferred arbitral institutions are the ICC, the Singapore International Arbitration (SIAC), the Hong Kong International Arbitration (HKIAC), the London Court of International Arbitration (LCIA), and the China International Economic and Trade Arbitration Commission (CIETAC). Within such an atmosphere of cut-throat competition, African IACs and sub-regional international economic courts struggle to compete favourably. The chapter, however, argues that the African IACs should not despair. Their presence shows a desire and will to reclaim the market of disputes. The need for such reclamation is real and dire, especially in African-domiciled disputes involving African private or public disputants.

The final section argues that the proliferation of international arbitral institutions in Africa over the past two decades can be a blessing or a curse, depending on how it is handled. Africa currently boasts approximately 87 arbitration institutions of various sizes and structures. This development is commendable, particularly in a continent with 54 countries, as it signals the emergence of homegrown and competitive arbitration centres in Africa. However, this plurality of arbitral institutions on the continent might very well be the Achilles heel of arbitration in Africa, particularly where there is a lack of cooperation and collaboration among these institutions. Establishing a joint centre, the Chinese-Africa Joint Arbitration Centre (CAJAC), is a coordinated effort that may address potential collaborative and coordination deficits. This final section discusses six leading African arbitration centres: Arbitration Foundation of Southern Africa (AFSA) in South Africa, the Cairo Regional Centre for International Commercial Arbitration (CRCICA) in Cairo, Egypt, the Kigali International Arbitration Centre (KIAC) in Kigali, Rwanda, the Lagos Court of Arbitration (LCA) in Lagos, Nigeria, the Nairobi Centre for International Arbitration (NCIA) in Nairobi, Kenya, and the Chinese-Africa Joint Arbitration Center (CAJAC).

2. TRANSNATIONAL LAW, JUDICIALISED ARBITRATION, AND AFRICAN SUB-REGIONAL INTERNATIONAL ECONOMIC COURTS AND TRIBUNALS

For recent scholarship, transnational law[7] has mainly covered the spillage of mostly private law outside the boundaries of the nation-state.[8] This spillage

[7] *See* Gregory Shaffer, 'Theorizing Transnational Legal Ordering' (2016) 12 *Annual Review of Law and Social Science* 231.

[8] Roger Cotterrell, 'What is Transnational Law' (2012) 37 *Law & Social Inquiry* 500.

is covered in both public and private international commercial arbitration. Although many legal relations, influences, controls, regimes, doctrines, and systems in international commercial arbitration can be easily categorised under the category' transnational law,' the broader involvement of nation states in public international law still marks the outer boundaries of this sub-branch of law.[9] The nation state plays a facilitative and indirect role in international commercial arbitration by allowing parties to exercise contractual freedom in directing their dispute settlement towards compulsory and binding arbitration.[10] Here, we see the role that the state essentially plays in international arbitration, as actors still rely on national courts at various stages of the arbitration process.[11]

The state's role here is indirect regulation, with national law remaining visible in the shadow of transnational law. If we then define international arbitration based on the presence of nation states, it means that, within the historical arc of international law, international arbitration must appear after the emergence of nation states. Additionally, the current mainstream, yet disputed,[12] understanding of international law and the nation state emerged around 1648 in Westphalia. Most African nation states only fully emerged in the mid-twentieth century after mass decolonisation in the 1960s.[13] It follows that international commercial arbitration as part of private transnational law appears in Africa only after the mid-twentieth century.

The Westphalian date of 1648,[14] the origins of the sovereignty doctrine,[15] and the emergence of nation-states in Africa are historical occurrences that have all been challenged in critical scholarship.[16] The current study has focused on international economic dispute settlement in Africa in the twenty-first century. In this century, international arbitration has been widely accepted as a well-established and structured mode of dispute settlement at both the domestic and international levels. Other appropriate forms of dispute settlement indigenous to African societies are still marginalised in the current century in favour of state-sanctioned adjudication.[17] This marginalisation is part of the continuation

[9] Robert S Wai, 'Transnational Private Law and Private Ordering in a Contested Global Society' (2005) 46 *Harv Intl LJ* 475 (2005).

[10] ibid at 476.

[11] Robert S Wai, 'Transnational Liftoff and Juridical Touchdown: The Regulatory Function of Private International Law in an Era of Globalization' (2001–2002) 40 *Colum J Transnatl L* 209.

[12] Carl Landauer, 'Regionalism, Geography, and the International Legal Imagination' (2011) 11 *Chi J Intl L* 581.

[13] See Basil Davidson, *The Black Man's Burden: Africa and the Curse of the Nation-State* (James Currey, 1992).

[14] Stephen D Krasner, 'Westphalia and All That' in Judith Goldstein (eds), *Ideas and Foreign Policy: Beliefs, Institutions, and Political Change Robert Keohane* (Cornell University Press, 1993) 235.

[15] Antony Anghie, *Imperialism, Sovereignty and the Making of International Law* (Cambridge University Press, 2005).

[16] Davidson (n 13).

[17] Roseline Njogu, 'Gods at War: Religion and Law-Making' in Muna Ndulo and Cosmas Emeziem (eds), *The Routledge Handbook of African Law* (Routledge, 2022) 78–99.

of the colonial paradigm of centralising power, including judicial power, by the nation-state inherited in Africa from the European colonial powers.

These appropriate, indigenous, and autochthonous modes of dispute settlement now form part of the law sub-discipline referred to as ADR. Arbitration (outside continental Europe), mediation, and 'traditional' forms of dispute settlement form part of ADR. The framing of these modes of dispute settlement as 'traditional' also forms part of the renowned British historian Terence Ranger's argument that Europe invented tradition in colonial Africa.[18] Ranger argued that in the late nineteenth century, British administrators in Africa sought to invent 'traditions' by favourably looking at what they perceived as traditional in Africa.[19] Once they identified it, they set about codifying and promulgating it in restatements as African customary law, transforming flexible custom into rigid prescriptions.[20] ADR, as is currently practised in Africa, is a panoply of legal techniques invented as appropriate modes of dispute settlement in Africa.

At the domestic (municipal) level, in its judicialised form, arbitration in Africa is a transplanted mode of dispute settlement. Broadly, the contributionist stream of African international comparative law scholars might argue that the concept of arbitration was known in pre-colonial Africa.[21] It is unlikely that the highly judicialised mode of arbitration witnessed in the twenty-first century was present. By judicialisation, I adopt Alec Stone Sweet's deductive formulation: 'the process by which a third-party dispute resolution process leads to the mutation of social, economic, and political relations or actors into polities'.[22] Judicialisation encompasses the process of significant norm-creation within a given polity, transforming or influencing societal outcomes in politics, the economy and even culture.

Judicialised arbitration is therefore a form of governance led and shaped by a critical mass of lawyers and 'lawyer-made' professionals within the Pierre Bourdieu sociological legal habitus.[23] Interestingly, even in medieval Europe, where the idea of arbitration ostensibly emerged, it was not birthed 'judicialised' in the form described above.[24] The following section demonstrates that the process gradually evolved through the efforts of individual normpreneurs, institutions, and geopolitics. Historically, it emerged through *lex mercatoria* in Europe without the strong hand of the nation-state. The nation-state gradually

[18] Terence Ranger, 'The Invention of Tradition in Colonial Africa' in Eric Hobsbawm and Terence Ranger (eds), *The Invention of Tradition* (Cambridge University Press, 1983) 212–262.

[19] ibid.

[20] ibid at 212–262.

[21] *See* Ditaba Rantsane, 'The Origin of Arbitration Law in South Africa' (2020) 23 PER/PELJ 1.

[22] Alec Stone Sweet, 'Judicialization and The Construction of Governance' (1999) 32 *Comp Pol Stud* 147.

[23] Pierre Bourdieu, 'The Force of Law: Toward a Sociology of the Juridical Field' (1987) 38 *Hastings LJ* 805; *see also* Pierre Bourdieu, *Outline of s Theory of Practice* (Cambridge University Press, 1977) 72.

[24] Edward Powell, 'Settlement of Disputes by Arbitration in Fifteenth-Century England' (1984) 2 *L & Hist Rev* 21.

incorporated and co-opted transnational actors through the exercise of sovereign state power in arbitration. There are numerous lessons that the African sub-regional International Economic Courts and Tribunals can learn from this history and process in their arbitration structure. One of the most glaring ones is that arbitral disputes are part of a limited market, and IACs are constantly and carefully jostling to have the largest market share.

As we saw in chapter 2 of this book, at the regional level, all the main African sub-regional International Economic Courts and Tribunals: ECOWAS Community Court of Justice (ECCJ), the East African Court of Justice (EACJ), the COMESA Court of Justice (CCJ), and the OHADA Common Court of Justice and Arbitration (OHADA CCJA), all have varied arbitration jurisdiction. The following sections of this chapter interrogate how this jurisdictional grant to all these international courts has affected the current dockets of economic disputes in these regional judiciaries. The assessment and analysis in this chapter are critical and novel because one of the additional avenues for shifting international economic law-based disputes in Africa is international arbitration administered by an increasing number of global, regional, and national arbitration centres.

While the prominent REC courts in Africa all have jurisdictional setups on international arbitration, they face significant competition from globally renowned regional and national commercial arbitration centres. The international ones include the likes of the International Chamber of Commerce's (ICC) International Court of Arbitration in Paris, France; the London Court of International Arbitration (LCIA) in London, United Kingdom; the international division of American Arbitration Association, International Center of Dispute Resolution (ICDR) in New York, United States; the Hong Kong International Arbitration Center (HKIAC) in Hong Kong, China; the Singapore International Arbitration Center (SIAC) in Singapore; the Stockholm Chamber of Commerce (SCC) in Stockholm, Sweden; and the China International Economic and Trade Arbitration Commission (CIETAC) in Beijing, China. Regional centres include the Cairo Regional Centre for International Arbitration, the Kigali International Arbitration Centre (KIAC), and the Nairobi Centre for International Arbitration (NIAC).

Additionally, national centres such as the Ghana Arbitration Centre, the Kenya national branch of the Chartered Institute of Arbitrators in London (CIArb), the Arbitration, Mediation, and Conciliation Centre of Ouagadougou (CAMC-O), the Lagos Court of Arbitration in Lagos, Nigeria, the 'Centro de Resolução Extrajudicial de Litígios' (CREL) in Luanda, Angola, and the Tunisia Chamber of Conciliation and Arbitration also attract international economic law (commercial) disputes that could form part of the economic disputes docket at the sub-regional African courts. While no sovereign legislator exists within these networks of IACs, the older IACs have a greater transnational reach. The elites who govern them are tightly networked in a stable, competitive, and market-based field.[25]

[25] Yves Dezalay and Bryant G Garth, *Dealing in Virtue: International Commercial Arbitration and the Construction of a Transnational Legal Order* (University of Chicago Press,1996).

In this atmosphere of IACs' market-based competition for a limited market, the African sub-regional International Economic Courts and tribunals, as well as African regional IACs, cannot compete favourably or even equally against the globally renowned, independent, and some state-supported IACs. Most African regional IACs are modelled around the Paris-based International Chamber of Commerce (ICC). The ICC has had a significant head start, with nearly 100 years of commercial advocacy, policy lobbying, and dispute settlement.[26] It is essential to distinguish the ICC as a chamber of commerce, which is a separate entity administratively, from its dispute settlement service: the International Court of Arbitration (ICA), and its secretariat. The ICC performs various functions, including advocacy and promoting the free movement of goods, services, and capital across borders. It also operates a dispute resolution service that encompasses mediation, arbitration, and expert proceedings. For arbitration, the ICC has the ICA, an arbitral institution that administers arbitration under defined rules.

The third section of this chapter argues that IACs with a global, transnational reach, such as the ICC, LCIA, and CIETAC, are well-networked, financially resourced, and connected to a business elite, and therefore have a vast competitive advantage over African IACs and sub-regional international courts and tribunals. Before presenting this argument, the following section outlines the historical trajectory of judicialised arbitration and the lessons that African IACs, sub-regional international economic courts, and tribunals can draw from.

3. THE EUROPEAN MEDIEVAL ORIGINS OF ARBITRATION AND LESSONS FOR AFRICA

The concept of arbitration, in both its judicialised and non-judicialised forms, is an invented tradition in medieval Europe and contemporary Africa. By 'invented tradition,' I mean a system of practice that did not develop organically within the currently practised society. An invented tradition can be created by internal participants or through external participants. To understand the trajectories of the idea and practice of arbitration in the twenty-first century in and for Africa, it is essential to trace its non-judicialised origins. A judicialised dispute settlement system is one in which a third-party dispute resolution (TDR) process influences the broader processes and outcomes of future disputes, politics, economics, and culture.[27]

The third-party dispute resolution process is highly judicialised if it is norm-creating and generating in the municipal and international scene. In medieval

[26] ibid at 45 (arguing that as the history indicates, history is the key legitimator in the legal field. No one can compete with tradition without ending underscoring that one group is a new arrival and another an established elite, akin to the aristocracy).

[27] *See* Joseph Weiler, 'The Transformation of Europe' (1990–1991) 100 *Yale LJ* 2405.

Europe, between the eleventh and twelfth centuries, a system emerged among traders whose influence extended beyond their local boundaries.[28] The traders designed the system to be for and by themselves. It was thus voluntarily produced, voluntarily adjudicated, and voluntarily enforced.[29] The traders wanted to escape the feudal system, the city-state, local guilds, and the church's domestic rules, customs, and courts. They intended to create their own tailored-made third-party dispute resolution (TDR) process free of any centralised authority. Thus, it was an institution-building and governance-generating process. Institutions should be understood here in both the legal and political science senses. In the legal sense, they are legally generated systems. And in their political science sense, they are 'norms (principles, standards, rules, procedures, and cultural dispositions) that constrain choices, fix roles and duties, enable the exercise of legitimate authority, and organise the evolution of social systems in path-dependent manners'.[30]

Contrary to this narrative, in England and arguably in the United Kingdom, the growth of the common law generally led to the ghettoisation of arbitration as a mode of justice dispensation. According to Edward Powell, the development of the common law legal system was always assumed to be linear and progressive.[31] The progression replaced consent-based, rudimentary dispute settlement systems with more advanced legal systems backed by the Crown's authority.[32] The rise of arbitration in medieval England is explained in relation to the breakdown of the central authorities of the monarchical systems, rather than as a separate system that develops independently, as seen in the accounts of Alec Sweet and Florian Griesel above. According to scholars J. G. Bellamy and Robin Lyndsey Storey, the presence of arbitration in England was symptomatic of the dysfunction of the central judiciary.[33]

Arguably, this is the historical origin of common law courts' resistance to arbitration and the uneasy sharing of competence between arbitration and courts in the countries that have inherited the common law heritage.[34] This history also explains the relegation of arbitration as an 'alternative' form of dispute settlement in the United Kingdom and the common law world. Despite these analytical assumptions, Edward Powell demonstrates that resolving disputes through extra-judicial means, such as negotiation, mediation, and arbitration, was widespread in medieval Europe.[35] His view confirms that even in England, the use of arbitration was not a mere 'alternative' to litigation, even in its origins.

[28] Alec Stone Sweet and Florian Grisel, *The Evolution of International Arbitration: Judicialization, Governance, Legitimacy* (Oxford University Press, 2017) 39.

[29] ibid.

[30] ibid at 7.

[31] Powell (n 24).

[32] ibid.

[33] ibid.

[34] Won Kidane, *The Culture of International Arbitration* (Oxford University Press, 2017) 32.

[35] Powell (n 24).

The individuals who conjured up arbitration in medieval Europe were themselves outsiders in the polities where they operated. As long-distance merchants who conducted long-distance trade between feudal manors, city-states, and the Holy Roman Empire, they operated with a social 'field'. In sociological research, a 'field' refers to an arena of activity in which separate actors who had previously operated autonomously or independently begin to act in ways that influence each other.[36] The process of economic integration around various regions of the world is an excellent example of how new fields emerge over time. The rationalist and deductive theories developed by Alec Stone Sweet and Florian Grisel explain international arbitration as a legal system and arbitration as a system of transnational governance.[37] To do so, they trace the history of arbitration from medieval Europe to the twenty-first century. They show how 'skilled social actors,' whom this study has referred to as normpreneurs, consolidated institutions that have enabled arbitration to develop as a legal system and to defend its autonomy and claims of normative and social legitimacy.[38]

Sweet's and Florian's deductive theory of judicialisation begins with some fundamental social assumptions in trade relations. They ask us to assume two or more traders who are strangers and want to trade with each other profitably; these traders will face three overlapping hurdles: commitment, high transaction costs, and institutional choice. If these traders are engaged with each other locally (face-to-face) and can see each other, the risks of non-commitment hurdles remain present but not as high as in the case of long-distance engagements. The transaction costs are also higher and riskier for long-distance trade than for local trade. Ultimately, these traders would be interested in establishing a system of governance that ensures consistent and predictable outcomes in contractual interpretation and effective enforcement.[39] A highly judicialised system overcomes these three hurdles: commitment, transaction costs, and establishing a secure, stable, and predictable dispute settlement system with effective enforcement.[40]

The first norms created in the assumed scenario above are intended to deal with the challenge of commitments and non-commitment. These norms are those of trustworthiness, reciprocity, and good faith. Individuals in a social system with an assumption of a rationalist prisoner dilemma and game theoretic cooperation account will act rationally to secure relationships with other trusted individuals. Such is a reputational system firmly grounded on the rule

[36] Neil Fligstein and Doug McAdam, *A Theory of Fields* (Oxford University Press, 2012).

[37] Sweet and Grisel (n 28).

[38] *See* Allen Buchanan and Robert O Keohane, 'The Legitimacy of Global Governance Institutions' in Lukas H Meyer(ed), *Legitimacy, Justice and Public International Law* (Cambridge University Press, 2010) 29 (defining normative legitimacy as an institution's right to rule ie promulgating rules and attempting to secure compliance with the rules by attaching costs to non-compliance; and sociological legitimacy as a belief by others that the institutions have a right to rule).

[39] Sweet and Grisel (n 28) 36.

[40] ibid.

that parties will keep their promises: *pacta sunt servanda*. Here, the difficulty of compliance is absent, as it is assumed that each party wants to maintain a reputable position in the system to make a profit or to retain trust in the eyes of other actors. Many non-judicialised domestic justice dispensing systems would have shared such an attribute before the advent of long-distance or globalised trade. It is possible that such a system still exists among many communities of interest that engage in close and face-to-face transactions and have low transaction costs involved. Additionally, even under current international law, where mounting literature on neo-realist compliance is present,[41] the Vienna Convention on the Law of Treaties (VCLT) still maintains the idea of *pacta sunt servanda* as a primary norm.[42]

The European medieval law merchant established a high reputation system early in the process, as merchants had strong incentives for trustworthiness, reciprocity, and good faith.[43] The third-party dispute resolution process was simply in place to restore and revitalise contractual relations when they had broken down. The third-party resolver was another merchant who was well-versed in the customs and usages among merchants, ie, the law merchant.[44] The decision was to be brief, without the need to provide reasons, and as it was a reputational system, there was no fear of non-enforcement.[45] The system bore all the advantages of what in the twenty-first century could be considered an effective legal system: it was expeditious, harnessed specific expertise, was cheap for its users and possessed high levels of compliance.[46] The outlook here is a system with high normative and sociological legitimacy levels. While not highly judicialised, this system exhibits some signs of judicialisation. The customs and trade practices that emerged during this era have persisted to date. An excellent example is the International Chamber of Commerce's (ICC) 'INCOTERMS,' a compendium of basic commercial and trade contract terms.Consequently, arbitration as a TDR process grew from medieval to the industrial revolution Europe from a mode of dispute settlement only within a small geographical 'field' to a state-backed dispute resolution process that was highly institutionalised and judicialised.

This medieval European arbitration operated with a sociological field of involved merchants and used similar scripts of social governance. This attribute gave the system both sociological and legal legitimacy, as well as a strong social

[41] Andrew T Guzman, 'A Compliance-Based Theory of International Law' (2002) 90 *Calif L Rev* 1823. 1823; Eric A Posner and John C Yoo, 'Judicial Independence in International Tribunals' (2005) 93 *Calif L Rev* 3; *contra* Robert Howse and Ruti Teitel, 'Beyond Compliance: Rethinking Why International Law Really Matters' (2010) 2 *Global Policy* 27.

[42] Vienna Convention on the Law of Treaties (VCLT), 23 May 1969, 1155 UNTS 331, art 26.

[43] Harold J Berman, *Law and Revolution: The Formation of the Western Legal Tradition* (Harvard University Press 1983) 333–356.

[44] Leon E Trakman, *The Law Merchant: The Evolution of Commercial Law* (Fred B Rothman & Co 1983), 7–10.

[45] ibid at 7–12.

[46] ibid.

glue of trustworthiness and good faith. The third-party dispute resolvers, ie, the arbitrators, were specialised as merchants themselves. They were thus quintessential experts in their fields, not by profession but by social practice. The recognition and enforcement of arbitration awards were assured, not by fear of state coercion, but by fear of reputational damage. The system was consensual and delocalised from the nation-states' adjudicatory authority in a way that the consensual theorists of international arbitration would only envy today.

For this reason, this system compares favourably to living customary dispute systems in the past and present among African communities. Such autonomous justice dispensing systems are expeditious, utilise non-professional third-party resolvers, prioritise common sense reasoning over formal legal reasoning, and achieve high rates of compliance based on their reputational foundations. I would call such a system a low-judicialised system. It is indeed favourable for certain disputes and specific contexts. Yet such a system is also, as we will see below, disadvantageous in some cases. The lesson for twenty-first-century African dispute settlement from the history above is that indigenous dispute settlement systems, anchored in living customary law, should be allowed to thrive and evolve organically.[47] There are still communities of interest in commercial and non-commercial engagements that maintain flexible, reputational, and voluntary systems. Of course, these modes of dispute settlement are not as sophisticated or advanced as they need to be to deal with the highly bureaucratic, international, and globalised business and trade environment that many African states face today. This atmosphere does not mean there is no space for such systems to be used and thrive, especially in informal cross-border trade. Importantly, this outlook supports the need for more judicialisation, which is discussed below in the context of arbitration. Such judicialisation is not inherently nefarious, and this chapter does not argue that the judicialisation of arbitration is, in itself, a negative development.

3.1 The Nation-State and the Emergence of Judicialised International Arbitration

The emergence of the modern iteration of nation states from the fifteenth century onwards would significantly impact the legal and institutional structure of arbitration that persisted into the twenty-first century. The nation state (or Westphalian state) demanded and coveted a strong centralisation of judicial power. All the power to make binding judicial pronouncements was vested in the state, and the state would delegate or entrust it at will to different organs. Thus, the centralised judiciary exercises and continues to exercise a strong centripetal force in modern constitutional democracies and republics. In these constitutional

[47] *See* Marc Galanter, 'Justice in Many Rooms: Courts, Private Ordering, and Indigenous Law' (1981) 19 *Journal of Legal Pluralism and Unofficial Law* 1.

democracies, the state's sovereign power is vested in the people, who are the original mandate providers to the state, who then act on their behalf.

The Western European tripartite constitutional structure, characterised by the separation and dispersal of public power among the executive, parliament, and judiciary, has also been adopted by many states worldwide. Unlike the executive and parliament, in many twenty-first-century countries, the judiciary remains a non-majoritarian institution. A non-majoritarian institution is a public entity that possesses two specific attributes: (a) it exercises some grant of specialised public authority, separate from other institutions, and (b) it is neither directly elected by the people nor directly managed by elected officials.[48] This puts the exercise of arbitral power further away from the state. Indeed, Jan Paulsson has referred to it as the exercise of private power.[49] Yet this distance from the state also significantly weakens arbitral power in a system in which the parties are involved in possible one-off transactions with very low reputational risks.

Before delving further into the seismic transformations that the modern nation state brought to the European medieval arbitral governance, it is crucial to outline the favourable attributes of the medieval European arbitration system. In comparison to judicial adjudication by the state, medieval arbitration was expeditious, relatively inexpensive, harnessed expertise, flexible, autonomous, and had high compliance rates, even without a violence- or sanctions-backed state behind it. However, arguably, with the birth of written constitutions in 1787 in the United States, the idea of enumerated rights constitutionally enshrined and enforceable by courts also emerged. In the twenty-first century, the idea is no longer novel, but such a system did not exist in the world in the late eighteenth century.[50] The increase of territorially defined nation states possessing prescriptive jurisdiction over their territories resulted in the monopolisation of justice dispensation. As expected, this posed a challenge to medieval European merchants' reputational and effective arbitration system.

The growth and increase of the central power of nation states, recognised both domestically and internationally, also coincided with the advent of the Industrial Revolution and the globalisation of trade. While these medieval merchants had already dealt with the challenges of long-distance trade through accepted customs and usages, such as the International Commercial Terms (INCOTERMS), the challenges posed by centralised judicial power were multipronged. First and foremost, the system required a means to utilise the state's enforcement powers both nationally and internationally. Second, the system required the establishment of internal and external doctrines of autonomy to limit the municipal court's intervention in arbitration. Third, an appropriate set

[48] Mark Thatcher and Alec Stone Sweet, 'Theory and Practice of Delegation to Non-Majoritarian Institutions' in Mark Thatcher and Alec Stone Sweet (eds) *The Politics of Delegation* (Routledge, 2005) 2.

[49] Jan Paulsson, *The Idea of Arbitration* (Oxford University Press, 2013) 1.

[50] Sweet and Grisel (n 28) 159–177.

of administrative tools and institutions had to be established to conduct arbitration in a procedural and effective manner.

It is only in the early twentieth century that historians and other social scientists have carefully unearthed the origins and arguments of neoliberalism, which were firmly established in the 1920s rather than the late 1970s.[51] If these thinkers are correct, we can easily conclude that the ideology for sustaining neo-colonialism was planted decades before colonialism, and judicialised international arbitration is part of the legal mechanism to ring-fence the gains made in a world order that protects capital. The story of the establishment and gradual development of arguably the world's leading IAC, the ICC, headquartered in Paris, France, explains the evolution and judicialisation of international arbitration, especially from the beginning of the twentieth century.

3.2 The End of Empire, Private Capital Protection, and International Arbitration: The Case of the International Chamber of Commerce

The International Chamber of Commerce (ICC) was founded in Paris in June 1920 as a crucial international institution to promote the idea of a single global economy.[52] According to its constitution, the ICC's fundamental objective is 'to further the development of an open world economy with the firm conviction that international commercial exchanges are conducive to both greater global prosperity and peace among nations'.[53] Its crafters were principally businessmen who formed what historian Quinn Slobodian calls the public sphere of capitalists.[54] Together with the League of Nations and the pre-war Allied powers (the United States, Great Britain, and France), the ICC was part of the post-empire institutional building to maintain the Allied global economic hegemony following World War I.[55]

The founders of the ICC advocated for the central codification of international economic statistics, the removal of trade barriers, and the free movement of capital as processes that would ostensibly ensure world peace. The rhetoric of peace and free trade concealed the businesspeople's connections to the Allied Powers' corporate manipulation of markets and the continued

[51] *See* Quinn Slobodian, *Globalists: The End of Empire and the Birth of Neoliberalism* (Harvard University Press, 2018); Shane R Tomashot, 'Selling Peace: The History of the International Chamber of Commerce, 1919–1925' (2015) (unpublished PhD dissertation, Georgia State University) www.semanticscholar.org/paper/Selling-Peace%3A-The-History-of-the-International-of-Tomashot/9879844fb6b34f743b4ed549fd88e29f56ccfe4d; Jessica Whyte, *The Morals of the Market: Human Rights and the Rise of Neoliberalism* (Verso Books, 2019).

[52] JH Fahey, 'The International Chamber of Commerce' (1921) *The Annals of the American Academy of Political and Social Science* 126.

[53] Dominic Kelly, 'The International Chamber of Commerce' (2005) 10 New Political Economy 260.

[54] Quinn Slobodian, Globalists: The End of Empire and the Birth of Neoliberalism (Harvard University Press, 2018) 34.

[55] Shane R Tomashot (n 51).

economic exploitation (through direct and indirect transnational corporation (TNC) control) of colonised or protected territories.[56] From its inception, the ICC was an instrument for early European neoliberal thinkers, such as the Austrian economist Ludwig von Mises.[57] Yet one of the earliest books written on the history of the ICC is titled *Merchants of Peace: Twenty Years of Business Diplomacy through the International Chamber of Commerce*, which offers a strenuous attempt at crafting a narrative of benevolence for the ICC.[58] Its author, historian George L. Ridgeway, who was initially connected to the ICC, states that 'the strength of the ICC at the early stage was its ability to co-opt, in-person and business executives, capital itself for the service of world peace'.[59]

To meet its internationalist, liberal, and neoliberal goals of reducing trade barriers and resolving private commercial disputes, the ICC established the ICA. The ICA is the dispute settlement service provider of the ICC and had its first set of institutional Arbitration rules in 1923.[60] The ICC's dispute settlement service operates as a single, cohesive IAC that administers and manages disputes before arbitral tribunals.[61] Here, it is essential to distinguish between *ad hoc* arbitration and institutional arbitration. Ad hoc arbitration occurs when no institution administers the arbitration process, while institutional arbitration occurs when an arbitration centre administers the arbitration process.[62] Parties in ad hoc arbitration can carefully tailor a procedure to meet the particular needs of their dispute.[63] They can decide to draft their own rules or to choose the United Nations Commission on International Trade (UNCITRAL) Arbitration Rules, which are frequently used in *ad hoc* arbitrations.[64]

The influence of the UNCITRAL arbitration rules has grown significantly to encompass *ad hoc* arbitrations that require self-standing arbitration rules. The ICC, ICDR, and other arbitral institutions discourage disputing parties from using their rules if they are not using the institutions. So, although parties in ad hoc arbitrations sometimes select institutional rules (after being modified), it is generally frowned upon and criticised by the arbitral institutions. If a party wants to have an ad hoc arbitration, it is highly advisable to use the UNCITRAL Rules or for the party to draft its own rules.

[56] ibid.

[57] Slobodian (n 50).

[58] George L Ridgeway, *Merchants of Peace: Twenty Years of Business through the International Chamber of Commerce* (Columbia University Press, 1938).

[59] ibid at 7.

[60] ICC, 'ICC International Court of Arbitration' iccwbo.org/dispute-resolution-services/icc-international-court-arbitration (hereinafter ICC Arbitration Rules, 2021).

[61] *See* ICC Arbitration Rules, 2021, art 2, iccwbo.org/content/uploads/sites/3/2020/12/icc-2021-arbitration-rules-2014-mediation-rules-english-version.pdf.

[62] Moses (n 6).

[63] ibid.

[64] ibid (reminding us that UNCITRAL itself does not administer arbitrations and is not an arbitral institution).

The ICC non-dispute settlement divisions operate strong political advocacy and lobbying aimed at national governments, international organisations, and business actors. The ICC serves as an administrative centre for resolving arbitral disputes. Its creation is a strong force in the nation states' involvement in judicialising arbitration, as it offers an institutional structure for arbitral governance. The ICC then functions with quasi-legislative powers for the parties who accept its codes, rules, and procedures. For the ICC, many actors, including individual and powerful TNCs, local, regional, bilateral, transnational, public-law, and private-law chambers of commerce, are members of the World Chambers Federation. The sheer number of these members makes the ICC's de facto legislative powers extend to many organisations globally. The ICC has therefore created a powerful, near-global 'rule by consent' island of by governance.[65] It has successfully done this powerful institutionalisation while remaining behind the cloak of its nonpolitical character.[66]

The creation of any rules system cannot be apolitical. The crafters and makers of such systems are generating norms within specific worldviews that are influenced by their moral, political, and societal context. Such normpreneurs are involved in legal imagination,[67] which creates or invents traditions[68] that form obvious and acceptable societal norms. The point here is not that the ICC, in its dispute settlement service, generates norms directly. It does, however, benefit from the business generated by its accepted customs, usages, and contractual documents, many of which have an ICC-selected standard arbitration clause.

The ICC made one of its enduring marks of judicialising arbitration in 1924 when it announced that it would check the 'phraseology' of awards.[69] The process of scrutiny and supervision of arbitral awards has become rigorous in all IACs of the twentieth and twenty-first centuries. The ICC is established under Article 1 of the ICC Arbitration Rules, 2021.[70] The ICC Rules describe it as an independent arbitration body of the ICC with its own separate statute.[71]

[65] Kelly (n 53) *citing* Helmut O Maucher, 'Ruling by Consent' *Financial Times* (London, 11 December 1997) (who stated: "Business has no political power and aspires to none." Helmut O. Maucher was a former ICC President and former chief executive of Nestlé); Yves Dezalay and Bryant G Garth, *Dealing in Virtue: International Commercial Arbitration and the Construction of a Transnational Legal Order* (University of Chicago Press, 1996) 45 (reporting that a longtime British observer pointed out that: 'But the ICC is a great institution in the world by a long way'. Potential clients see the ICC as trustworthy and respectable because of its senior status, and because it has preserved the missionary idealism of its origins).

[66] George L Ridgeway, *Merchants of Peace: Twenty Years of Business through the International Chamber of Commerce* (Columbia University Press, 1938) 5.

[67] Nicolás M Perrone, *Investment Treaties and the Legal Imagination: How Foreign Investors Play by Their Own Rules* (Oxford University Press, 2021).

[68] Ranger (n 18).

[69] Sweet and Grisel (n 28).

[70] ICC Arbitration Rules, 2021.

[71] ibid art 1.

As stated, the ICC does not resolve disputes itself. It only administers the resolution of disputes by ICC-mandated arbitral tribunals.[72] The ICC-mandated arbitral tribunals are required to resolve disputes in accordance with the ICC Rules of Arbitration.[73] The administration of arbitration by the ICC explicitly includes the scrutiny and approval of awards rendered in accordance with the ICC Rules.[74]

The creation of the ICC arbitration and its move to ensure that arbitrators justify their awards with reasons is fundamentally a commercialisation approach with significant social ramifications.[75] The requirement that arbitral awards be justified by reasons (in many cases, legal reasons) is also an early twentieth-century innovation, or, as I call it in this chapter, an invented tradition. In the medieval era described above, there was no such requirement. It was enough to offer unreasoned awards (ie, awards in equity rather than law)[76] as long as the fundamental rules of natural justice and due process were adhered to. The legal 'reasons-based' requirement fundamentally moves the arbitral process more towards the legal, sociological field or what Pierre Bourdieu refers to as the 'legal habitus.'[77] Part of the judicialisation of arbitration is therefore a sociological monopolisation of the arbitration process for and by the legal profession. These two forms of judicialisation are both necessitated by the competition that IACs face against each other. While the justification for scrutinising an award is consistent and ensures awards rendered are enforceable under the New York Convention, IACs have an excellent reason to develop rules to guarantee the product they sell.[78]

For African sub-regional international economic courts and tribunals that only emerged on the scene towards the latter part of the twentieth century, there were possibly two broad options that the normpreneurs who developed the systems had. The first would have been an attempt to invent new traditions that would appropriately fit the African context of economic dispute settlement. I think this is a deviant approach. Such an approach has been firmly rejected, primarily due to its complete lack of use. The second was to conform to the already invented structures and work within an established framework of international economic dispute settlement. As we will see below, the African sub-regional international economic courts and tribunals' crafters adopted the second approach. One of the promises of the second approach, which I label the conformity approach, was that the global harmonisation of international economic dispute settlement is directly correlated to improved economic

[72] ibid art. 2.
[73] ibid.
[74] ibid.
[75] Sweet and Grisel (n 28).
[76] ibid at 100.
[77] Pierre Bourdieu, 'The Force of Law: Toward a Sociology of the Juridical Field' (1987) 38 *Hastings LJ* 805.
[78] Sweet and Grisel (n 28).

development. However, the empirical studies that have tested this promise in international investment law have yielded mixed or, in some cases, agnostic results.[79] There is no specific evidence that adopting harmonised dispute settlement systems (judicialised arbitration) – in this case setting up arbitration in the African sub-regional international economic courts and tribunals – would increase foreign direct investment.

4. THE INVENTED AND COMPETITIVE LEGAL TRADITIONS OF INTERNATIONAL ARBITRATION CENTRES

There are two different angles that the analysis of the invented legal traditions of international arbitration centres can take. The first, directly linked to this chapter's argument, is the marketisation or commercialisation that creates fierce competition among international arbitration centres to offer arbitral justice. Whether international, regional, or national, an arbitration centre is an institution established either by a state, privately, or jointly by a state and a private entity, with its main function being the administration of arbitrations. The arbitration centre thus establishes its rules on administering the arbitration and sets up procedures for conducting such arbitration. Its primary role is administrative, rather than decisional, since disputes are heard by arbitrators who are, in many cases, appointed by the parties. The arbitration centre can, in some cases, have a robust complementary role in appointing arbitrators. The goal is to make the arbitral process as smooth as possible in terms of case management, venue, fee processing, and other incidental and administrative matters.

The competition among arbitration centres can be linked to the competition among arbitration seats. The most popular seats in surveys have consistently been located in the global North, including London, Paris, Geneva, and New York, which correspond with the homes of the most active arbitration centres.[80] Happily, Singapore and Hong Kong are upsetting the status quo on the most critical seats of arbitration of global repute.[81] We also see nation states involved

[79] Mary Hallward-Driemeier, 'Do Bilateral Investment Treaties Attract FDI? Only a bit…and they could bite' (Policy Research Working Paper: No 3121 2003); Michael Frenkel and Benedikt Walter, 'Do Bilateral Investment Treaties attract Foreign Direct Investment? The Role of International Dispute Settlement Provisions' (2018) 42 *World Economics* 1316; Eric Neumayer and Laura Spess, 'Do Bilateral Investment Treaties Increase Foreign Direct Investment to Developing Countries?' (2005) 33 *World Development* 1567; Terence K Teo, 'BITs and FDI Revisited: A Matching Approach' (2021) 11 *Open Journal of Political Science* 116; Lauge N Skovgaard Poulsen, 'The Importance of BITs for Foreign Direct Investment and Political Risk Insurance: Revisiting the Evidence' in Karl Sauvant (ed) *Yearbook on International Investment Law & Policy* 2009–2010 (Oxford University Press, 2010) 539–574.

[80] White & Case, 'Current Choices and Future Adaptations' (6 May 2021) www.whitecase.com/insight-our-thinking/current-choices-and-future-adaptations.

[81] ibid.

in a regulatory competition to protect arbitration agreements and awards in domestic legislation.[82]

The second angle referenced above for invented traditions in international arbitration involves the legal doctrines or techniques invented by these centres and endorsed by states that maintain and legally legitimise judicialised arbitration. There are two essential doctrines developed to safeguard arbitration, particularly from the encroachment of domestic courts and statutory or common-law doctrines. These the crucial doctrines of Kompetenz-Kompetenz and Separability. Additionally, IACs continually lobby international and domestic business industries and states to ensure they attract as many cases as possible, and thus displace other competitors in the attraction of cases.

4.1 International Arbitration Centres Competition to offer Arbitral Justice

International commercial arbitration, provided in arbitration centres, is a business and has been so since the early days of the ICC.[83] With fierce competition between IACs, states, national chambers of commerce, and private entities establishing arbitration houses for cases, IACs robustly market themselves as the best venues for dispute settlement. With a singularly consensual arbitration paradigm, the social function of dispute settlement, which benefits the entire community, can easily be lost. When justice dispensation becomes completely commercialised, the holders and purveyors of capital can easily manipulate the system for their benefit. When entities such as IACs view potential disputes as opportunities to generate business and gain global prestige, the concept of an effective justice dispensation system can easily be overlooked. However, allowing this fierce competition is also beneficial, from a rationalist point of view, as more competition arguably enables consumers to obtain the best services at the most affordable and effective rates.

However, the reality is that IACs that currently operate globally are interested in attracting as many cases as possible. In Africa, where the market for commercial or economically driven cases is limited, the impact of these IACs cannot be overstated. Their effects on the dockets of African sub-regional international economic courts and tribunals, which are presumably competing for the same market, can also be significant.

There is no precise or conclusive data on the number of IACs. Most IACs, except for the International Centre for the Settlement of Investment Disputes (ICSID) and the Permanent Court of Arbitration (PCA), as well as some defunct

[82] Tariq Khan, 'Making India a Hub of Arbitration: Bridging the Gap Between Myth and Reality' (*SCC Online Blog* 17 February 2021) www.scconline.com/blog/post/2021/02/17/making-india-a-hub-of-arbitration-bridging-the-gap-between-myth-and-reality/.

[83] Stéphanie Papazoglou, 'The Battle for Survival among Arbitral Institutions' (*Kluwer Arbitration Blog* 19 June, 2020 arbitrationblog.kluwerarbitration.com/2020/06/19/the-battle-for-survival-among-arbitral-institutions/.

mixed tribunals, such as the Eritrea-Ethiopia Claims Commission (EECC), are private institutions. For many years, the ICC was, expectedly, the international citadel among the IACs with a broad international reach. Since its inception in 1923, the ICC has received over 25,000 cases from all the world's major regions, including Africa.[84] In 2020, the ICC registered 946 arbitration cases, comprising 929 cases under the ICC Arbitration Rules and 17 cases under the ICC Appointing Authority Rules.[85] In the same year, the ICC received a record number of cases from 145 countries and independent territories; only 5 per cent of these cases came from the Sub-Saharan Africa region.

Additionally, in 2020, the ICC took steps to build capacity in the Sub-Saharan Africa region by enhancing awareness of the ICC in Africa. To meet this goal, the ICC appointed Ms. Diamana Diawara as the Regional Director for Africa.[86] This positionworks with the ICC Africa Commission, established in 2018, to promote the ICC's work on the continent. Valentine Mintah, an Executive Board member of the ICC representing Anglophone Africa, captured the role of the ICC in Africa in the following words:

> As a business leader myself, I understand the importance of dispute resolution to keep commerce flowing. I also know that what businesses want is a trusted and neutral institution for resolving those disputes if, and when they arise. That is why more and more parties, including of African representation, are turning to ICC. They do so in the knowledge that the case will be supervised by independent and impartial decision makers and managed by an experienced institution that cares about their needs.[87]

In recent years, other international arbitration institutions have emerged that directly and fiercely compete with the ICC. All these institutions are constantly competing to secure, keep, and expand their share of arbitration cases. They all aim to build their brands and enhance their influence and reputation. A 2020–21 survey by the Queen Mary University of London and White and Case LLP concluded that the five most preferred arbitral institutions are the ICC, the Singapore International Arbitration (SIAC), the Hong Kong International Arbitration (HKIAC), the London Court of International Arbitration (LCIA), and the China International Economic and Trade Arbitration Commission (CIETAC).[88] The other notable missing entities in this list are the American Arbitration Association (AAA), the International Centre for Dispute Resolution (ICDR), and the Stockholm Chamber of Commerce (SCC).

[84] ICC, 'ICC Dispute Resolution 2019 Statistics' (2020) iccwbo.be/shop/icc-dispute-resolution-statistics-2019/#:~:text=The%20ICC%20Court%20registered%20a,its%20almost%20100%2Dyear%20history 9.

[85] ibid.

[86] ibid.

[87] ICC, 'Regional Director role to bolster ICC reach' (2021), iccwbo.org/media-wall/news-speeches/regional-director-role-to-bolster-icc-reach-in-africa/.

[88] Queen Mary University of London and White and Case LLP, '2021 International Arbitration Survey: Adapting arbitration to a changing world' (2021) www.whitecase.com/sites/default/files/2021-05/quml-international-arbitration-survey-2021-web.pdf.

The same survey found the five most preferred seats for arbitration are London, Singapore, Hong Kong, Paris, and Geneva. When expanded to the top ten arbitration seats, still no African city emerges.[89] The point to note here, and as we will see below, is that neither African national nor regional centres nor seats appear in this list. Yet, as we saw with the ICC, it is competing to expand its reach into Sub-Saharan Africa. With these arbitration centres competing for a limited market share in Africa, it is unlikely that the African IACs and sub-regional international economic courts and tribunals, as currently constituted, can compete favourably when directly competing with these international centres.

Through targeted surveys, these five major arbitration centres deploy various marketing tools to ensure that parties use them as institutional centres for arbitration. Lobbying industry and business players, lobbying their host states, and organising training, conferences, and moot court competitions are all ways in which these centres make their work visible. When we add the small cadre of elite arbitrators, mainly from the global North, who continue to dominate the lucrative appointments and top management positions in these IACs, we see a highly judicialised system structured in favour of these strong IACs and against the sub-regional African international economic courts and tribunals.

Following on the heels of the ICC, which structures and forms the gold standard in terms of activities and rules, all IACs, whether global or international, claim or seek to claim the following attributes:

(a) to respect the freedom of the contracting parties to determine how cases will proceed, while offering adaptable rules and in-house appointment of arbitrators when desired;
(b) to provide neutral, expert, flexible, efficient, and predictable administration of cases, including complex disputes involving three or more parties;
(c) to maintain a roster of highly competent, impartial arbitrators;
(d) to guarantee the confidentiality of awards, subject to waiver by the parties;
(e) to furnish modern facilities, equipped with state-of-the-art hearing rooms and technology, near comfortable hotels and world-class restaurants;
(f) to offer less costly substitutes to arbitration, in the form of mediation and simplified, 'fast-track' procedures;
(g) to produce final, binding awards that will be enforceable in state courts, with little or no judicial review on the merits.[90]

Some of these attributes require substantial support and financial resources to follow through. Most African sub-regional international economic courts and tribunals face structural difficulties that easily make the attainment of some of these aims difficult. Housing these African sub-regional international economic courts and tribunals, as well as arbitration houses, in the same premises as

[89] ibid (the ten are London, Singapore, Hong Kong, Paris, Geneva, New York, Beijing, Shanghai, Stockholm, and Dubai).
[90] Sweet and Grisel (n 28) 48.

the international courts is considered disadvantageous. While some of these courts are based in stable and easily accessible African cities, others, such as the COMESA Court of Justice, have faced structural and accessibility issues in Khartoum, Sudan (now based in Lusaka, Zambia). The OHADA Common Court of Justice and Arbitration (CCJA), housed in the court in Abidjan, Côte d'Ivoire, has also faced some criticisms.[91] Global and regional IACs boast a comparative advantage based on their location, scope of operations, administrative capacity, procedural rules, and costs.

5. THE EMERGING COMPETITIVE LEGAL TRADITIONS OF AFRICAN REGIONAL ARBITRATION CENTRES

There has been a proliferation of international arbitral institutions in Africa over the past two decades. Most African states have established some form of framework for arbitration. Approximately 87 arbitration institutions of various sizes and located in different parts of Africa offer arbitration services.[92] This progress is laudable, especially across a continent comprising 55 states, since it reflects the rise of indigenous and competitive arbitration centres throughout Africa. Nonetheless, this multiplicity of arbitral bodies within the continent could very easily become the Achilles heel of arbitration in Africa, particularly where there exists a deficiency of cooperation and coordination between these institutions, with every institution striving to surpass the other. The Chinese-Africa Joint Arbitration Centre (CAJAC) represents a collaborative initiative that enhances competitiveness.The 2020 SOAS,University of London Arbitration in Africa Survey Report identified five key arbitral centres chosen by respondents. These are the Arbitration Foundation of Southern Africa (AFSA) in South Africa, the Cairo Regional Centre for International Commercial Arbitration in Egypt, the Kigali International Arbitration Centre in Rwanda, the Lagos Court of Arbitration in Nigeria, and the Nairobi Centre for International Arbitration in Kenya.[93] The Ouagadougou Arbitration and Mediation & Conciliation Centre (OAMCC) in Burkina Faso was also ranked among the top five arbitral institutions by an independent coding exercise. This subsection discusses the five key arbitral institutions, assessing their structure, rules, and activities since their establishment.

[91] Global Arbitration Review (GAR), 'White List/Institutions Worth a Closer Look- Middle East & Africa' (2021) https://globalarbitrationreview.com/survey/the-guide-regional-arbitration/2025/article/white-list-institutions-worth-closer-look-middle-east-africa.

[92] Herbert Smith Freehills, '2016 ICC Dispute Resolution Statistics: Record Year for the ICC, Arbitration notes' (15 September 2017) hsfnotes.com/arbitration/2017/09/15/2016-icc-dispute-resolution-statistics-record-year-for-the-icc/.

[93] Emiilia Onyema, '2020 Arbitration in Africa Survey Report: Top African Arbitral Centres and Seats' (30 June 30 2020), <https://eprints.soas.ac.uk/33162/1/2020%20Arbitration%20in%20Africa%20Survey%20Report%2030.06.2020.pdf.> accessed 24 November 2021.

5.1 Arbitration Foundation of Southern Africa (AFSA)

As mentioned above, the compelling requirements of international trade, investment, and finance have prompted many African countries to subscribe to international arbitration through various mechanisms, including the creation of centres such as AFSA.[94] AFSA was established in 1996 as a non-profit partnership venture by legal, business, and accounting professionals to develop the most effective process for resolving private disputes.[95] Its headquarters are in Johannesburg, South Africa. It manages and administers a wide range of local and international disputes through mediation, adjudication, arbitration, and other related processes. AFSA has handled 4134 cases between 1996 and 2020.[96] South Africa's international arbitration has increased after it promulgated a new statute in 2017. South Africa signed the New York Convention in 1976; however, its Arbitration Act No. 42 was criticised for lacking teeth and thus limiting international arbitration.[97]

The South African Arbitration Act No. 42 of 1965 gave municipal courts discretionary powers to hinder the arbitration process. In response to demands from the international arbitration community, South Africa's parliament passed a new Arbitration Act No.15 of 2017. Act 42 of 1965 still governs domestic arbitrations.[98] The 2017 Act adopts the UNCITRAL Model Law on International Commercial Arbitration as the cornerstone of international arbitration.[99] This UNCITRAL model law adoption appeals to parties who have already used the model law because it gives a recognisable structure for arbitration.

Further, the 2017 Act requires an arbitration agreement and international arbitral award to be recognised and enforced as required by the New York Convention.[100] The International Arbitration Act empowers the courts to support arbitration when needed but limits court interference. These reforms have enhanced international commercial arbitration in South Africa by creating an environment that protects the arbitration process from domestic litigation. The AFSA released its draft International Arbitration Rules in August 2020. These arbitral rules are specifically intended to entice parties to choose the AFSA. Expectedly, the AFSA rules incorporate methods developed by prominent global arbitration centres. They attempt to strike a careful balance on

[94] Samuel KB.Asante, 'The Perspectives of African Countries on International Commercial Arbitration' (1993) 6 *Leiden JIL* 331, 336.

[95] AFSA, 'A Brief History' arbitration.co.za/history/.

[96] Emilia Onyema (n 89) 12.

[97] Stephan Wilske, 'Why South Africa Should Update its International Arbitration Legislation – An Appeal from the International Arbitration Community for Legal Reform in South Africa' (2011) 28 *Journal of International Arbitration* 1.

[98] Danika Balusik, 'The Know How to Enforcing Foreign Arbitration Awards in South Africa' (*Kluwer Arbitration Blog* 17 February 2019) arbitrationblog.kluwerarbitration.com/2019/02/17/the-know-how-to-enforcing-foreign-arbitration-awards-in-south-africa/.

[99] ibid.

[100] International Arbitration Act No 15 of 2017.

sensitive issues, such as expedited procedures, early dismissal, confidentiality versus transparency, and third-party funding.[101] They also allow distance hearings, effectively reflecting post-COVID realities.

5.2 Cairo Regional Centre for International Commercial Arbitration (CRCICA)

CRCICA is Africa's oldest arbitral organisation, established by the Asian-African Legal Consultative Committee (AALCC) in its 19th session.[102] The AALC was founded in 1956, following the Bandung Conference, and is an intergovernmental organisation comprising 43 countries from Asia and Africa.[103] AALCC dispute settlement concerns arose from the need for a fair method to resolve business disputes within the emerging international economic order.[104] It had been noted that economic disputes in developing countries were settled through arbitration under the auspices of private institutions or chambers of commerce in the West.[105] AALCC's promotion of African international arbitration centres thus aligns with this chapter's view that these centres should be actively promoted to counter the strong influence of global and influential arbitration centres, such as the ICC and LCIA.

At its 1974 Tokyo session, the AALCC decided to develop institutional arbitration in Asia and Africa to limit the flow of disputes to arbitral centres outside these regions. At the 1978 Doha session, the AALCC decided to establish three centres: one in Kuala Lumpur, one in Cairo, and another in an African country to be determined after consultation with the relevant governments.[106] The AALCC's dispute settlement scored two goals through the establishment of these regional centres: first, a system through which disputes arising out of transactions in which both parties belong to the Asian-African region could

[101] Alon Meyerov and Giles Hutt, 'Arbitration in South Africa Receives Another Boost' (*Kluwer Arbitration Blog* 14 August 2020), arbitrationblog.kluwerarbitration.com/2020/08/14/arbitration-in-south-africa-receives-another-boost/.

[102] Regional Centre for International Commercial Arbitration Cairo, 'Arbitration Under the Auspices of the Cairo Regional Centre' (1987) 2 *Arab Law Quarterly* (1987) 185 www.jstor.org/stable/i276430.

[103] Asian African Legal Consultative Organization, 'Member States' www.aalco.int/Members (Bahrain; Bangladesh; People's Republic of China; Brunei Darussalam; Cameroon; Cyprus; Arab Republic of Egypt; Gambia; Ghana; India; Indonesia; Islamic Republic of Iran; Iraq; Japan; Jordan; Kenya; Democratic People's Republic of Korea; Republic of Korea; Kuwait; Lebanon; Libya; Malaysia; Mauritius; Mongolia; Myanmar; Nepal; Nigeria; Oman; Pakistan; State of Palestine; Qatar; Republic of Philippines; Saudi Arabia; Senegal; Sierra Leone; Singapore; Somalia; South Africa, Sri Lanka; Sudan; Syria; Tanzania; Thailand; Republic of Türkiye; Uganda; Socialist Republic of Vietnam; and Republic of Yemen).

[104] Amazu A Asouzu, *International Commercial Arbitration and African States: Practice, Participation and Institutional Development* (Cambridge University Press, 2001) 3.

[105] Regional Centre for International Commercial Arbitration Cairo, 'Arbitration Under the Auspices of the Cairo Regional Centre' 190.

[106] ibid at 191.

be settled under fair, inexpensive and adequate procedures;[107] and second, they encourage parties to have their arbitrations in the region where the investment is made, if it involves a country in the region.[108]

On January 28, 1978, Egypt and the AALCC agreed to establish the Regional Centre for International Arbitration in Cairo, providing financial and other facilities for a period of three years. The agreement was renewed several times between 1978 and 1986. The CRCICA was established as a non-profit entity to provide a method for resolving trade and investment disputes within the region. The CRCICA uses the 1976 UNCITRAL Arbitration Rules with some modifications. The Centre has international autonomy and enjoys privileges accorded to other international organisations.[109] English, French and Arabic are the Centre's official languages.[110] In 2018, 70 per cent of CRCICA cases were in Arabic, and 30 per cent were in English. CRCICA's ability to conduct arbitral procedures in Arabic makes it a good choice for Middle Eastern parties contracting in Africa. CRCICA ranks among Africa's top five arbitral institutes, having handled 1,385 cases as of 2019, including 82 new cases. By 2020, CRCICA had handled 1408 cases.

5.3 Kigali International Arbitration Centre (KIAC)

In 2011, KIAC was established by Law No. 51/2010, being Rwanda's only trade arbitration institution.[111] It has a broad mandate to resolve economic disputes. The KIAC's board is comprised of seven members appointed by professional associations.[112]The 2020 Arbitration in Africa Survey Report states that KIAC has handled 137 cases since its inception in 2011.[113] KIAC funds its operations through contributions from regional and international stakeholders, user fees and charges, gifts and grants from donors, and government grants as needed.[114]

The government is only marginally involved in funding KIAC activities, although it strongly promotes an investor-friendly climate in Rwanda.[115] On May 5, 2015, the Rwandan Government ordered that KIAC arbitrate any disputes concerning the government, unless the Minister of Justice/Attorney

[107] S A F Haridi and others, 'The Cairo Regional Centre for International Commercial Arbitration (CRICA) Newly Revised Arbitration Rules'; Incorporating the New UNICTRAL Model Rules of 2010 and expanding the Centre's Role as an Appointing Authority, 8 *TDM* 1, 3 (2011)

[108] Regional Centre for International Commercial Arbitration Cairo (n 101).

[109] Statute of the Regional Centre for International Commercial Arbitration at Cairo, art 2(1).

[110] ibid, art 20.

[111] Article 5, Law N°51/2010 of 10/01/2010 establishing the Kigali International Arbitration Centre and determining its organisation, functioning and competence – via Official Gazette n°09 bis of 28/02/2011 kiac.org.rw/wp-content/uploads/2023/06/The-Law-Establishing-the-KIAC.pdf.

[112] Article 4, Law N°51/2010 of 10/01/2010.

[113] Onyema (n 89).

[114] Article 18, Law N°51/2010 of 10/01/2010.

[115] Fidèle Masengo, 'A regional success story: the development of arbitration in Rwanda' (*Herbert Smith Freehills* 1 February 2017).

General opined otherwise.[116] To attract cases, KIAC regulations reduce party expenses and empower emergency arbitrators to award interim relief before the arbitral panel is assembled.

KIAC provides parties with the flexibility to choose between its institutional rules and UNCITRAL's rules. KIAC institutional rules are a compendium of provisions from the ICC, LCIA, and SIAC rules. Accession to the New York Convention is a criterion in determining the seat of arbitration. Rwanda joined the New York Convention on November 3, 2008, and ratified it on January 29, 2009. KIAC Rules include party autonomy and enhanced party control over the arbitration process, from the choice of seat to the relevant rules of procedure, the separability of the arbitration agreement, competence-competence, and limited state court interference in arbitration.

The KIAC rules also provide that the doctrine of separability applies to its arbitration. The doctrine recognises that the arbitration clause survives the contract, which is crucial in effectuating the parties' intent.[117] Rwandan courts have recognised the limited involvement of courts in the arbitral process. In *Minani Valens. v Cogebanque Ltd,* the Commercial Court of Nyarugenge cited article 10 of the Rwandan Arbitration Law and held that: 'Minani Valens and Cogebanque Ltd agreed to refer any dispute arising from their contract to arbitration, and therefore the court does not have jurisdiction to entertain the disputes arising from the contract containing an arbitration clause'.[118]

5.4 Lagos Court of Arbitration (LCA)

The LCA was established by an Act of Parliament under the Lagos Court of Arbitration Law No. 17 of 2009 to provide institutionalised arbitration and ADR services.[119] The LCA was launched on November 9, 2012, and is headquartered at the International Centre for Arbitration and ADR (ICAA), which also houses the Chartered Institute of Arbitrators (UK) Nigeria Branch, the Chartered Institute of Arbitrators Nigeria, the Lagos Chamber of Commerce International Arbitration Centre, and the Maritime Arbitration Association of Nigeria.[120] When selecting an arbitration institution, parties may look for well-equipped physical and technological facilities, which the ICCA provides.

The LCA Law No. 17 of 2009 established its institutional framework. The LCA, however, is independent of government supervision and interference.

[116] Dieudonné Nzafashwanayo, 'Arbitration Proceedings before the Kigali International Arbitration Centre' (24 November 2018) 4 ssrn.com/abstract=3289963. See *Minani Valens v Cogebanque Ltd*, R. com 1173/14/TC/Nyge, 05/01/2015.

[117] Jeremy Cantor, 'Rwanda and the Kigali International Arbitration Centre: The Future face of East African Arbitration and Growth' (2017) 19 *CJCR* 93, 110.

[118] Nzafashwanayo (n 112) para 8.

[119] Lagos Court of Arbitration Law No. 17 of 2009, art 1(1).

[120] Lagos Court of Arbitration Home of dispute resolution (26 February 2016) www.lca.org.ng.

Grants, membership fees, and dispute resolution services fund its operation and services.[121] The LCA has a three-tiered structure: the General Meeting of registered members, who pay annual dues; the Board of Directors, comprising 15 respected ADR specialists led by the President; and the Secretariat, led by the Executive Secretary. The LCA is also partly funded by ADR users who subscribe annually.[122]

The LCA Arbitration Rules are modelled on UNCITRAL's arbitration rules. The UNCITRAL model laws provide for the successful enforcement of arbitral awards, as courts can only refuse enforcement in limited circumstances. An essential element in selecting a seat is ensuring that the country has a supportive arbitration law and a supportive but non-interventionist judiciary.[123]The Nigerian Court of Appeal in *Nigerian National Petroleum Corporation v. Statoil (Nigeria) Limited and Others* refused to terminate arbitral proceedings because doing so would undermine the parties' agreement to arbitrate the dispute.[124]

5.5 Nairobi Centre for International Arbitration (NCIA)

The NCIA was created in 2013 by an Act of Parliament (NCIA Act).[125] The NCIA promotes, supports, and stimulates international commercial arbitration in conformity with the Act; manages domestic and international arbitrations and alternative dispute resolution approaches; and creates conciliation and mediation regulations.[126] The Centre consists of a Board of Directors made up of East African professionals who appoint a Registrar to oversee the day-to-day operations of the Centre.[127] The Act also establishes an Arbitral Court that has exclusive original and appellate jurisdiction to hear matters referred to it under the Act.[128] The court consists of a President, two Deputy-Presidents, a Registrar, and 15 leading international arbitrators.[129]

The NCIA's arbitration rules and the Kenyan Arbitration Act, 1995, are modelled on the 1985 UNCITRAL Model Law. Kenya's 1995 Arbitration Act specifies that international arbitration awards are binding and enforced according to the New York Convention or any other agreement Kenya has signed.

[121] Megha Joshi, 'National Arbitration Institutions/Centres: Lagos Court of Arbitration – International Centre for Arbitration and ADR' in The Role of Arbitration Institutions in the Development of Arbitration in Africa at Arbitration Institutions in Africa Conference, 23 July 2015.

[122] Law N°51/2010 of 10/01/2010, art 2.

[123] Cantor (n 113) 108.

[124] Stuart Dutson, '"Africa's Century" – The Rise of International Arbitration in Africa and what it means for users of Arbitral Institutions in Africa' in The Role of Arbitration Institutions in the Development of Arbitration in Africa at Arbitration Institutions in Africa Conference, 23 July 2015. eprints.soas.ac.uk/20421/1/Addis%20Arbitration%20Conference%202015.pdf.

[125] National Centre for International Arbitration Act No 26 of 2013, s 2.

[126] National Centre for International Arbitration Act No 26 of 2013, s 5.

[127] ibid, s 9.

[128] ibid, s 21.

[129] ibid.

This recognition reflects Kenya's commitment to a legal framework that favours international arbitration, which may attract arbitration disputes to the country. Judicialised arbitration needs enforceable awards.[130] In 2015, 65 per cent of respondents claimed award enforceability influenced arbitration seat choice.

The NCIA functions through dispute resolution, government grants, and public donations. Government money is the NCIA's main source of funding. Dispute settlement and public donations contribute little to its activities and expenses. This funding structure might easily cripple the NCIA if government financing is withheld. It may also reflect government involvement in NCIA activities, hindering dispute resolution. The Kenyan Arbitration Act limits the intervention of national courts in arbitration procedures, except for the recognition of awards and their execution.[131]

5.6 Chinese Africa Joint Arbitration Centre (CAJAC)

Although African states have contributed to the development of several arbitral systems, the main centres of international arbitration were established long before these states gained independence.[132] In 2015, China and 50 African states, represented by the Forum of Chinese African Cooperation (FOCAC), adopted the Johannesburg Action Plan and decided to establish CAJAC in South Africa. Its primary role is to resolve international disputes between Chinese and African entities based in China or on the African continent.[133]

CAJAC is the umbrella institution housing the accredited Centres in China and Africa, providing mediation, conciliation, and arbitration to resolve disputes presented by the parties. These centres include:

(i) CAJAC Johannesburg (AFSA);
(ii) Nairobi Centre for International Arbitration's CAJAC (NCIA);
(iii) Beijing International Arbitration Centre's CAJAC (BIAC);
(iv) Shanghai International Arbitration Centre's CAJAC (SHIAC) and
(v) Shenzhen International Court of Arbitration CAJAC (SCIA).[134]

CAJAC uses a shared panel to ensure parties have the same choice of arbitrators. CAJAC arbitrators have diverse knowledge and are conversant in Chinese and African cultures. When investing in Africa, China faces distinct legal systems, cultural disparities, linguistic obstacles, political instability, and the continent's image as corrupt and uncivilised. This move is arguably an impressive stride in

[130] Wilfred Mutubwa, 'The Making of an International Arbitration Hub: A Critical Appraisal of the Nairobi Centre for International Arbitration Act 2013' (2016) 82 *IJLA* 135,140.

[131] National Centre for International Arbitration Act No 26 of 2013, s 10.

[132] Samuel K B Asante, 'The Perspectives of African Countries on International Commercial Arbitration' (1993) 6 *Leiden JIL* 331, 335.

[133] CAJAC Rules, art 1.

[134] CAJAC Rules, Appendix A.

arbitration, as it will allow conflicts to be resolved swiftly and within the context in which they arise.[135]

6. CONCLUSION

This chapter has argued that the judicialised form of arbitration emerged in Europe and is slowly spreading to Africa. The lesser version of judicialisation of arbitration emerged with the strengthening of the powers of nation states. The chapter has demonstrated how a system with minimal state regulation gradually developed into a highly judicialised governance system in the twenty-first century. The chapter traced the origins of arbitration as a non-judicialised reputational mode of dispute settlement among medieval European merchants. The system bore all the advantages of what in the twenty-first century could be considered an effective legal system: it was expeditious, harnessed specific expertise, was cheap for its users and possessed high levels of compliance. Over the centuries, other normpreneurs, especially holders of transnational capital, gradually worked towards the judicialisation of arbitration to favour them and protect their capital. This move was led by the International Chamber of Commerce (ICC), now one of the world's leading international arbitration centres.

Taken together, this history of ICC demonstrates that its arbitration regime is best understood not as neutral technical facilitator of dispute settlement, but as historically situated institution embedded in particular political, economic, and sociological projects. From its origins in post-war efforts to stabilise capitalist hegemony, through its role in codifying mercantile norms and judicialising arbitration, the ICC has exercised significant normative power under the guise of private ordering and consent. Its institutionalisation of arbitration, especially the scrutiny of awards and the entrenchment of reason-giving, has profoundly reshaped arbitral practice, aligning it more closely with the legal profession and the broader legal habitus. For African sub-regional economic courts and tribunals, the decision to conform to these established frameworks reflects not merely technical choice but ideological alignment with a global dispute settlement model whose developmental promises remain empirically uncertain. This historical and structural context is essential for understanding both the appeal and the limitations of judicialised arbitration as it has been transplanted into African regional economic governance.

Furthermore, the evolution of IACs is driven by two primary forces: the commercial marketization of arbitral justice and the development of legitimising legal doctrines. As these centers compete globally to offer efficient administrative dispute settlement services. There have traditionally been dominated by Global North cities like London and Paris but increasingly challenged

[135] The Arbitration Brief, '*Chinese Africa Joint Arbitration Center: A solution to trade disputes between Africa and China*' (2019) thearbitrationbrief.com/2019/02/11/chinese-africa-joint-arbitration-center-a-solution-to-trade-disputes-between-africa-and-china%EF%BB%BF/.

by Asian hubs like Singapore and Hong Kong. These IACs simultaneously rely on "invented traditions" such as *Kompetenz-Kompetenz* and separability to maintain autonomy from domestic judicial interference. Ultimately, this synergy between competitive market dynamics and protective legal frameworks allows arbitration centers to solidify their roles as essential, self-regulating fixtures in the global resolution of commercial disputes. Increasingly, the rise of modern arbitration centers across Africa signals a shift toward a more multipolar competitive market. Even though the face and continue to face fierce competition from the more established Global North and Asian IACs their rise is a welcome and enviable development that also shows the diversification of the global arbitration scene.

ANNEX I

Table 3 List of Arbitration Centres in Africa:

	Institution	**Location**	**Date Established**
1	Center de médiation et d'arbitrage de la Chambre algérienne de commerce et d'industrie	Algeria, Algiers	2003
2	Center de médiation et d'arbitrage d'Annaba	Algeria, Annaba	
3	Centre for Extra-Judicial Resolution of Disputes (CREL)	Angola	
4	Angolan Centre for Arbitration of Disputes	Angola	
5	CEFA Arbitration Centre	Angola	
6	Harmonia Dispute Resolution Centre	Angola	
7	Arbitral Juris	Angola	
8	Centre for Mediation and Arbitration of Angola	Angola	
9	Mediation and Arbitration Centre of the Angolan Industrial Association	Angola	
10	Center d'arbitrage de médiation et de conciliation (CAMeC) de la Chambre de commerce et d'industrie du Bénin	Benin, Cotonou	2003
11	Chambre de conciliation et d'arbitrage de l'Association interprofessionnelle du coton	Benin, Cotonou	2003

(Continued)

Table 3 (*Continued*)

	Institution	Location	Date Established
12	EV Arbitrage & Mediation Cotonou	Benin	
13	Center d'Arbitrage, de Médiation et de Conciliation de Ouagadougou (CAMC-O) de la Chambre de Commerce, d'Industrie et d'Artisanat	Burkina Faso, Ouagadougou	2005
14	Botswana Institute of Arbitrators	Botswana	1999
15	Burundi Center for Arbitration & Mediation	Burundi	2007
16	Center d'arbitrage du GICAM (Groupement interpatronal du Cameroun)	Cameroon, Douala,	2005
17	Le Center Permanent d'Arbitrage et de Médiation du CADEV (CPAM), Yaounde	Cameroon, Yaounde	
18	Center d'Arbitrage, de Mediation et de Conciliation de Centrafrique (CAMC-CA),	Central African Republic, Bangui	
19	Centre d'Arbitrage et de mediation attached to the Brazzaville Chamber of Commerce, Industry, Agriculture and Jobs,	Chad	2016
20	Centre d'Arbitrage et de mediation attached to the Brazzaville Chamber of Commerce, Industry, Agriculture and Jobs, Libreville	Congo	
21	Center de mediation et d'arbitrage au Congo	Congo	2014
22	Cour commune de justice et d'arbitrage de l'Organisation pour l'harmonisation en Afrique du droit des affaires (OHADA)	Cote d'Ivoire, Abidjan	1993
23	Cour d'Arbitrage de Côte d'Ivoire (CACI)	Cote d'Ivoire, Abidjan	1997
24	Center de mediation et d'arbitrage au Congo	Congo	2014

	Institution	Location	Date Established
25	Center National d'Arbitrage, de Conciliation et de Médiation (CENACOM)	Democratic Republic of Congo	2004
26	Center d'arbitrage du Congo (CAC)	Democratic Republic of Congo, Kinshasa	2003
27	Intergovernmental Authority on Development (IGAD) Business Arbitration Centre	Djibouti	2016
28	Cairo Regional Centre for International Commercial Arbitration	Egypt, Cairo	1979
29	Dr. A. Kheir Law & Arbitration Centre (AKLAC)	Egypt, Cairo	1994
30	Sharm El Sheikh International Arbitration Centre	Egypt, Sharm El Sheikh	1994
31	The Egyptian Arbitration and Mediation Centre	Egypt	
32	The Egyptian Centre for Voluntary Arbitration and the Settlement of Non-Banking, Financial Disputes	Egypt	
33	Conciliation, Mediation and Arbitration Commission (CMAC)	Eswatini, Mbabane	2000
34	Addis Ababa Chamber of Commerce & Sectorial Association [AACCSA] Arbitration Institute	Ethiopia, Addis Ababa	2002
35	Center d'Arbitrage, de Mediation et de Conciliation (CAMC-GA)	Gabon	2011
36	Ghana Arbitration Center	Ghana	1997
37	Ghana Association of Certified Mediators & Arbitrators (GHACMA)	Ghana, Accra	
38	Copyright Office Ghana Arbitration Center	Ghana, Accra	
39	Ghana ADR Hub	Ghana	
40	Arbitration Center Chambre d'Arbitrage de la Guinee	Guinea, Conakry	

(Continued)

Table 3 (*Continued*)

	Institution	Location	Date Established
41	Nairobi Center for International Arbitration (NCIA)	Kenya, Nairobi	2013
42	Strathmore Dispute Resolution Center (SDRC)	Kenya, Nairobi	2012
43	The Directorate of dispute Prevention and Resolution (DDPR)	Lesotho, Maseru	2001
44	Liberia Chamber of Commerce	Liberia,	1951
45	Center Libyen de Médiation et d'Arbitrage	Libya, Tripoli	2004
46	Libyan Center for International Commercial Arbitration	Libya	
47	Center d'arbitrage et de médiation de Madagascar (CAMM)	Madagascar, Antananarivo	2001
48	Agricultural Commodity Exchange for Africa	Malawi	
49	Center de conciliation et d'arbitrage du Mali (CECAM-CCIM)	Mali, Bamako	
50	Arbitration and Mediation Centre (MARC) of the Mauritius Chamber of Commerce & Industry (MCCI)	Mauritius	1996
51	Mauritius International Arbitration Centre (MIAC)	Mauritius, Port-Louis	2011
52	Permanent Court of Arbitration at the Mauritius Chamber of Commerce and Industry	Mauritius, Port-Louis	1996
53	Center de conciliation et d'arbitrage d'Agadir (CCISA)	Morocco, Agadir	
54	Casablanca International Mediation and Arbitration Center (CIMAC)	Morocco, Casablanca	2016
55	Center de Médiation et Arbitrage, created by the Chambre de Commerce d'Industrie et de Services de Casablanca	Morocco, Casablanca	2001
56	Center international de médiation et d'arbitrage de Rabat (CIMAR)	Morocco, Rabat	1999
57	Centro de Arbitragem, Conciliação e Mediação (CACM)	Mozambique, Maputo	2002

	Institution	Location	Date Established
58	Center de Mediation et d'Arbitrage de Niamey (CMAN) attached to the Niger Chambre de Commerce, d'Industrie et d'Artisan	Niger	2014
59	Regional Centre for International Commercial Arbitration	Nigeria, Lagos	1989
60	Maritime Arbitrators Association of Nigeria (MANN)	Nigeria	2005
61	Lagos Court of Arbitration Centre	Nigeria	2012
62	International Centre for Arbitration & Mediation, Abuja (ICAMA)	Nigeria	2012
63	Lagos Chamber of Commerce International Arbitration Centre (LACIAC)	Nigeria	2014
64	Janada International Centre for Arbitration & Mediation	Nigeria	
65	Kigali International Arbitration Centre (KIAC)	Rwanda	2011
66	Center d'arbitrage de la Chambre de commerce, d'industrie et d'agriculture de Dakar	Senegal, Dakar	1998
67	Arbitration Foundation of Southern Africa (AFSA)	South Africa, Johannesburg	1996
68	Equillore Group	South Africa	1997
69	The Association of Arbitrators	South Africa	1979
70	Commission for Conciliation, Mediation and Arbitration	South Africa, Johannesburg	1995
71	Tokiso Dispute Settlement Pty Ltd	South Africa	2001
72	China-Africa Joint Arbitration Centre	South Africa, Johannesburg	2015
73	South Sudan Chamber of Commerce, Industry & Agriculture, Juba.	South Sudan	2005
74	Arabic Centre for Arbitration	Sudan	2007
75	International Chamber of Arbitration	Sudan	

(Continued)

Table 3 (*Continued*)

	Institution	Location	Date Established
76	The Sudanese Centre for Conciliation & Arbitration	Sudan	2006
77	The National Construction Council	Tanzania, Dar es Salaam	1981
78	East African Court of Justice (Arbitration Institution)	Tanzania, Arusha	2001
79	Tanzania Institute of Arbitrators (TIA)	Tanzania, Dar es Salaam	1999
80	Center de conciliation et d'arbitrage de Tunis	Tunisia, Tunis	1996
81	Al Insaf Local and International Arbitration Centre	Tunisia, Tunis	
82	Arbitration Court CATO,	Togo, Lome	2011
83	Centre for Arbitration & Dispute Resolution (CADER)	Uganda	2000
84	Centre for Arbitration & Dispute Resolution (CADER)	Zambia	2001
85	Commercial Arbitration Centre in Harare	Zimbabwe, Harare	1995
86	Africa Institute of Arbitration and Mediation	Zimbabwe, Harare	2013
87	Alternative Dispute Solutions Centre	Zimbabwe, Harare	2020

7

The Three Main Emerging Transnational Actors within the African International Arbitration Scene

I. INTRODUCTION

CURRENT INTERNATIONAL LAW SCHOLARSHIP focuses on international law as a professional enterprise around four main themes or strands. The first is the fragmentation of international law (including the 'invisible college').[1] This theme focuses on the origins, increased, and continuing role of international lawyers in shaping and reshaping the contours of international law.[2] International lawyers thus serve as intermediaries between law, politics, and global governance.[3] This theme also romanticises the role of international lawyers as guardians of international affairs in pursuit of the noble goals of peace and the well-being of humankind.[4] However, its earliest proponent conceded that the international lawyer profession serves a *'dédoublement fonctionnel'*, ie 'jurists move from one functional role to another, each with different

[1] *See* Martti Koskenniemi, 'Fragmentation of International Law: Difficulties Arising from the Diversification and Expansion of International Law' (Report of the Study Group of the International Law Commission, International Law Commission, UN Doc A/CN.4/L.682, 13 April, 2006); *see also* Jose E Alvarez, 'The Democratization of the Invisible College' (*American Society of International Law Post: President's Column*, 8 November 2007); David Kennedy, 'The Politics of the Invisible College: International Governance and the Politics of Expertise (2001) 5 *EHRLR* 463; *see also* Oscar Schachter, 'Invisible College of International Lawyers' (1977-1978) 72 *North Western University School of Law Review* 217 (he was arguably the first to coin the use of the metaphor 'invisible college of international lawyers').

[2] Wounter Werner, Marieke de Hoon, and Alexis Galán, 'Introduction: The Law of International Lawyers' in Wouter Werner, Marieke de Hoon and Alexis Galán (eds), *The Law of International Law: Reading Martti Koskenniemi* (Cambridge University Press, 2017)3; *see also* Martti Koskenniemi, *From Apology to Utopia – The Structure of International Legal Argument* (Cambridge University Press, 2005) 569.

[3] Martti Koskenniemi, International Law as "Global Governance" in Searching For Contemporary Legal Thought (Cambridge University Press, 2017) 199.

[4] *Compare* Martti Koskenniemi, 'Legal Cosmopolitanism: Tom Franck's Massianic World' (2003) 35 *NYU J Intl L & Pol* 471 (arguing that both indeterminacy of cosmopolitan values and their dependence on institutional arrangements as weaknesses and suggests that cosmopolitanism is utopian and a facade). Suggests that cosmopolitanism is utopian and a facade.

perspectives and frames of reference'.[5] The fragmentation of international law into different specialised subareas or subdisciplines has fractured the initial vision of a unified field of international lawyers pursuing cosmopolitan aims.[6]

The second theme is the 'club' or 'mafia' idea in international arbitration.[7] This theme already concedes a fragmented international law and focuses on a specific field of international law. It argues that international arbitration is composed of a few recurring names of arbitrators forming a part of the 'grand old men'.[8] Previously, this group consisted entirely of men, but it has recently included a select few women, who are predominantly white.[9] A 2012 report furthered this theme by showing that just 15 per cent of arbitrators, nearly all from Europe, the US, and Canada, had decided over 55 per cent of all known Investor-State Dispute Settlements (ISDS).[10] The report refers to this small group of heavily interconnected, cohesive international lawyers as an 'inner mafia' that acts as arbitrators, counsels, and even calls on each other as witnesses in arbitration.[11] A negative response to this labelling of an 'inner mafia' argues that the reference is an overstatement that ignores and dismisses the general dynamics of many social networks, including the arbitrator network.[12] This view dismisses the mafia tag since the group lacks a level of coordinative mastermind, with the arbitrators' network resulting from different actors behaving rationally and independently in a convenient and constantly evolving environment.[13] Despite the dismissal, the 'mafia' tag is used by detractors and by members of the inner circle of the relatively small and tight-knit arbitration community.[14]

[5] Oscar Schachter, 'The Role of the Institute of International Law and its Methods of Work – Today and Tomorrow' in Institut De Droit International (ed), *Livre Du Cententainaire 1873–1973, Évolution Et Perspectives Du Droit International* (S Karger, 1973)403–451; Schachter, 'Invisible College of International Lawyers' (n 1) (arguing that the mingling of the scholarly and the official often creates tension as individuals move from one role to another or perceive themselves as acting in the dual capacity of objective scientist and government advocate).

[6] *See* Sean D Murphy, 'Deconstructing Fragmentation: Koskenniemi's 2006 ILC Project' (2013) 27 *Temp Int'l & Comp LJ* 293.

[7] Yves Dezalay and Bryant G Garth, *Dealing in Virtue: International Commercial Arbitration and the Construction of a Transnational Legal Order* (University of Chicago Press,1996) 10; Sergio Puig, 'Social Capital in the Arbitration Marketplace' (2014) 25 *EJIL* 423.

[8] Dezalay and Garth (n 7) 10–11

[9] Andrea K Bjoklund and others, 'The Diversity Deficit in International Investment Arbitration' (2020) 21 *JWIT* 410 (arguing that a study (including a sample period up to 2017) covering arbitrators in ICSID as well as non-ICSID cases found that 11 per cent of arbitrators were female. Yet two women – Gabrielle Kaufmann-Kohler and Brigitte Stern – account for 57 per cent of all appointments given to female arbitrators); *see* Daniel Behn, Malcolm Langford and Laura Létourneau-Tremblay, 'Empirical Perspectives on Investment Arbitration: What do We Know? Does it Matter?' 21 (2020) *JWIT* 188.

[10] Pia Eberhardt and Cecilia Olivet, 'Profiting From Injustice: How Law Firms, Arbitrators And Financiers are Fuelling An Investment Arbitration Boom (2012), www.tni.org/files/download/profitingfrominjustice.pdf.

[11] ibid.

[12] Puig (n 7).

[13] ibid.

[14] Sara Dezalay and Yves Dezalay, 'From the Shadow of State Diplomacy to the Pull of the Market for Commercial Arbitration' in Jean d'Aspermont and others, *International Law as a Profession* (Cambridge University Press, 2017) 311.

The third theme is 'the international bar' in the International Court of Justice (ICJ).[15] Scholars who have explored this theme have found that most practitioners in the ICJ are academics (59 per cent). Of the inner circle of 17 lawyers who had appeared more than four times, over 70 per cent were academics.[16] Additionally, the studies under this theme have found that counsel before the ICJ during oral proceedings are overwhelmingly men from developed countries who are usually professors of public international law.[17] These men are the core of the 'ICJ Bar', which is well dominated by UK- and French-based academics.[18] The ICJ bar thus consists of individuals, mostly men from the global North,

> who have practised and continue to practice as oral advocates before the court. They represent a variety of foreign states other than their own governments. They are well-known to the judges and Registrar of the court, who know how things work out in practice, and who understand by experience the trade's difficulties, pitfalls, and tricks.[19]

Some studies' conclusions on numbers are surprisingly low for an international organisation of the ICJ's magnitude. One study concluded that the ICJ Bar comprises only 17 lawyers (8 per cent of the 205 lawyers studied), who accounted for 42 per cent of the court's speaking time. One of them was the academic Alain Pellet, who accounted for 10 per cent of all oral arguments before the court between 1999 and 2012.[20]

The fourth stream of scholarship complicates challenges and further clarifies the three themes above. It is a sociologically grounded account that views the three strands of scholarship above as obfuscating rather than clarifying the origins of developments in international dispute settlement.[21] This account seeks to explain the evolutions that have produced and legitimised the perceived polarisation in the ICJ between the public form of justice dealing with inter-state disputes and the private or hybrid form dealing with ISDS and international commercial arbitration.[22] This account argues that the three themes above also complicate the growing connections between the two poles of international justice, specifically state-to-state dispute settlement and private and public international arbitration.[23] It views the increasing role of legal profes-

[15] Shashank Kumar and Cecily Rose, 'A Study of Lawyers Appearing Before the International Court of Justice, 1999–2012' (PIL, Grotius Centre Working Paper 2014); Kurt Taylor Gaubatz and Matthew MacArthur, 'How International Is International Law' (2001) 22 *Mich J Intl L* 239.

[16] Kumar and Rose (n 15); *see also* Anthea Roberts, *Is International Law International*? (Oxford University Press, 2017) 30.

[17] Shashank P Kumar and Cecily Rose, 'A Study of Lawyers Appearing Before the International Court of Justice, 1999–2012' (2014) 25 *EJIL* 893.

[18] ibid.

[19] Keith Highet, 'A Personal Memoir of Eduardo Jiménez de Aréchaga' (1994) 88 *ASIL Proc* 577, 579.

[20] Roberts (n 16) 118.

[21] Dezalay and Dezalay (n 14) 312.

[22] ibid.

[23] ibid.

sionals circulating between the two poles, or whose careers or positions span these two poles of international justice, as an appropriate explanation for the evolutions in international adjudication.[24] These circulating professionals are appointed ICJ judges and arbitrators in state-to-state disputes and ISDS. This multiple-appointments phenomenon has been described as 'double-hatting' and denounced by the ICJ (and its former President, Judge Abuldqawi Yusuf).[25] These scholars also point to the entry of multinational corporate law firms into the 'international bar' of the ICJ.[26]

The four strands above contribute to understanding the cartelisation of international legal practice.[27] However, most of this scholarship has not focused specifically on African international lawyers and arbitrators. Thus, the African marketplace of international professional dispute settlement analysis remains somewhat of a black box. This final chapter of this book aims to fill a small section of this gap by focusing on the three emerging transnational actors within the African arbitration scene: international lawyers, law firms, and law training institutions. Relying more on the fourth sociological account-based analysis, I argue that three different but interconnected transnational socio-legal actors are emerging in the field of African international arbitration. These three are: First, well-established and emerging arbitrators; second, African top-tier corporate law firms connecting regionally and globally; and finally, African arbitration training institutions and professional centres.

Importantly, all three actors have African international lawyers at their core. The three actors are increasingly interconnected, navigating, and intermediating the African international arbitration scene. These actors are essential in shaping how arbitration practice is both globalised and localised for various interested parties. Lawyers, law firms, and law training institutions in Africa are now intricately involved in shaping the market space and legitimacy of arbitration.[28] African lawyers strategically position themselves in influential positions using their social, legal, political, and economic capital to create powerful nodes of international arbitration governance.[29]

These lawyers can position themselves as either 'intermediary elites' or 'double agents'.[30] As 'double agents' in positions of power, they can balance the

[24] ibid.

[25] Speech By H E Mr. Abdulqawi A. Yusuf, President Of The International Court Of Justice, 'On The Occasion Of The Seventy-Fifth Session Of The United Nations General Assembly' (2 November 2020) 6–7 www.icj-cij.org/public/files/press-releases/0/000-20201102-STA-01-00-EN.pdf; *see also* Yasachandra Devarakonda, 'Restricting Double-Hatting to Safeguard International Arbitrations' (2022) 22 *Pepperdine Dispute Resolution LJ* 65.

[26] *See* Sara Dezalay, 'Law Firms and International Adjudication' in Hélène Ruiz Fabri (ed), *The Max Planck Encyclopedia of International Procedural Law* (Oxford University Press, 2021).

[27] Dezalay and Dezalay (n 14) 311.

[28] *See* Yves Dezalay and Bryant G Garth, 'Introduction' in Yves Dezalay and Bryant G Garth (eds), *Lawyers and the Rule of Law in an Era of Globalizaiton* (Routledge, 2011) 1–16.

[29] ibid 2.

[30] *See* Sara Dezalay, 'Lawyers in Africa: Brokers of the State, Intermediaries of Globalization: A Case Studt of the "Africa" Bar in Paris' (2018) 25 *Ind J Global Legal Stud* 639, 643.

influence of neo-colonial corporate transnational interests with the promotion of the rule of law through arbitration. As 'intermediary elites', lawyers help to structure, fix, and define private law doctrines and concepts that undergird arbitration.[31] In the highly judicialised format of arbitration described in the previous chapter, lawyers negotiate the contracts that submit cases to arbitration, represent parties in arbitration proceedings and are selected as arbitrators in arbitral proceedings. Lawyers are thus undeniably 'intermediaries' between the transnational elites who are the primary builders of capital and capitalism and the nation state. In their role as 'double agents', lawyers present the law as apolitical 'in order to distance themselves from politics, as a condition to protect the autonomy of the law, and with it their professional practices'.[32]

The chapter is divided into three sections; the first section starts with discussing the first limb of the three main emerging transnational actors within the African international arbitration scene: the well-established and emerging African arbitrators. This section profiles two African international lawyers as a representative sample of one of the chapter's arguments: that a core group of diversified African lawyers is emerging to animate the arbitration scene. These two are Egyptian academic, legal practitioner, and arbitrator Professor Mohamed Abdel Wahab and Kenyan Hague-based international lawyer and practitioner Ndanga Kamau. These two present the attributes of an oscillating group of arbitrators maintaining a strong presence in the global North while remaining deeply connected to power structures within African settings. They are more in line with the fourth sociological approach discussed in this introduction to international law professions, which occupy multiple spaces to influence their fields of engagement.

Section 2 carefully analyses the role of emerging top-tier corporate law firms in African international arbitration. The section argues that many large international corporate law firms are increasingly looking to Africa for internal collaboration and networking. They aim to acquire a slice of 'the Global Economy's last frontier.' African top-tier corporate law firms are also looking externally to international and regional law firms for similar needs. The result is a robust environment of collaboration, cooperation, and the merging of law firms in Africa. Accordingly, this chapter presents the following four models of collaboration and new developments among African corporate top-tier law firms: Foreign branches, Association with Local Firms, Networking Arrangements, and Boutique Arbitration Law firms.

The final section completes the discussion by analysing the third actor of the three main emerging transnational actors within the African international arbitration scene: African arbitration training institutions and professional centres. This section discusses two vital actors in the arbitration training scene: the

[31] *See* Ambreena Manji, *The Politics of Land Reform in Africa* (Zed Books Ltd, 2006), (presenting the role of lawyers in the global network of land reform).

[32] *See* Dezalay (n 30).

African Arbitration Academy (AAA) and the African Institute of International Law (AIIL). Within these two institutions, we see the concept of oscillating professionals resurface. Individuals discussed in the other sections also appear in this section through the increasing practice by the AAA and the East Africa International Arbitration Conference (EAIAC) of creating halls of fame, power lists, lists of promising arbitrators, and the Africa Arbitration Awards. I caution against this increasingly pervasive practice, which some commentators have condemned as the manufacturing of reputations.

2. THE WELL-ESTABLISHED AND EMERGING AFRICAN ARBITRATORS

One enduring attribute of seasoned African arbitrators is the maintenance of a strong presence in the global North while remaining deeply connected to power structures within African settings. Without this dual presence, these arbitrators cannot hold the required symbolic capital, ie, the social class, education, career, and expertise needed to influence the field.[33] One avenue to join this elite class of arbitrators is through connecting with and operating within major arbitral institutions, such as the ICC.[34] To gain and project influence in African international arbitration, one has to amass significant recognition within international arbitration circles.[35] Educational degrees from institutions in the global North, especially those in international arbitration hubs such as Paris, Geneva, London, and now Singapore, hold greater value as social and symbolic capital.[36] The faculties of law are indeed involved in the reproduction of knowledge that projects the desires and enhances hierarchies of expertise in international arbitration.[37] Ascending to the position of a seasoned African arbitrator requires a 'massive, sustained, planned, and practised investment' by the individual to acquire the legal, social, and political capital necessary for visibility within the international arbitration industry.[38]

Unlike the well-known current and former arbitrators from the global South who easily fit Yves Dezalay and Bryant G. Garth's description of 'grand old men', these African arbitrators are keen to influence the arbitration scene in Africa, which is more diversified. They do not depend on familial capital but more on social, meritocratic, and scholarly capital within the field. Yet they do

[33] Dezalay and Garth, (n 7).

[34] ibid at 18.

[35] ibid.

[36] *See also* Roberts (n 16) (Martti Koskenniemi arguing in the foreward of the book that joining centres of influence in international law requires a socialisation into a professional vocabulary and set of cultural scripts conveyed in well-known academic insititutions).

[37] Yves Dezalay and Bryant G Garth, The Internalization of Palace Wars: Lawyers, Econonomists, and the Contest to Transform Latin American States (University of Chicago Press, 2002) 5.

[38] Yvez Dezalay and Bryant G Garth, *Law as Reproduction and Revolution: An Interconnected History* (University of California Press, 2021) 4.

also share some of the social capital and symbolic markers of influence with the 'grand old men' described by Dezalay and Garth. They hold educational degrees from the former metropolises of London, Paris, and, more commonly now, the United States. Some still maintain a path straddling academia and practice. They publish articles and books in the field of international arbitration in leading and emerging journals to influence the field. They also maintain a strong presence in the main hubs of arbitration, with some setting and running boutique arbitration law firms in the global North. They also maintain close ties with the ICC as one of their institutional launching pads.

They are, however, different from the 'grand old men' in the vital sense of gender, age, and geographical diversity. The group includes some ambitious and relentless, relatively young women who have carved out a niche in a sector that had long maintained a preference for the male and relatively old, with an accumulated legal and social aura. I offer two short biographical examples: Prof Mohamed Abdel Wahab and Ms. Ndanga Kamau. Both can fall within Dezalay and Garth's formulation of international arbitration 'technocrats' as they have developed and accumulated their credentials within the field of international arbitration.[39] Biographically, they also appear to want to display the additional sociological marker of the current generation leading arbitrators: strong management abilities.[40]

2.1 Prof Mohamed Abdel Wahab

Mohamed Abdel Wahab is an Egyptian law professor, legal practitioner, and arbitrator who does not fit the traditional marker of the 'grand old men' because he is relatively young. Since he graduated with his *Licence en Droit* (equivalent to LLB) in 1998 from Cairo University, a plausible assumption is that, in terms of age, he is not yet or is only close to his fifties by 2025.[41] He holds a Ph.D. and a Master of Philosophy (MPhil) from the University of Manchester, UK, and a diploma from the Chartered Institute of Arbitrators, in collaboration with Balliol College, Oxford University.[42] He is a professor of International Arbitration, Private International Law, and English Contract Law at Cairo University. He is also the founding partner and head of the arbitration, construction, and energy groups at Zulficar and Partners law firm in Egypt.[43]

He holds and has held numerous roles in the domestic and international arbitration scene, including the following: Chair of the International

[39] Dezalay and Garth (n 7).

[40] Thomas Schultz and Robert Kovacs, 'The Rise of a Third Generation of Arbitrators? Fifteen Yeares after Dezalay and Garth' (2012) 28:2 *Arbitration International* 161.

[41] Zulficar and Partners, 'Profile Mohamed Abdel Wahab' www.zulficarpartners.com/people/mohamed-s-abdel-wahab/.

[42] ibid.

[43] ibid.

Expert Committee of the Permanent Forum for China Construction Law; Vice Chair of the ICC Governing Body for Dispute Resolution Services; Co-Chair, International Bar Association (IBA) Arab Regional Forum; Vice-Chair of the Advisory Committee of the Cairo Regional Centre for International Commerical Arbitration (CRCICA); Member of the Casablanca International Mediation and Arbitration Centre (CIMAC) Court of Arbitration; Member of the Advisory Board of the Mauritius International Arbitration Centre (MIAC); Member of the Lagos Chamber of Commerce International Arbitration Centre (LACIAC) Court of Arbitration; Member of the Board of Trustees of the Chartered Institute of Arbirators (CIArb); Member of the Institute for Transnational Arbitration (ITA) Academic Council; Member of the Advisory Board, Indonesian Arbitration Centre; Member of the Court, Permanent Court of Arbitration (PCA); Member of the International Council for Online Dispute Resolution's (ICODR) Governing Board; Member of the International Academy for Construction Lawyers; Former Vice President of the ICC International Court of Arbitration (2015 – 2021); and Former Court Member of the LCIA (2014–2019).[44]

Additionally, according to his profile on Transnational Dispute Management (TDM), a network for international arbitration, mediation, and ADR, Prof Abdel Wahab has also served as 'arbitrator,' 'legal expert,' and 'counsel' in more than 235 arbitrations.[45] He has received numerous awards, including the 2017 LAW Magazine Best Legal Practitioner Award, the 2018 ASA International Arbitration Advocacy Prize, the 2019 AYA Hall of Fame African Arbitrator Award, and the 2020 Client Choice International Award. He also features in WWL Global Elite Thought Leaders: International Arbitration, WWL Construction Thought Leaders, Chambers & Partners Global: International Arbitration, the 2021 Lawdragon Global Litigation 500 Lawyers Guide, the Legal500 Africa Powerlist, and the AYA's Africa's Top 30 Powerlist.[46] He is also widely published in the fields of international arbitration, private international law, and Islamic shari'a law. In this regard, he has authored one book and co-edited two others, all of which focus on international arbitration. It is also worth noting that he serves on numerous editorial boards and advisory committees of leading law journals and holds visiting teaching posts at universities in Egypt, the UK, and the US.

The roles he holds leave little doubt that he has accumulated significant social capital in various settings within the world of international commercial arbitration. He also holds the enviable position of being the first Dean of the

[44] ibid.

[45] TDM, 'Professor Dr. Mohamed S. Abdel Wahab' www.transnational-dispute-management.com/about-author-a-z-profile.asp?key=2526.

[46] Arbitration Africa, 'Africa *Arbitration Academy publishes Africa's* 30 Arbitration Powerlist 2020' < africaarbitration.org/2021/02/02/africa-arbitration-academy-publishes-africas-30-arbitration-powerlist-2020/.

Lagos-based AAA (discussed in detail below).[47] All these, in addition to the fact that he speaks Arabic, English, and French, all languages that make him quite marketable for arbitrations in Africa, the Middle East, and Europe. It is therefore no surprise that Prof Abel Wahab's name appears as one of the 16 commissioners of the ICC's Africa Commission, established in 2018 to coordinate the ICC's expanding range of activities and growth on the continent.[48]

His name appears in the ICC Africa Commission alongside other key players, influencing the three markers of influence that this section analyses. The other 16 commissioners are: Thierry Ngoga, Managing Partner, Line Partners, Rwanda; Ahmed Abdourahman, lawyer, Cabinet Abayazid & Abdourahman, Djibouti; Babatunde Ajibade, lawyer, S.P.A Ajibade & Co., Nigeria; Laura Alakija, arbitrator, Primera Africa Legal, Nigeria; Karim Anjarwalla, Managing Partner, Africa Legal Network, Kenya; Sylvie Bebohi Ebongo, Arbirtrator, HBE Avocats, Cameroon; Lino Diamvutu, Professor, Agostinho Neto University, Angola, Emmanuel Ugirashebuja, lawyer, Emmanuel Ugirashebuja-Independent (former judge and president at the EACJ); Guled Yusuf, lawyer, Allen & Overy, Somalia; Mouhamed Kebe, lawyer, Geni & Kebe, Senegal; Won Kidane, professor, Seattle University Law School, Ethiopia; Jimmy Kodo, independent arbitrator, Benin/France; Namaal E. Liebenthal, lawyer, AME & Co. Legal Practitioners, Zambia; Jimmy Ngoy Tshamala, lawyer, Barreau de Kinshasha Matete, Democratic Republic of Congo; Tafadzwa Pasipanodya, partner Foley Hoag, Zimbabwe; and Eunice Shang-Simpson, arbitrator, Shangress Limited, Ghana. The commission is chaired by Thierry Ngoga, Managing Partner of Legal Line Partners in Rwanda, and its secretary is Diamana Diawara, Regional Director for Africa at ICC Dispute Resolution Services from Mali.

The extensive list of lawyers above confirms that Prof. Abdel Wahab has created significant social capital both domestically in Egypt, regionally in Africa, and internationally at the ICC. His development can be compared to that of Ibrahim Shihata, another influential Egyptian in the field of international arbitration. Shihata would fit the description of the 'old grand men' from the global South as described by Yves Dezalay and Bryant G. Garth.[49] Educated in Cairo and holding an SJD degree from Harvard in 1964, Shihata primarily explored opportunities outside of his native Egypt and Africa.[50] He served in the Vienna-based Organisation of the Petroleum Exporting Countries (OPEC) Fund for International Development, later as President and General Counsel of the World Bank, and Secretary-General of the International Centre for Settlement of Investment Disputes (ICSID).[51]

[47] African Arbitration Academy, 'Dean of the Academy' www.africaarbitrationacademy.org/dean-of-the-academy/.

[48] ICC, 'ICC Court to Launch Africa Commission' iccwbo.org/media-wall/news-speeches/icc-court-launch-africa-commission/.

[49] Dezalay and Garth (n 7) 26.

[50] ibid.

[51] ibid.

The ICC Africa Commission list also confirms the first argument made in this chapter that one of the enduring attributes of seasoned African arbitrators is maintaining a strong presence in the global North while remaining deeply connected to power structures within African settings. All of these individual lawyers and arbitrators, selected by the ICC, and except, for one: Won Kidane, practice in Africa; all also seek to maintain international ties, especially with the ICC. This connection has a dual advantage. It serves as a gateway for themselves personally, as well as for their law firms, to the lucrative market of arbitration cases on the continent and beyond. Outside of the one, arguably full-time academician, most the other members of the commission have a strong incentive to promote the dispute resolution service from the vantage position of building substantial social capital in international commercial arbitration. As we will see below, these actors repeatedly appear as partners in top-tier corporate law firms connected to international arbitration, as well as being founders and members of African arbitration training institutions. One of their best examples is Prof. Abel Wahab. He has been exceptionally able to create a profile of an academic, practitioner, and arbitrator with a broad reach in both Africa and the global hubs of arbitration, ie Paris and London.

The list of commissioners above underscores another critical point about the diversity challenge within this 'invisible college' of African arbitrators.[52] This point is that the ICC deliberately ensures a sense of gender parity within this group. Using this group as a tiny representative sample, we can deduce a few issues regarding diversity in African international commercial arbitration. Of the 17 (plus the chair) commissioners and the secretary, we can add 22 more names selected by the ICC as ICC Africa Commission ambassadors.[53] Out of the 40 individuals in the commission, 19 are women, representing 47.5 per cent of all the selected individuals in the commission. Based on this list, the ICC must have deliberately maintained some level of gender parity. Using another representative sample from the 2020 Africa's 30 arbitration power list, we find that out of

[52] Susan D Franck and others, 'The Diversity Challenge: Exploring the Invisible College of International Arbitration' (2015) 53 *Col J Transnatl L* 429.

[53] Girgis Abd El-Shahid, Lawyer, Shahid Law Firm, Egypt; Mohamed Abdel Raouf, Arbitrator, Abdel Raouf Law Firm, Egypt; Sabrina Aïnouz, Partner, Squire Patton Boggs, Algeria; Martial Akakpo, Lawyer, Martial Akakpo & Associes, Togo; Marietta Brew Appiah-Opong, Lawyer, Lithur Brew & Company, Ghana; Sana Bellaid, In-house Counsel, Cisco Systems Canada Co., Tunisia; Affef Ben Mansour, Lawyer, Cabinet D'Avocat Affef Ben Mansour, Tunisia; Joachim Bile-Aka, Arbitrator, Bile-Aka, Brizoua-Bi & Associés, Côte d'Ivoire; Aïcha Brahma, Partner, Cabinet Aicha Brahma, Morocco; Bobson Coulibaly, Lawyer, SCP Yanogo Bobson, Burkina Faso; Nadine Ahouefa Dossou-Sakponou, In-house Counsel, SCPA Robert M Dossou, Benin; Njeri Kariuki, Arbitrator, Njeri Kariuki Advocate, Kenya; Azzedine Kettani, Founder and Partner, Kettani Law Firm, Morocco; Madeline Kimei, Arbitrator, iResolve, Tanzania; Mamadou Konaté, Arbitrator, Jurifis Consult, Mali; Salim Moollan QC, Brick Court Chambers, Mauritius; Adedoyin Rhodes-Vivour, Arbitrator, Doyin Rhodes-Vivour & Co., Nigeriachille Ngwanza, Arbitrator, Jus Africa, Cameroon; Yejide Osunkeye, Tomás Timbane, Partner, TTA – Sociedade de Advogados, Mozambique; Mahlape Sello, Lawyer, Duma Nokwe Group of Advocates, South Africa; Des Williams, Arbitration Director and Head of Dept., Werksmans Attorneys, South Africa.

the 30 listed arbitrators, 10 are women.[54] This lower proportion (~33 per cent) perhaps more accurately approximates the true level of under-representation of women among the top African arbitrators.

2.2 Ndanga Kamau

Ms. Ndanga Kamau is a Kenyan international lawyer, arbitrator, and counsel based in The Hague, Netherlands, who has amassed considerable social, meritocratic, and scholarly capital in international arbitration.[55] She is the founder of Ndanga Kamau Law, an international law practice based in the Hague.[56] She obviously does not fit the classical view of the 'grand, old, men' arbitrators, but can easily be described as a 'young and ambitious woman arbitrator of African descent.' Attributes that would have meant little, or could even be disadvantageous, in the twentieth century, but can now carry enormous social capital, especially when deployed strategically. But this does not mean it is easy for a black woman to make a mark in the competitive field of international arbitration.[57] It is still true that women, regardless of their background, may need to work twice as hard to get half as far as the 'grand old men' in arbitration. This difficulty arises because, for women to become arbitrators, they still have to be hired by industries that men dominate. Black women face the double bind of gender and race, making the ladder even more difficult to climb.

It is, therefore, neither an easy nor mean feat that Kamau has become visible within the pool of impactful arbitrators in Africa. She has had to beat and is still struggling to beat the odds of the 'famous clique' and an 'old boy network.'[58] Hers is a story of breaking the glass ceiling from below by strategically placing herself in avenues that could influence international arbitrations in Africa.

Still, the path to establishing oneself as a leading arbitrator within Africa and internationally is the well-trodden one of receiving education at the great institutions in the metropolitan hubs of international arbitration and maintaining close links with the ICC. Kamau has carefully followed through on some of these identity markers while breaking the glass ceiling in others. She holds an LLM in International Dispute Settlement from the prestigious University of Geneva and the Graduate Institute (MIDS program), a postgraduate diploma from the

[54] Arbitration Africa, 'Africa Arbitration Academy publishes Africa's 30 Arbitration Powerlist 2020' <africaarbitration.org/2021/02/02/africa-arbitration-academy-publishes-africas-30-arbitration-powerlist-2020/.

[55] Ndanga Kamau Law, 'Ndanga Kamau, Arbitrator, Counsel' ndangakamau.com/.

[56] ibid.

[57] *See* Anne-Marie Slaughter, 'Why Women Still Can't Have It All' *The Atlantic* (July/August 2012) www.theatlantic.com/magazine/archive/2012/07/why-women-still-cant-have-it-all/309020/; *see also* Destiny Peery, Paulette Brown and Eileen Letts, 'Left Out and Left Behind: The Hurdles, Hassles, and Heartaches of Achieving Long-Term Legal Careers for Women of Color' (American Bar Association, 2020).

[58] Ndanga Kamau Law (n 55).

City Law School in London, and an undergraduate degree in Economics from the University of Cape Town, South Africa. She currently specialises in the practice of international dispute settlement, including arbitration.[59] Having studied in Geneva and London, two hubs of international arbitration, and having the privilege of setting up practice in The Hague, another Hub of international law, comes with some obvious advantages. She was additionally the vice president of the ICC and the inaugural president of the ICC Africa Commission (2018–2021).

Unsurprisingly, she has been recognised as a Future Leader in the Who's Who global legal guide in 2022 in the category of Arbitration Future Leaders-Partners. She has amassed some legal, social, and political capital by, among others, being a member of the following institutions: the International Law Association (ILA) Committee on Rule of Law and international investment law, visiting scholar at the Max Planck Institute of Comparative Public Law and international law, observer delegate at the UNCITRAL WG III on ISDS reform, a PRIME Foundation expert in dispute resolution, a member of the Global Advisory Board of the New York International Arbitration Center (NYIAC), member of the Executive Committee of the Foundation for International Arbitration Advocacy (FIAA), and the director of programs of the African Association of International Law (AAIL).[60] She is also listed in the panels of the following international arbitration centres: China International Economic and Trade Arbitration Commission (CIETAC), Shanghai Arbitration Commission (SHAC), and the Kigali International Arbitration Centre (KIAC).[61]

With the above credentials and further qualifications, Ms. Kamau easily meets the criteria of a seasoned African arbitrator, maintaining a strong presence in the global North while remaining deeply connected to power structures within African settings. In this way, she can, directly and indirectly, influence the trajectory of international commercial arbitration in Africa. She is already building an impressive career as a 'broker' between the ICC and the market of arbitration in Africa. Unlike Prof. Abdel Wahab above, Ms. Kamau has connected with African arbitration institutions through training and membership in African-based training institutions, such as the AIIL, based in Arusha, Tanzania. The idea of individuals like Ms. Kamau is not only a strong belief in arbitration generally, but also the belief that arbitration as a mode of dispute settlement ensures the rule of law. Thus, African countries that do not maintain arbitration-friendly solid laws and institutions would easily lose out on attracting foreign direct investment. The broad consequence would be the decline or lack of development in these countries. In this sense, arbitration institutions and emerging arbitrators, such as Prof. Adel Wahab and Ms. Kamau, are not gaining in terms of building strong careers; they are also promoting a version of 'law

[59] ibid.
[60] ibid.
[61] ibid.

and development.' This is similar to the version promoted by prominent groups of consultants, think tanks, philanthropic foundations, and national and transnational actors as 'good governance' in Africa.[62] Such groups argue that 'good governance' requires the 'rule of law' and better judicial remedies – in this case including judicialised arbitration – would preserve it.[63]

3. AFRICAN TOP-TIER CORPORATE LAW FIRMS CONNECTING REGIONALLY AND GLOBALLY

In recent years, African top-tier law firms have formed regional and global alliances to capture new markets, increase market share, and acquire access to specialised skills and expertise.[64] One such market is international arbitration. The increase in cross-border corporate dealings involving African states or parties has made the continent 'the Global Economy's last frontier.'[65] The demand for corporate lawyers and corporate law firms in Africa has created a supply of Anglo-American-type' big' corporate law firms with the following characteristics: high prestige, high-salaried partners, and hiring based on merit from top law schools.[66] These international corporate law firms are aiming for the enormous economic potential in Africa.

Entering the African law firm market, however, is not an easy task as one might imagine. Africa is a diverse continent with different legal traditions, cultures, and the ever-present shadow of colonialism. Leading African law firms, such as Nairobi-based Anjarwalla and Khanna (A&K), while adopting a fast-paced American-type corporate law firm structure, still maintain their roots as a familial and quasi-familial establishment. The continued presence of abundant mineral wealth, the need and thirst for infrastructure, and the growth of corporate and financial legal needs have made Africa attractive for international law firms based in the global North.[67] International law firms such as Dentons, Norton Rose, Clifford Chance (CC), Allen & Overy, DLA Piper, Hogan Lovells, and Jones Day, among others, have been actively seeking a share of Africa's

[62] *See* David M Trubek and Marc Galanter, 'Scholars in Self Estrangement: Reflections on the Crisis in Law and Development Studies' (1974) 4 *Wisconsin L Rev* 1062; *see also* David M Trubek, 'Law and Development: Forty Years after Scholars in Self-Estrangement' (2016) 66 *University of Toronto LJ* 301.

[63] See Yves Dezalay and Bryant G Garth, *The Internationalization of Palace Wars: Lawyers, Economists, and the Contest to Transform Latin America* (University of Chicago Press, 2002).

[64] Jonathan Klaaren, 'African Corporate Lawyering and Globalization' (2015) 22 *International Journal of the Legal Profession* 226.

[65] Kingsley Chiedu Moghalu, *Emerging Africa: How the Global Economy's 'Last Frontier' can Prosper and Matter* (Bookcraft Ltd, 2013).

[66] *See* David B Wilkins, David M Trubek and Bryon Fong, 'Globalization, Lawyers, and Emerging Economies: The Rise, Transformation, and Significance of the New Corporate Legal Ecosystem in India, Brazil, and China' (2020) 61 *Harv IntL LJ* 281.

[67] Maria Jackson, 'Race for Africa' *Legal Business*, (November 2011) www.vda.pt/xms/files/v1/Noticias/Legal_Business_-_219_Africa_-_NC_-November_2011-.pdf.

legal market in recent years. African top-tier corporate law firms are a core of the African' corporate legal elite.' The African corporate legal elite comprises lawyers who work in firms that serve a clientele primarily composed of TNCs.[68] International law firms look internally to Africa for collaboration and networking, while African corporate firms look externally for similar opportunities. There are four models of such collaborations and new developments among African corporate law firms: Foreign branches, Association with Local Firms, Networking Arrangements, and Boutique Arbitration Law firms. All these models are present in Africa.[69]

3.1 Foreign Branches

Foreign branches are established in foreign jurisdictions under the same name as the parent firm. Allen & Overy has branches in Casablanca, Morocco, and Johannesburg, South Africa.[70] DLA Piper has offices in Morocco and South Africa, but as we will see below, it has established its African presence mainly through association with existing local firms and lawyers.[71] Herbert Smith Freehills also has a branch in Johannesburg, South Africa.[72] Other law firms with branches or associations across Africa include Clifford Chance, Eversheds, Lefèvre Pelletier & Associés, and UGGC avocats.[73] The English firm Clyde & Co has branches in Cape Town, South Africa; Dar es Salaam, Tanzania; and Johannesburg, South Africa. Another firm employing this model is Baker McKenzie, which has branch offices in South Africa. This model is employed by setting up shop in a single stable and attractive city; in this case, South Africa has offered the best cities and uses these as bases to serve the continent.[74]

3.2 Association with Local African Firms

Associations between international law firms and local African law firms have also increased in recent years. Such associations sometimes involve the firm's

[68] David B Wilkins and Mihaela Papa, 'The Rise of the Corporate Legal Elite in the BRICS: Implications for Global Governance' (2013) 54 *B C L Rev* 1149.

[69] Tung-Lung S Chang, Cheng-Min Chuang and Wen-Shiung Jan, 'International Collaboration of Law Firms: Modes, Motives, and Advantages' (1998) 33 *Journal of World Business* 245; *see also*, Andrew Mizner, 'Law Firms Balance Competition and Collaboration in Africa' (*African Law & Business* 14 October 2022), iclg.com/alb/18162-law-firms-balance-competition-and-collaboration-in-africa.

[70] Allen & Overy, 'Africa' www.allenovery.com/en-gb/global/global_coverage/africa.

[71] DLA Piper, 'DLA Piper offices in Africa' www.dlapiper.com/en/africa/focus/africa-offices/.

[72] Herbert Smith Freehills, 'Africa Group' www.herbertsmithfreehills.com/where-we-work/africa-group.

[73] Crasner Consulting, 'Law firms Scramble for Africa' (18 October 2016) www.crasnerconsulting.com/news/law-firms-scramble-for-africa/.

[74] Mizner (n 69).

name change or mere association by reference. Dentons, a large international corporate law firm, merged in 2010 across the UK, Canada, and the US.[75] In 2015, it doubled in size again with a merger with Chinese firm Dacheng, becoming the world's largest law firm in terms of headcount.[76] The firm describes its mergers as combinations, and within five years, it had a presence in Latin America, Western Europe, and the Asia-Pacific region.[77] Before merging with Dacheng, Dentons already had branch offices in Johannesburg and Casablanca.[78] By 2017, Dentons had 15 associate firms in Africa, located in Algeria, Angola, Cabo Verde, Ghana, Guinea-Bissau, Kenya, Libya, Mauritania, Mauritius, Mozambique, Nigeria, Rwanda, São Tomé and Principe, Uganda, and Zambia.[79] In 2017, Dentons decided to launch a new African region, separate from the UK and Middle East region, which the African region had previously been part of. They stated their aim as one of establishing a Pan-African capability.[80]

DLA Piper is the closest comparison to Denton's strategy in Africa. Like Dentons, it is another of the world's largest firms, with branch offices established across the globe. In Africa, DLA Piper has decided to move towards a 'one firm' approach.[81] It has previously had two branch offices and 17 associated law firms across the continent for many years.[82] Kenyan partner of IKM-DLA Piper James Kamau, who also served as the chairperson of DLA Piper, captures the idea on the interest of international firms as follows: 'governments want work done locally, but the market continues to demand that cases are taken to international hubs in Paris, London or New York, as an example of where an international firm with a local office comes into its own'.[83] We see the tension between African states, business actors, and international and local law firms in international arbitration.[84] While African states work to promote arbitrations in African seats, the forces of supply and demand in the market still point to the metropoles. Clyde & Co, Eversheds Sutherland, and Clifford Chance also have associated law firms or operate regional groups in Africa.[85] Clyde & Co is associated with Kangwana & Co in Nairobi, Kenya.[86]

[75] Andrew Mizner, 'Dentons Doing its Own Thing in Africa'(*African Law & Business* 12 December 2022)iclg.com/alb/18162-law-firms-balance-competition-and-collaboration-in-africa.

[76] ibid.

[77] ibid.

[78] ibid.

[79] ibid.

[80] ibid.

[81] Mizner (n 69).

[82] Andrew Mizner, 'DLA Looks for an Integrated Future in Africa' (*African Law & Business* 6 July 2018) iclg.com/alb/18162-law-firms-balance-competition-and-collaboration-in-africa.

[83] ibid.

[84] *See* Joseph Otoo and Kwadwo Sarkodie, 'The Rise and Rise of Arbitration in Africa' (*African Law & Business* 4 May 2018) www.africanlawbusiness.com/news/8105-the-rise-and-rise-of-arbitration-in-africa.

[85] Andrew Mizner, 'New Leadership as Eversheds eyes Africa's Growing Legal sector Rewards' (*African Law & Business* 3 March 2022) www.africanlawbusiness.com/news/8095-newz-leadership-as-eversheds-eyes-africa-s-growing-legal-sector-rewards.

[86] Clyde & Co, 'Africa' www.clydeco.com/en/locations/africa.

3.3 Networking Arrangements

The third model of collaboration is that of networking arrangements. It is also booming in Africa. The arguable leader here is the African Legal Network (ALN), founded in 2004 by the Kenyan law firm of Anjarwalla and Khanna (A&K). The ALN describes itself as an alliance of leading corporate firms, currently in 15 African countries.[87] The firms are set up to work as a one-stop shop solution for African clients. The heart of the ALN is the Nairobi top-tier corporate law firm of Anjarwalla and Khanna. Its managing partner, Karim Anjarwalla, is, as we saw earlier in the analysis of leading arbitrators above, also unsurprisingly linked with the ICC as one of the commissioners of the ICC Africa Commission. The strength of ALN is its African orientation. The network is comprised solely of African law firms and does not include any non-African law firms.

The ALN has also established an academic department called the ALN Academy. The ALN academy seeks to provide unique legal training and expert exchange opportunities on the continent.[88] Following up on the rule of law and good governance narrative of the 1970s and 1980s, the ALN Academy is set up to 'play an influential role in enhancing the rule of law (the new term for law and development) in Africa'.[89] For an academy established within a network of law firms that serve corporate clients and diverse corporate interests, ALN Academy's 'rule of law' and 'good governance' mandate framing is both curious and neoliberal at the same time. This framing again calls attention to the continued questioning of the 'law and development'/'rule of law' project in the current century.[90] The idea of having such an academy nestled within a network of law firms harkens back to the early belief among law and development scholars that legal education was essential for legal reforms in developing countries.[91] In this case, legal education is called upon for the benefit of African lawyers, who form the core of the corporate legal elite. The outcome would arguably be a privatised rule of law framework that would benefit corporate clients and engender economic gains only for the capitalist class. The ALN Academy, therefore, might knowingly or unknowingly only serve the interests of a narrow neo-liberal elite.

3.4 Boutique Arbitration Law Firms

In addition to these international and top-tier law firms' collaborations and associations, one other development is essential to mention in international

[87] ALN, 'About us' https://aln.africa/.
[88] ibid.
[89] ibid.
[90] David M Trubek, 'Law and Development: Forty Years after Scholars in Self-Estrangement' (2016) 66 *University of Toronto* LJ 301.
[91] ibid at 305.

arbitration. This is the development of boutique law firms. A boutique law firm is one that specialises in a specific aspect of the law rather than offering a general legal service. A notable example worth mentioning is the Nairobi-based JMiles & Co. The firm specialises in international arbitration, investigation, and legal consultancy services. Its managing partner, John Miles, was part of the prestigious Legal 500 Africa Arbitration power list of 2021. The firm was also voted the leading arbitration service provider in 2019 and 2020 at the inaugural African Arbitration Awards hosted by the EAIAC.[92]

4. AFRICAN ARBITRATION TRAINING INSTITUTIONS AND PROFESSIONAL CENTRES

Legal education and training in the era of mega-commercial law practice are structured to support the existing needs and demands of corporate practice.[93] Given that the teaching of international arbitration has not received as much attention in African law schools, arbitration training institutions have sought to fill this gap. As international commercial arbitration has gotten more professionalised, so has the demand and supply of training institutions increased.[94] One sure way of gaining entry into the area is to possess the requisite qualifications in the field. At this point, it goes without saying that lawyers have dominated the field, even though domestic and international arbitration is not strictly considered an area of exclusive law practice. Post and pre-graduate school entrants in Africa have to enter the field as qualified 'professionals' in international arbitration.

The increase in training institutions and professional associations reflects the legal professionalisation of the field of international commercial arbitration in Africa.[95] Arbitration training institutions are set up for three primary purposes. The first is to supply a cadre of trained and thus well-prepared arbitrators and arbitral practice lawyers. The second is to professionalise the field, ie, the process of making a profession. The third and final role is to inculcate a distinct culture of international commercial arbitration.[96] Such inculcation reminds us of the concept of interpellation, as discussed by structural Marxist Louis Althusser in various parts of his book, *On the Reproduction of Capitalism: Ideology and Ideological State Apparatuses*. The culture of international arbitration encompasses the following normative values and principles: party autonomy,

[92] Mauritius Mediation and Arbitration Center, 'African Arbitration Awards-2nd edition-2020' (28 August 2020).

[93] Dezalay and Garth (n 38) 7.

[94] Mikaël Schinazi, *The Three Ages of International Commercial Arbitration* (Cambridge University Press,Cambridge University Press, 2021) 195.

[95] ibid at 197.

[96] ibid at 199.

the primacy of business interests, neutrality, and internationalism.[97] For African arbitration training institutions, we can add the objective of increasing the number of qualified African arbitrators and arbitral practice lawyers. This section analyses two African arbitration institutions: the AAA and the AIIL.

4.1 The African Arbitration Academy

The Association of Young Arbitrators (AYA) founded and set up the AAA.[98] The AYA is an association of young arbitration practitioners in Africa under the age of 40.[99] Abayomi Okubote, who founded AYA,[100] was, until 2021, a senior associate and team lead in international arbitration in Olaniwun Ajayi LP, a leading Nigerian commercial law firm based in Lagos.[101] He exited in 2021 to start a boutique commercial law firm – Pensbury Attorneys & Solicitors – in Abuja, Nigeria.[102] At the time of writing, he is also a Ph.D. candidate at Queens University, Kingston, Canada, under the supervision of Prof. Joshua Karton.[103] Mr. Okubote has also appeared in the 2021 Legal 500 Arbitration Powerlist: Africa. Legal 500 asserts that his peers have described him as one of the 'future leaders of arbitration in Africa' and as 'innovative and exceptional'.[104]

Mr. Okubote appears in the Powerlist together with 30 other leading practitioners in Africa, including Mr. Khrushchev Ekwueme, Partner and head of dispute settlement at Olaniwun Ajayi LP; Mr. George Oraro, Senior Partner at Oraro & Company Advocates in Nairobi, Kenya;[105] Prof Mohamed S. Abdel Wahab (already profiled above); Mr. Zaeem Soofie, Partner, director, and national CEO at Dentons in South Africa; Ms. Adedoyin Rhodes-Vivour, Managing partner at Doyin Rhodes-Vivour & Co based in Nigeria; Mr. John

[97] Joshua D H Karton, *The Culture of International Arbitration and the Evolution of Contract Law* (Cambridge University Press,Cambridge University Press, 2013) ch 4.

[98] ICSID, 'Association of Young Arbitrators Africa Arbitration Academy' icsid.worldbank.org/fr/actualites-et-evenements/evenements/association-young-arbitrators-africa-arbitration-academy.

[99] Association of Young Arbitrators, 'About Us' https://www.linkedin.com/company/association-of-young-arbitrators-aya/?originalSubdomain=ng.

[100] ibid.

[101] *See* Olaniwun Ajayi, 'The Firm' www.olaniwunajayi.net/the-firm/.

[102] Africa Arbitration, 'Africa's Rising Star, Abayomi Okubote, Exits Top Law Firm…Starts a boutique Arbitration Firm!' africaarbitration.org/2021/12/13/africas-rising-star-exits-top-law-starts-a-boutique-arbitration-firm/.

[103] Queens Law, 'Abayomi Okubote: PhD Candidate'.

[104] Africa Arbitration Blog, "The Legal 500's Arbitration Powerlist: Africa 2021 Recognises our Co-Founder-Abayomi Okubote" africaarbitration.org/2021/05/04/the-legal-500s-arbitration-powerlist-africa-2021-recognises-our-co-founder-abayomi-okubote-mciarb/#:~:text=The%20Powerlist%20recognizes%20Africa%20Arbitration's,the%20views%20of%20Africa%20Arbitration.

[105] Has been a successful legal practitioner for very many years and can fit Dezalay and Garth's designation of a 'grand, old, man' because of having risen to the pinnacle of Kenya's legal profession yet not known so much in the field of arbitration even in Kenya.

Miles, Managing director at JMiles & Co (already profiled above); and Ms. Jackie Oyuyo Githinji, Managing Partner at Umsizi based in Nairobi, Kenya.[106]

The AAA, according to its website, states that it was established 'due to the demand for improved expertise and training of arbitration practitioners in Africa and to expose young practitioners to the current trends and developments in international commercial and investment arbitration'.[107] Its overall objective is to 'provide the much-needed specialised training to arbitration practitioners from Africa and to equip them with the right set of skills to succeed within the international community'.[108] It held its flagship training program in London in June 2019, though it is based and stationed in Abuja, Nigeria.[109]

The AAA was voted 'Innovation of the Year' at the 2019 Africa Arbitration Awards.[110] The Africa Arbitration Awards were first held in 2019 and are hosted by the EAIAC.[111] By 2025, the EAIAC had hosted 12 annual conferences that brought together stakeholders interested in and working on international arbitration in Africa.[112] It is run by an organising committee of

> 'four members: Agnes Gitau, Partner at GBS Africa, a London-based Africa investment advisory; Wairimu Karanja, Director, Wairimu & Co.; Leyou Tameru, Director at I-Arb Africa, an Africa-focused international arbitration resource platform; and Elodie Dulac, Partner at King & Spalding, Singapore and Ethiopia University lecturer'.[113]

It is a periodic mass gathering in Africa that is quickly becoming another essential ritual for stakeholders in the field of international arbitration in Africa.[114] As we will see below, entering the awards market is part of a sociological narrative aimed at influencing who acquires more symbolic capital in the African international arbitration arena.

As most of the profiled arbitrators in this chapter, including the specifically profiled ones, have invariably appeared in one or another lawyer, law firm, arbitrator rankings, and power lists, a word on such rankings is vital in this section. As we will see below, the AAA and other associations dealing with arbitration have also launched their own lists and rankings of arbitrators.[115] The Legal 500,

[106] The Legal 500, 'Arbitration Powerlist 2021: Africa' indd.adobe.com/view/07527242-bd96-4ac8-b1ff-03b60f37787a.

[107] Africa Arbitration Academy, 'About Us' www.africaarbitrationacademy.org.

[108] ibid.

[109] ibid.

[110] ibid.

[111] Mauritius Mediation and Arbitration Center, 'African Arbitration Awards -1st edition 2019'.

[112] EAIAC, 'About EAIAC 2025' www.eastafricaarbitration.com/.

[113] The East Africa International Arbitration Conference, 'About EAIAC' www.eastafricaarbitration.com/about-eaiac/.

[114] Emmanuel Gaillard, 'Sociology of International Arbitration' (2015) 31 *Arbitration International* 10–13 (describing three arbitrations rituals: arbitral hearings, recognition tournaments, and periodic mass gatherings).

[115] ibid (referring to them as recognition tournaments similar to the Grammy Awards).

Chambers Global, and Global Arbitration Review (GAR) are examples of such professional guides, reviews, online directories, and law firm/lawyers/arbitrators ranking service providers. Emmanuel Galliard (himself a former elite global North arbitrator) referred to such service providers as the 'merchants of recognition.'[116] Indeed, absence from such rankings might easily mean being absent from the international arbitration market altogether. Absence in the field is an outcome that, as we have seen above, is detrimental to the individual arbitrator and the law firm they trade-in. Going back to the theoretical framework of this book, and based on Pierre Bourdieu's notion of symbolic capital, we can understand the need for honour, prestige, and recognition generated by these arbitration rankings.[117]

The notion of symbolic capital was deployed powerfully by Dezalay and Garth in their most cited book, *Dealing in Virtue*.[118] Dezalay and Garth deploy symbolic capital as the prestige and professional 'virtue' required to legitimise private justice in a transnational arena. This capital is built on a combination of high-level academic credentials, national judicial status, and a reputation for disinterested neutrality, which together allow elite arbitrators, whom they refer to as the 'Grand Old Men', to command authority over global corporations. By transforming their personal status and legal expertise into a recognized form of power, these actors create the 'credit' necessary to bypass state courts, effectively turning their social and intellectual standing into the foundational trust upon which the entire international arbitration market is built. Bourdieu demonstrated that actors in any field, which he referred to as 'habitus', actively seek symbolic capital, ie, in economic terms, money and welfare, and in symbolic terms, honours, prestige, and recognition.[119] In international commercial arbitration, acquiring symbolic capital is arguably more important than economic capital. This is a truism in Africa as it is anywhere else in the world.

Arbitrator rankings and power lists can pose a potential ethical danger to African international arbitration. For lawyers, law firms, and arbitrators seeking to create a favourable reputation, such rankings and power lists offer an excellent source of marketing their skills and abilities. In an arena where symbolic capital plays a vital role, rankings and power lists can easily manufacture reputations. In instances in which the selection methodologies are revealed and independently audited, the possibility of 'insider trading,' ie, ranking individuals who are only known or who pay the service provider, also increases.

To be sure, not all ranking systems use dubious methodologies. Sometimes, these service providers can offer an excellent avenue for arbitrators and law firms to establish well-deserved reputations, recognition, and prestige. In the US

[116] ibid at 7.

[117] See Pierre Bourdieu, *Distinction-A Social Critique of the Judgment of Taste* (Harvard University Press, 1984).

[118] Dezalay and Garth (n 7).

[119] *See* Pierre Bourdieu, 'The Force of Law: Toward a Sociology of the Juridical Field' (1987) 38 *Hastings LJ* 805.

state of New York, the New York Bar Association Committee on Standards of Attorney Conduct adopted new standards requiring a professional rating to be unbiased and non-discriminatory.[120] The standards also require the service to use objective criteria or legitimate peer review in a manner that is unbiased by the service provider's economic interests.[121] In the case of the African economy, we can also add personal interests to the economic considerations.

As if on cue, the AAA and Africa Arbitration (also co-founded by Mr. Abayomi Okubote)[122] published Africa's 30 arbitration power list in 2020. The AAA now has three rankings in addition to its 'Hall of Fame' (which includes two individuals: Mrs. Funke Adekoya SAN & Prof Mohamed Abdel Wahab): the Africa Arbitration Awards, the Power List, and Most Promising.[123] According to AAA, the power list is meant to celebrate the leaders in the African dispute settlement market. The problem is that AAA does not provide any additional information on the methodology beyond calling for nominations and outlining the nomination requirements. The mode and method of arriving at the final power list remain a mystery. The list has the following individuals: Mohamed Abdel Wahab, Funke Adekoya, Samaa Haridi, Christopher Ojo, Tunde Fagbohunlu, Sami Houerbi, Harry Matovu, John Ohaga, Marie-Andrée Ngwe, Konyin Ajayi, Doyin-Vivour, Njeri Kariuki, Ace Ankomah, Dorothy Ufot, Kamal Shah, Oba Nsugbe QC SAN, Azzedine Kettani, Ismail Selim, Suzanne Rattray, Emmanuel Amofa, Gaston Kenfack, Githu Muigai, Mohamed Abdel Raouf, Emilia Onyema, Nagla Nassar, Tafadzwa Pasipanodya, Mohamed Shelbaya, Edward Luke II, Hon. Justice Edward Torgbor, and Salim Moollan QC.[124]

In 2022, the AAA published a list of 30 promising arbitration practitioners. The announcement on the social media site LinkedIn begins with the following disclaimer: 'The directors of the Africa Arbitration Academy – Dr. Abayomi Okubote, Dr. Ademola Bamgbose, Femi Gbede, Anita Omonuwa Ogbalu, Solomon Ebere, Kate Okoh-Kpina, and Ngo-Martins Okonmah, who are themselves deserving of this recognition, have been deliberately excluded from the List'.[125] The bias involved in this case is hiding in plain sight. The other awardees are as follows: Diamana Diawara, Isaiah Bozimo, Nania Owusu Ankomah, Hamid Abdulkareem, Guled Yusuf, Tolu Obamuroh, Laura Alakija, Madeline Kimei, Noella Lubano, Noreen Kidunduhu, Tsegaye Laurendeau, Youssef Al Saman, Dr. Wilfred Mutubwa, Patson Wilbroad Arinaitwe, Jackwell Feris, Leyou Tameru, Amr Omran, Naomi Tarawali, Leah Njoroge-Kibe,

[120] Fred C Zacharias, 'Effects of Reputation on the Legal Profession'(2008) 65 *Washington and Lee Law Review* 173.

[121] ibid.

[122] Africa Arbitration, 'Co-Founders' africaarbitration.org/management/.

[123] Africa Arbitration Academy www.africaarbitrationacademy.org/.

[124] Arbitration Africa, 'Africa Arbitration Academy publishes Africa's 30 Arbitration Powerlist 2020' africaarbitration.org/2021/02/02/africa-arbitration-academy-publishes-africas-30-arbitration-powerlist-2020/.

[125] Africa Arbitration Academy, www.linkedin.com/feed/update/urn:li:activity:7011254773874126848/.

Mulopa Ndalameta, Kimbeng T. Tah, Sally Kotb, Mohamed Hafez, Sylvie Bebohi Ebongo, Victoria Kigen, Mohamed Sweify, Diane Okoko, Alexandra do Nascimento Gonçalves, Mercy A. Okiro, and Benjamin Ng'eno. Although many, if not all, of these young Africans deserve such recognition, one cannot ignore the reputational risks involved in such an exercise. One can surmise that this is also a move to slowly create an African' club' or 'mafia' of arbitrators, as directly imitating the practice in the global North.

A few issues related to conscious or unconscious bias can be raised regarding the power list and promising arbitrators' lists above.[126] Prepared by AAA, an institution headed by Mr. Abayomi Okubote, the inclusion of Prof Mohamed Abdel Wahab, the AAA's unsurprising first dean, and Mr. Konyin Ajayi, partner at Olaniwun Ajayi LP, which is Mr. Okubote's former employer, could easily raise some eyebrows. One would respond by arguing that Prof Abdel Wahab is also on the Legal 500 power list of 2021 and is, therefore, a worthy and meritorious addition. The same, however, is arguably not true for Mr. Ajayi. The list includes two notable Kenyans, Prof. Githu Muigai and Mr. John Ohaga. While Mr. John Ohaga is also selected in the 2021 Legal 500 power list, which is arguably a well-earned recognition, Prof. Muigai is absent from that list.

Observers of the African field of international arbitration would also argue that the Kenyan arbitrator, Dr. Kariuki Muigua's, absence from these lists is telling. According to the African Arbitration Association, he has been listed as a top arbitrator by Chambers Global for five years running.[127] Chambers Global celebrates him as: 'having an astute understanding of arbitration and as respected for litigation that touches on commercial, constitutional, and environmental law'.[128] These examples are not intended to indicate who should or shouldn't be included in these lists, but rather to highlight the pitfalls and criticisms that may arise in cases in which undisclosed methodologies are used without named and independent selection juries. We must hold all service providers accountable. This call to accountability is vital because soon the increasing competition among these merchants of recognition might undermine the noble quest of rewarding well-earned recognition and reputation in the field.

The danger lies in accusations of offering a service for arbitrators to manufacture reputations, rather than celebrating excellence and well-earned reputations. The neo-Marxist critique that such recognition tournaments naturalise and justify the hegemony of elites in a social field could be valid in this analysis.[129]

[126] *See* Maya Sen, 'How Judicial Qualification Ratings May Disadvantage Minority and Female Candidates' (2014) 2 *Journal of Law and Courts* 33; *see also* Rebecca D Gill, Sylvia R Lazos and Mallory M Waters, 'Are Judicial Performance Evaluations Fair to Women and Minorities – A Cautionary Tale from Clark County, Nevada' (2011) 45 *Law and Society Review* 731.

[127] African Arbitration Association, 'Dr. Kariuki Muigua Ranked by Chambers as Top Arbitrator for the 5th Year' afaa.ngo/page-18443.

[128] ibid.

[129] *See* Steven Lukes, 'Political Ritual and Social Integration' (1975) 9 *Sociology* 289.

Exceptionally and to its credit, the African Arbitration Awards run by the EAIAC discussed above has a nomination criterion that includes demonstrated knowledge and experience in international arbitration, use of innovation, teamwork, and collaboration, observance of confidentiality, use of African centres, and training and mentorship.[130] It also annually announces its nomination and selection panel of judges.[131]

4.2 The African Institute of International Law (Institut Africain de Droit International)

The AIIL prides itself on being the only institution in Africa dedicated to capacity building for the dissemination of international law, African Union (AU) law, and the promotion of the rule of law through training and teaching activities.[132] The institute began as an initiative of the current ICJ Somali judge, Abdulqawi Yusuf, under the auspices of the African Foundation of International Law.[133] The institute was also supported by the government of Tanzania and is hosted in Arusha, Tanzania, which is considered the international law city of Africa.[134] The AU endorsed AIIL in 2012 during its 18th Ordinary Session as an essential institution in building the capacity of African faculties of law and African lawyers to deal with various aspects of international and African Union law.[135] The United Nations General Assembly (UNGA) also welcomed its creation and encouraged the UN secretariat to cooperate with the institute.[136]

The AIIL has the general objective of being an

> autonomous international educational and research institution, with the mission of advancing, through sustainable capacity-building in the field of international law, the rule of law, legal predictability and certainty, and more stable and rule-based intergovernmental relations within the African continent and with the outside world.[137]

After consultations with African governments and institutions, one of AIIL priority areas is 'negotiation and conclusion of bilateral investment treaties and arbitration'.[138]

[130] Africa Arbitration Awards, 2020, 'Spotlingting Africa's International Arbitration expertise at 2nd Annual Africa Arbitration Awards, 2002' www.addleshawgoddard.com/globalassets/insights/celebrating-africas-international-arbitration-expertise.pdf.

[131] ibid.

[132] African Institute of International Law, 'About the Institute' aiil-iadi.org/the-aiil; *see also* Statutes of the African Institute of International Law, art 1 [hereinafter AIIL statutes], aiil-iadi.org/statutes-of-the-african-institute-of-international-law/.

[133] African Institute of International Law, 'Presentation' April 2021.

[134] ibid.

[135] ibid.

[136] ibid.

[137] AIIL statutes, art II (1).

[138] African Institute of International Law, 'Presentation' (n 133).

Unlike the AAA, the AIIL has a broader mandate and is more connected with African governments and international organisations. This mandate is not surprising, considering that its founder, Judge Abdulqawi Yusuf, has amassed an impressive amount of social capital within the AU and UN systems. It is easy to see the intended reach of the institute by examining its lead governing body, known as the curatorium.[139] The curatorium consists of the following individuals: Judge Abdulqawi Yusuf, the president of the curatorium; Prof Sabine von Schorlemer; Judge Nicholas Michel; Ms. Sandie Okoro; Ms. Amina Mohamed Jibril; Prof Chris Maina Peter; Prof Sean Murphy; Judge Fatsah Ouguergouz; Prof Mads Adenaes, and Amb. Sani Mohamed (ex-officio and rector of the institute).[140] For an organisation that is firmly rooted in training and promoting Africans, it is not clear why its leading organ has a representation of individuals who are non-African.[141] Its trainings and agenda on arbitration are also linked to the broader ecosystem of international commercial arbitration in Africa. Take, for example, a March 2022 workshop organised by the institute together with the African Arbitration Association (AfAA) on international investment law and dispute resolution.[142] This workshop featured Ms. Ndanga Kamau as one of the faculty members, again highlighting how we often find the same actors recurring in the international commercial arbitration scene in Africa.

5. CONCLUSION

This chapter began by pointing out that the African marketplace of international professional dispute settlement analysis remains somewhat of a black box. The chapter attempted to fill a small section of this gap by focusing on the three emerging transnational actors within the African arbitration scene: Well-Established and Emerging African Arbitrators, African top-tier corporate law firms, and African Arbitration Law Training Institutions. Using a sociological account-based analysis focused on the oscillating and circulating roles of international lawyers, the chapter argued that three different but interconnected transnational socio-legal actors are emerging in the field of African international arbitration. First, regarding well-established and emerging arbitrators, the chapter profiles two African international lawyers as a small but arguably representative sample of international lawyers. One of this chapter's arguments

[139] AIIL statutes, art IV (the other two organs of the institute are the Administrative Committee and the Rector).

[140] ibid.

[141] *See* AIIL statutes, art V (listing the composition requirements of the curatorium).

[142] African Institute of International Law & African Arbitration Association, 'Advanced Introduction Workshop on International Investment Law and Dispute Resolution' www.afronomicslaw.org/sites/default/files/pdf/AfAAAIIL%20Advanced%20Workshop%20on%20International%20Investment%20Law%20%203%20March%202022.pdf.

on this count was that a core group of diversified African arbitrators is emerging and animating the arbitration scene.

The second actor is African top-tier corporate law firms connecting regionally and globally. In this chapter, novel arguments and illustrations are presented on the emerging competitive field of international law firms, which are scrambling for the African market. This section argued that many large international corporate law firms are increasingly looking to Africa for collaboration and networking opportunities. They aim to acquire a slice of 'the Global Economy's last frontier.' African top-tier corporate law firms are also looking externally to international and regional law firms for similar needs. The result is a robust environment of collaboration, cooperation, and the merging of law firms in Africa. Accordingly, I presented the following four models of collaboration and new developments among African corporate top-tier law firms: Foreign branches, Association with Local Firms, Networking Arrangements, and Boutique Arbitration Law firms.

Finally, the chapter analysed the role of African arbitration training institutions and professional centres within the African international arbitration scene. This section focused on two institutions: The AAA and the AIIL. An analysis showed that the same legal professionals who influence the other two actors are also connected within these institutions. The interconnectedness and interrelatedness of these professionals easily support the overarching claim that these three actors are central to the evolution and mutations in African international arbitration. To the best of my knowledge, the insights in this chapter represent the first sociologically grounded analysis of the role of international arbitration professionals in Africa. The space for future research is endless.

8

General Conclusion: New Frontiers and Failed Imaginations

I. THE AFRICAN CONTINENTAL FREE TRADE AGREEMENT AND ITS DISPUTE SETTLEMENT MECHANISMS

The African Continental Free Trade Area (AfCFTA) Agreement entered into force on 30 May 2019 and was operationalised in 2021. It stands as a landmark initiative in African economic integration.[1] Encompassing 55 African Union (AU) Member States and a combined population of over 1.3 billion, the AfCFTA aims to create a single continental market for goods and services, fostering intra-African trade, which currently ranges between 16–18 per cent of total trade.[2] This ambitious project seeks not only to liberalise tariffs but also to harmonise rules on investment, intellectual property and competition policy.[3] The AfCFTA is anchored on the Agreement Establishing the AfCFTA and is operationalised through several protocols, including those on trade in goods, trade in services, investment, competition policy, intellectual property rights, and dispute settlement.[4]

Despite this ambitious attempt by the AU to ensure a single market, the AfCFTA's operationalisation has been marked by slow ratification, contradictions, and unfinished negotiations.[5] At the time of writing, the AfCFTA Agreement marks five years since its entry into force, on 1 January 2021. This concluding chapter therefore only assesses the 'new frontiers' that the AfCFTA

[1] African Union, 'The African Continental Free Trade Area' (African Union, 2 November 2025) au.int/en/african-continental-free-trade-area.

[2] United Nations Economic Commission for Africa, 'Celebrating the Adoption of New Protocols on Investment, Intellectual Property Rights, Competition Policy and Digital Trade under the AfCFTA' (UNECA, 16 March 2023) uneca.org/stories/%28blog%29-deepening-the-afcfta-celebrating-the-adoption-of-new-protocols-on-investment> accessed 22 September 2025.

[3] Iza Lejarraga, 'Trading aims: The value of Africa's deep integration trade agreement' (European Council on Foreign Relations, policy brief 3 May 2022) ecfr.eu/publication/trading-aims-the-value-of-africas-deep-integration-trade-agreement/.

[4] Agreement Establishing the African Continental Free Trade Area (adopted 21 March 2018), art 8.

[5] Kiiza Africa, '*Assessing Five Years of the African Continental Free Trade Area (AfCFTA): Proposal on Potential Ammendments*' (South Centre, 215 Research Paper, 23 January 2025) 4. www.econstor.eu/handle/10419/312875.

has brought and uncovers some of the 'failed imaginations' of the AfCFTA. It is prudent to do this given that the AfCFTA Agreement provides that '...[it] shall be subject to review every five (5) years after its entry into force, by State Parties, to ensure effectiveness . . .'.[6] This chapter therefore proceeds in three parts: first, it examines the new frontiers embodied in the AfCFTA, with particular emphasis on the distinct features and innovations of its protocols. Second, it interrogates the failed legal imaginations of the AfCFTA, focusing on the dispute settlement mechanism, stalled negotiations, the shortcomings of the Guided Trade Initiative (GTI), and the unnegotiated annexes. Finally, it offers a broad and general conclusion to this book.

2. THE NEW FRONTIERS

The AfCFTA is replete with both new and innovative trade aspects as embodied in various protocols that reflect the continent's socioeconomic realities and the specific needs of Africans. These include protocols on investment, competition policy, digital trade, and women and youth in trade. The characterisation of these protocols as 'new frontiers' is made in contrast to the World Trade Organization (WTO), which, as is argued below, has largely been replicated in the AfCFTA dispute settlement framework. Describing them as new frontiers, however, is not to suggest that they have been fully realised or implemented; rather, it highlights their potential to reshape Africa's trade governance if effectively operationalised.

2.1 The Investment Protocol

The Investment Protocol is a testament of African Countries' attempts to reclaim the investment regime through an Afro-centric legal landscape that coheres with the continental priorities.[7] Evidently, the WTO does not directly govern investments made between Member States, but rather, as already shown in this book, the dispute settlement in investment is often governed within the purview of ad hoc or institutional arbitral tribunals commonly referred to as Investor-State Dispute Settlements (ISDSs). Investment based disputes are also increasingly resolved within the jurisdiction of national judicial authority of the host states. The enabling frameworks for such regulation have been bilateral investment treaties (BITs) or Trade and Investment Framework Agreements

[6] AfCFTA Agreement, art 28.

[7] Muhammad Siddique Ali Pirzada, 'The AfCFTA Investment Protocol: A new age for regional Investment and dispute resolution' (Harvard ILJ, 11 April 2025) journals.law.harvard.edu/ilj/2025/04/the-afcfta-investment-protocol-a-new-age-for-regional-investment-and-dispute-resolution/.

(TIFAs), which vary considerably depending on the contracting parties.[8] These investment arrangements have generally been skewed in favour of investors, constraining host states and undermining public policy space.[9] International Investment law generally and International Investment Arbitration, have attracted enormous controversy in the first two decades of the twenty-first century.[10] These controversies are also historical as this area of international commerce has been stepped by controversy from its inception.[11] In recent times, especially in the first three decades of the twenty-first century, there is a broad emerging consensus that international investment law and international investment arbitration (including ISDS) are in crisis.[12] Some commentators labeled the current situation a legitimacy crisis,[13] while others called it a backlash to international investment law.[14] It is now uncommon to meet any stakeholder in the area who doesn't think that the area currently needs reform.[15]

The AfCFTA makes a landmark departure from traditional investment governance by carving out its own Investment Protocol.[16] The Protocol, in

[8] United Nations Conference on Trade and Development, International Investment Agreements Trends: The Increasing Dichotomy between New and Old Treaties (IIA Issues Note No 2, October 2024) UNCTAD/DIAE/PCB/INF/2024/4 unctad.org/publication/international-investment-agreements-trends-increasing-dichotomy-between-new-and-old.

[9] Patrick Dumbery, 'Suggestions for Incorporating Human Rights Obligations into BITs' in Kavaljit Singh and Burghard Ilge (eds) *Rethinking Bilateral Investment Treaties* (Both ENDS and SOMO, 2016) 212–214.

[10] Muthucumaraswamy Sornarajah, *International Law on Foreign Investment* (3rd edn, Cambridge University Press, 2010); Pia Eberhardt and Cecilia Olivet, *Profiting from Injustice: How Law Firms, Arbitrators and Financiers Are Fuelling an Investment Arbitration Boom* (Corporate Europe Observatory and Transnational Institute, 2012); Muthucumaraswamy Sornarajah, *Resistance and Change in the International Law on Foreign Investment* (Cambridge University Press, 2015).

[11] ibid, see also Kate Miles, *The Origins of International Investment Law: Empire, Environment and the Safeguarding of Capital* (Cambridge University Press, 2013).

[12] See Gabrielle Kaufmann-Kohler and Michele Potestà, *Can the Mauritius Convention Serve as a Model for the Reform of Investor-State Arbitration in Connection with the Introduction of a Permanent Investment Tribunal or an Appeal Mechanism?: Analysis and Roadmap* (CIDS Research Paper, 2016) lk-k.com/wp-content/uploads/2016/05/KAUFMANN-KOHLER-POTESTA-CIDS-Research-Paper-Reform-of-Investor-State-Arbitration-2016.pdf; Robert Howse and Günes Ünüvar, 'Sowing the Seeds of an ISDS Legitimacy Crisis? The Notorious First Wave of NAFTA Chapter 11 Awards' in Hélène Ruiz Fabri and Edoardo Stoppioni (eds), *International Investment Law: An Analysis of the Major Decisions* (Edward Elgar, 2022) 99.

[13] Susan D Franck, 'The Legitimacy Crisis in Investment Treaty Arbitration: Privatizing Public International Law through Inconsistent Decisions' (2005) 73 *Fordham L Rev* 1521.

[14] Malcolm Langford, Daniel Behn and Ole Kristian Fauchald, 'Backlash and State Strategies in International Investment Law' in Tanja Aalberts and Thomas Gammeltoft-Hansen (eds), *The Changing Practices of International Law* (Cambridge University Press, 2018) 70; *see also* Claire Balchin, Liz Kyo-Hwa Chung, Asha Kaushal and Michael Waibel, *The Backlash against Investment Arbitration: Perceptions and Reality* (Kluwer Law International, 2010); Asha Kaushal, 'Revisiting History: How the Past Matters for the Present Backlash against the Foreign Investment Regime' (2009) 50 *Harvard Intl LJ* 491; Olivia Chung, 'The Lopsided International Investment Law Regime and Its Effect on the Future of Investor-State Arbitration' (2007) 47 *Virginia J Intl L* 953.

[15] Lee M Caplan, 'ISDS Reform and the Proposal for a Multilateral Investment Court' (2019) 46 *Ecology LQ* 53.

[16] Gerhard Erasmus, 'An Protocol for the AfCFTA' (TRALAC Blog 23 March 2021) www.tralac.org/blog/article/15152-an-investment-protocol-for-the-afcfta.html.

essence, bears a plethora of innovative provisions whose bottom line is to safeguard African Countries' right to regulate and to freely pursue their sustainable or economic goals.[17] It attempts to re-balance the scale of investment by imposing obligations on investors. In view of the Investment protocol, the following provisions are the 'new frontiers':

(i) Article 1 on the definition of an 'investment' adopts an enterprise-based approach and requires that such investment must make a significant contribution to the Host State's sustainable development.[18] This departs from the open-ended, asset-based definitions common in BITs. It also builds upon the *Salini* criteria by expressly linking investment to state developmental goals,[19] thereby preventing purely speculative or extractive ventures from enjoying treaty protection.

(ii) Article 17 replaces the notorious Fair and Equitable Treatment (FET) standard with a high threshold of Administrative and Judicial Treatment standard.[20] The drafters of the AfCFTA appreciated the unsettled and ambiguous nature of the FET and carefully replaced it with a standard defined by a closed list of elements rather than the unwinding elements of FET.[21] This arguably renders the FET jurisprudence inapplicable within the AfCFTA and sets the stage for new beginnings.[22] This shift also potentially resolves the long-standing debate over whether FET exceeds the minimum standard of treatment under customary international law.

(iii) Article 18 reformulates the wording of the traditional Full Protection and Security (FPS) clause to a narrower Physical Protection and Security (PPS) clause. This confines the duty of host states to safeguarding the physical integrity of investments,[23] rather than extending protection to legal or regulatory frameworks.[24] The provision is further qualified by two elements: 'subject to capabilities' and 'no less favourable', which

[17] Hamed El-Kady and Mustaqeem De Gama, 'The Reform of the International Investment Regime: An African Perspective' (2019) 34(2) *ICSID Review*, 482, 486.

[18] AfCFTA Investment Protocol, art. 1.

[19] *Salini Construttori S.P.A and Italstade S.P.A. V. Morocco*, ICSID Case No. ARB/00/4, Decision on Jurisdiction, 23 July 2001, 52.

[20] Alexandre Genest and Letizia Busso, 'The AfCFTA's Investment Protocol: the bell tolls for first-generation intra-African BITs and their more conventional investor protections' (Global Trade & Investment Law Blog, July 2024) www.steptoe.com/en/news-publications/global-trade-and-investment-law-blog/the-afcftas-investment-protocol-the-bell-tolls-for-first-generation-intra-african-bits-and-their-more-conventional-investor-protections.html?utm_source=chatgpt.com.

[21] Yuliya Chernyk, 'Contract Interpretation in Investment Treaty Arbitration' (2022) 12 *Brill Nijhoff*, 38.

[22] AfCFTA Investment Protocol, art 17(2).

[23] Romesh Weeramantry, 'Full Protection and Security and Its Overlap with Fair and Equitable Treatment' in Julien Chaisse, Leila Choukroune and Sufian Jusoh (eds), *Handbook of International Investment Law and Policy*, (Springer Nature, 2021) 4–6, link.springer.com/rwe/10.1007/978-981-13-5744-2_53-1.

[24] Nartnirun Junngam, 'The Full Protection and Security Standard in International Investment Law: What and Who is Investment Fully [?] Protected and Secured From? (2018) 7(1) *American University Business Law Review* 48.

contextualise state obligations and reflect the diverse capacities of African states.

(iv) The provisions under PART IV embody the prioritisation of African Countries' right to regulate and to exercise their sovereignty by having the liberty to pursue their developmental and sustainable goals. This is complemented by the Protocol's audacious act of imposing obligations on investors under PART V. These provisions reflect a sharp break from traditional BITs that vest the investor with limitless rights, while usurping the state's right to regulate.

(v) Lastly, perhaps the most ambitious provision, Article 49 mandates the termination of all 183 intra-African BITs within five years of the Protocol's entry into force.[25] This move seeks to replace the patchwork of bilateral arrangements with a coherent continental framework.[26] If achieved, it would mark a significant consolidation of Africa's investment governance landscape and a historic assertion of collective sovereignty.

The above-discussed provisions are illustrative of the new frontiers that the Investment Protocol seeks to pursue. In general, the protocol deviates from an investor-centred regime to a regime of equals in which both parties bear different but equally important obligations. But, as argued in chapter five of this book, the AfCFTA Investment protocol like the Pan-African Investment Code (PAIC) before it bears the marks of benign Africanisation as it focuses only on the regulation of intra-African investment.

2.2 The Competition Policy

The integration of competition provisions within the AfCFTA represents both a 'new frontier' in supranational regulation and a reflection on 'failed imagination' in global trade frameworks, such as the omission of comprehensive competition rules in the WTO established by the 1994 Marrakesh Agreement.[27] To understand a multilateral competition policy, I draw on the failed attempts under the WTO. The roots of international competition policy trace back to the post-World War II era, in which the 1948 Havana Charter for the International

[25] AfCFTA Investment Protocol, art 49(1).

[26] Alexandre Genest and Letizia Busso, 'The AfCFTA's Investment Protocol: the bell tolls for first-generation intra-African BITs and their more conventional investor protections' (Global Trade & Investment Law Blog, July 2024) www.steptoe.com/en/news-publications/global-trade-and-investment-law-blog/the-afcftas-investment-protocol-the-bell-tolls-for-first-generation-intra-african-bits-and-their-more-conventional-investor-protections.html?.

[27] Mitsuo Matsushita, 'International Cooperation in the Enforcement of Competition Policy' (2002) 1 *Washington University Global Studies Law Review*, 464 www.worldtradelaw.net/document.php?id=articles/matsushitacompetition.pdf&mode=download.

Trade Organization (ITO) envisioned a comprehensive global trade organisation.[28] Chapter V of the Charter specifically addressed 'Restrictive Business Practices', mandating Member States to curb private enterprise behaviours that restrained international trade, such as price-fixing, market allocation, and exclusionary tactics.[29] The ITO aimed to foster consultations and recommendations, promoting fair competition as integral to economic recovery and global stability.[30] However, the Charter's ambitious scope clashed with national interests, particularly in the United States, where business lobbies and congressional opposition viewed it as an unpermissible infringement on sovereignty.[31] The US failure to ratify the Charter in 1950 doomed it to failure, leaving the General Agreement on Tariffs and Trade (GATT) 1947 as a provisional alternative that was focused narrowly on tariff reductions and non-discrimination principles.[32]

Following the failure of the Havana charter, any competition policy that encompasses regulations against cartels, abuse of dominance and anti-competitive mergers has been firmly rooted in the domain of sovereign states or of regional trade agreements.[33] National authorities tailor these laws to local economic contexts, allowing for exemptions that align with developmental goals, such as protecting employment or promoting industrialisation.[34] This sovereignty-centric approach has persisted due to fears of external interference, yet it has left gaps in addressing cross-border anti-competitive practices.

The AfCFTA's Competition Policy, adopted in February 2023, challenges this paradigm by introducing a continental framework that balances national autonomy with unified enforcement.[35] In contrast to the WTO's shortcomings, the AfCFTA embodies a 'new frontier' by explicitly embedding competition policy within its architecture. The Protocol on Competition Policy seeks to establish an integrated and unified African continental competition regime that promotes fair markets, inclusive growth, and innovation while addressing the continent's unique challenges, such as low intra-regional trade and economic disparities.[36]

[28] Giorgio Sacerdoti, 'Havana Charter (1948)' (Oxford Public International Law, June 2014) opil.ouplaw.com/display/10.1093/law:epil/9780199231690/law-9780199231690-e1529.

[29] Havana Charter (1948), art 46–54.

[30] Mitsuo Matsushita, 'International Cooperation in the Enforcement of Competition Policy' 464.

[31] Daniel Drache, 'The short but significant life of the International Trade Organization: Lessons for our time' (2000 CSGR Working paper No. 62/00) 21–22; Daniel Steiner, 'The International Convergence of Competition Laws' (1997) 24(3) *Manitoba Law Journal* 602– 603.

[32] Daniel Drache, 'The short but significant life of the International Trade Organization: Lessons for our time' Working papers (University of Warwick. Centre for the Study of Globalisation and Regionalisation) 22.

[33] AfCFTA Competition Policy, preamble.

[34] AfCFTA Protocol on Competition Policy: Factsheet (5 October 2023) www.tralac.org/resources/infographic/16150-afcfta-protocol-on-competition-policy-factsheet.html.

[35] United Nations Economic Commission for Africa, 'Celebrating the Adoption of New Protocols on Investment, Intellectual Property Rights, Competition Policy and Digital Trade under the AfCFTA' (UNECA, 2023) uneca.org/stories/%28blog%29-deepening-the-afcfta-celebrating-the-adoption-of-new-protocols-on-investment%2C#:~:text=In%20a%20step%20that%20takes,)%2C%20and%20on%20competition%20policy.

[36] AfCFTA Competition Policy, preamble.

This marks a shift from purely national domains toward supranational elements, drawing lessons from global failures and regional successes.

The Protocol prohibits a range of anti-competitive practices, including horizontal agreements (cartels, bid-rigging), vertical restraints (exclusive dealing), abuse of dominance (predatory pricing), and mergers that substantially lessen competition. It also introduces novel provisions on abuse of economic dependence, targeting digital platforms and gatekeepers that impose unfair terms on smaller players.[37]

Institutionally, the Protocol creates the AfCFTA Competition Authority, an autonomous body with a Board for decision-making, an Investigative Body, and an Executive Director.[38] A Committee on Competition Policy facilitates coordination, while the AfCFTA Competition Tribunal handles appeals.[39] This structure empowers the Authority to investigate cross-border issues, impose fines of up to 10 per cent of global turnover, approve mergers and conduct market inquiries; functions that go beyond the WTO's state-centric model.[40]

Cooperation is central, with mandates for state parties to harmonise laws, share information, and provide technical assistance to build capacity in under-resourced jurisdictions.[41] This networked approach mitigates the WTO's 'failed imaginations' by tailoring integration to Africa's context, where only about half of the countries have operational competition authorities. By addressing issues like food price cartels or Big Tech dominance, the AfCFTA aims to unlock economic potential, potentially increasing GDP by 3.9 per cent by 2035 through enhanced competition and trade.[42]

2.3 Protocol on Digital Trade

The Protocol on Digital Trade is a major milestone for African countries. It governs digitally enabled trade in goods and services, whether delivered digitally or physically, and involving both natural and juridical persons.[43] The complexities of digital trade are numerous and require deliberate regulation to ensure adherence to free market principles. African countries bypassed a systemic problem that has plagued the WTO since 1998. The WTO has no binding agreement governing digital trade, nor a definition of digital transmissions. As a result, the

[37] Andrew T Guzman, 'Is International Antitrust Possible?' (1998) 73 *NYU L Rev*, 1538–1540 nyulawreview.org/wp-content/uploads/2018/08/NYULawReview-73-5-Guzman.pdf.

[38] AfCFTA Competition Policy, art. 13(2).

[39] ibid at art 24(2).

[40] ibid at art 17.

[41] ibid at art 22.

[42] United Nations Economic Commission for Africa, 'Celebrating the Adoption of New Protocols on Investment, Intellectual Property Rights, Competition Policy and Digital Trade under the AfCFTA'.

[43] Protocol to the Agreement Establishing the African Continental Free Trade Area on Digital Trade, art 1.

elimination of customs duties and tariffs on such transmissions remains elusive. [44] Instead, WTO Members rely on the temporary e-commerce Moratorium, renewed at every Ministerial Conference since 1998. At the thirteenth Ministerial Conference in 2024, Members agreed to maintain the moratorium until the earlier of the fourteenth Ministerial Conference or 31 March 2026, when it will expire.[45]

The protocol on digital trade, therefore, serves as a launching pad for a continental regulatory reform, harmonisation and investment in digital public infrastructure.[46] While Africa faces challenges concerning digital exclusion, low quantum of intra-African digital trade, data protection concerns and lack of broadband infrastructure,[47] the Protocol can alleviate them by facilitating a digitally friendly environment that incentivises governments to ratify and implement the protocol.

The Protocol is attuned to the realities of African countries, particularly the challenge of limited infrastructure, which remains a major impediment to the full realisation of trade in digital products. Article 18 addresses this by calling for deliberate actions by State Parties to enhance digital infrastructure through measures such as creating an enabling regulatory environment, fostering partnerships, promoting interoperability and interconnectivity, and increasing the affordability of broadband, among others.[48] In addition, the Protocol promotes cross-border payments, which can only be realised through the interoperability of digital payment and settlement systems.[49] The Pan-African Payment and Settlement System (PAPSS) provides a practical example of such an initiative.[50]

2.4 Protocol on Women, Youth and Trade

The Protocol on Women, Youth and Trade represents a significant frontier in the AfCFTA because it addresses the intersection between trade and social inclusion,[51] an area largely absent from the WTO framework. By contrast, the AfCFTA explicitly integrates gender and youth considerations into its legal

[44] OECD, 'The WTO Moratorium on Custom Duties on Electronic Transmissions: What is really at stake?' (2023) OECD unpublished working paper, 2–3 www.intracen.org/file/2023icc-itc-joint-icc-itc-policy-brief-edition-1-wto-moratoriumpdf.

[45] World Trade Organization, Work Programme on Electronic Commerce, Draft Ministerial Decision of 1 March 2024, WTO Doc WT/MIN(24)/17 (1 March 2024) https://docs.wto.org/dol2fe/Pages/SS/directdoc.aspx?filename=q:/WT/MIN24/W26R1.pdf&Open=True.

[46] John Stuart, 'Implementing the AfCFTA'S Digital Trade Protocol' (Policy Briefing 303, December 2024) 1 saiia.org.za/wp-content/uploads/2024/12/PB-303-ERIP-stuart-FINAL.pdf.

[47] Aberto Lemma, Prachi Agarwal and Dirk Willem te Velde, 'Implementing the Digital Trade Protocol of the African Continental Free Trade Area' (2025) *ODI Global Working Paper* 20–21 <odi.org/en/publications/implementing-the-afcfta-digital-trade-protocol-expected-impacts-early-experiences-and-challenges-ahead/.

[48] AfCFTA Digital Trade Protocol, art 18.

[49] ibid at art 15.

[50] Annabel Nanjira and Nwamaka Okany, 'African perspective in International Economic Law 2022 – 2023' (2024) 4 *African Journal of International Economic Law* 105, 109.

[51] AfCFTA Protocol on Women, Youth and Trade, Preamble, recital 5.

framework, recognising that structural inequalities have historically limited the ability of these groups to engage in cross-border commerce.[52] This inclusion signals a paradigm shift away from a purely market-driven model of trade governance to one that embeds socio-economic realities within its operations.[53]

A second dimension of novelty is the Protocol's design of affirmative obligations on State Parties to facilitate the participation of women- and youth-led businesses.[54] These include commitments to eliminate non-tariff barriers, improve access to finance, protect intellectual property, and enhance digital trade opportunities for women and youth entrepreneurs. The Protocol goes further by operationalising ownership and management thresholds that qualify businesses as 'women- or youth-led' or 'women- or youth-owned,' ensuring that preferential measures are targeted and measurable.[55] This is a radical departure from the WTO model, in which inclusivity concerns are often left to soft law instruments, side initiatives or capacity-building projects without binding obligations.

Finally, the Protocol illustrates how non-trade aspects can directly contribute to trade by recognising the economic potential of women and youth as drivers of structural transformation. Access to trade finance,[56] protection of intellectual property, and integration into digital platforms are not simply social policy objectives but are crucial mechanisms for unlocking productive capacity and boosting intra-African trade.[57] By treating inclusivity as a trade issue, the Protocol underscores that sustainable and broad-based economic growth cannot be achieved without dismantling barriers that exclude marginalised groups from markets.[58]

2.5 Failed Legal Imaginaries

The concept of legal imagination refers to 'the space in which our ideas about the limits and purposes of [the law] take shape'.[59] The imagination here is sociologically grounded and goes beyond just ideas but includes practices.[60] AfCFTA legal framework offers both African diplomats and norm entrepreneurs

[52] Laura Naliaka, 'The AfCFTA protocol on women and youth in trade-Africa's blueprint for inclusive trade' (UNECA, 16 April 2025) www.uneca.org/stories/blog-the-afcfta-protocol-on-women-and-youth-in-trade-%E2%80%93-africa%E2%80%99s-blueprint-for-inclusive?utm_source=chatgpt.com.

[53] Katrin Kuhimann and Amrita, 'Gender mainstreaming in trade agreement: "A Potemkin Façade"?' (2023) *Georgetown Law Faculty Publications and other Works*, 235 <scholarship.law.georgetown.edu/cgi/viewcontent.cgi?params=/context/facpub/article/3529/&path_info=Kuhlmann_Bahri_Gender_Potemkin_Facade_May_2023.pdf.

[54] Nanjira and Okany (n 50) 112.

[55] John Stuart, 'The AfCFTA Protocol on Women and Youth in Trade and Trade-Driven Development in Africa' (TralacBog 24 February 2024) www.tralac.org/blog/article/16324-the-afcfta-protocol-on-women-and-youth-in-trade-and-trade-driven-development-in-africa.html.

[56] AfCFTA Protocol on Women, Youth and Trade, art 10.

[57] ibid at art 11

[58] ibid at Preamble, recital 9.

[59] Nicolás M Perrone, *Investment Treaties and the Legal Imagination: How Foreign Investors Play by Their Own Rules* (Oxford University Press, 2021) 4.

[60] Charles Taylor, *Modern Social Imaginaries* (Duke University Press 2004) 63

an opportunity to reorient the direction of international economic law generally to favour African states. I, however, show that in certain areas principally in the dispute settlement Protocol, there is a failed imaginary that is directly linked to the path dependency of directly transplanting the WTO dispute settlement system.

3. AfCFTA DISPUTE SETTLEMENT

AfCFTA represents a bold ambition to unite a 1.3 billion-person market under a single continental trade framework.[61] From the outset, drafters recognised that a robust dispute resolution mechanism would be central to the success of the agreement. Indeed, Article 20 of the AfCFTA Agreement establishes a compulsory dispute settlement mechanism for Member States, and the Protocol on Rules and Procedures on the Settlement of Disputes (DSP) affirms that this mechanism is 'a central element in providing security and predictability to the regional trading system'.[62] In theory, an effective Dispute Settlement Mechanism (DSM) is an assurance to the AfCFTA that its commitments are enforceable and that disagreements over interpretation can be resolved fairly. Just as the WTO relies on its dispute settlement system to maintain security and predictability,[63] the AfCFTA's DSM was intended as the cornerstone for Africa's rules-based trade regime.[64]

In design, the AfCFTA's DSM closely mirrors the WTO model.[65] It is an inter-state system: only governments of Member States can bring a case, and disputes are defined as disagreements between state parties over the interpretation or application of the AfCFTA Agreement.[66] A two-tier adjudicative structure is envisaged. First, ad hoc Dispute Settlement Panels hear cases and issue reports;[67] then a standing Appellate Body of seven members review panel decisions on appeal.[68] This framework, outlined in the Dispute Settlement Protocol, aims to

[61] Regis Simo, 'A Future Court without Cases? On the Question of Standing in the AfCFTA Dispute Settlement Mechanism' (AfronomicsLaw Blog, 19 August 2019) www.afronomicslaw.org/2019/08/19/a-future-court-without-cases-on-the-question-of-standing-in-the-afcfta-dispute-settlement-mechanism#:~:text=operational%20phase%20au,obligation%20for%20all%20Member%20States.

[62] AfCFTA Agreement, art 20.

[63] ibid at art 4(1).

[64] Tomasz Milej, 'The Dispute Settlement Mechanism under the African Continental Free Trade Area as a Preserve of Elites – A Missed Opportunity for Regional Integration in Africa' (2023) *SSRN Electronic Journal* 1–2.

[65] James T Gathii, 'Evaluating the Dispute Settlement Mechanism of the African Continental Free Trade Agreement' AfronomicsLaw Blog, 10 April 2019 www.afronomicslaw.org/2019/04/10/evaluating-the-dispute-settlement-mechanism-of-the-african-continental-free-trade-agreement.

[66] Regis Simo 'Non-exclusivity and an ocean of Possibilities: The AfCFTA Jurisdictional Lex Specialis' (2023) 20(2) Transnational Dispute Management 6.

[67] Protocol on Rules and Procedures on the Settlement of Disputes, Annex to the Agreement Establishing the African Continental Free Trade Area (adopted 21 March 2018, entered into force 30 May 2019) art 12.

[68] DSP, art 20.

provide neutral, law-based resolutions. Like the WTO's process, it begins with consultations and allows for mediation or arbitration alternatives, but ultimately empowers panels to make binding decisions if diplomacy fails.[69] In short, on paper, the AfCFTA DSM aspires to combine flexibility (through consultations and optional arbitration) with judicial certainty (through panel rulings and appeals). Such a structure, if fully operational and utilised, would arguably be a cornerstone of the AfCFTA project, deterring violations and giving businesses confidence that trade rules will be upheld.

However, as we turn from the textbook design to the emerging reality, cracks in this foundation become apparent. The AfCFTA DSM may have been carefully modelled after the WTO DSM, but the African context presents different challenges.[70] A dispute mechanism is only as effective as the willingness and ability of parties to use it. African states have rarely litigated trade disputes against each other in existing forums. In the WTO, African member countries have made very little use of the dispute system.[71] The AfCFTA drafters were certainly aware of this pattern, as it has been prevalent not only in the WTO but also within Regional Economic Communities (RECs).[72] The drafters thus failed to imagine a system beyond the reality that African states historically avoid adjudicating trade disputes.

3.1 State-Centrism as a Flawed Design

A core criticism is that the AfCFTA's dispute settlement is entirely state-centric, to the exclusion of non-state actors. Only governments can initiate a dispute under AfCFTA rules; private businesses, trade associations, civil society, and individuals have no direct standing.[73] This was a deliberate choice by the negotiators, aligning with many traditional trade agreements. But this chapter sees this as a *failure of imagination* for lack of courage to break the mould and craft a

[69] Olabisi Akingube, 'Dispute Settlement under the African Continental Free Trade Area Agreement: A Preliminary Assessment' (2020) 28 African Journal of International and Comparative Law, 145–148 digitalcommons.schulichlaw.dal.ca/cgi/viewcontent.cgi?article=1483&context=scholarly_works.

[70] Regis Simo, 'A Future Court without Cases? On the Question of Standing in the AfCFTA Dispute Settlement Mechanism' (Afronomicslaw Blog 19 August 2019), www.afronomicslaw.org/2019/08/19/a-future-court-without-cases-on-the-question-of-standing-in-the-afcfta-dispute-settlement-mechanism.

[71] Edwin Kessie and Kofi Addo, 'African Countries and the WTO Negotiations on the Dispute Settlement Understanding' (2007) *International Centre for Trade and Sustainable Development* 1–3.

[72] Desiderio Consultants Ltd, 'AfCFTA Dispute Settlement Body goes operational' (International Trade & Customs Regulation, 27 April 2021) www.ddcustomslaw.com/index.php?option=com_content&view=article&id=481:afcfta-dispute-settlement-body-goes-operational-&catid=1:ultime&Itemid=50&lang=it#:~:text=from%20other%20RECs%20,been%20initiated%20by%20private%20parties.

[73] Tomasz Milej, 'The Dispute Settlement Mechanism under the African Continental Free Trade Area as a Preserve of Elites – A Missed Opportunity for Regional Integration in Africa' Proceedings of the National University of Lesotho – World Trade Organization (NUL-WTO) Research Chairs' 2nd Annual Conference (October 6 2023) dx.doi.org/10.2139/ssrn.4644827.

more expansive system for Africa. By 'copying and pasting' the WTO's intergovernmental model,[74] the AfCFTA overlooked lessons from Africa's own regional courts, some of which allow direct access and have thereby developed meaningful jurisprudence. For example, the East African Court of Justice (EACJ) is notably accessible to individuals and companies,[75] a feature that has led to the institution of trade-related cases, strengthening the rule of law in that region.[76] In contrast, under AfCFTA's DSM, disputes can only be initiated by states, a design that leaves no room for non-state actors.[77] Far from pioneering a uniquely African dispute model, the AfCFTA mechanism ended up not significantly different from the dispute settlement mechanisms, but as a replica.

Critics argue that this state-centricity is not a trivial technical detail, but a fundamental mistake in achieving AfCFTA's aims.[78] By depriving non-state actors of any capacity to directly invoke AfCFTA rules, the system effectively disincentivises the small and medium-sized enterprises (SMEs), whereas they account for a bigger fraction of intra-Africa trade.[79] In any case, SMEs, unlike large transnational corporations, lack sufficient resources and political influence to lobby states to file disputes on their behalf when their interests are harmed. As such, the dispute settlement system could become a preserve of elites, addressing only those issues that align with big market players. The AfCFTA DSM's design struggles to fulfil the aspirations of AU's Agenda 2063, particularly concerning inclusive growth and people-driven development, by failing to increase the bargaining power of SMEs.[80] The nature of the DSM defeats the essence of grassroots participation and equitable benefits by excluding the people meant to drive and benefit from integration.

The consequences of this limited standing are both practical and principled. Practically, trade in Africa is marred with non-tariff barriers and regulatory issues that individual traders or firms encounter, such as cumbersome customs

[74] David Luke, 'Making the case for the African Continental Free Trade Area' in David Luke and Jamie MacLeod (eds), *Inclusive Trade in Africa: The African Continental Free Trade Area in Comparative Perspective* (Routledge, 2019) 11.

[75] Treaty for the Establishment of the East African Community (signed 30 November 1999, entered into force 7 July 2000) 2144 UNTS 255, art 30.

[76] Milej (n 73).

[77] Akinyi J Eurallyah, 'Conflict of Laws and Intra-African Commercial Disputes: To what Extent Does (Lack of) a Harmonized Pan-African Conflict of Laws Regime Support the AfCFTA Liberalization Agenda?' (AfronomicsLaw Blog, 12 December 2021) www.afronomicslaw.org/category/analysis/conflict-laws-and-intra-african-commercial-disputes-what-extent-does-lack.

[78] Milej (n 73) at 1.

[79] Mariam Olafuyi, 'Mainstreaming Non-State Actors in African Regional Integration' (AfronomicsLaw Blog 1 May 2019) www.afronomicslaw.org/2019/05/01/mainstreaming-non-state-actors-in-african-regional-integration.

[80] Lily Sommer and Jamie MacLeod, 'How important is special and differential treatment for an inclusive AfCFTA?' in David Luke and Jamie MacLeod (eds), *Inclusive Trade in Africa: The African Continental Free Trade Area in Comparative Perspective* (Routledge, 2019) 69.

procedures, discriminatory regulations, etc.[81] Without direct access, many legitimate grievances will go unaddressed, which hinders the identification and removal of trade barriers that the AfCFTA is supposed to eliminate. Principally, the state-centric model distances the people from running and contributing to the dispute settlement system and as a result, conflicts with the notion of a people-centred principle as envisioned by REC regimes such as in the East Africa Community Treaty (EAC Treaty).[82] As Regis Simo noted, broad access to justice in trade agreements can advance legal integration and rights – for instance, a case at the EACJ saw a private company successfully challenge a Member State's trade restriction (an excise duty by Uganda) as violating the community's treaty.[83] AfCFTA's DSM, by contrast, offers no such opportunity; if Uganda's action had violated the AfCFTA, only another government could contest it, and in all likelihood no one would, leaving the violation (and its harm to traders) unchecked. This underscores the need to broaden access to truly deepen integration.

Furthermore, the exclusive reliance on states raises doubts about the DSM's effectiveness and usage. This goes to the sincerity of AfCFTA members in establishing this mechanism, noting that no African state has ever brought a pure trade dispute against another in existing regional courts.[84] Given that track record, expecting the same governments to suddenly litigate under AfCFTA might be wishful thinking. Regis Simo has pointedly observed that one might cynically suspect the negotiators intentionally designed an inter-state DSM 'to nip the project in the bud'.[85] In other words, the negotiators created a dispute settlement system they knew would likely remain dormant, thereby avoiding any real transfer of adjudicative power. While that claim may be provocative, it reflects a genuine concern: that AfCFTA's DSM could exist largely on paper, while in reality, trade conflicts continue to be resolved (or not be resolved) through political bargains or through other means. A dispute mechanism that no one uses is, effectively, a failed one. It risks becoming an empty shell that diminishes the credibility of the AfCFTA as a 'rules-based' system.

[81] Stephen Drinkwater and Catherine Robinson, 'The impact of customs and trade regulations on the operation of African firms' (2023) 165(C) Journal of Business Research, 3 www.sciencedirect.com/science/article/pii/S0148296323004046.

[82] Petro Protas and Theophil Romward, 'Reflections on 'People Centered Principle' in the East African Community: The current legal Controversy' (2015) 42(2) Eastern African Law Review, 6 www.researchgate.net/publication/333674193_Reflections_on_'People_Centered_Principle'_in_the_East_African_Community_The_Current_Legal_Controversy.

[83] Harrison O Mbori, 'Case Commentary on the British American Tobacco v. Attorney General of Uganda (EACJ) and GETMA International v. The Republic of Guinea (OHADA CCJA)' (2020) 1 *African Journal of International Economic Law* 344-371.

[84] Olabisi Akingube, 'What African Continental Free Trade Agreement Protocol on Dispute Settlement Says about the culture of African States to Dispute Resolution' (AfronomicsLaw Blog 9 April 2019) www.afronomicslaw.org/2019/04/09/what-the-african-continental-free-trade-agreement-protocol-on-dispute-settlement-says-about-the-culture-of-african-states-to-dispute-resolution.

[85] Simo (n 70).

4. CONCLUSION

The African Continental Free Trade Agreement represents a pivotal moment in the continent's quest for economic sovereignty and integration, yet its first five years reveal a landscape of bold innovations shadowed by persistent shortcomings. The new frontiers charted through protocols on investment, competition, digital trade, and women and youth in trade demonstrate a commitment to an Africanised model that prioritises sustainable development, regulatory autonomy, and inclusive participation, diverging from global precedents like the WTO to address Africa's unique challenges and opportunities. These elements hold the potential to foster resilient markets, empower marginalised groups, and drive intra-continental growth in ways that traditional trade frameworks have overlooked.

Nevertheless, the failed imaginations embedded in the AfCFTA's structure, particularly its state-centric DSM underscore the risks of replicating external models without sufficient adaptation. These gaps not only hinder enforcement and predictability but also perpetuate elitism, forum shopping, and delays that erode confidence among traders and investors. As the Agreement approaches its mandated review under Article 28, state parties must seize this opportunity to amend the dispute framework for broader access, finalise pending annexes with clear timelines, and strengthen institutional capacity to translate aspirations into actionable outcomes. Only through such reforms can the AfCFTA evolve from a promising vision into a transformative force for Africa's economic future.

This book has demonstrated that the judicial and arbitral institutions in sub-regional that African states have mandated to settle economic disputes are not just mere copies of the counterparts in other parts of the world. They are impactful institutions that generate a complex matrix of social, political, historical, and legal variations for understanding the trajectory of international law generally and international economic law specifically. African international economic dispute settlement was presented as a 'field' in the Bourdieusian sense of an area of structured, socially patterned activity or 'practice', and as a site of struggle for control.[86] This field is heavily influenced by five socio-legal actors: African states, Transnational corporations (TNCs), African international law legal scholars and experts, International and Transnational Organisations (IOs), and African emerging transnational actors in arbitration. These five socio-legal actors were used as the launchpad to present a Third World Approaches to International Law (TWAIL) analysis of the legitimacy, role, and authority of African sub-regional judiciaries and arbitral institutions in resolving economic disputes.[87]

[86] Pierre Bourdieu, 'The Force of Law: Toward a Sociology of the Juridical Field' (1987) 38 *Hastings Law Journal* 805.

[87] Obiora Chinedu Okafor, 'Critical Third World Approaches to International Law (TWAIL): Theory, Methodology, or Both' (2008) 10 *International Community Law Review* 375.

The book argued that the jurisdictional mandates of Africa's sub-regional economic courts and tribunals are complex and that commentators should avoid purely positivistic or doctrinal analyses of these courts. It also demonstrated that a socio-historical appraisal of the jurisdictional posture of the African sub-regional economic courts and tribunals reveals a complex matrix of social, political, historical, and legal variation. In the process, the book also unearthed the role of international dispute settlement in embedding the deep structures of imperialism, colonialism and its continuities, and crony capitalism. The book thus shows how the actions of these five actors have produced and reproduced both unfair and neutral economic, legal, political, and social outcomes for the peoples of Africa. African states and African international economic actors are also poorly represented in terms of a very low number of economic or commercial disputes in these sub-regional economic courts and tribunals. The book shows that paltry dockets are a source of three broad reactions: the first one is one of general and selective neglect by mainstream international law practitioners, other international institutions, and academics. The second is one of path dependence produced by European regional economic integration experimental triumphalism. The third is analytical subject matter, linguistic, and regional segregation by international economic law practitioners, other international institutions, and academics. These three interrelated factors formed the backbone of this book's analysis and argumentation of the role of socio-legal actors in international economic dispute settlement in Africa.

Africa boasts the highest number of regional and sub-regional international courts and tribunals of all the other regions of the world. It thus offers an excellent laboratory of experiments in the judicialisation of international law. Altogether, Africa is home to the following eight active international courts:

1. The African Court on Human and Peoples' Rights (ACtHPR) (established 1998);
2. The East Africa Court of Justice (EACJ) (established in 2001);
3. The Economic Community for West African States (ECOWAS) Court of Justice (ECCJ) (established in 2001);
4. The South African Development Community (SADC) Tribunal (established 2005);
5. The West African Economic and Monetary Union (WAEMU) Court of Justice (established in 1995);
6. The Organization for the Harmonization of Business Law in Africa Common Court of Justice and Arbitration (OHADA CCJA) (established in 1997);
7. The Common Market for Eastern and South Africa (COMESA) Court of Justice (established in 1998); and the
8. The Court of justice for the Central African Economic and Monetary Community (CEMAC) (established in 2000).

Despite this enviable outlook, this book has shown that most scholarship focusing on these courts remains pessimistic and gloomy. In many cases, these courts are viewed as bad copies of their counterparts, especially in Europe. Such narratives are present in both avenues of international dispute settlement: international court litigation and international arbitration. This book has, however, demonstrated that these courts exist within a context of pernicious colonial, post-colonial, and imperial continuities structured around the five select socio-legal actors involved in international economic dispute settlement in Africa. There are thus both successes and continuing experiments or 'trials and errors' within this field.

The aim of mainstreaming these African institutions remains urgent as ever. International law as we know it today remains a limited geography of spaces and ideas that marginalises non-Western institutions.[88] This book has engaged directly with this challenge and forms part of a project aimed at increasing the visibility and showcasing the relevance of African international judiciaries in the existing academic literature. The book has focused in varied style and format on the on economic (including international investment) disputes settlement institutions in African sub-regional level. A distinction was drawn between African sub-regional international and regional international courts. The regional ones are established at the continental level, mainly by the AU while the sub-regional ones are established at the sub-regional level mainly by RECs. The book typologised the existing African international courts into four types: judicial, quasi-judicial, FTAs, DSMs and non-operational international courts. The main regional dispute settlement mechanism is the dispute settlement body of AfCFTA, which at the time of writing in 2025, is yet to be fully operationalised.

This book also displayed how International law remains a purveyor of and bulwark against the complex web of persistent and violent exploitative relationships that order the quotidian lives of Africans today.[89] International law offers an avenue for the quest for social, economic and political justice for many Africans.[90] These two opposing views form the paradox of rejectionism and reformism of international law that this book engaged with through a focus on institutions of economic dispute settlement. Part of the central claim of TWAIL is international law's constitutive attributes of concepts, doctrines, and practices that have been unfair and unfavourable to non-Europeans (now including the United States of America and Australia) generally and Africans specifically.[91] Western nation states not only used international law to acquiesce to the violent

[88] James T Gathii, 'The Promise of International Law: A Third World View' (2021) 36 *AUILR* 377.

[89] Ibrahim J Gassama, 'International Law, Colonialism, and the African' in M S Shanguhyia and T Falola (eds), *The Palgrave Handbook of African Colonial and Postcolonial History* (Palgrave Macmillan, 2018) 550.

[90] Muthucumaraswamy Sornarajah, 'Power and Justice: Third World Resistance in International Law' (2006) 10 *Singapore Yearbook of International Law* 19–57.

[91] Antony Anghie, *Imperialism, Sovereignty and International Law* (Cambridge University Press, 2005).

practices of the empire like slavery and colonialism, they used it to constitute these practices that still plays a role that remains unfavourable to Africans and non-Europeans generally through supporting neoliberal laws, institutions and practices.[92]

For Africa and international law, there are three frames of analysis that can analyze these paradoxes of reformism and rejectionism. The first frame references African state practice on international law, especially following their mass independence in the 1960s, and on the second level we can reference the scholarship of African international law thinkers that has emerged in the twentieth century. These two levels of analysis can then be divided into three additional analytical frameworks that deal with thinking, writing, critiquing, engaging, producing, and practicing international law in Africa. The first is the inevitable and unconscious embrace of international law by African states in the international relations. The second frame is the contribution that African states have had on international law since their mass independence in the 1960s. The African sub-regional international economic courts and tribunals are a direct manifestation of the contribution and footprints of African states on international law. The third and final frame is the critical, rejectionist and firm reformist stance by African states. This third framing is the most difficult and controversial to implement for African states and even scholars. It is associated with the stronger scholarship of international law in Africa that has one of its main sources in the TWAIL scholarship.[93]

On the first frame of analysis, here, many African states involuntarily find themselves bound by rules, principles, and doctrines of international law formulated when their sovereignty was denied or was exercised on their behalf.[94] These rules are referenced as customary international law (CIL) and are therefore binding on all states despite their formulation in the Euro-American praxis.[95] This is in addition to the strong critique that most customary international law norms lack legitimacy and authority as they are not customary in the sense of widespread, consistent, and legal binding force.[96] This critique is premised on the view that while customary international law is intended to be inductive, inferred from the repeated acts of states believed to be in adherence to the law, 'these norms have become a device for judges, advocates, and self-interested states (mainly from the global North) to deduce or create new norms without regard to the beliefs or participation of the vast majority of states and their peoples'.[97]

[92] James T Gathii, 'Neoliberalism, Colonialism, and International Governance: Decentering the International Law of Governmental Legitimacy' (2000) 98 *Michigan Law Review* 1996.

[93] James T Gathii, 'Africa and the History of International Law' in Bardo Fassbender & Anne Peters eds., *The Oxford Handbook of the History of International Law*.

[94] Bhupinder S Chimni, 'Customary International Law: A Third World Perspective' (2018) 112:1 *American Journal of International Law* 1–46.

[95] ibid.

[96] Patrick J Kelly, 'The Twilight of Customary International Law' (2000) 40(2) *Virginia Journal of International Law* 449–543.

[97] ibid.

The setting up of African international courts offers a space for entrenchment of these norms as the interpellated vocabulary for many international law lawyers.

This does not mean that the deductive version of customary international law produced especially by dedicated norm entrepreneurs and especially by ISDS arbitral tribunals has not affected the trajectory of current customary international law for African states.[98] The current clamor for reform in international investment law is historically linked to the norms of reform generated by Third World states that form part of the New International Economic Order (NIEO).[99] Additionally, recent reform claims are anchored on the expansive interpretations of international investment standards such as fair and equitable treatment (FET) and most-favored nation (MFN) standards by ISDS tribunals. Thus, ISDS tribunals have continued the involuntary deductive production of customary international law for African states.[100] Such a risk is also possible for both judicialised and arbitral processes in Africa.

On the second frame of analysis, African states have also voluntarily accepted and voraciously defended doctrines of international law that have proved disadvantageous to them. A good example of this is the doctrine of *uti possidentis juris* that the Organization of African Unity (OAU) Member States unreservedly accepted in 1964.[101] The doctrine cast in stone the European set colonial boundaries at the time of independence. This was without any considerations to social, cultural or ethnic make-up of the communities present in those localities at the time of independence.[102] Here, the critique of earlier[103] and more recent[104] scholarship is that the positive contribution of African states to international law has been downplayed and only aspects of non-contribution have been displayed. In chapter 5, this book criticised Olabisi Akingube's agnostic review of African states' participation at the International Centre for the Settlement

[98] Bernard Kishoiyian, 'The Utility of Bilateral Investment Treaties in the Formulation of Customary International Law' (1993) 14(2) *Northwestern Journal of International Law & Business*, 327–375.

[99] Mohamed Bedjaoui, Towards a New International Economic Order (New York: Holmes & Meier, 1979); Jagdish Bhagwati, (ed) *The New International Economic Order: The North South Dialogue* (Cambridge, Mass, MIT Press, 1977).

[100] John Linarelli, Margot E Salomon, Muthucumaraswamy Sornarajah, *The Misery of International Law: Confrontations with Injustice in the Global Economy* (Oxford University Press, 2015) ch 3.

[101] Organization of African Unity (OAU), 'Border Disputes Among African States' Resolution AHG/Res 16 (I), July 1964.

[102] Makau Mutua, 'Why Redraw the Map of Africa: A Moral and Legal Inquiry' (1995) 16(4) *Michigan Journal of International Law* 1113–117.

[103] Chuks F Okoye, *International Law and The New African States* (1972); Taslim O Elias, 'Africa and the Development of International Law' (Richard Akinjide ed, 2nd edn, 1988); and Josephmarie Bipoum-Woum, *Le Droit International Africain: Problèmes Généraux, Règlement Des Conflits* (1970).

[104] Jeremy Levitt, 'Introduction—Africa: A Maker of International Law,' in *Africa: Mapping New Boundaries In International Law*, at vii (Jeremy Levitt ed, 2008); Tiyanjana Maluwa, 'Reassessing Aspects of the Contribution of African States to the Development of International Law Through African Regional Multilateral Treaties,' (2020) 41 *Mich. J. Int'l L.* 327-415.

of Investment Disputes (ICSID). Akingube labeled this a form of intermediate contribution as 'reverse' contributionism.[105] In this form of contribution, African states have contributed to international investment law as active respondents in pioneering cases at ICSID. The African contribution to international law is a complex narrative that can be divided into many different streams. This book also foregrounded and critiqued the scholarship of celebrated Nigerian scholar and international practitioner Taslim Olawale Elias that African contribution to international law should be acknowledged and celebrated. The book also acknowledged and strived towards the credible and well-established narrative that Taslim Olwale Elias' scholarship falls into the milder version of weak contributionism to international law in Africa.[106]

The third and final frame of analysis that this book explored is African states' critical, rejectionist and firm reformist stance. This frame of analysis is controversial and has in many cases set African states against their global North counterparts. This stance centers on the processes of colonialism and neocolonialism and how they continue to constitute injustice for Africans. Acknowledging such a posture and the positioning to reject and firmly reform international law norms to different orientations is the main agenda of this frame of analysis. Its examples in state practice are far and wide apart because of the fear of backlash, the interpellation of the past and the former African elites that mediate between international law doctrines and their application to ordinary Africans, and the false triumphalism of Western modernity, especially its ideas and practice of neoliberalism. Chapter 3 of this book on the complexities of Africa's Sub-Regional International Economic Courts and Tribunals addressed how this frame of analysis informs and affects the jurisdictional set-ups, the disputational modes and the current dearth of economic disputes in these courts.

The example of the EACJ is prescient here. The EAC Treaty explicitly states the EACJ shall have a human rights jurisdiction 'as will be determined by the [EAC] Council of Ministers at a suitable subsequent date once Partner States 'conclude a protocol to operationalise the extended jurisdiction'.[107] Thus, the EACJ, unlike its counterparts, the ECOWAS Court of Justice (after 2005 amendments) and the SADC Tribunal (which can interpret a sub-regional treaty that arguably includes human rights commitments), does not have an express/textual human rights jurisdiction.[108] The reality, however, is that as it stands at the time of writing, the docket of the EACJ is replete with human rights-related cases. This is so much so that the opposite question of why the Court has not

[105] Olabisi D Akinkugbe, 'Reverse Contributors? African State Parties, ICSID and the Development of International Investment Law' (2019) 32(2) *ICSID Review* 434–454.

[106] Carl Landauer, 'Things Fall Together: The Past and Future Africas of TO Elias's *Africa and the Development of International Law*' (2008) 21 *Leiden Journal of International Law*, 351–375.

[107] EAC Treaty, art 27 (2).

[108] Karen J Alter, James T Gathii, & Laurence R Helfer, 'Backlash against International Courts in West, East and Southern Africa: Causes and Consequences' (2016) 27(2) *The European Journal of International Law* 301.

attracted or received more cases in its core areas of community trade, business, or commerce was at the core of this book's analysis.[109] Scholars have referred to this reality as a 'repurposed mandate'[110] or as an 'implied jurisdiction'.[111] This repurposed mandate emerges from the EACJ's judgment in the *James Katabazi and 21 others v. Secretary General of the East African Community and Attorney General of the Republic of Uganda*, in which, for the first time, in 2007 the EACJ found that: 'While the Court will not assume jurisdiction to adjudicate on human rights disputes, it will not abdicate from exercising its jurisdiction of interpretation under Article 27(1) merely because the reference includes allegation(s) of human rights violation'.[112] It is through this invocation (Katabazi doctrine) that the Court has – despite the provisions in Article 27(2) and the lack of a protocol granting the Court explicit human rights jurisdiction – that the Court has, nevertheless, received human rights cases.

The example of the *British American Tobacco (U) LTD v The Attorney General of Uganda*, (BAT Case),[113] which was the first case that dealt with a purely international trade law issue in the EACJ might offer an explanation as to why the court has had a paltry docket in relations to trade, commerce, and business cases.[114] This is an observational inference drawn from the main elements of the case. Thus, to have more trade or business-related cases, the African sub-regional economic courts and tribunals would require two essential features to attract more international trade law disputes. The first is the product test. Here, the product at issue needs to be commercially, socially, politically, or culturally controversial. Tobacco is a good example, but many more products in the era of climate change and global pandemics might also fulfill this characteristic. The second is the producer test. Here, TNCs easily qualify as the best examples of entities with the financial, legal, political, and even cultural power to drive international litigation, both directly and indirectly. The converse is thus correct in answering the vital question of why there has been low judicialisation of international trade law disputes within African sub-regional economic courts and tribunals: in many disputes, the conjunctive product and producer tests articulated above are not present.

Additionally, the book has shown that international arbitration can generally cover public arbitration involving two disputing nation states or a nation state on the one hand and a private entity on the other, such as an investor-state

[109] James T Gathii, 'The East African Court of Justice: Human Rights and Business Actors Compared' in Karen J. Alter, Laurence R Helfer, & Mikael Rask Madsen, eds, *International Court Authority* (Oxford University Press, 2018) 59–81.

[110] James T Gathii, 'Mission Creep or a Search for Relevance: The East African Court of Justice's Human Rights Strategy, (2013) 24 *Duke J. Comp. & Int'l L.* 249.

[111] Tomasz P Milej, 'Human Rights Protection by International Courts-What Role for the East African Court of Justice' (2018) 26(1) *African Journal of International and Comparative Law*.

[112] *James Katabazi v Attorney General of Uganda*, where the EACJ Ref No. 1 of 2007, p 16.

[113] *British American Tobacco (U) LTD v The Attorney General of Uganda*, Reference No. 7 of 2017, East African Court of Justice [EACJ] (March 26 2019).

[114] Mbori (n 83).

dispute settlement (ISDS).[115] Additionally, private international arbitration, commonly referred to as international commercial arbitration, covers disputes between private disputants. Chapter 6 engaged with the historical, substantive, institutional, and administrative setups of private and public arbitration. Most international arbitrations are now administered by national or International Arbitration Centers (IACs). It was argued that African regional IACs are emerging and increasing the competition for arbitration disputes involving African parties with more established IACs like the International Chamber of Commerce (ICC). With its broad economic, political, and social tentacles, competing with the ICC is a challenge and will continue to remain so in the foreseeable future. However, the emergence and presence of these African regional IACs is a fact to be celebrated and encouraged. As long as they maintain a credible and increasingly high appeal for their services, in many cases supported by the state, the dominance of the more recognised IACs in the metropoles will not remain unchallenged.

Finally, the book grounded an a socially inspired account demonstrated how there are three emerging transnational actors within the African arbitration scene. Chapter 7 of this book aimed to fill a small section of the gap in the study of the professionalisation of the arbitration scene in Africa by focusing on the three emerging transnational actors within the African arbitration scene: international lawyers, law firms, and law training institutions. Relying on a sociological account-based analysis, it was argued that these three different but interconnected transnational socio-legal actors are emerging in the field of African international arbitration. The book thus profiled two emerging arbitrators: Prof Mohamed Abdel Wahab and Ms. Ndanga Kamau. Both can fall within Dezalay and Garth's formulation of international arbitration 'technocrats' as they have developed and accumulated their credentials within the field of international arbitration. For African law firms, it was demonstrated how African top-tier law firms have formed regional and global alliances to capture new markets, increase market share, and acquire access to specialised skills and expertise. The book presented four models of such collaborations and new developments among African corporate law firms: Foreign branches, Association with Local Firms, Networking Arrangements, and Boutique Arbitration Law firms. For African arbitration training institutions, two institutions, the African Arbitration Academy and the African Institute of International Law were analysed as being emblematic of the growing desire to increase the number of qualified African arbitrators and arbitral practice lawyers.

Importantly, all three actors have African international lawyers at their core. The actors are increasingly interconnected, navigating, and intermediating the African international arbitration scene. These actors are essential in shaping how arbitration practice is both globalised and localised for various interested

[115] Margaret Moses, *Principles and Practice of International Commercial Arbitration* (Oxford University Press, 2017) 15.

parties. Lawyers, law firms, and law training institutions in Africa are now intricately involved in shaping the market space and legitimacy of arbitration.[116] African lawyers strategically position themselves in influential positions using their social, legal, political, and economic capital to create powerful nodes of international arbitration governance.[117] These lawyers can position themselves as either 'intermediary elites' or 'double agents'.[118] As 'double agents' in positions of power, they can balance the influence of neo-colonial corporate transnational interests with the promotion of the rule of law through arbitration. As 'intermediary elites,' lawyers help to structure, fix and define private law doctrines and concepts that undergird arbitration.[119] In the highly judicialised format of arbitration described in the previous chapter, lawyers negotiate the contracts that submit cases to arbitration, represent parties in arbitration proceedings and are selected as arbitrators in arbitral proceedings. Lawyers are thus undeniably 'intermediaries' between the transnational elites who are the primary builders of capital and capitalism and the nation state. In their role as 'double agents,' lawyers present the law as apolitical 'in order to distance themselves from politics, as a condition to protect the autonomy of the law, and with it their professional practices'.[120]

[116] *See* Yves Dezalay and Bryant G Garth, 'Introduction' in Yves Dezalay and Bryant G Garth (eds), *Lawyers and the Rule of Law in an Era of Globalizaiton* (Routledge, 2011) 1–16.

[117] ibid at 2.

[118] *See* Sara Dezalay, 'Lawyers in Africa: Brokers of the State, Intermediaries of Globalization: A Case Study of the "Africa" Bar in Paris' (2018) 25 *Ind J Global Legal Stud* 639, 643.

[119] *See* Ambreena Manji, *The Politics of Land Reform in Africa* (Zed Books Ltd, 2006), (presenting the role of lawyers in the global network of land reform).

[120] *See* Dezalay (n 118).

Bibliography

BOOKS

Achebe C, *The Education of a British-Protected Child: Essays* (Penguin, 2009).

Alschner W, *Investment Arbitration and State-Driven Reform: New Treaties, Old Outcomes* (Cambridge University Press, 2022).

Alter KJ and Helfer LR, *Transplanting International Courts: The Law and Politics of the Andean Tribunal of Justice* (Oxford University Press, 2017).

Alter KJ, *The European Court's Political Power: Selected Essays* (Oxford University Press, 2009).

Alter KJ, *The New Terrain of International Law: Courts, Politics, Rights* (Princeton University Press, 2014).

Althusser L, *On the Reproduction of Capitalism: Ideology and Ideological State Apparatuses* (Verso, 1971).

Anghie A, *Imperialism, Sovereignty, and the Making of International Law* (Cambridge University Press, 2005).

Asouzu AA, *International Commercial Arbitration and African States: Practice, Participation and Institutional Development* (Cambridge University Press, 2001).

Balchin C, Chung L.K, Kaushal A and Waibel M, *The Backlash against Investment Arbitration: Perceptions and Reality* (Kluwer Law International, 2010).

Bedjaoui M, *Towards a New International Economic Order* (Martinus Nijhoff, 1979).

Bhagwati J (ed), *The New International Economic Order: The North–South Dialogue* (Macmillan, 1977).

Bipoum-Woum J, *Le Droit International Africain: Problèmes Généraux, Règlement des Conflits* (L'Harmattan, 1970).

Blackaby N et al, *Redfern and Hunter on International Arbitration* (Oxford University Press, 2015).

Bliss P, *Of Sovereignty* (Scribner, 1885).

Block-Lieb S and Halliday TC, *Global Lawmakers: International Organizations in the Crafting of World Markets* (Cambridge University Press, 2017).

Bourdieu P, *Distinction: A Social Critique of the Judgment of Taste* (Harvard University Press, 1984).

Bourdieu P, *Outline of a Theory of Practice* (Cambridge University Press, 1977).

Brownlie I, *Principles of Public International Law* (7th edn, Oxford University Press, 2008).

Chakrabarty D, *Provincializing Europe: Postcolonial Thought and Historical Difference* (Princeton University Press, 2000).

Chimni BS, *International Law and World Order: A Critique of Contemporary Approaches* (Cambridge University Press, 2017).

Craig P and de Búrca G, *EU Law: Text, Cases, and Materials* (Oxford University Press, 2008).

Curtin P, Feierman S et al, *Africa History* (Cambridge University Press, 1978).

Davidson B, *The Black Man's Burden: Africa and the Curse of the Nation-State* (James Currey, 1992).

de Brouwer A-M and Smeulers A (eds), *The Elgar Companion to the International Criminal Tribunal for Rwanda* (Edward Elgar 2016).

de Sousa Santos B, *Epistemologies of the South: Justice Against Epistemicide* (Routledge, 2016).

de Sousa Santos B, *The End of the Cognitive Empire* (Duke University Press, 2018).

Dezalay Y and Garth BG, *Dealing in Virtue: International Commercial Arbitration and the Construction of a Transnational Legal Order* (University of Chicago Press, 1996).

Dezalay Y and Garth BG, *Law as Reproduction and Revolution: An Interconnected History* (Cambridge University Press, 2021).

Dezalay Y and Garth BG, *The Internalization of Palace Wars: Lawyers, Economists, and the Contest to Transform Latin American States* (University of Chicago Press, 2002).
Dezalay S, *Lawyering Imperial Encounters: Negotiating Africa's Relationship with the World Economy* (Cambridge University Press, ed, 2nd edn 2024).
Drahozal CR and Gibson CS, *The Iran–US Claims Tribunal at 25: The Cases Everyone Needs to Know for Investor–State and International Arbitration* (Oxford University Press, 2007).
Du Bois WEB, *The Souls of Black Folk* (A.C. McClurg, 1903).
Du Bois WEB, *The World and Africa: Color and Democracy* (International Publishers, 1965).
Dzah G, *Sustainable Development, International Law, and a Turn to African Legal Cosmologies* (Cambridge University Press, 2024).
Elias T.O, *Africa and the Development of International Law* (Richard Akinjide ed, 2nd edn, 1988)
Fanon F, *The Wretched of the Earth* (Grove Press, 1963).
Fligstein N and McAdam D, *A Theory of Fields* (Oxford University Press, 2012).
Frimpong Oppong R, *Legal Aspects of Economic Integration in Africa* (Routledge, 2011).
Franceschi L, The African Human Rights Judicial System: Viewed from a Foreign Affairs Perspective (Cambridge Scholars Publishing, 2014).
Gandhi L, *Postcolonial Theory: A Critical Introduction* (Columbia University Press, 1998).
Garten JE, *Three Days at Camp David: How a Secret Meeting in 1971 Transformed the Global Economy* (Penguin, 2021).
Gathii JT, *African Regional Trade Agreements as Legal Regimes* (Cambridge University Press, 2011).
Geertz C, *The Interpretation of Cultures* (Basic Books, 1973).
Getachew A, *Worldmaking After Empire: The Rise and Fall of Self-Determination* (Princeton University Press, 2019).
Gordon LR, *An Introduction to Africana Philosophy* (Cambridge University Press, 2008).
Jalloh C, Clarke K and Nmehielle V (eds), *The African Court of Justice and Human and Peoples' Rights in Context* (Cambridge University Press, 2019).
Jessup PC, *Transnational Law* (Yale University Press, 1956).
Karton JDH, *The Culture of International Arbitration and the Evolution of Contract Law* (Cambridge University Press, 2013).
Kelsall T, *Culture under Cross-Examination: International Justice and the Special Court for Sierra Leone* (Cambridge University Press, 2009).
Khan R, *The Iran–United States Claims Tribunal: Controversies, Cases, and Contribution* (Martinus Nijhoff, 1990).
Kidane W, *The Culture of International Arbitration* (Oxford University Press, 2017).
Kleis J, *African Regional Community Courts and Their Contribution to Continental Integration* (Routledge, 2016).
Koskenniemi M, *From Apology to Utopia: The Structure of International Legal Argument* (Cambridge University Press, 2005).
Kurtz J, *The WTO and International Investment Law: Converging Systems* (Cambridge University Press, 2016).
Lim CL, Ho J and Paparinskis M, *International Investment Law and Arbitration: Commentary, Awards and Other Materials* (Cambridge University Press, 2018).
Linarelli J, Salomon ME and Sornarajah M, *The Misery of International Law: Confrontations with Injustice in the Global Economy* (Cambridge University Press, 2015).
Loughlin M, *The Idea of Public Law* (Oxford University Press, 2004).
Luxemburg R, *The Accumulation of Capital* (Routledge 1913).
Mamdani M, *Citizen and Subject: Contemporary Africa and the Legacy of Late Colonialism* (Princeton University Press, 1996).
Manji A, *The Politics of Land Reform in Africa* (Zed Books, 2006).
Mann FA, 'Lex Facit Arbitrum' in Pieter Sanders (ed), *International Arbitration: Liber Amicorum for Martin Domke* (Martinus Nijhoff, 1967).
Masiko T, *Flexible Regional Economic Integration in Africa: Lessons and Implications for the Multilateral Trading System* (Routledge, 2022).

Mazrui A, *The Africans: A Triple Heritage* (Little, Brown, 1986).

Merry SE, *Colonizing Hawai'i: The Cultural Power of Law* (Princeton University Press, 2000).

Mignolo WD and Walsh CE, *On Decoloniality: Concepts Analytics Praxis* (Duke University Press, 2018).

Miles Kate, *The Origins of International Investment Law: Empire, Environment and the Safeguarding of Capital* (Cambridge University Press, 2013).

Moghalu KC, *Emerging Africa: How the Global Economy's 'Last Frontier' Can Prosper and Matter* (Hurst & Company, 2014).

Moses M, *Principles and Practice of International Commercial Arbitration* (Cambridge University Press, 2017).

Mouloul A, *Understanding The Organization For The Harmonization Of Business Laws In Africa* (OHADA, 2009).

Mudimbe VY, *The Invention of Africa: Gnosis, Philosophy, and the Order of Knowledge* (Indiana University Press, 1988).

Murray R, *The African Commission on Human and Peoples' Rights and International Law* (Martinus Nijhoff 2000).

Oduntan G, *Sovereignty and Jurisdiction in the Airspace and Outer Space: Legal Criteria for Spatial Delimitation* (Routledge, 2012).

OECD, *Foreign Direct Investment for Development: Maximizing Benefits, Minimizing Costs* (OECD Publishing, 2002).

Okoye CF, *International Law and the New African States* (Sweet & Maxwell, 1972).

Onuma Y, *International Law in a Transcivilizational World* (Cambridge University Press, 2017).

Oppenheim L, *International Law* (9th edn, Longman, 1992).

Oppong R & Agyebeng K (eds.), *A Commitment to Law, Development and Public Policy: A Festschrift in Honour of Nana Dr. SKB Asante* (Wildy, Simmonds & Hill Publishing, 2016)

Orford A, *International Law and the Politics of History* (Cambridge University Press, 2021).

Pahuja S, *Decolonising International Law: Development, Economic Growth and the Politics of Universality* (Cambridge University Press, 2011).

Paulsson J, *The Idea of Arbitration* (Oxford University Press, 2013).

Peery D, Brown P and Letts E, *Left Out and Left Behind: The Hurdles, Hassles, and Heartaches of Achieving Long-Term Legal Careers for Women of Color* (American Bar Association, 2020).

Perrone NM, *Investment Treaties and the Legal Imagination: How Foreign Investors Play by Their Own Rules* (Cambridge University Press, 2021).

Pigeaud F and Sylla NS, *Africa's Last Colonial Currency: The CFA Franc Story* (Thomas Fazi tr, Pluto Press, 2020).

Pouemi JT, *Monnaie, Servitude et Liberté: La Répression Monétaire de l'Afrique* (L'Harmattan, 2000).

Powell EJ, *Islamic Law and International Law: Peaceful Resolution of Disputes* (Oxford University Press, 2019).

Reydams L, *Universal Jurisdiction: International and Municipal Legal Perspectives* (Oxford University Press, 2004).

Ridgeway GL, *Merchants of Peace: Twenty Years of Business through the International Chamber of Commerce* (Columbia University Press, 1938).

Roberts A, *Is International Law International?* (Oxford University Press, 2017).

Rothstein R, *The Color of Law: A Forgotten History of How Our Governments Segregated America* (Liveright, 2017).

Roucounas E, *A Landscape of Contemporary Theories of International Law* (Brill, 2019).

Roy T, *The East India Company: The World's Most Powerful Corporation* (Penguin, 2012).

Ryle G, *Collected Papers: Volume 2 1929–1986* (Routledge, 2009).

Ryngaert C, *Jurisdiction in International Law* (2nd edn, Oxford University Press, 2015).

Saito NT, *Settler Colonialism, Race, and the Law: Why Structural Racism Persists* (Cambridge University Press, 2020).

Schinazi M, *The Three Ages of International Commercial Arbitration* (Oxford University Press, 2021).

Shany Y, *Questions of Jurisdiction and Admissibility Before International Courts* (Oxford University Press, 2015).
Shivji IG, *Accumulation in an African Periphery: A Theoretical Framework* (Mkuki na Nyota Publishers, 2009).
Sinha SP, *Legal Polycentricity and International Law* (Martinus Nijhoff, 1996).
Slobodian Q, *Globalists: The End of Empire and the Birth of Neoliberalism* (Harvard University Press, 2018).
Sornarajah M, *International Law on Foreign Investment* (Cambridge University Press, 2010).
Sornarajah M, *Resistance and Change in International Law on Foreign Investment* (Cambridge University Press, 2015).
Steingruber AM, *Consent in International Arbitration* (Oxford University Press, 2012).
Sweet A & Grisel F, *The Evolution of International Arbitration: Judicialization, Governance, Legitimacy* (Oxford University Press, 2017).
Taylor Charles, *Modern Social Imaginaries* (Duke University Press, 2004).
UNCTAD, *Economic Development in Africa Report 2019: Made in Africa, Rules of Origin for Enhanced Intra-African Trade* (United Nations, 2019).
Viner J, *The Customs Union Issue* (University of Chicago Press, 1950).
von Bogdandy A and Venzke I, *In Whose Name? A Public Law Theory of International Adjudication* (Oxford University Press, 2014).
von Jhering R, *Law as a Means to an End* (Harvard University Press, 1913).
wa Thiong'o N, *Decolonising the Mind: The Politics of Language in African Literature* (Heinemann, 1981).
Welch CE, *Protecting Human Rights in Africa: Roles and Strategies of Non-Governmental Organizations* (University of Pennsylvania Press, 1995).
Whyte J, *The Morals of the Market: Human Rights and the Rise of Neoliberalism* (Cambridge University Press, 2019).
Yakpo E and Boumedra T (eds), *Liber Amicorum Mohammed Bedjaoui* (Martinus Nijhoff, 1999).
Zartman WI, *Government and Politics in Northern Africa* (Van Nostrand, 1964).

BOOK CHAPTERS

Ajayi JFA, 'Africa at the Beginning of the Nineteenth Century: Issues and Prospects' in Ajayi JFA (ed), *General History of Africa VI: Africa in the Nineteenth Century until the 1880s* (Heinemann, 1989).
Akinkugbe OD, 'Dispute Settlement: African Continental Free Trade Area (AfCFTA)' in Ruiz Fabri H (ed), *The Max Planck Encyclopedia of International Procedural Law* (Oxford University Press, 2021).
Ando N, 'Permanent Court of Arbitration' in Wolfrum R (ed), *The Max Planck Encyclopedia of Public International Law* (Oxford University Press, 2006).
Anghie A, Chimni B, Mickelson K and Okafor O, 'Introduction' in Anghie A, Chimni B, Mickelson K and Okafor O (eds), *The Third World and International Order: Law, Politics and Globalization* (Martinus Nijhoff, 2003).
Asmelash H, 'The Legacy of the SADC Tribunal in International Investment Law' in Ruiz Fabri H and Stoppioni E (eds), *International Investment Law: An Analysis of the Major Decisions* (Edward Elgar, 2020).
Bhagwati J, 'U.S Trade Policy: The Infatuation with Free Trade Agreements' in Bhagwati J and Krueger AO (eds), *The Dangerous Drift to Preferential Trade Agreements* (AEI Press, 1995).
Boahen AA, 'Africa and the Colonial Challenge' in Boahen AA (ed), *General History of Africa VII: Africa under Colonial Domination 1880–1935* vol 2 (Heinemann, 1989).
Broberg M, 'Preliminary Ruling: European Court of Justice (ECJ)' in Ruiz Fabri H (ed), *The Max Planck Encyclopedia of International Procedural Law* (Oxford University Press, 2018).

Broches A, 'The Present Need for a Permanent Arbitral Tribunal', Address at the Institute on Permanent International Courts organised by the Minnesota State Bar Association (13 June 1962) in *Broches MA, Articles and Speeches (1951–1982).*

Buchanan A and Keohane RO, 'The Legitimacy of Global Governance Institutions' in Meyer LH (ed), *Legitimacy, Justice and Public International Law* vol 29 (Oxford University Press, 2010).

Chang HJ, 'Globalization, Transnational Corporations, and Economic Development: Can the Developing Countries Pursue Strategic Industrial Policy in a Globalizing World Economy?' in Baker D et al (eds), *Globalizing and Progressive Economic Policy* (Cambridge University Press, 1998).

Chen L, 'Contextualizing Legal Transplant: China and Hong' in Monateri G (ed), *Methods of Comparative Law* 192 (Edward Elgar 2012).

Chimni BS, 'An Outline of a Marxist Course on Public International Law' in Marks S (ed), *International Law on the Left: Re-examining Marxist Legacies* (Routledge 2008).

Chimni BS, 'International Organizations, 1945–Present' in Katz J et al (eds), *The Oxford Handbook of International Organizations* (Oxford University Press, 2016).

Cuyvers A, 'Preliminary References under EU Law' in Ugirashebuja E, Ruhangisa JE, Ottervanger T and Cuyvers A (eds), *East African Community Law: Institutional, Substantive and Comparative EU Aspects* (Oxford University Press, 2017).

Dezalay S and Dezalay Y, 'From the Shadow of State Diplomacy to the Pull of the Market for Commercial Arbitration' in d'Aspermont J, Gazzini T, et al (eds), *International Law as a Profession* 311 (Springer 2017).

Dezalay S, 'Law Firms and International Adjudication' in Ruiz Fabri H (ed), *The Max Planck Encyclopedia of International Procedural Law* (Oxford University Press, 2021).

Dezalay Y and Garth BG, 'Introduction' in Dezalay Y and Garth BG (eds), *Lawyers and the Rule of Law in an Era of Globalization* 1 (Cambridge University Press, 2011).

Diagne P, 'African Political, Economic and Social Structures during this Period' in Ogot BA (ed), *General History of Africa V: Africa from the Sixteenth to the Eighteenth Century* (Heinemann, 1992).

Dutson S, '"Africa's Century" – The Rise of International Arbitration in Africa and what it means for users of Arbitral Institutions in Africa' in *The Role of Arbitration Institutions in the Development of Arbitration in Africa* (Arbitration Institutions in Africa Conference, 2015).

Ebobrah ST, 'International Human Rights Courts' in Romano C, Alter K, & Shany Y (eds), *The Oxford Handbook of International Adjudication* 227 (Oxford University Press, 2014).

Eslava L, Fakhri M and Nesiah V, 'The Spirit of Bandung' in Eslava L, Fakhri M and Nesiah V (eds), *Bandung, Global History, and International Law* (Cambridge University Press, 2017).

Fagbayibo B, 'African Approaches to International Law' in *Oxford Bibliographies* (Oxford University Press, 2021).

Falola T and Jennings C, 'Introduction' in Falola T and Jennings C (eds), *Africanizing Knowledge: African Studies Across the Disciplines* 1 (Routledge, 2002).

Gassama IJ, 'International Law, Colonialism, and the African' in Shanguhyia MS and Falola T (eds), *The Palgrave Handbook of African Colonial and Postcolonial History* (Palgrave Macmillan, 2018).

Gathii JT and Mbori HO, 'Reference Guide to Africa's International Courts: An Introduction' in J T Gathii (ed), *The Performance of Africa's International Courts: Using International Litigation for Political, Legal, and Social Change* (Cambridge University Press, 2020).

Gathii JT, 'Africa and the History of International Law' in Fassbender B and Peters A (eds), *The Oxford Handbook of the History of International Law* 407 (Oxford University Press, 2012).

Gathii JT, 'Introduction: The Performance of Africa's International Courts' in Gathii JT (ed), *The Performance of Africa's International Courts* (Cambridge University Press, 2020).

Gathii JT, 'Sub-Regional Court or Employment Tribunal? The Legacy and Legitimacy of the COMESA Court of Justice' in Howse R, Ruiz Fabri H and Ulfstein G (eds), *The Legitimacy of International Trade Courts and Tribunals*(Cambridge University Press, 2018).

Gathii JT, 'The Agenda of the Third World Approaches to International Law (TWAIL)' in Dunoff J and Pollack M (eds), *International Legal Theory: Foundations and Frontiers* 158 (Cambridge University Press, 2019).

Gathii JT, 'The COMESA Court of Justice' in Howse R, Ruiz Fabri H and Ulfstein G (eds), *The Legitimacy of International Trade Courts and Tribunals* (Cambridge University Press, 2018).
Gathii JT, 'The East African Court of Justice: Human Rights and Business Actors Compared' in Alter KJ, Helfer LR and Madsen MR (eds), *International Court Authority* (Oxford University Press, 2018).
Giorgetti C, 'Introduction' in Giorgetti C (ed), *The Rules, Practice, and Jurisprudence of International Courts and Tribunals* 1 (Oxford University Press, 2012).
Halliday TC and Shaffer G, 'Transnational Legal Orders' in Halliday TC and Shaffer G (eds), *Transnational Legal Orders* 5 (Cambridge University Press, 2015).
Howse R, Ruiz-Fabri H, et al, 'Introduction' in Howse R, Ruiz-Fabri H, Ulfestein G, & Zang MQ (eds), *The Legitimacy of International Trade Courts and Tribunals* (Oxford University Press, 2018).
Howse R and Ünüvar G, 'Sowing the Seeds of an ISDS Legitimacy Crisis? The Notorious First Wave of NAFTA Chapter 11 Awards' in Hélène Ruiz Fabri and Edoardo Stoppioni (eds), *International Investment Law: An Analysis of the Major Decisions* (Edward Elgar 2022) 99.
Hunter E, 'The History of Political Thought in the African Political Present' in Brett A, Donaldson M and Koskenniemi M (eds), *History, Politics, Law: Thinking Through the International* (Oxford University Press, 2021).
Illy O, 'The WAEMU Court of Justice' in Howse R, Ruiz Fabri H and Ulfstein G (eds), *The Legitimacy of International Trade Courts and Tribunals* (Oxford University Press, 2018).
Jackson JH, 'Sovereignty: Outdated Concept or New Approaches' in Shan W, Simons P and Singh D (eds), *Redefining Sovereignty in International Economic Law* (Oxford University Press, 2008).
Joshi M, 'National Arbitration Institutions/Centres: Lagos Court of Arbitration – International Centre for Arbitration and ADR' in *The Role of Arbitration Institutions in the Development of Arbitration in Africa* (Arbitration Institutions in Africa Conference, 2015).
Kennedy D, 'The "Rule of Law," Political Choices, and Development Common Sense' in Trubek DM (ed), *The New Law and Economic Development: A Critical Appraisal* (Cambridge University Press, 2006).
Klabbers J, 'International Courts and Informal International Law' in Pauwelyn J, Wessel RA and Wouters J (eds), *Informal International Lawmaking* (Oxford University Press, 2012).
Klabbers J, 'Introduction' in Klabbers J (ed), *The Cambridge Companion to International Organizations Law* 1 (Cambridge University Press, 2022).
Koskenniemi M, 'International Law as "Global Governance"' in Desautels-Stein J and Tomlins C (eds), *Searching for Contemporary Legal Thought* (Cambridge University Press, 2017).
Krasner SD, 'Westphalia and All That' in Goldstein J (ed), *Ideas and Foreign Policy: Beliefs, Institutions, and Political Change Robert Keohane* 235 (Cornell University Press, 1993).
Krishna P, 'The Economics of PTAs' in Lester S and Mercurio B (eds), *Bilateral and Regional Trade Agreements* (Edward Elgar 2009).
Kurtz J, 'Building Legitimacy Through Interpretation in Investor-State Arbitration: On Consistency, Coherence, and the Identification of Applicable Law' in Douglas Z, Pauwelyn J and Viñuales JE (eds), *The Foundations of International Investment Law* (Oxford University Press, 2014).
Lagrange E, 'SPP v Egypt, AAPL v Sri Lanka: Some Revolutionary Steps?' in Ruiz Fabri H and Stoppioni E (eds), *International Investment Law: An Analysis of the Major Decisions* (Edward Elgar, 2022).
Langford M, Behn D and Fauchald OK, 'Backlash and State Strategies in International Investment Law' in Tanja Aalberts and Thomas Gammeltoft-Hansen (eds), *The Changing Practices of International Law* (Cambridge University Press, 2018) 70.
Lei C, 'Contextualizing Legal Transplant: China and Hong', in Pier Giuseppe Monateri (ed.) *Methods of Comparative Law* (Edward Elgar Publishing, 2012)
Levitt J, 'Introduction—Africa: A Maker of International Law' in Levitt J (ed), *Africa: Mapping New Boundaries in International Law* vii (Martinus Nijhoff, 2008).

Mbaye K, 'L'OHADA: Une Intégration Juridique en Afrique' in Yakpo E and Boumedra T (eds), *Liber Amicorum Mohammed Bedjaoui* (Brill, 1999).
Mbengue M, 'African Perspectives on Inter-State Litigation' in Klein N (ed), *International Law Disputes: Weighing the Options* (Oxford University Press, 2014).
Mbori H, '*International Trade Solidarity Governance Split: Bretton Woods Solidariry vs Bandung Solidarity*' in Cecial M Baillet(ed), *Research Handbook on International Solidarity and the Law* (Edward Elgar, 2024), 178-202.
Michaels R, 'Roles and Role Perceptions of International Arbitrators' in Mattli W and Dietz T (eds), *International Arbitration and Global Governance: Contending Theories and Evidence* (Oxford University Press, 2014).
Milej T, 'Reclaiming African Agency: The Right to Regulate, the Investor-State Dispute Settlement and "Africanisation" of International Investment Law' in Hofmann R, Scheu J, et al (eds), *Investment Protection, Human Rights, and International Arbitration in Extraordinary Times* (Brill, 2021).
Njogu R, 'Gods at War: Religion and Law-Making' in Ndulo M and Emeziem C (eds), *The Routledge Handbook of African Law* 78 (Routledge, 2022).
Pauwelyn J, Wessel RA and Wouters J, 'Informal International Lawmaking: Framing the Concept and Research Questions' in Pauwelyn J, Wessel RA and Wouters J (eds), *Informal International Lawmaking* (Oxford University Press, 2012).
Ranger T, 'The Invention of Tradition in Colonial Africa' in Hobsbawm E and Ranger T (eds), *The Invention of Tradition* 212 (Cambridge University Press, 1983).
Rodney W, 'The Colonial Economy' in Boahen AA (ed), *General History of Africa: Africa under Colonial Domination 1880–1935* 337 (Heinemann, 1985).
Romano C, 'The Shadow Zones International Judicialization' in Romano C, Alter K and Shany Y (eds), *The Oxford Handbook of International Adjudication* (Oxford University Press, 2014).
Romano C, 'Trial and Error in International Judicialization' in Romano C, Alter K and Shany Y (eds), *The Oxford Handbook of International Adjudication* (Oxford University Press, 2014).
Schachter O, 'The Role of the Institute of International Law and its Methods of Work – Today and Tomorrow' in *Institut De Droit International, Livre Du Centenaire 1873–1973, Évolution Et Perspectives Du Droit International* (1973).
Seck SL, 'Transnational Corporations and Extractive Industries' in Alam S, Atapattu S, et al (eds), *International Environmental Law and the Global South* 380 (Routledge, 2015).
Shahabuddin M, 'The Colonial "Other" in the Nineteenth Century German Colonisation of Africa, and International Law' in Yusuf A (ed), *The African Yearbook of International Law* vol 15 (Brill, 2013).
Sipalla H, 'Not too Many Faces, One Mask: A Kéba Mbaye Biographic' in Viljoen F, Sipalla H and Adegalu F (eds), *Exploring African Approaches to International Law* (Brill, 2022).
Skovgaard Poulsen LN, 'The Importance of BITs for Foreign Direct Investment and Political Risk Insurance: Revisiting the Evidence' in Sauvant K (ed), *Yearbook on International Investment Law & Policy 2009–2010* (Oxford University Press, 2010).
Sornarajah M, 'The Battle Continues: Rebuilding Empire through Internationalization of State Contracts' in von Bernstorff J and Dann P (eds), *The Battle for International Law: South–North Perspectives on the Decolonization Era* (Brill, 2019).
Sornarajah M, 'The Return of the NIEO and the Retreat of Neo-Liberal International Law' in Bhuiyan S, Schrijver N and Sands P (eds), *International Law and Developing Countries: Essays in Honour of Kamal Hossain* (Brill, 2017)
Squatrito T, Young OR, et al, 'A Framework for Evaluating the Performance of International Courts and Tribunals' in Squatrito T, Young OR, et al (eds), *The Performance of International Courts and Tribunals* 1 (Oxford University Press, 2018).
Thatcher M and Stone Sweet A, 'Theory and Practice of Delegation to Non-Majoritarian Institutions' in Thatcher M and Stone Sweet A (eds), *The Politics of Delegation* (Oxford University Press, 2005).

Ugirashebuja E, 'Preliminary References under EAC Law' in Ugirashebuja E, Ruhangisa JE, Ottervanger T and Cuyvers A (eds), *East African Community Law: Institutional, Substantive and Comparative EU Aspects* (Oxford University Press, 2017).

Vansina J, 'Population Movements and Emergence of New Socio-Political Forms in Africa' in Ogot BA (ed), *General History of Africa V: Africa from the Sixteenth to the Eighteenth Century* (Heinemann, 1992).

Viljoen F, Sipalla H and Adegalu F(eds), *Exploring African Approaches to International Law* (Pretoria University Law Press, 2022)

Viñuales JE, 'Experiments in International Adjudication: Past and Present' in De La Rasilla I and Viñuales JE (eds), *Experiments in International Adjudication: Historical Accounts* (Oxford University Press, 2019).

von Bogdandy A and Venzke I, 'Framing the Issue' in von Bogdandy A and Venzke I (eds), *International Judicial Lawmaking* (Oxford University Press, 2012).

Werner W, de Hoon M and Galán A, 'Introduction: The Law of International Lawyers' in Werner W, de Hoon M, & Galán A (eds), *The Law of International Law: Reading Martti Koskenniemi* 3 (Oxford University Press, 2017).

Zeleza PT, 'The Inventions of African Identities and Languages: The Discursive and Developmental Implications' in Arasanyin OF and Pemberton MA (eds), *Selected Proceedings of the 36th Annual Conference on African Linguistics: Shifting the Center of Africanism in Language Politics and Economic Globalization* (Ohio University Press, 2006).

Zenker O and Hoehne MV, 'When the State has to deal with Customary Law' in Zenker O and Hoehne MV (eds), *The State and the Paradox of Customary Law in Africa* (Brill, 2018).

JOURNAL ARTICLES

Abdoullah Cisse, 'L'harmonisation du Droit en Afrique: L'experience OHADA à l'épreuve de sa Première Décenie' (2004) *Revue internationale de droit économique* 198.

Adamantia Rachovitsa, 'On New "Judicial Animals": The Curious Case of an African Court with Material Jurisdiction of a Global Scope' (2019) 19 *Human Rights Law Review* 255.

Ademola Abass, 'The Proposed International Criminal Jurisdiction for the African Court: Some Problematical Aspects' (2013) 60 *Netherlands International Law Review* 31.

Akbar Rasulov, 'Nameless Rapture of the Struggle: Towards a Marxist Class-Theoretic Approach to International Law' (2008) 19 *Finnish Yearbook of International Law* 268.

Akeret Muna, 'Is OHADA "Common Law Friendly"?' (2001) 3 *International Law Forum du Droit International* 176.

Alec Stone Sweet, 'Judicialization and the Construction of Governance' (1999) 32 *Comparative Political Studies* 147.

Ally Possi, 'An Appraisal of the Functioning and Effectiveness of the East African Court of Justice' (2018) 21 *Potchefstroom Electronic Law Journal* 24.

Ally Possi, 'Striking a Balance Between Community Norms and Human Rights: The Continuing Struggle of the East African Court of Justice' (2015) 15 *African Human Rights Law Journal* 192.

Amr A Shalakany, 'Arbitration and the Third World: A Plea for Reassessing Bias under the Specter of Neoliberalism' (2000) 41 *Harvard International Law Journal* 419.

Anaclet Nzohabonayo, 'Préservation de la Sécurité Juridique et Judiciaire des Affaires à Travers les Formations: Cas de l'ERSUMA et des commissions nationales OHADA' (2018) 23 *Uniform Law Review* 131.

Andrea K Bjorklund, Daniel Behn et al., 'The Diversity Deficit in International Investment Arbitration' (2020) 21 *Journal of World Investment & Trade* 410.

Andrew T Guzman, 'A Compliance-Based Theory of International Law' (2002) 90 *California Law Review* 1823.

Aníbal Quijano, 'Coloniality and Modernity/Rationality' (2007) 21 *Cultural Studies* 168.
Anne Orford, 'Embodying Internationalism: The Making of International Lawyers' (1998) 19 *Australian Yearbook of International Law* 2.
Anne-Marie Slaughter, 'International Law in a World of Liberal States' (1995) 6 *European Journal of International Law* 503.
Annelise Riles, 'Aspiration and Control: International Legal Rhetoric and the Essentialization of Culture' (1993) 106 *Harvard Law Review* 723.
Antony Anghie and BS Chimni, 'Third World Approaches to International Law and Individual Responsibility in Internal Conflicts' (2003) 2 *Chinese Journal of International Law* 77.
Antony Anghie, 'Legal Aspects of the New International Economic Order' (2015) 6 *Humanity* 144.
Antony Anghie, 'The Evolution of International Law: Colonial and Postcolonial Realities' (2006) 27 *Third World Quarterly* 741.
Antony C Diala, 'The Concept of Living Customary Law: A Critique' (2017) 49 *Journal of Legal Pluralism and Unofficial Law* 143.
Antony J Colangelo, 'Spatial Legality' (2012) 107 *Northwestern University Law Review* 69.
Asha Kaushal, 'The Politics of Jurisdiction' (2015) 78 *Modern Law Review* 791.
Asha Kaushal, 'Revisiting History: How the Past Matters for the Present Backlash against the Foreign Investment Regime' (2009) 50 *Harvard Intl LJ* 491..
Awino Okech, 'African Feminist Epistemic Communities and Decoloniality' (2020) 12 *Critical African Studies* 314.
BJ George Jr, 'Extraterritorial Application of Penal Legislation' (1996) 64 *Michigan Law Review* 609.
Babatunde Fagbayibo, 'Some Thoughts on Centering Pan-African Epistemic in the Teaching of Public International Law in African Universities' (2019) 21 *International Community Law Review* 170.
Babatunde Fagbayibo, 'Towards the Harmonisation of Laws in Africa: Is OHADA the Way to Go?' (2009) 42 *Comparative and International Law Journal of Southern Africa* 309.
Bepyassi V Ouafo, 'Le droit issu de l'organisation pour l'harmonisation en Afrique du droit des affaires et les sociétés africaines: regard critique sur une illustration du déni de l'essence culturelle du droit' (2020) 61 *Les Cahiers de droit* 793.
Bernard Kishoiyian, 'The Utility of Bilateral Investment Treaties in the Formulation of Customary International Law' (1993) 14 *Northwestern Journal of International Law and Business* 327.
Bhupinder S Chimni, 'Capitalism, Imperialism, and International Law in the Twenty-First Century' (2012) 14 *Oregon Review of International Law* 17.
Bhupinder S Chimni, 'Customary International Law: A Third World Perspective' (2018) 112 *American Journal of International Law* 1.
Bhupinder S Chimni, 'The International Law of Jurisdiction: A TWAIL Perspective' (2022) 35 *Leiden Journal of International Law* 29.
Bjørn Letnes, 'Transnational Corporations and Human Rights: Silencing the Ontological Controversy' (2004) 4 *Public Organization Review* 259.
Bogumil Jewsiewicki and Valentin Y Mudimbe, 'Africans' Memories and Contemporary History of Africa' (1992) 31 *History and Theory* 1.
Carl Landauer, 'Regionalism, Geography, and the International Legal Imagination' (2011) 11 *Chicago Journal of International Law* 581.
Carl Landauer, 'Things Fall Together: The Past and Future Africas of TO Elias's *Africa and the Development of International Law*' (2008) 21 *Leiden Journal of International Law* 351.
Caroline Nalule, 'Defining the Scope of Free Movement of Citizens in the East African Community: The East African Court of Justice and its Interpretive Approach' (2018) 62 *Journal of African Law* 6.
Cesare PR Romano, 'A Taxonomy of International Rule of Law Institutions' (2011) 2 *Journal of International Dispute Settlement* 262.
Cesare PR Romano, 'The Proliferation of International Judicial Bodies: The Pieces of the Puzzle' (1999) 31 *New York University Journal of International Law and Politics* 713.
Cesare Romano, 'The Price of International Justice' (2005) 4 *Law and Practice of International Courts and Tribunals*281.
Charles Manga Fombad, 'Some Reflections on the Prospects for the Harmonisation of International Business' (2012) 59 *Africa Today* 51.

Charles N Brower and Stephan W Schill, 'Is Arbitration a Threat or a Boon to the Legitimacy of International Investment Law?' (2009) *Chicago Journal of International Law* 473.
Christof Heyns, 'The African Regional Human Rights System: In Need of Reform?' (2001) 21 *African Human Rights Law Journal* 167.
Daniel Abebe, 'Does International Human Rights Law in African Courts Make a Difference' (2016) 56 *Virginia Journal of International Law* 527.
Daniel Behn, Malcolm Langford and Laura Létourneau-Tremblay, 'Empirical Perspectives on Investment Arbitration: What Do We Know? Does It Matter?' (2020) 21 *Journal of World Investment & Trade* 188.
David B Wilkins and Mihaela Papa, 'The Rise of the Corporate Legal Elite in the BRICS: Implications for Global Governance' (2013) 54 *Boston College Law Review* 1149.
David B Wilkins, David M Trubek and Bryon Fong, 'Globalization, Lawyers, and Emerging Economies: The Rise, Transformation, and Significance of the New Corporate Legal Ecosystem in India, Brazil, and China' (2020) 61 *Harvard International Law Journal* 281.
David Kennedy, 'The Politics of the Invisible College: International Governance and the Politics of Expertise' (2001) 5 *European Human Rights Law Review* 463.
David Kennedy, 'When Renewal Repeats: Thinking Against the Box' (2000) 32 *New York University Journal of International Law and Politics* 497.
David L Levy, 'Political Contestation in Global Production Networks' (2008) 4 *Academy of Management Review* 943.
David M Trubek and Marc Galanter, 'Scholars in Self Estrangement: Reflections on the Crisis in Law and Development Studies' (1974) 4 *Wisconsin Law Review* 1062.
David M Anderson, 'Punishment, Race and "the Raw Native": Settler Society and Kenya's Flogging Scandals, 1895–1930' (2011) 37 *Journal of Southern African Studies* 496.
David M Trubek, 'Law and Development: Forty Years After Scholars in Self-Estrangement' (2016) 66 *University of Toronto Law Journal* 301.
Demba Mbow, 'L'attractivité juridique et économique de l'OHADA' (2020) *Université de Franche-Comté* 98.
Ditaba Rantsane, 'The Origin of Arbitration Law in South Africa' (2020) 23 *Potchefstroom Electronic Law Journal* 1.
Dominic Kelly, 'The International Chamber of Commerce' (2005) 10 *New Political Economy* 260.
Edward Powell, 'Settlement of Disputes by Arbitration in Fifteenth-Century England' (1984) 2 *Law and History Review* 21.
Elsa Sardinha, 'The New EU-Led Approach to Investor-State Arbitration: The Investment Tribunal System in the Comprehensive Economic Trade Agreement (CETA) and the EU-Vietnam Free Trade Agreement' (2017) 32 *ICSID Review* 628.
Emmanuel Gaillard, 'Sociology of International Arbitration' (2015) 31 *Arbitration International* 10.
Emmanuel T Laryea and Oladapo O Fabusuyi, 'Africanisation of International Investment Law for Sustainable Development: Challenges' (2021) 20 *Journal of International Trade Law and Policy* 42.
Eric A Posner and John C Yoo, 'Judicial Independence in International Tribunals' (2005) 93 *California Law Review* 3.
Eric Neumayer and Laura Spess, 'Do Bilateral Investment Treaties Increase Foreign Direct Investment to Developing Countries?' (2005) 33 *World Development* 1567.
Erika de Wet, 'The Rise and Fall of the Tribunal of the Southern African Development Community: Implications for Dispute Settlement in Southern Africa' (2013) 28 *ICSID Review* 45.
Esperanza Brizuela-Gracia, 'The History of Africanization and the Africanization of History' (2006) 33 *History in Africa* 85.
Federico Ortino, 'The Investment Treaty System as Judicial Review' (2013) 24 *American Review of International Arbitration* 437.
Frans Viljoen, 'Africa's Contribution to the Development of International Human Rights and Humanitarian Law' (2001) 1 *African Human Rights Law Journal* 18.
Fred C Zacharias, 'Effects of Reputation on the Legal Profession' (2008) 65 *Washington & Lee Law Review* 173.

Frederick A Mann, 'The Doctrine of International Jurisdiction Revisited After Twenty Years' (1984) 186 *Recueil des Cours de l'Académie de Droit International* 20.
Gabrielle Kaufmann-Kohler, 'The Arbitrator and the Law: Does He/She Know It? Apply It? How? And a Few More Questions?' (2005) 21 *Arbitration International* 631.
George Abi-Saab, 'Fragmentation or Unification: Some Concluding Remarks' (1999) 31 *New York University Journal of International Law and Politics* 919.
George Galindo, 'Splitting TWAIL?' (2016) 33 *Windsor Yearbook of Access to Justice.*
Gregory Shaffer, 'Theorizing Transnational Legal Ordering' (2016) 12 *Annual Review of Law and Social Science* 231.
Hans Bagner, 'How to Avoid Conflicting Awards: The Lauder and CME Cases' (2004) 5 *Journal of World Investment and Trade* 32.
Mathew Happold and Relja Radovic, 'The ECOWAS Court of Justice as an Investment Tribunal' (2018) 19 *Journal of World Investment and Trade* 95.
Harrison O Mbori, 'Benign and Radical Africanization in International Investment Law and Investor-State Dispute Settlement in Africa' 24 (2023) *Journal of World Investment and Trade* 633.
Harrison O Mbori, 'Case Commentary on the British American Tobacco v Attorney General of Uganda (EACJ) and GETMA International v The Republic of Guinea (OHADA CCJA)' (2020) 1 *African Journal of International Economic Law* 341.
Harrison O Mbori, 'Combating Unjustified Sanitary and Phytosanitary Measures in the African Tripartite Free Trade Area (COMESA-SADC-EAC): SPS-Plus or SPS-Minus?' (2017) 58 *Hungarian Journal of Legal Studies* 409.
Ian Laird and Rebecca Askew, 'Finality Versus Consistency: Does Investor-State Arbitration Need an Appellate System?' (2005) 7 *Journal of Appellate Practice and Process* 294.
Ibironke T Odumosu-Ayanu, 'South-South Investment Treaties, Transnational Capital and African Peoples' (2013) 21 *African Journal of International and Comparative Law* 172.
J H Fahey, 'The International Chamber of Commerce' (1921) *Annals of the American Academy of Political and Social Science* 126.
J Patrick Kelly, 'The Twilight of Customary International Law' (2000) 40 *Virginia Journal of International Law* 449.
James Gathii and Celestine Nyamu, 'Reflections on United States-Based Human Rights NGOs' Work on Africa' (1996) 9 *Harvard Human Rights Journal* 285.
James Gathii, 'Human Rights, the World Bank and the Washington Consensus: 1949–1999' (2000) 94 *Proceedings of the American Society of International Law* 144.
James T Gathii, 'Neoliberalism, Colonialism and International Governance: Decentering the International Law of Government Legitimacy' (2000) 98 *Michigan Law Review* 1996.
James T Gathii, Obiora Okafor and Antony Anghie, 'Africa and TWAIL' (2010) 18 *African Yearbook of International Law* 9.
James T Gathii, 'Africa and the Radical Origins of the Right to Development' (2020) 1 *Third World Approaches to International Law Review.*
James T Gathii, 'African Regional Trade Agreements as Flexible Legal Regimes' (2010) 35 *North Carolina Journal of International Law and Commercial Regulation* 571.
James T. Gathii, '*Beyond Samuel Moyn's Countermajoritatian Difficulty as a Model of Global Judicial Review*' (2019) 52 *Vanderbilt Journal of Transnational Law* 1237.
James T Gathii, 'Defining the Relationship between Human Rights and Corruption' (2009) 31 *University of Pennsylvania Journal of International Law* 125.
James T Gathii, 'International Law and Eurocentricity' (1998) 9 *European Journal of International Law* 189.
James T Gathii, 'Mission Creep or a Search for Relevance: The East African Court of Justice's Human Rights Strategy' (2013) 24 *Duke Journal of Comparative and International Law* 249.
James T Gathii, 'Popular Authorship and Constitution Making: Comparing and Contrasting the DRC and Kenya' (2008) 49 *William and Mary Law Review* 1109.
James T Gathii, 'Saving the Serengeti: Africa's New International Judicial Environmentalism' (2016) 16 *Chicago Journal of International Law* 386.

James T Gathii, 'The American Origins of Liberal and Illiberal Regimes of International Economic Governance in the Marshall Court' (2006) 54 *Buffalo Law Review* 765.

James T Gathii, 'The Neoliberal Turn in Regional Trade Agreements' (2011) 86 *Washington Law Review* 421.

James T Gathii, 'The Promise of International Law: A Third World View' (2021) 36 *American University International Law Review* 377.

James T Gathii, 'TWAIL: A Brief History of Its Origins, Its Decentralized Network, and a Tentative Bibliography' (2011) 3 *Trade, Law and Development* 26.

James T Gathii, 'Variation in the Use of Subregional Integration Courts between Business and Human Rights Actors: The Case of the East African Court of Justice' (2016) 79 *Law and Contemporary Problems* 37.

James T Gathii, 'The Under-Appreciated Jurisprudence of Africa's Regional Trade Judiciaries' (2010) 12 *Oregon Review of International Law* 245.

Jan Paulsson, 'Arbitration Without Privity' (1995) 10 *ICSID Review* 332.

Jeremy Cantor, 'Rwanda and the Kigali International Arbitration Centre: The Future Face of East African Arbitration and Growth' (2017) 19 *Cardozo Journal of Conflict Resolution* 93.

Joe Oloka-Onyango and Sylvia Tamale, '"The Personal is Political," or Why Women's Rights are Indeed Human Rights: An African Perspective on International Feminism' (1995) 7 *Human Rights Quarterly* 704.

John H Wood, 'The Demise of the Gold Standard' (1981) 5 *Economic Perspectives* 13.

John Kagochi and Nazif Durmaz, 'Assessing RTAs Inter-Regional Trade Enhancement in Sub-Saharan Africa' (2018) 6 *Cogent Economics and Finance*.

Jonathan Klaaren, 'African Corporate Lawyering and Globalization' (2015) 22 *International Journal of the Legal Profession* 226.

Jose E Alvarez, 'The Democratization of the Invisible College' (2007) 9 *American Society of International Law Insights: President's Column*.

Joseph G Ponterotto, 'Brief Note on the Origins, Evolution, and Meaning of the Qualitative Research Concept "Thick Description"' (2006) 11 *The Qualitative Report* 539.

Joseph H Beale, 'The Jurisdiction of a Sovereign State' (1923) *Harvard Law Review* 241.

Joseph Weiler, 'The Transformation of Europe' (1990–91) 100 *Yale Law Journal* 2405.

Judith Knieper, 'UNCITRAL's Working Group III Discussion on Dispute Prevention' (2021) 17 *University of St Thomas Law Journal* 455.

Kai Koddernbrock and Ndongo Samba Sylla, 'Towards a Political Economy of Monetary Dependency: The Case of the CFA Franc in West Africa' (2019) 19 *MaxPo Discussion Paper* 33.

Karen J Alter and Laurence R Helfer, 'Nature or Nurture? Judicial Law-Making in the European Court of Justice and the Andean Tribunal of Justice' (2010) 64 *International Organization* 563.

Karen J Alter, James T Gathii and Laurence Helfer, 'Backlash against International Courts in West, East and Southern Africa: Causes and Consequences' (2016) 27 *European Journal of International Law* 293.

Karen J Alter, Laurence R Helfer and Jaqueline R McAllister, 'A New International Human Rights Court for West Africa: The ECOWAS Community Court of Justice' (2013) 107 *American Journal of International Law* 737.

Karen J Alter, 'The European Court's Political Power' (1996) 19 *West European Politics* 458.

Karin Mickelson, Ibironke Odumosu and Pooja Parmar, 'Situating Third World Approaches to International Law (TWAIL): Inspirations, Challenges and Possibilities' (2008) 10 *International Community Law Review* 351.

Keith Highet, 'A Personal Memoir of Eduardo Jiménez de Aréchaga' (1994) 88 *Proceedings of the American Society of International Law* 577.

Kimberlé Williams Crenshaw, 'Race, Reform, and Retrenchment: Transformation and Legitimation in Antidiscrimination Law' (2011) 12 *German Law Journal* 247.

Kirsten Ainsley and Mark Kersten, 'Resilience and the Impacts of Hybrid Courts' (2020) *Leiden Journal of International Law*.

Kurt Taylor Gaubatz and Matthew MacArthur, 'How International Is International Law' (2001) 22 *Michigan Journal of International Law* 239.
Kwadwo Sarkodie and Joseph Otoo, 'GETMA v Republic of Guinea – Implications for African Arbitration' (2017) 33 *Arbitration International* 167.
L L Kato, 'The Court of Appeal for East Africa: From a Colonial Court to an International Court' (1971) 7 *East African Law Journal* 1.
Lauren Benton, 'Beyond Anachronism: Histories of International Law and Global Legal Politics' (2019) 21 *Journal of the History of International Law* 7.
Laurence R Helfer and Anne-Marie Slaughter, 'Toward a Theory of Effective Supranational Adjudication' (1997) 107 *Yale Law Journal* 273.
Laurence R Helfer and Karen J Alter, 'Legitimacy and Lawmaking: A Tale of Three International Courts' (2013) 14 *Theoretical Inquiries in Law* 480.
Lee M Caplan, 'ISDS Reform and the Proposal for a Multilateral Investment Court' (2019) 46 *Ecology LQ* 53.
Lucy Reed, 'Great Expectations: Where Does the Proliferation of International Dispute Resolution Tribunals Leave International Law?' (2002) 96 *Proceedings of the American Society of International Law* 219.
Mahmoud Cherif Bassiouni, 'In memoriam Kéba Mbaye' (2008) 79 *Revue Internationale de Droit Pénal* 299.
Makane Moïse Mbengue and Stefanie Schacherer, 'Africa as an Investment Rule-Maker: Decrypting the Pan-African Investment Code' (2018) 23 *African Yearbook of International Law* 81.
Makane Moïse Mbengue and Stefanie Schacherer, 'The "Africanization" of International Investment Law: The Pan-African Investment Code and the Reform of the International Investment Regime' (2017) 18 *Journal of World Investment and Trade* 414.
Makau Mutua, 'The African Human Rights Court: A Two-Legged Stool' (1999) 21 *Human Rights Quarterly* 342.
Makau Mutua, 'Typologies of Scholarship on Africa' (2014) 107 *Proceedings of the American Society of International Law* 191.
Makau Mutua, 'What is TWAIL' (2000) 94 *Proceedings of the American Society of International Law* 31.
Makau Mutua, 'Why Redraw the Map of Africa: A Moral and Legal Inquiry' (1995) 16 *Michigan Journal of International Law* 1113.
Malcolm Langford, Michele Potestà and others, 'Special Issue: UNCITRAL and Investment Arbitration Reform: Matching Concerns and Solutions: An Introduction' (2020) 21 *Journal of World Investment and Trade* 167.
Marc Galanter, 'Justice in Many Rooms: Courts, Private Ordering, and Indigenous Law' (1981) 19 *Journal of Legal Pluralism* 1.
Marcel Fontaine, 'Note Explicative à l'avant-projet d'Acte Uniforme OHADA sur le droit des Contrats' (2008) 13 *Uniform Law Review* 561.
Mark Fathi Massoud, 'International Arbitration and Judicial Politics in Authoritarian States' (2014) 39 *Law and Social Inquiry* 1.
Martin Kirsch, 'Historique de l'Organisation pour l'Harmonisation du Droit des Affaires en Afrique (OHADA)' (1998) *Revue Penant* 130.
Martti Koskenniemi, 'Legal Cosmopolitanism: Tom Franck's Messianic World' (2003) 35 *New York University Journal of International Law and Politics* 471.
Mathew Happold and Relja Radovic, 'The ECOWAS Court of Justice as an Investment Tribunal' (2018) 19 *Journal of World Investment and Trade* 95.
Mathew Happold, 'Investor-State Dispute Settlement using the ECOWAS Court of Justice: An Analysis and Some Proposals' (2019) 34 *ICSID Review* 496.
Max du Plessis and Lee Stone, 'A Court not Found?' (2007) 7 *African Human Rights Law Journal* 538.
Maya Sen, 'How Judicial Qualification Ratings May Disadvantage Minority and Female Candidates' (2014) 2 *Journal of Law and Courts* 33.

Michael Bühler, 'Out of Africa: The 2018 OHADA Arbitration and Mediation Law Reform' (2018) 35 *Journal of International Arbitration* 517.
Michael Frenkel and Benedikt Walter, 'Do Bilateral Investment Treaties Attract Foreign Direct Investment? The Role of International Dispute Settlement Provisions' (2018) 42 *World Economy* 1316.
Michael W Apple, 'The Politics of Official Knowledge: Does a National Curriculum Make Sense?' (1993) 14 *Discourse* 1.
Mikael Rask Madsen, Pola Cebalak and Micha Wiebusch, 'Backlash against International Courts: Explaining the Forms and Patterns of Resistance to International Courts' (2018) 14 *International Journal of Law in Context* 197.
Mohammad Shahabuddin, 'The Colonial "Other" in the Nineteenth Century German Colonisation of Africa, and International Law' (2013) *African Yearbook of International Law* 15.
Mohsen al Attar, 'Reframing the Universality of International Law in a Globalizing World' (2013) 59 *McGill Law Journal* 95.
Mohsen al Attar, 'Peculiar Double-Consciousness of TWAIL' (2022) 19 *Indonesian Journal of International Law* 239.
Muthucumaraswamy Sornarajah, 'Power and Justice: Third World Resistance in International Law' (2006) 10 *Singapore Yearbook of International Law* 19.
Muthucumaraswamy Sornarajah, 'The New International Economic Order, Investment Treaties and Foreign Investment Law in ASEAN' (1985) 27 *Malaya Law Review* 440.
Muthucumaraswamy Sornarajah, 'The Unworkability of "Balanced Treaties" and the Importance of Diversity of Approach among the BRICS' (2018) 112 *American Journal of International Law Unbound* 223.
Nazifa Rashid, 'British Colonialism in East-Africa during the Nineteenth Century' (2013) 1 *International Journal of Art and Art History* 23.
Ndanga Kamau, 'Investment Law and Treaty Reform in Africa: Fragments and Fragmentation' (2020) 1 *African Journal of International Economic Law* 216.
Ndongo Samba Sylla, 'Fighting Monetary Colonialism in Francophone Africa: Samir Amin's Contribution' (2021) 48 *Review of Political Economy* 33.
Nienke Grossman, 'Legitimacy and International Adjudicative Bodies' (2009) 41 *George Washington International Law Review* 107.
Obiora C Okafor, 'Newness, Imperialism, and International Legal Reform in Our Time: A TWAIL Perspective' (2005) 43 *Osgoode Hall Law Journal* 171.
Obiora Chinedu Okafor, 'Critical Third World Approaches to International Law (TWAIL): Theory, Methodology, or Both' (2008) 10 *International Community Law Review* 375.
Olabisi D Akinkugbe, 'Dispute Settlement under the African Continental Free Trade Area Agreement: A Preliminary Assessment' (2020) 28 *African Journal of International and Comparative Law* 138.
Olabisi D Akinkugbe, 'Reverse Contributors? African State Parties, ICSID and the Development of International Investment Law' (2019) 32 *ICSID Review* 434.
Olivia Chung, 'The Lopsided International Investment Law Regime and Its Effect on the Future of Investor-State Arbitration' (2007) 47 *Virginia J Intl L* 953.
Oscar Schachter, 'Compensation for Expropriation' (1984) 78 *American Journal of International Law* 121.
Oscar Schachter, 'Invisible College of International Lawyers' (1977–1978) 72 *Northwestern University Law Review* 217.
Patrice SA Badji, 'Réflexions sur l'attractivité du droit OHADA' (2014) 2 *Bulletin de Droit Économique* 51.
Patrick J Kelly, 'The Twilight of Customary International Law' (2000) 40 *Virginia Journal of International Law* 449.
Paul Craig, 'The Jurisdiction of the Community Courts Reconsidered' (2001) 36 *Texas International Law Journal* 559.
Pemmaraju Sreenivasa Rao, 'Multiple International Judicial Forums: A Reflection of the Growing Strength of International Law or Its Fragmentation' (2004) 25 *Michigan Journal of International Law* 929.

Pierre Bourdieu, 'The Force of Law: Toward a Sociology of the Juridical Field' (1987) 38 *Hastings Law Journal* 805.

Raj Kumar Trivedi, 'The Role of Imperial British East Africa Company in the Acquisition of East African Colony in the Second Half of the Nineteenth Century' (1971) 33 *Indian History Congress*.

Rajeev Bhargava, 'Overcoming the Epistemic Injustice of Colonialism' (2013) 4 *Global Policy*.

Ralf Michaels, 'Private Law Theory and the "Global Legal Community"' (2022) 23 *German Law Journal* 851.

Rebecca D Gill, Sylvia R Lazos and Mallory M Waters, 'Are Judicial Performance Evaluations Fair to Women and Minorities – A Cautionary Tale from Clark County, Nevada' (2011) 45 *Law and Society Review* 731.

Reginald Chikere Keke, 'Southern Cameroons/Amabazonia Conflict: A Political Economy' (2020) 23 *Theory & Event* 329.

Regional Centre for International Commercial Arbitration Cairo, 'Arbitration under the Auspices of the Cairo Regional Centre' (1987) 2 *Arab Law Quarterly* 185.

Richard Frimpong Oppong, 'The African Union, the African Economic Community and Africa's Regional Economic Communities: Untangling a Complex Web' (2010) 18 *African Journal of International and Comparative Law* 99.

Robert Howse and Ruti Teitel, 'Beyond Compliance: Rethinking Why International Law Really Matters' (2010) 2 *Global Policy* 27.

Robert S Wai, 'Transnational Liftoff and Juridical Touchdown: The Regulatory Function of Private International Law in an Era of Globalization' (2001–2002) 40 *Columbia Journal of Transnational Law* 209.

Robert S Wai, 'Transnational Private Law and Private Ordering in a Contested Global Society' (2005) 46 *Harvard International Law Journal* 475.

Roger Cotterrell, 'What is Transnational Law' (2012) 37 *Law and Social Inquiry* 500.

Roger P Alford, 'The Proliferation of International Courts and Tribunals: International Adjudication in Ascendance' (2000) 94 *American Society of International Law Proceedings* 160.

Rose Rameau, 'The African Perspective: The Development of Investment Laws, the Pan-African Investment Code (PAIC), and the African Continental Free Trade Area in the "New Economic World Order"' (2020) 114 *American Society of International Law Proceedings* 62.

S.A.F Haridi et al, 'The Cairo Regional Centre for International Commercial Arbitration (CRICA) Newly Revised Arbitration Rules; Incorporating the New UNICTRAL Model Rules of 2010 and Expanding the Centre's Role as an Appointing Authority' (2011) 8 *Transnational Dispute Management* 1.

Salvatore Caserta, 'Western Centrism, Contemporary International Law, and International' (2021) 34 *Leiden Journal of International Law* 321.

Salvatore Mancuso, 'Trends on the Harmonization of Contract Law in Africa' (2007) 13 *Annual Survey of International and Comparative Law* 157.

Samuel K.B. Asante, 'The Perspectives of African Countries on International Commercial Arbitration' (1993) 6 *Leiden Journal of International Law* 331.

Samuel Moyn, 'International Law and the Politics of History' (2022) 116 *American Journal of International Law* 895.

Samuel Moyn, 'On Human Rights and Majority Politics: Felix Frankfurter's Democratic Theory' (2019) 52 *Vanderbilt Journal of Transnational Law* 1135.

Sara Dezalay, 'Lawyers in Africa: Brokers of the State, Intermediaries of Globalization: A Case Study of the "Africa" Bar in Paris' (2018) 25 *Indiana Journal of Global Legal Studies* 639.

Sean D. Murphy, 'Deconstructing Fragmentation: Koskenniemi's 2006 ILC Project' (2013) 27 *Temple International and Comparative Law Journal* 293.

Sergio Puig, 'Social Capital in the Arbitration Marketplace' (2014) 25 *European Journal of International Law* 423.

Shashank P. Kumar and Cecily Rose, 'A Study of Lawyers Appearing Before the International Court of Justice, 1999–2012' (2014) 25 *European Journal of International Law* 893.

Solomon T. Ebobrah, 'A Rights-Protection Goldmine or a Waiting Volcanic Eruption: Competence of, and Access to, the Human Rights Jurisdiction of the ECOWAS Community Court of Justice' (2007) 7 *African Human Rights Law Journal* 307.

Solomon T. Ebobrah, 'Critical Issues in the Human Rights Mandate of the ECOWAS Court of Justice' (2010) 54 *Journal of African Law* 1.

Solomon T. Ebobrah, 'Human Rights Developments in African Sub-Regional Economic Communities during 2009' (2010) 10 *African Human Rights Law Journal* 233.

Solomon T. Ebobrah, 'Human Rights Developments in African Sub-Regional Economic Communities during 2010' (2011) 11 *African Human Rights Law Journal* 216.

Solomon T. Ebobrah, 'Human Rights Developments in African Sub-Regional Economic Communities during 2011' (2012) 12 *African Human Rights Law Journal* 223.

Solomon T. Ebobrah, 'Human Rights Developments in African Sub-Regional Economic Communities during 2012' (2013) 13 *African Human Rights Law Journal* 178.

Solomon T. Ebobrah, 'Human Rights Developments in Subregional Courts in Africa during 2008' (2009) 9 *African Human Rights Law Journal* 312.

Solomon T. Ebobrah, 'Tackling Threats to the Existence of the SADC Tribunal: A Critique of Perilously Ambiguous Provisions in the SADC Treaty and the Protocol on the SADC Tribunal' (2010) 4 *Malawi Law Journal* 199.

Stephan Wilske, 'Why South Africa Should Update its International Arbitration Legislation – An Appeal from the International Arbitration Community for Legal Reform in South Africa' (2011) 28 *Journal of International Arbitration* 1.

Steven Lukes, 'Political Ritual and Social Integration' (1975) 9 *Sociology* 289.

Susan D. Franck et al, 'The Diversity Challenge: Exploring the Invisible College of International Arbitration' (2015) 53 *Columbia Journal of Transnational Law* 429.

Susan D. Franck, 'The Legitimacy Crisis in Investment Treaty Arbitration: Privatizing Public International Law Through Inconsistent Decisions' (2005) 73 *Fordham Law Review* 1521.

Terence K. Teo, 'BITs and FDI Revisited: A Matching Approach' (2021) 11 *Open Journal of Political Science* 347.

Thomas Buergenthal, 'Proliferation of International Courts and Tribunals: Is it Good or is it Bad?' (2001) 14 *Leiden Journal of International Law* 267.

Thomas Schultz and Robert Kovacs, 'The Rise of a Third Generation of Arbitrators? Fifteen Years after Dezalay and Garth' (2012) 28 *Arbitration International* 161.

Tiyanjana Maluwa, 'Reassessing Aspects of the Contribution of African States to the Development of International Law Through African Regional Multilateral Treaties' (2020) 41 *Michigan Journal of International Law* 327.

Tom Gerald Daly and Micha Wiebusch, 'The African Court on Human and Peoples' Rights: Mapping Resistance against a Young Court' (2018) 14 *International Journal of Law in Context* 294.

Tomasz P. Milej, 'Human Rights Protection by International Courts-What Role for the East African Court of Justice' (2018) 26:1 African Journal of International and Comparative Law.

Tung-Lung S. Chang, Cheng-Min Chuang and Wen-Shiung Jan, 'International Collaboration of Law Firms: Modes, Motives, and Advantages' (1998) 33 *Journal of World Business* 245.

Wilfredi Mutubwa, 'The Making of an International Arbitration Hub: A Critical Appraisal of the Nairobi Centre for International Arbitration Act 2013' (2016) 82 *International Journal of Law and Arbitration* 135.

William I. Robinson and Jerry Harris, 'Towards a Global Ruling Class? Globalization and the Transnational Capitalist Class' (2000) 64 *Science & Society* 11.

Won Kidane, 'Civil Liability for Violations of International Humanitarian Law: The Jurisprudence of the Eritrea-Ethiopia Claims Commission in the Hague' (2009) 23 *Journal of Ethiopian Law* 36.

Yasachandra Devarakonda, 'Restricting Double-Hatting to Safeguard International Arbitrations' (2022) 22 *Pepperdine Dispute Resolution Law Journal* 65.

Yuval Shany, 'Assessing the Effectiveness of International Courts: A Goal-Based Approach' (2012) 106 *American Journal of International Law* 225.

Yuval Shany, 'No Longer a Weak Department of Power? Reflections on the Emergence of a New International Judiciary' (2009) 20 *European Journal of International Law* 73.
Zongnan Wu, 'Orascom TMT Investments v Algeria: A New Trend on the Doctrine of Abuse of Rights in the Context of Parallel Proceedings' (2019) 34 *ICSID Review* 197.

REPORTS, WORKING PAPERS, DISSERTATIONS

Working Papers

Craig K. Elwell, *Brief History of the Gold Standard in the United States* (Congressional Research Service, June 23, 2011), sgp.fas.org/crs/misc/R41887.pdf
Dieudonné Nzafashwanayo, *Arbitration Proceedings before the Kigali International Arbitration Centre* (Dec. 16, 2018) 4, SSRN, papers.ssrn.com/sol3/papers.cfm?abstract_id=3289963
ECMR, *Intra-African Foreign Direct Investment (FDI) and Employment: A Case Study* (African Development Bank Working Paper Series No 335), www.afdb.org/sites/default/files/documents/publications/wps_no_335_intra-african_foreign_direct_investment_fdi_and_employment_a_case_study_e_0.pdf
Gabrielle Kaufmann-Kohler and Michele Potestà, *Can the Mauritius Convention Serve as a Model for the Reform of Investor-State Arbitration in Connection with the Introduction of a Permanent Investment Tribunal or an Appeal Mechanism?: Analysis and Roadmap* (CIDS Research Paper, 2016) lk-k.com/wp-content/uploads/2016/05/KAUFMANN-KOHLER-POTESTA-CIDS-Research-Paper-Reform-of-Investor-State-Arbitration-2016.pdf accessed 27 September 2025
Gustav Kalm, *Building Legal Certainty Through International Law: OHADA Law in Cameroon* 11 (Buffett Centre for International & Comparative Studies, Working Paper No. 11-005, 2011) www.academia.edu/38335634/Building_Legal_Certainty_Through_International_Law_OHADA_Law_in_Cameroon.
James T. Gathii, *Reform and Retrenchment in International Investment Law* (13 January 2021) ssrn.com/abstract=3765169
Mary Hallward-Driemeier, *Do Bilateral Investment Treaties Attract FDI? Only a bit . . . and they could bite'* (Policy Research Working Paper: No. 3121. 2003), openknowledge.worldbank.org/handle/10986/18118
Pia Eberhardt & Cecilia Olivet, *Profiting from Injustice. How Law Firms, Arbitrators and Financiers Are Fuelling an Investment Arbitration Boom* (Corporate Europe Observatory (CEO) & Transnational Institute (TNI), 2012), www.tni.org/files/download/profitingfrominjustice.pdf
Shashank Kumar & Cecily Rose, *A Study of Lawyers Appearing Before the International Court of Justice, 1999–2012* (PIL, Grotius Centre Working Paper 2014), papers.ssrn.com/sol3/papers.cfm?abstract_id=2435621

Reports

Emilia Onyema, *2020 Arbitration in Africa Survey Report: Top African Arbitral Centres and Seats*, (30 June 2020), eprints.soas.ac.uk/33162/1/2020%20Arbitration%20in%20Africa%20Survey%20Report%2030.06.2020.pdf
Lombe Chibesakunda, *COMESA: Dispute Settlement and Arbitration Developments* TRALAC Annual Conference (6–7 April 2017) https://comesacourt.org/blog/2016/03/08/capacity-building-programme-for-comesa-court-judges/

John Eudes Ruhangisa, *The East African Court of Justice: Ten years of Operation (Achievements and Challenges)* Sensitisation Workshop on the Role of the EACJ in the EAC Integration, Imperial Royale Hotel, Kampala, Uganda, (1-2 November 2011), *available at* www.eacj.org/wp-content/uploads/2013/09/EACJ-Ten-Years-of-Operation.pdf

Jonathan Bonnicha, *Assessing the Impacts of Investment Treaties: Overview of the Evidence* (IISD September 2017) www.iisd.org/publications/report/assessing-impacts-investment-treaties-overview-evidence

Martti Koskenniemi, *Fragmentation of International Law: Difficulties Arising from the Diversification and Expansion of International Law* (Report of the Study Group of the International Law Commission, International Law Commission, UN Doc A/CN.4/L.682, 13 April 2006)

Open Society Foundations, *Counterterrorism and Human Rights Abuses in Kenya and Uganda: The World Cup Bombing and Beyond* (2013) www.justiceinitiative.org/uploads/1b4cef46-0f2f-498a-a16c-cfcefd9897ae/counterterrorism-human-rights-abuses-kenya-uganda-20130403.pdf

Queen Mary University of London & White and Case LLP, *2021 International Arbitration Survey: Adapting Arbitration to a Changing World* (2021), www.whitecase.com/sites/default/files/2021-05/quml-international-arbitration-survey-2021-web.pdf

H.E. Mr. Abdulqawi A. Yusuf, *Speech by the President Of The International Court Of Justice, On The Occasion Of The Seventy-Fifth Session Of The United Nations General Assembly* (2 November 2020), www.icj-cij.org/public/files/press-releases/0/000-20201102-STA-01-00-EN.pdf

Dissertations

Ally Possi, *The East Africa Court of Justice: Towards Effective Protection of Human rights in the East African Community* (unpublished PhD dissertation, University of Pretoria, November 2014), repository.up.ac.za/bitstream/handle/2263/46232/Possi_East_2015.pdf?sequence=1&isAllowed=y

Shane R. Tomashot, *Selling Peace: The History of the International Chamber of Commerce, 1919-1925* (unpublished PhD dissertation, Georgia State University, 2015), www.semanticscholar.org/paper/Selling-Peace%3A-The-History-of-the-International-of-Tomashot/9879844fb6b34f743b4ed549fd88e29f56ccfe4d

Solomon T. Ebobrah, Legitimacy and Feasibility of Human rights Realisation through Regional Economic Communities in Africa: The Case of the Economic Community of West African States (unpublished PhD dissertation, University of Pretoria, September 2009), repository.up.ac.za/bitstream/handle/2263/27990/Complete.pdf?sequence=9&isAllowed=y

Victor Lando, The Domestic Effect of the East African Community's Human Rights Practice (LLD Thesis, University of Pretoria Faculty of Laws, September 2017), hdl.handle.net/2263/64619

NEWSPAPERS, BLOGS,OTHERS

News

Anne-Marie Slaughter, '*Why Women Still Can't Have It All*' *The Atlantic* (Jul/Aug. 2012), www.theatlantic.com/magazine/archive/2012/07/why-women-still-cant-have-it-all/309020/

Boubacar Boris Diop, 'Françafrique: A Brief History of a Scandalous *Word' NewAfrican* (3 March 2018), newafricanmagazine.com/opinions/francafrique-a-brief-history-of-a-scandalous-word/

Luke Anami, 'Lawyers fight Kenya-US Trade Deal' *The East African* (21 March 2020) www.theeastafrican.co.ke/tea/business-tech/lawyers-fight-kenya-us-trade-deal-1439086

Luke Anami, 'Tanzanian Glass Company takes KRA to Court over a 25% Import Tax' *The East African* (Jun. 7, 2020) www.theeastafrican.co.ke/business/Tanzanian-glass-company-takes-KRA-to-court/2560-5572644-g0engkz/index.html

BLOGS

Afronomics Law

AfronomicsLAW, www.afronomicslaw.org/ (last visited 14 December 2022).
Harrison Mbori, 'Exit is the Only Way Out: A Polemic Response to John Nyanje's "Hegemony in Investor State Dispute Settlement: How African states need to Approach Reforms"' *AfronomicsLaw* (10 September 2020), www.afronomicslaw.org/2020/09/10/exit-is-the-only-way-out-a-polemic-response-to-john-nyanjes-hegemony-in-investor-state-dispute-settlement-how-african-states-need-to-approach-reforms
John Nyanje, 'Hegemony in Investor State Dispute Settlement: How African States Need to Approach Reforms' *AfronomicsLaw* (7 September 2020) www.afronomicslaw.org/2020/09/07/hegemony-in-investor-state-dispute-settlement-how-african-states-need-to-approach-reforms
Oladapo Fabusuyi, 'Africanisation of International Investment Law: Prospects and Challenges' *AfronomicsLaw* (18 October 2019) www.afronomicslaw.org/2019/10/18/africanisation-of-international-investment-law-prospects-and-challenges

Kluwer Arbitration Blog

Alon Meyerov & Giles Hutt, 'Arbitration in South Africa Receives Another Boost' *Kluwer Arbitration Blog* (14 August 2020) arbitrationblog.kluwerarbitration.com/2020/08/14/arbitration-in-south-africa-receives-another-boost/
Clement Fouchard & Marc Krestin, 'The Judgment of the CJEU in Slovak Republic v Achmea – A Loud Clap of Thunder on the Intra-EU BIT Sky!' *Kluwer Arbitration Blog*, (7 March, 2018), legalblogs.wolterskluwer.com/arbitration-blog/the-judgment-of-the-cjeu-in-slovak-republic-v-achmea-a-loud-clap-of-thunder-on-the-intra-eu-bit-sky/
Danika Balusik, 'The Know How to Enforcing Foreign Arbitration Awards in South Africa' *Kluwer Arbitration Blog* (17 February 2019) arbitrationblog.kluwerarbitration.com/2019/02/17/the-know-how-to-enforcing-foreign-arbitration-awards-in-south-africa/
Deyan Draguiev, '2018 in Review: The Achmea Decision and Its Reverberations in the World of Arbitration' *Kluwer Arbitration Blog*, (16 January 2019), arbitrationblog.kluwerarbitration.com/2019/01/16/2018-in-review-the-achmea-decision-and-its-reverberations-in-the-world-of-arbitration/
Marike Paulsson, 'UNCITRAL Working Group III: Reforms in the Realm of Investor-State Disputes – UNCITRAL's Proposals for an Appellate Mechanism and its Impact on Duration and Cost' *Kluwer Arbitration Blog* (26 March 2020), arbitrationblog.kluwerarbitration.com/2020/03/26/uncitral-working-group-iii-reforms-in-the-realm-of-investor-state-disputes-uncitrals-proposals-for-an-appellate-mechanism-and-its-impact-on-duration-and-cost/?print=print
Stéphanie Papazoglou, 'The Battle for Survival among Arbitral Institutions' *Kluwer Arbitration Blog* (19 June 2020) arbitrationblog.kluwerarbitration.com/2020/06/19/the-battle-for-survival-among-arbitral-institutions/

Others

Andrew Mold & Samiha Chowdhury, 'Why the Extent of Intra-African Trade is much Higher than Commonly believed-and what this means for the AfCFTA' *Brookings* (19 May 2021), www.brookings.edu/blog/africa-in-focus/2021/05/19/why-the-extent-of-intra-african-trade-is-much-higher-than-commonly-believed-and-what-this-means-for-the-afcfta/

Anna Hankings-Evans, 'The Africanization of International Investment Disputes-from Past to Present,' *Verfassungsblog*, (23 July 2020) verfassungsblog.de/the-africanization-of-international -investment-disputes-from-past-to-present/

Andrew Mizner, 'Dentons Doing its Own Thing in Africa' *African Law & Business* (6 December 2022), iclg.com/alb/18381-dentons-doing-its-own-thing-in-africa

Andrew Mizner, 'DLA Looks for an Integrated Future in Africa' *African Law & Business* (8 June 2018), iclg.com/alb/8258-dla-looks-for-an-integrated-future-in-africa

Andrew Mizner, 'Law Firms Balance Competition and Collaboration in Africa' *African Law & Business* (14 September 2022), iclg.com/alb/18162-law-firms-balance-competition-and -collaboration-in-africa

Andrew Mizner, '*New Leadership as Eversheds eyes Africa's Growing Legal Sector Rewards' African Law & Business* (29 March 2022) www.africanlawbusiness.com/news/8095-new -leadership-as-eversheds-eyes-africa-s-growing-legal-sector-rewards

Africa Arbitration, '*Africa's Rising Star, Abayomi Okubote, Exits Top Law Firm . . . Starts a boutique Arbitration Firm!'* africaarbitration.org/2021/12/13/africas-rising-star-exits-top-law -starts-a-boutique-arbitration-firm/ (last visited 8 March 2021).

Africa Arbitration, 'Africa Arbitration Academy publishes Africa's 30 Arbitration Powerlist 2020' africaarbitration.org/2021/02/02/africa-arbitration-academy-publishes-africas-30-arbitration -powerlist-2020/ (last visited on 22 February 2022).

African Arbitration Association, '*Dr. Kariuki Muigua Ranked by Chambers as Top Arbitrator for the 5th Year'* afaa.ngo/page-18443 accessed 14 March 2022.

Africa Arbitration Awards, 2020, '*Spotlingting Africa's International Arbitration expertise at 2nd Annual Africa Arbitration Awards, 2002'* www.addleshawgoddard.com/globalassets/insights /celebrating-africas-international-arbitration-expertise.pdf

Anabel Gonzalez, Senior Director, World Bank Group, Statement by Anabel Gonzalez at the Fourth China-WTO Accessions Roundtable: International Economic Cooperation and African Perspectives on the Future of the Multilateral Trading System, Nairobi, Kenya (Dec. 14, 2015), www.worldbank.org/en/news/speech/2015/12/14/deepening-african-integration-intra-africa -trade-for-development-and-poverty-reduction

Calestous Juma & Francis Mageni, 'The Benefits of Africa's New Free Trade Area', *Belfer Center for Science and International Affairs* (11 June 2015) www.belfercenter.org/publication/benefits -africas-new-free-trade-area-0

Christine Zhenwei Qiang, Peter Kusek, *Victor Steebergen & Brody Viney, 'The Road to Recovery in Sub-Saharan Africa: Capitalizing on Transformative Opportunities from shifting FDI Patterns' World Banks Blogs* (27 May 2021), blogs.worldbank.org/africacan road-recovery-sub-saharan-africa-capitalizing-transformative-opportunities-shifting-fdi

Emmanuel Kagisye, '*Environnement Institutionnel des Affaires en Afrique: Contexte et Structure d'harmonisation du droit OHADA,' Hal* (2017), hal-auf.archives-ouvertes.fr/hal-01495556 /document

Global Arbitration Review (GAR), 'White List/Institutions Worth a Closer Look- Middle East & Africa' (29 July 2022) globalarbitrationreview.com/survey/the-guide-regional-arbitration/2022 /article/white-list-institutions-worth-closer-look-middle-east-africa

Joseph Otoo & Kwadwo Sarkodie, '*The Rise and Rise of Arbitration in Africa,' African Law & Business* (5 April 2018), www.africanlawbusiness.com/news/8105-the-rise-and-rise-of-arbitration -in-africa

Lise Johnson, '*CME v Czech Republic, Lauder v Czech Republic' Investment Treaty News: International Institute for Sustainable Development*, (18 October 2018) www.iisd.org/itn /en/2018/10/18/cme-v-czech-republic-lauder-v-czech-republic/

Maria Jackson, '*Race for Africa' Legal Business*, (November 2011), www.vda.pt/xms/files/v1/Noticias /Legal_Business_-_219_Africa_-_NC_-November_2011-.pdf

Mohsen al Attar, '*Subverting Racism in/through International Law Scholarship' OpinioJuris* (24 November 2022, 3:37 PM), opiniojuris.org/2021/03/03/subverting-racism-in-international-law -scholarship/

re A Request by the Council of Ministers of the East African Community for an Advisory Opinion, Appl. No. 1 of 2008 (First Instance Division 2009), www.eacj.org/wp-content/uploads/2019/03/Advisory-Opinion-No.-1-of-2008-The-Council-of-Ministers-of-the-East-African-Community.pdf accessed 1 November 2022.

Tariq Khan, '*Making India a Hub of Arbitration: Bridging the Gap Between Myth and Reality' SCC Online Blog* (17 February 2021) www.scconline.com/blog/post/2021/02/17/making-india-a-hub-of-arbitration-bridging-the-gap-between-myth-and-reality/

TDM, '*Professor Dr. Mohamed S. Abdel Wahab'*, www.transnational-dispute-management.com/about-author-a-z-profile.asp?key=2526 (last visited on 22 February 2022).

The Arbitration Brief, '*Chinese Africa Joint Arbitration Center: A solution to trade disputes between Africa and China*'(2019) thearbitrationbrief.com/2019/02/11/chinese-africa-joint-arbitration-center-a-solutionto-trade-disputes-between-africa-and-china%EF%BB%BF / thearbitrationbrief.com/2019/02/11/chinese-africa-joint-arbitration-center-a-solution-to-trade-disputes-between-africa-and-china%EF%BB%BF/

Thibaud Roujou de Boubee & Thomas Kendra, '*The Paris court upholds the supranational nature of OHADA in dismissing annulment application (CA Paris 16/25484, December, 20, 2018)' JDSUPRA*, (14 February 2019), www.jdsupra.com/legalnews/the-paris-court-upholds-the-76318/

Organisation Websites

African Committee of Experts on the Rights and Welfare of the Child (ACERWC), reporting. acerwc.africa/committeeexperts reporting.acerwc.africa/en

Africa Arbitration Academy, www.africaarbitrationacademy.org/

Africa Arbitration, Co-Founders, africaarbitration.org/management/ (last visited 8 March 2022).

African Institute of International Law, aiil-iadi.org/

Allen & Overy, Africa, www.allenovery.com/en-gb/global/global_coverage/africa

ALN, *About Us*, aln.africa/about-us/ (last visited 1 March 2022).

African Institute of International Law & African Arbitration Association, Advanced Introduction Workshop on International Investment Law and Dispute Resolution afaa.ngo/event-4688310 (last visited 25 December 2022).

Statutes of the African Institute of International Law, www.aiil-iadi.org/wp-content/uploads/2021/03/Statutes-of-the-African-Institute.pdf accessed 14 March 2022.

African Union, 'AfCFTA: African Continental Free Trade Area' au.int/en/ti/cfta/about

AFSA, arbitration.co.za/history/

Asian African Legal Consultative Organization, Member States, www.aalco.int/Members

Association of Young Arbitrators, About Us

Clyde & Co, Africa, www.clydeco.com/en/locations/africa

COMESA-EAC-SADC Tripartite, East African Community (7 September 2020) www.eac.int/tripartite

Crasner Consulting, Law firms Scramble for Africa (18 October 2016), www.crasnerconsulting.com/news/law-firms-scramble-for-africa/

DLA Piper, *DLA* Piper offices in Africa, www.dlapiper.com/en-ma/locations/africa

EAC, Court President pays courtesy to the Chief Justice & Minister of Industry, Trade and EAC Affairs in Rwanda *(12 June 2017)* www.eac.int/press-releases/153-legal-judicial-affairs/795-court-president-pays-courtesy-to-the-chief-justice-minister-of-industry,-trade-and-eac-affairs-in-rwanda.

EAC, *Investment Framework: Key Features*, www.eac.int/investment/investment-framework

Fidèle Masengo, A regional success story: the development of arbitration in Rwanda Herbert Smith Freehills (1 February 2017) www.herbertsmithfreehills.com/latest-thinking/a-regional-success-story-the-development-of-arbitration-in-rwanda

Herbert Smith Freehills, 2016 ICC Dispute Resolution Statistics: Record Year for the ICC (15 September 2017), hsfnotes.com/arbitration/2017/09/15/2016-icc-dispute-resolution-statistics-record-year-for-the-icc/

Herbert Smith Freehills, Africa Group, www.herbertsmithfreehills.com/where-we-work/africa-group
ICC Arbitration Rules (1 January 2021) iccwbo.org/publication/arbitration-rules-and-mediation-rules/
ICC, ICC Court to Launch Africa Commission (19 July 2018) iccwbo.org/media-wall/news-speeches/icc-court-launch-africa-commission/
ICC, ICC Dispute Resolution 2019 Statistics, (2020) www.iccwbo.be/shop/icc-dispute-resolution-statistics-2019/#:~:text=The%20ICC%20Court%20registered%20a,its%20almost%20100%2Dyear%20history
Lagos Court of Arbitration, www.lca.org.ng/ (last visited 25 December 2022).
Ndanga Kamau Law, Ndanga Kamau, Arbitrator, *Counsel* ndangakamau.com/
Olaniwun Ajayi, Our Firm, www.olaniwunajayi.net/the-firm/
Queens Law, Abayomi Okubote https://law.queensu.ca/news/Queens-Law-doctoral-student-developing-a-framework-to-regulate-third-party-funding-in-international-arbitration.
Regional Director role to bolster ICC reach, ICC (11 May 2021), iccwbo.org/media-wall/news-speeches/regional-director-role-to-bolster-icc-reach-in-africa/
The East Africa International Arbitration Conference, *About EAIAC*, www.eastafricaarbitration.com/about-eaiac/
The Legal 500, Arbitration Powerlist 2021: Africa indd.adobe.com/view/07527242-bd96-4ac8-b1ff-03b60f37787a
UNCTAD, COVID-19 slashes Foreign Direct Investment in Africa by 16% (21 June 2021), unctad.org/news/covid-19-slashes-foreign-direct-investment-africa-16
White & Case, Current Choices and Future Adaptations, (6 May 2021), www.whitecase.com/insight-our-thinking/current-choices-and-future-adaptations
Zulficar & Partners, Mohamed Abdel Wahab, www.zulficarpartners.com/people/mohamed-s-abdel-wahab/

Social Media

Africa Arbitration Academy, LINKEDIN www.linkedin.com/feed/update/urn:li:activity:7011254773874126848/

Index

References are to page number.

www.ingramcontent.com/pod-product-compliance
Ingram Content Group UK Ltd.
Pitfield, Milton Keynes, MK11 3LW, UK
UKHW020251290926
15470UKWH00002B/861

9 781509 99287